The Transformation of Title IX

The Transformation of Title IX

Regulating Gender Equality in Education

R. SHEP MELNICK

BROOKINGS INSTITUTION PRESS
Washington, D.C.

The Brookings Institution is a private nonprofit organization devoted to research,
education, and publication on important issues of domestic and foreign policy. Its
principal purpose is to bring the highest quality independent research and analysis
to bear on current and emerging policy problems. Interpretations or conclusions in
Brookings publications should be understood to be solely those of the authors.

Library of Congress Cataloging-in-Publication Data

Names: Melnick, R. Shep, 1951– author.
Title: The transformation of Title IX : regulating gender equality in education /
    R. Shep Melnick.
Description: Washington, D.C. : Brookings Institution Press, 2018. | Includes
    bibliographical references and index.
Identifiers: LCCN 2017048747 (print) | LCCN 2017049939 (ebook) |
    ISBN 9780815732402 (ebook) | ISBN 9780815732228 (pbk. : alk. paper)
Subjects: LCSH: Educational equalization—United States. | Women—
    Education—United States. | Sex discrimination in education—United States. |
    United States. Education Amendments of 1972. Title IX.
Classification: LCC LC213.2 (ebook) | LCC LC213.2 .M45 2018 (print) |
    DDC 379.2/6—dc23
LC record available at https://lccn.loc.gov/2017048747

9 8 7 6 5 4 3 2 1

Typeset in Adobe Garamond Pro

Composition by Westchester Publishing Services

For Joanne

Contents

Part III
Sexual Harassment

Part IV
Expansion and Retrenchment

Preface

When I began studying Title IX in 2009, I expected my research to culminate in a single chapter in a book about the larger American civil rights state. Like most Americans, I associated Title IX primarily with athletics. And like many parents, I was grateful to Title IX for contributing to the expansion of educational and athletic opportunities for my daughter.

Little did I know then that the Obama administration was about to announce a series of Title IX policies that would significantly extend the reach of federal regulation and spark intense controversy. Most important were its detailed guidelines on sexual assault and harassment on college campuses. Meanwhile the Office for Civil Rights (OCR) in the Department of Education was tightening its rules on intercollegiate athletics and for the first time investigating athletic opportunities for girls at the high school level. The more OCR did, the more I wrote. By early 2016 I realized the chapter had morphed into a book.

A few months later OCR issued yet another novel and controversial rule, this one on transgender students' use of sex-segregated facilities. Title IX had entered the "bathroom wars." This required more research and more pages. After I finished the first draft of the manuscript, Donald Trump shocked much of the country by being elected president. The Trump administration quickly revoked the transgender guidelines and soon thereafter announced it would reevaluate OCR policy on sexual assault and sexual harassment. With all these developments to cover, the small book grew into this 300-plus-page volume.

Writing a scholarly book about hotly contested regulations that might soon be altered presents both dangers and opportunities. On the one hand, I have often felt like an explorer stepping into a fast moving river: the movement around me has at times left me off-balance, uncertain how the surrounding landscape will look in a few years. On the other hand, I have been troubled by the shallowness of the current debate on Title IX issues and believe that detailed analysis of the evolution of these policies will help us think more clearly about them. Many of the deficiencies of current policies can be traced to the convoluted policymaking process I describe in the pages that follow. I hope that a better understanding of the history of and rationale for the current regulatory regime will improve the quality of debate over proposals to change it.

As my topic evolved, I benefited from comments and criticisms in a variety of forums: the Center for American Political Studies and the Program on Constitutional Government at Harvard; the Institute for Governmental Studies and Program on Jurisprudence and Social Policy at the University of California, Berkeley; the Program on Law and Public Affairs at Princeton; the Miller Center at the University of Virginia; the political science departments at the University of California, San Diego, the University of Colorado, Colorado Springs, and the University of Texas at Austin; and panels at the American Political Science Association and New England Political Science Association conventions. Earlier versions of my work on the civil rights state appear in Jeffrey A. Jenkins and Sidney M. Milkis, eds., *The Politics of Major Policy Reform in Postwar America* (Cambridge University Press, 2014), Thomas F. Burke and Jeb Barnes, eds., *Varieties of Legal Order: The Politics of Adversarial and Bureaucratic Legalism* (New York: Routledge, 2017), and Lynda G. Dodd, ed., *The Rights Revolution Revisited: Institutional Perspectives on the Private Enforcement of Civil Rights in the U.S.* (Cambridge University Press, 2017).

I would particularly like to thank William Finan of Brookings Press for his enthusiastic support for this project; Philip Wallach for his skillful combination of encouragement and criticism; Peter Schuck, not only for his detailed comments, but for providing a model of how to combine the study of law and politics; Jeremy Rabkin, whose suggestions helped me fill out my argument; Welch Suggs for his comments on Part II; Leor Sapir and Hale Melnick for their valuable assistance in the editing process; and an anonymous reader whose comments made this a much better book. My political science colleagues at Boston College not only helped me think more clearly about these issues, but encouraged me to keep slogging.

Over the years my work on the civil rights state has been supported by grants from the Smith Richardson Foundation, the Earhart Foundation, the Harvard Program on Constitutional Government, and the American Enterprise Institute's National Research Initiative. I am glad finally to deliver the book I have been promising them for many years.

My biggest thanks must go to members of my family, who put up with my absorption with Title IX and forced me to defend (and at times amend) my positions. Since my son, Hale, is now a lawyer, my daughter, Hanna, a research associate at an education policy think tank, and my wife, Joanne Linden, a clinical psychologist at a counseling center named Womankind, this has been a demanding audience. (The lacrosse stick on the cover of this book is a tip-of-the-hat to Hanna and Hale's dedication to that sport.) Joanne not only read and commented on the entire manuscript, but quietly tolerated many weekends lost to work on this book. For that and so many other reasons, this book is dedicated to her.

Part I

Title IX in the Civil Rights State

ONE

Rights Regulation

A s Title IX of the Education Amendments of 1972 approached its half-century mark, Americans could look back with pride and amazement at the progress we have made in opening the doors of educational opportunity for women and girls. In 1972, 58 percent of college students were male and only 42 percent female. By 2010 those numbers had flipped: 57 percent of college students were women, and that number keeps creeping up. From 1970 to 2008 the percentage of white men ages twenty-five to thirty-four with a bachelor's degree (B.A.) rose only modestly, from 20 percent to 26 percent. Meanwhile the proportion of white women of this age with a B.A. nearly tripled, shooting up from 12 percent to 34 percent. Among African Americans, women receive two-thirds of all B.A.s. Women now earn more graduate degrees than men. In 1970 men earned eight times as many Ph.D.s as women; today women earn more doctorates than do men (53 percent). Once all but shut out of medical, dental, and law schools, women have reached parity with men. Women earn more degrees in the sciences than men, although not as many in engineering and math. Female undergraduates are more likely to be selected for Phi Beta Kappa, to serve in student government, to write for college newspapers, and to engage in every extracurricular activity other than sports.[1]

Girls' performance at the elementary and secondary levels is no less impressive. Girls get better grades than boys, in part because they do more homework and misbehave less frequently. They now have higher educational aspirations, take more advanced placement courses, and participate in more extracurricular and out-of-school activities. They write better. Their advantage on verbal standardized tests is growing. Conversely, boys' advantage on math tests has shrunk, almost to the point of disappearing. Boys are falling farther and farther behind. At many colleges only affirmative action for boys keeps their proportion in the undergraduate student body above 40 percent. One finds these trends for every race and ethnicity.[2] As Thomas DiPrete and Claudia Buchmann put it in *The Rise of Women*, "Women have not merely gained educational equality with men; on many fronts they have surpassed men by a large and growing margin."[3]

Even in intercollegiate and interscholastic athletics, one of the few areas where males still predominate, the change has been dramatic. When Title IX was enacted, only 15 percent of college varsity athletes were women; four decades later that proportion was 43 percent. Between 1972 and 2015 the number of female varsity athletes at National Collegiate Athletic Association schools increased sevenfold. At the high school level female participation is now ten times what it was in 1970, rising from less than 300,000 to well over 3 million. In 1970 only 7 percent of interscholastic athletes were female. Today that number is 42 percent.[4]

Mission Accomplished?

At the heart of Title IX lies this simple prohibition: "No person in the United States shall, on the basis of sex, be excluded from participation in, be denied the benefits of, or be subject to discrimination under any educational program or activity receiving Federal financial assistance." Since every public elementary, middle, and high school in the country and virtually every college and university—private as well as public—receives federal money, these thousands of institutions are all subject to the rules established by the courts and by the Department of Education's Office for Civil Rights (OCR) under Title IX. Although Title IX has long been associated in the public mind primarily with intercollegiate athletics, it covers all aspects of education, from English and math courses to sex education and intramural sports, from schools' treatment of pregnant students to first-graders' interaction on the playground, from sexual relations between college students to the pronouns used by transgender students. Over the past half century, judges and administrators have produced hundreds of pages of rules, guidelines, and interpretations to explain what educational institutions must do to stay on what one judge described as the "sunny side" of Title IX.[5]

Despite the stunning changes described above, Title IX has become more controversial than ever. Starting in 2011 the Obama administration issued detailed and demanding rules on what schools must do to combat sexual violence and other forms of sexual harassment. In 2016 it announced guidelines—soon revoked by the Trump administration—on the rights of transgender students. These Title IX initiatives were part of the Obama administration's We Can't Wait campaign. "We can't wait for an increasingly dysfunctional Congress to do its job," the president told a crowd in Nevada. "When they won't act, I will."[6] Not surprisingly, this drew a heated response from the Republican Party. Its 2016 platform devoted a separate section to Title IX, charging that the original purpose of Title IX had been perverted "by bureaucrats—and by the current President of the United States—to impose a social and cultural revolution upon the American people."[7] A year later Secretary of Education Betsy DeVos announced that her department would review and revise the controversial guidelines on sexual harassment and assault issued during the Obama years.

Title IX is both a powerful symbol of our broad national commitment to gender equality in education and a complex, controversial regulatory regime. Most of the advances in opportunities for female students occurred not because the law demanded them, but because our culture had profoundly shifted. In the late 1960s and early 1970s—before Title IX was enacted or enforced—the doors of educational opportunity began to swing open for women, and they quickly rushed through. Colleges and universities that had previously accepted only men started to admit women, including Yale, Princeton, Johns Hopkins, the University of Virginia, Williams, Bowdoin, Brown, Dartmouth, and Duke. Despite the fact that Title IX does not apply to admissions policy at private undergraduate schools, there are almost no all-male colleges left in the United States.

Title IX was itself the product of this cultural shift. It passed with little debate in 1972 because no one was left to defend (at least in public) practices that limited the educational and employment opportunities of women. In that year both houses of Congress also approved by wide margins the Equal Rights Amendment (ERA) to the Constitution, and sent it to the states for what at the time looked like quick ratification. As Congresswoman Bella Abzug (D-N.Y.) put it, "1972 was a watershed year. We put sex discrimination provisions into everything. There was no opposition. Who'd be against equal rights for women?" Birch Bayh, the primary sponsor of both the ERA and Title IX in the Senate, explained, "Once you get by the ERA, Title IX is a piece of cake."[8] The previous year the Supreme Court had for the first time ruled that a sex-based classification violated the Equal Protection clause of the Fourteenth Amendment.[9] Two years later the Court suggested that gender based classifications might be subject to the "strict scrutiny" previously reserved for judging racial classifications.[10] In light of these changes, passage of Title IX seemed inconsequential. President Nixon did not even mention the mandate when he signed the omnibus legislation that contained it, nor was it covered in the next day's *New York Times*.

In fact, DiPrete and Buchmann's data show that there is hardly a country in the developed world that has not experienced this remarkable cultural transformation.

The "reversal from a male advantage to a female advantage in educational attainment," they conclude, "has unfolded not only in the United States but also in most industrialized societies."[11] Hanna Rosin, author of the provocatively titled *The End of Men and the Rise of Women*, claims that "women's dominance on college campuses is possibly the strangest and most profound change of the century, even more so because it is unfolding in a similar way pretty much all over the world."[12] Few of these countries have a Title IX equivalent.

Initially this made the job of enforcing Title IX far easier than enforcing prohibitions of racial discrimination. Nowhere did enraged alumni of men's colleges stand in the doorway of the admissions office vowing, "Gender Segregation Now, Gender Segregation Forever." Instead they flooded admissions offices with requests for interviews for their daughters.[13] Despite the frequency with which sex discrimination and racial discrimination are equated (a central theme of subsequent chapters), the differences are huge and obvious.

Because so many barriers to educational opportunity for women fell so quickly in the 1960s and 1970s, the focus of the regulatory regime shifted from overt exclusion and discrimination to more subtle educational practices. Federal regulators paid less and less attention to what goes on in the classroom, and more attention to what happens on the playing fields, in the bedroom, and in restrooms and locker rooms. Their focus shifted from the policies and practices of educational institutions to the beliefs of students and their teachers. No longer was the goal simply to provide equal opportunity to female students. Now it was to break down a wide array of stereotypes—those held by women as well as men; those common outside schools as well as inside; and those related to the meaning of masculinity, femininity, sexual orientation, and gender identity. In 1972 few would have predicted that sports, sexual harassment, and transgender rights would become the major elements of Title IX regulation. Indeed, it took OCR nearly a quarter of a century to issue its first regulations on sexual harassment, and two decades more to announce guidelines on transgender rights. Certainly no one who voted for Title IX in 1972 thought that OCR would eventually write rules allowing students to choose for themselves whether to be treated as male or female.

This book traces the slow transformation of Title IX from its original focus on ending exclusionary institutional practices to its current emphasis on deconstructing stereotypes about sex and gender. Much of it is devoted to understanding Title IX policy on athletics (part II) and sexual harassment (part III). The shorter transgender story is examined in the penultimate chapter. Parts II and III both begin with a discussion of the issues addressed by regulators (chapter 5 on athletics, chapter 9 on sexual harassment), and then offer a detailed look at the evolution of regulatory policy in OCR and the courts. These stories are long and complicated. Policymaking has usually occurred in fits and starts (to use the title of chapter 6), featuring incremental expansion and what I describe as institutional "leapfrogging." Such complexity and incrementalism often make the story hard to follow, but are essential elements of the politics of Title IX. They hide the significance of policy innovations not just from regulated institutions and the public, but at times from the regulators themselves.

Part I of the book provides the context for these detailed case studies by presenting an overview of the broader civil rights state (chapter 2), explaining the key features of Title IX (chapter 3), and offering a first look at the Department of Education's Office for Civil Rights (chapter 4). The final two chapters of the book examine the logic behind the expansion of Title IX regulation and the prospects for significant retrenchment in coming years.

Title IX in Action

Title IX speaks in grand phrases with uncertain meaning. Court decisions and administrative guidelines tend to be more specific. But they, too, often remain coy or ambiguous on key terms. To get a sense of the "law in action"—what federal regulation really means for those on the receiving end—it is useful to examine developments at three much different schools, Quinnipiac University in suburban Connecticut, Harvard Law School in Cambridge, Massachusetts, and Palatine Township High School in Illinois. These vignettes offer a glimpse at how Title IX has evolved and why regulatory efforts under it have become so contentious.

Quinnipiac University, 2010–14

In July 2010 a federal district court judge in Connecticut addressed this civil rights issue: should "competitive cheer and tumbling" be considered an intercollegiate sport? Despite acknowledging that "competitive cheer and tumbling" is a form of team gymnastics rather than traditional sideline pom-pom waving, Judge Stefan Underhill ruled that Quinnipiac University could not count the members of that team as varsity athletes under Title IX. That meant that to comply with federal law, Quinnipiac would either have to add another women's varsity team or eliminate a men's team. Judge Underhill's ninety-five-page, heavily footnoted opinion also concluded that Quinnipiac had not properly reported the number of male and female cross-country runners, and had failed to apply uniform roster rules to male and female teams. His initial order required Quinnipiac to reinstate the previously disbanded women's volleyball team and to change the way it counts varsity athletes.[14]

After three and a half years of litigation Quinnipiac signed a twenty-five-page agreement with the volleyball players and the Connecticut chapter of the American Civil Liberties Union (ACLU) that cost the school more than $8 million: at least $5 million to upgrade athletic facilities for women; over $600,000 for coaches, training, and equipment for women's teams; and nearly $2 million in attorneys' fees for the plaintiff. In addition to retaining the volleyball team, the college upgraded two other women's teams. The agreement established a monitor who would report to the court annually on the college's compliance—and be paid up to $150,000 per year for his efforts. This $8 million does not include the legal expenses the college ran up during those years of litigation.[15]

The Quinnipiac case received considerable media attention—and ridicule. To some it represented yet another case of overreach by federal regulators and judges. Just as the Supreme Court had tried to establish the rules of "classic, Platonic golf" in a 2001 Americans with Disabilities Act case,[16] now federal judges (with the help of bureaucrats in the Department of Education) were telling schools that synchronized swimming is a competitive sport, but competitive cheer and tumbling is not (or at least not yet). The most acerbic critique came from the sports and political commentator Gregg Easterbrook. Title IX, he wrote on ESPN .com, "has become an exemplar of the kind of government action that initially was justified but since has taken on a life of its own grounded in legal and bureaucratic nonsense." The law has generated "increasingly incongruous legal intrusion into minor matters," created "perverse results," and "mainly serve[s] to make government look ridiculous." Title IX, he fumed, "has become a Monty Python sketch," degrading our understanding of civil rights. "Whether a college offers volleyball or cheer," Easterbrook insisted, "is not a civil rights issue!"[17]

Easterbrook's column drew a spirited response from Nancy Hogshead-Makar, a former Olympic gold medal swimmer and director of advocacy for the Women's Sports Foundation (WSF).[18] She pointed out that the case involved not just the status of competitive cheer and tumbling, but the court's finding that the college had "deliberately reported fraudulent numbers" to inflate the number of female athletes on team rosters. This, she argued, was a widespread problem in college sports. Despite the fact that Title IX had been on the books for almost forty years, male athletes still receive more scholarship money than females, and at the high school level boys still outnumber girls on varsity teams by a wide margin. Expanding athletic opportunities for women and girls is a legitimate government responsibility because "a large body of research continues to confirm with certainty that a sports experience leads to higher educational achievement and success in the workplace, life-time lower rates of obesity, breast cancer, osteoporosis, heart disease and depression." She also noted that Judge Underhill was not making up his own definition of intercollegiate sports, but was simply applying rules developed by the Department of Education's Office for Civil Rights to distinguish sports from other extracurricular activities.

Intercollegiate and interscholastic athletics have attracted so much attention under Title IX not because sports is such an essential element of "equal educational opportunity"—at best it is a valuable extracurricular activity, at worst it is a serious distraction and a corrupting influence—but because it is one of the few activities that we continue to segregate by sex. Under Title IX the central rule for high school and college sports is "separate but equal." How do we measure equality in this context? By spending? By the number of varsity athletes or varsity roster spots? By the number and range of teams or activities? By participation rates in comparison to interest by male and female students? All these measures have flaws. All can be manipulated. And each reflects a somewhat different understanding of gender equality. Moreover, each measure creates its own set of incentives for schools, often unintended, occasionally silly, and all too frequently perverse. This serves as a useful reminder that Title IX cannot escape the challenges, dilemmas, and pathologies characterizing most forms of government regulation.

Harvard Law School, 2014–16

In 2014 the Office for Civil Rights launched investigations of scores of colleges across the country, alleging that they had failed to follow the agency's recently announced guidelines on preventing sexual violence and other forms of sexual harassment. Like most of the schools under investigation, Harvard University quickly agreed to change disciplinary rules for all its students, undergraduate and graduate alike, to conform to OCR's directives. A diverse group of Harvard Law School professors dissented, arguing that the rules Harvard had instituted under pressure from OCR violated basic principles of due process. The university, they maintained, was "jettisoning balance and fairness in the rush to appease certain federal administrative officials."[19] Soon thereafter one-third of the University of Pennsylvania Law School faculty signed a letter claiming that the agreement their school had reached with OCR "requires subordinating so many protections long deemed necessary to protect from injustice those accused of serious offenses." They also charged that "OCR has used threats of investigation and loss of federal funding to intimidate universities into going further than even the guidance requires."[20]

Harvard Law School eventually struck a separate deal with OCR. The law school reintroduced disciplinary hearings, which the university had replaced with the OCR-favored "single-investigator model" in sexual harassment cases. It allowed both the accuser and the accused to consult with a lawyer throughout the process, and it offered to "provide financial assistance to parties unable to afford an attorney who would like to do so." The law school acknowledged that this was a measure very few schools could afford.[21]

Shortly after these procedural matters were resolved, another sexual miscon duct controversy rocked Harvard Law. *The Hunting Ground*, a widely publicized documentary about sexual violence on campus, castigated the school for readmitting a "rapist" who had been suspended for several semesters for sexual misconduct. This referred to Brandon Winston, an African American law student who in a criminal trial had been found not guilty of rape but guilty of misdemeanor nonsexual touching. To Winston's accuser, Kamilah Willingham, and the producers of the documentary, this demonstrated that universities are unwilling to take steps necessary to eliminate the "rape culture" on college campuses. Nineteen Harvard Law professors—including several noted African American and feminist scholars—took issue with this characterization both of the accused student and the school's handling of the matter. They charged that "Winston was subjected to a long, harmful ordeal for no good reason," that the film "prolong[ed] his ordeal with its unfair and misleading portrayal of the facts of his case," and that it presented "a seriously false picture" not only of events at Harvard, but of "the general sexual assault phenomenon at universities."[22] Willingham, who is also African American, responded by demanding an apology from Harvard for "remain[ing] silent while 19 of the professors who presumably helped overturn my assailant's sanction very publicly doubled down on his side, expending my rape trial into the court of public opinion and joining my assailant's effort to brand me as a vindictive, slutty liar." In 2016 she formed an organization called Survivors Eradicating Rape Culture to "end gender violence using culture change and social justice."[23]

Meanwhile across the street in the Yard, Harvard undergraduates were completing a "climate check," a survey devised by a consortium of universities to get a better handle on the frequency of sexual misconduct on campus. Such "climate checks" constitute a key part of every compliance agreement OCR has negotiated with schools. Harvard's participation rate was unusually high (63 percent), giving its results more credibility than most such surveys. Among its many findings, two stood out. Nearly 15 percent of women seniors reported having experienced during their four years on campus the most serious form of sexual assault—"attempted or completed nonconsensual penetration through use of physical force or incapacitation." In other words, more than one out of seven female undergraduates said they had been the victim of assaults serious enough to constitute a crime in every state. Incongruently, nearly 70 percent of the female Harvard College students "who indicated they experienced an incident of penetration by force did not formally report it," and 80 percent of female students "who indicated they experienced an incident of penetration by incapacitation" did not report it either. "The most frequently cited reason for not reporting was a belief that it was not serious enough to report."[24]

During its first year and a half, Harvard's Office for Sexual and Gender-Based Dispute Resolution, the unit established to handle sexual harassment complaints, received sixteen allegations of sexual assault—only about ten per year from the university's more than 20,000 students, a tiny fraction of 1 percent.[25] Does this mean that these students consider the emotional and social costs of reporting too onerous to bear? That they believe the punishment might be too severe? That they remain ambivalent about their relationship with the perpetrator? We do not know.

Surveys at other schools report a similar reluctance to consider such conduct "serious enough" to report. Moreover, despite the extensive publicity given to the problem of sexual violence on campus and despite changes in college reporting systems designed to make them more victim friendly, the number of reports of sexual assault remains very small—at most schools less than 1 percent of the undergraduate population.[26]

If the Quinnipiac case has more than a touch of comedy, the events at Harvard have all the makings of a tragedy. Compelling demands for protection of women from sexual assault collide with compelling demands for due process, especially for racial minorities that have been subject to so many unsubstantiated accusations in the past. Race and sex, violence and fairness, federal rules and institutional autonomy, law and culture, the complexities of intense interpersonal relationships—all were thrown into this volatile mix. After years of discussion and investigation, the extent and the causes of sexual assault on campus remain elusive, and OCR's guidelines have become more controversial than ever. Although the Trump administration withdrew two key guidance documents issued by OCR in 2011 and 2014, it has yet to explain what will take their place. Most schools have been reluctant to change their disciplinary codes until the Department of Education issues rules that are upheld in court. In short, the issue continues to roil campuses, with no workable solution yet in sight.

Palatine Township School District, 2015–17

On November 2, 2015, OCR sent to the superintendent of schools in Palatine, Illinois, a fourteen-page, single-spaced letter regarding his high school's treatment of "Student A," a transgender teenager who was born biologically male but for many years had identified as female. The school had previously acquiesced to almost all the requests made by Student A, including being listed as a girl, being referred to by female pronouns, using the girls' bathrooms, and playing on girls' sports teams. Citing the privacy concerns of other female students, though, the school refused to allow Student A to change clothes and shower in the girls' locker room. Instead, it offered Student A individual changing and showering facilities either next door or down the hall.

After many days of negotiation, OCR ruled that the school district had violated Title IX because the law requires schools to treat transgender students who identify as female exactly as they would treat any other female student. Shortly thereafter, the school agreed to give Student A full access to the girls' locker room, to hire a consultant "with expertise in child and adolescent gender identity," and to establish a "support team to ensure that Student A has access and opportunity to participate in all programs and activities, and is otherwise protected from gender-based discrimination at school." The agreement further stipulated that if other students object to Student A's presence in the locker room, they can use the alternative changing areas previously rejected by Student A.[27]

A local group calling itself Students and Parents for Privacy then filed suit against the school district in federal court, alleging that girls at the high school "live in constant anxiety, fear and apprehension that a biological boy will walk in at any time while they use the locker rooms and showers and see them in a state of undress or naked." Representing Student A, the Illinois chapter of the ACLU charged that "the plaintiffs and their counsel have insisted on cruelly mis-gendering our client" and that their description of transgender students was "outside the mainstream of medical and scientific understanding." After Students and Parents for Privacy lost the court case, they took their cause to the voters, running a slate of candidates against the school board members who had signed the agreement with OCR. The *Chicago Tribune*'s story on the election reported that "transgender access has overshadowed all other issues." The challengers lost, and the agreement remained in place.[28]

Palatine proved to be an opening salvo in a rapidly escalating battle over the treatment of transgender students. In May 2016, OCR and the Department of Justice (DOJ) issued a Dear Colleague Letter (DCL) requiring schools to "treat a student's gender identity [as defined by the student] as the student's sex for purposes of Title IX." They insisted that "the desire to accommodate others' discomfort cannot justify a policy that singles out and disadvantages a particular class of students." This applied not just to restrooms and locker rooms, but to single-sex classes, sports, housing, and overnight accommodations.[29]

Meanwhile the state of North Carolina was enacting legislation requiring that access to restrooms in all public buildings (including schools) be determined on the basis of the "biological sex" listed on a person's birth certificate. The Department of Justice sued North Carolina, arguing that the state's bathroom law stigmatizes the transgendered, adding to "their isolation and exclusion" and "perpetuat[ing] a sense that they are not worthy of equal treatment and respect." Announcing the lawsuit, Attorney General Loretta Lynch equated the state's opposition to the department's guidelines with southern states' "fierce and widespread resistance to *Brown v. Board*" in the 1950s and 1960s. "It was not so very long ago," Lynch said, that states like North Carolina "had signs above restrooms, water fountains and on public accommodations keeping people out based upon a distinction without a difference." The country has "moved beyond those dark days, but not without pain and suffering. . . . Let us write a different story this time."[30] North Carolina countersued, arguing that the prohibition against sex discrimination in Title IX and Title VII of the 1964 Civil Rights Act do not require states to accept students' "gender identification" when it conflicts with their biology at birth. Governor Pat McCrory charged that "the Obama administration is bypassing Congress by attempting to rewrite the law and set restroom policies for public and private employers across the country."[31]

Eleven states filed a similar suit in a federal district court in Texas, and won an injunction barring OCR from enforcing its transgender DCL anywhere in the country.[32] But the Fourth Circuit took a much different stance, holding that a Virginia high school *must* follow the policies established by OCR.[33] The Supreme Court decided to review that decision, scheduling oral argument for the spring of 2017. Before that could happen, though, OCR and the Department of Justice withdrew the transgender DCL, and the Supreme Court sent the case back to the Fourth Circuit for reconsideration in light of the new circumstances.[34] While that case was pending, the Seventh Circuit read Title IX to require schools to defer to students' gender identity.[35] The "bathroom war" suddenly became the latest battleground in the ongoing American culture war.

Title IX as Regulatory Regime

These stories offer a quick first look at the extensive regulatory regime described in this book. What can one learn from these stories? Five distinctive features of this policy area stand out. Each will be developed and supported at greater length in subsequent chapters.

1. *The growth of the American civil rights state.* Most obviously, these stories illustrate the reach of the American civil rights state. By "civil rights state" I mean the extensive set of statutes, court decisions, and administrative regulations, guidelines, interpretations, and settlement agreements designed to prevent and rectify discrimination based on race, ethnicity, religion, national origin, sex, disability, age, and sexual orientation. Although the term "civil rights state" will no doubt sound strange to many ears, it reminds us that since 1964 we have constructed an impressive edifice of nondiscrimination rules that apply to nearly every business, school, nonprofit, and government unit in the country. These rules are enforced by judges and administrators armed with formidable sanctions. Like its cousin, the American welfare state, the civil rights state has a distinctive form that reflects both our unusual constitutional system and our long history of struggle over civil rights.

Although we often associate "civil rights" with constitutional decisions such as the Supreme Court's 1954 landmark ruling in *Brown v. Board of Education*, the contemporary American civil rights state rests primarily on *statutory* rather than constitutional foundations. The key texts are the civil rights laws of the 1960s—the Civil Rights Act of 1964, the Voting Rights Act of 1965, and the Fair Housing Act of 1968—and subsequent legislation barring discrimination based on sex, disability, language, religion, and age. Over the years these laws have been amended to cover more actors and activities and to promote more aggressive and effective enforcement.

Just as important, since 1964 we have created a variety of federal agencies to interpret and enforce civil rights laws, which (like most statutes) remain silent on crucial policy matters. These bureaucracies include not just the two mentioned above, the Department of Education's Office for Civil Rights and the Civil Rights Division of the Department of Justice, but also the Equal Employment Opportunity Commission (EEOC), the Department of Labor's Office of Federal Contract Compliance Programs, and several units in the Department of Housing and Urban Development. In addition, all federal departments and many agencies have their own civil rights offices.

Together these agencies issue thousands of pages of rules, covering not just sex discrimination in schools and racial discrimination in housing and employment, but also how employers must "accommodate" employees with disabilities; what constitutes an "appropriate education" for English-language learners and children with disabilities; and what forms of electoral redistricting illegally "dilute" the voting power of racial and linguistic minorities. The level of detail in these regulations can be surprising: one EEOC guidance document explains when employers can and cannot base an employment decision on a candidate's foreign accent.[36] HUD devotes ten dense, double-column pages of the *Code of Federal Regulations* to "Pet Ownership for the Elderly or Persons with Disabilities."[37] Because the central mandates in most civil rights laws are so vague—they prohibit discrimination without explaining what that key term means—writing these rules and guidelines means making civil rights policy.

Civil rights regulation is one form of the "social regulation" that has grown in leaps and bounds since the mid-1960s. This includes environmental and consumer protection and rules designed to reduce a wide array of health and safety risks. Social regulation differs from traditional "economic regulation" in several important ways. Traditional economic regulation tends to focus narrowly on one particular industry—railroads, aeronautics, electric power, nuclear energy, or oceangoing shipping. Its daily fare is limited to mundane matters of prices and service levels. Usually the regulatory body is a multimember commission partially insulated from presidential control. In contrast, new agencies such as the Environmental Protection Agency (EPA) and the Occupational Safety and Health Administration (OSHA) regulate all sorts of business, are led by a single executive appointed by the president, and routinely make controversial decisions about what constitutes "acceptable risk" and fair outcomes. The cost of social regulation dwarfs that of all previous forms of federal regulation. Traditional regulation usually became the preserve of a small group of self-interested parties. Social regulation, in contrast, raises cultural and partisan issues that attract far wider and more impassioned attention.

2. *Courts, agencies, and institutional "leapfrogging."* In building the administrative apparatus of the civil rights state, Congress not only divided authority among a number of executive branch agencies, but gave federal courts substantial enforcement authority. This is particularly apparent for employment dis-

crimination. As Sean Farhang has explained, in 1964 Congress was unwilling to create a strong administrative agency, and instead handed responsibility for determining guilt and imposing sanctions in employment discrimination cases to the courts. Although civil rights organizations first opposed this approach, they eventually came to favor it over a more executive-centered enforcement framework. Since the 1990s, 15,000 to 20,000 employment discrimination suits have been filed in federal court every year.[38]

Title IX, in contrast, was designed to place primary enforcement authority in the hands of the federal administrators: it directs them to deny federal funding to any educational institution that engages in sex discrimination. But this enforcement strategy quickly proved ineffective. For decades the real enforcement teeth in Title IX have come from lawsuits filed by private parties—such as the volleyball players who sued Quinnipiac and the transgender student who sued the Virginia school district.

Several factors contribute to the large role courts play within the civil rights state. The provisions of some civil rights laws are designed to protect rights guaranteed by the Fourteenth and Fifteenth Amendments. As a result, the line between constitutional interpretation and statutory interpretation often blurs.[39] Given the Supreme Court's insistence that the federal judiciary is the preeminent interpreter of the Constitution, judges have not been willing simply to defer to agencies' reading of these statutes. Moreover, as we can see in the North Carolina case, civil rights issues often raise serious federalism concerns. Not only have the Rehnquist and Roberts Courts occasionally (if inconsistently) expressed concern for protecting the "sovereign dignity" of the states, but federal agencies do not have nearly as much leverage against state and local governments as they do against private parties. In addition, most civil rights laws enacted since 1970 were passed by Democratic Congresses when Republicans controlled the White House. The laws' sponsors tended to trust federal judges more than administrators appointed by GOP presidents.[40]

Although courts and agencies sometimes disagree on how to interpret civil rights statutes, in most instances each needs the other. Agencies rely on the courts for their superior political legitimacy, as well as their ability to issue injunctions and order the payment of money damages. Civil rights agencies seldom have authority to impose such sanctions by themselves. Courts, in turn, need agencies' ability to issue rules of general applicability, to investigate the thousands of complaints filed by private parties, and to negotiate and monitor a multitude of compliance agreements.

Throughout this book we will encounter examples of a process I call institutional "leapfrogging"—courts and agencies each taking a step beyond the other, expanding regulation without seeming to innovate.[41] This was apparent in the Quinnipiac case. The district court relied heavily on OCR's 1996 "clarification" of its 1979 "interpretation" of its 1975 regulations. That agency "clarification" rested in large part on circuit courts' reading of the 1979 "interpretation." The Quinnipiac court then adopted a reading of those administrative guidelines that went well beyond what OCR had previously required. Similarly, OCR's sexual harassment rules built on the Equal Employment Opportunity Commission's Title VII guidelines, which followed Supreme Court decisions that were in turn based on previous EEOC rules that incorporated earlier lower court decisions. The 2016 OCR/DOJ Dear Colleague Letter on schools' treatment of transgender students claimed to follow the sole federal court opinion on the topic, a circuit court ruling that had deferred to a previous policy statement by the agency that was in turn based on a few settlement letters similar to the one signed by the Palatine School District.[42] To describe this process as convoluted would be an understatement. Indeed that is one of its most important characteristics. Understanding how civil rights regulations evolved requires painstaking political archaeology, digging through one layer of judicial and administrative detail after another.

The court–agency leapfrogging so common in the 1970s and 1980s became somewhat less frequent by the late 1990s as the Supreme Court turned in a more conservative direction. This was most apparent with sexual harassment, where OCR adopted a far broader interpretation of Title IX than that announced by the Supreme Court in 1998–99. When courts and agencies see eye-to-eye (as they have with intercollegiate athletics), agencies can count on courts to provide the enforcement teeth and public legitimacy that the agencies themselves have lacked. But when courts and agencies diverge, agencies must scramble to invent new enforcement tools—as OCR did with sexual harassment.

It is important to remember, though, that the Supreme Court decides very few cases—fewer than eighty per year. Over the past forty-five years it has heard only eight Title IX cases, none on athletics, three on sexual harassment, and (so far at least) none on transgender rights.[43] This means that circuit courts usually have the final judicial word on interpretation of Title IX. They have been more inclined to adopt a broad reading of the law than has the Supreme Court.

3. *Educational exceptionalism.* Most forms of regulation are designed to change the behavior of business firms. Regulation is usually seen as an effort to address "market failures" such as monopoly, externalities, and imperfect information. Few of the educational institutions subject to Title IX are profit-making firms. The vast majority are public elementary and secondary schools that do not compete for "customers" and are not judged by their "bottom line." Colleges and universities (both public and private) obviously do compete for applicants, often intensely. Unlike business firms, though, they tend to maximize status rather than profits. These peculiar features of educational institutions change the politics of regulation, making the task of ensuring compliance with federal rules harder in some ways and easier in others.

On the one hand, schools are the type of bureaucracies James Q. Wilson has called "coping organizations." These are organizations in which it is difficult either to observe the work done by key personnel (in this case, teachers) or to measure with confidence the consequences of their work. "A school administrator," Wilson notes, "cannot watch teachers teach (except through classroom visits that momentarily may change the teacher's behavior) and cannot tell how much students have learned except by standardized tests that do not clearly differentiate between what the teacher has imparted and what the student has acquired otherwise."[44] Consequently schools tend to be decentralized, hard to control either from the top or through written rules. A federal agency with little more than 500 staff members can hardly expect to monitor or to control what goes on in the classrooms of the more than 20,000 schools subject to Title IX—however long and detailed its rulebook.

On the other hand, schools are filled with employees who consider themselves "professionals," which means not only that they are guided by the norms of their profession, but also that they are concerned with their reputation among peers outside their formal organization. This limits hierarchical control within schools and often creates tension between school professionals and the elected officials—school boards, mayors, governors, legislators—who hire them and provide their funding.

It also means that federal regulators can increase their chances of changing educational practices by negotiating informal alliances with the numerous professionals who staff the institutions being regulated: special education teachers, psychologists, bilingual education teachers, coaches of women's teams, diversity offices, human resources administrators, and many more. Professionals employed by schools in turn can use regulation and litigation as leverage to gain resources for the activities they consider especially important. As the lawyer in a seminal disability rights case told a gathering of specialists, "We have with some ease adopted the agenda that you, the professionals have set and we have taken them to court."[45] Norma Cantú, head of OCR under President Clinton, explained, "Our investigators and negotiators were good at figuring out what the people on the other side of the table wanted . . . and giving them political cover."[46] In recent years OCR has worked assiduously to build large, autonomous Title IX compliance offices within universities. Charles Epp's research on "legalized accountability" in state and local governments demonstrates the importance of these internal compliance offices for changing bureaucratic behavior.[47] It is not unusual for such offices to exaggerate the demands of federal administrators and judges in order to extend their authority and enhance their status.

4. *The language of rights.* Most regulatory agencies establish "policies." Civil rights agencies, as their name suggests, define legal rights. In practice there isn't much difference between the two. OCR's rules, like the rules issued by EPA or

OSHA, tell regulated institutions what they can and cannot do. Nonetheless, the language of rights has had a profound effect on the politics of regulation. Elsewhere the central regulatory standard is market efficiency; here it is "equality of opportunity." Economists have established themselves as the experts on the former; in the United States lawyers claim to be the experts on the latter. Interpretation of civil rights statutes takes place in the shadow of courts' interpretation of the Fourteenth Amendment's Equal Protection clause. Although these laws cover private parties—which are not subject to the Fourteenth Amendment's prohibitions—most judges and administrators believe that interpretation of civil rights statutes should track the evolving interpretation of constitutional provisions.

As Mary Ann Glendon has pointed out, "rights talk" tends to discourage exploration of costs, trade-offs, incentives, alternatives, consequences, and compromise by encouraging us to think in terms of moral absolutes.[48] The sort of policy analysis one finds in the rulemaking proceedings of EPA or OSHA is rarely found in OCR documents. In fact, OCR has virtually abandoned the standard rulemaking process, replacing it with unilateral statements about the evolving meaning of statutory rights. "Rights talk" also leads us to see the world in black and white, rather than in the shades of gray that characterize most policy debates. We expect one presidential administration to change many of the policies established by its predecessor. But we balk at "rolling back civil rights"— even when those rights are based on partisan interpretations of ambiguous legislation. As a result, the language of rights is frequently used to lock in preferred policies by delegitimizing opposition.

To complicate matters further, it is not unusual for one set of rights to collide with another. Consider the examples of rights in conflict found in our three stories. One student's right to be free from sexual violence can conflict with another student's right to due process. The right of transgender students to be treated according to their gender identity can conflict with other students' right to privacy. To comply with Title IX some men's teams have been eliminated while women's teams scramble to fill their rosters. Aggrieved college wrestlers and gymnasts have charged that this constitutes "reverse discrimination." In 2002 the executive director of the National Wrestling Coaches Association promised, "We're prepared to do whatever it takes to eliminate the gender quota. . . . There shouldn't be any gender discrimination, period, and there's serious discrimination going on against men."[49] Male students falsely accused of sexual assault made similar arguments a decade and half later. Rights are seldom as simple in practice as they sound in lofty political and academic debates. Behind the rhetoric of rights lies the messy complexity of regulatory politics.

5. *The idea of progress.* Soon after successfully defending the Civil Rights Act before the Supreme Court, former solicitor general Archibald Cox wrote, "Once

loosed, the idea of Equality is not easily cabined."[50] The American civil rights state was originally constructed to destroy the racial caste system in the South. Attacking state-sponsored segregation, discrimination, and disenfranchisement required an unprecedented assertion of federal authority. Before long these same powers were being employed to address sex discrimination, the barriers faced by English-language learners and students with disability, age-based rules on hiring and retirement, and social norms regarding sexual orientation and gender identity. Regulation slowly moved from the most public—state laws mandating segregation—to the most private—sexual relations among adults.

In almost all areas of discrimination law there has also been a strong tendency to move from bans on *intentional* discrimination (the original focus of the Civil Rights Act) toward an expectation of *proportional results*. Intentional discrimination is hard to prove and easy to disguise. Once intentional racial and sex discrimination became illegal, judges and administrators looked for ways to ferret out discrimination that is more subtle, based on sophisticated pretexts, or even unintentional. The standard approach has been to place the burden of proof on businesses, schools, and other institutions that fail to produce proportional results in hiring or admissions to demonstrate that they have not discriminated on the basis of race, sex, or any other prohibited criteria. Under such "disparate impact" rules, only business or educational "necessity" can justify practices that result in disproportionate outcomes.

This proportionality standard is particularly apparent in athletics: the only "safe harbor" for college athletic departments is a distribution of male and female varsity athletes and scholarships that mirrors the proportion of male and female undergraduate students at the institution. The central argument against this manifestation of the proportionality rule—an argument repeated loudly and frequently by coaches of discontinued men's teams—is that males and females differ in their relative interest in highly competitive sports. The distribution of athletic opportunities, they argue, should reflect students' interest, not enrollment numbers. Women's groups and OCR respond that interest often reflects opportunity, and Title IX is designed to upend gender stereotypes that all too often reflect decades of discriminatory practices rather than natural differences.

This means that civil rights regulation often seeks not just to change behavior, but to change the way all of us—employers and employees, teachers and students, and members of the public at large—think about race, sex, age, disability, language, religion, or ethnicity. As First Circuit judge Hugh Bownes claimed in an important Title IX case, "Title IX was enacted in order to remedy discrimination that results from stereotyped notions of women's interests and abilities."[51] According to this interpretation, Title IX must be used to change the way men view women and women view themselves. "Build it and they will come" is the motto of many advocates for women's sports: new opportunities will upend old gender stereotypes. One finds an even stronger effort to change how people think about sex in OCR's regulations on sexual harassment and gender identity. Their goal is not just to punish those who engage in misconduct, but to change students' understanding of what constitutes proper sexual behavior, the right way to think about sex, and even what it means to be male or female. This is a heady job for government regulators.

This book explores the gradual expansion of the goals of Title IX regulation and the corresponding authority of OCR and federal judges. This transformation took place not through congressional amendment of the law, but through administrative and judicial reinterpretation of a statute that has changed little since 1972. On the one hand, this shows that the common complaining about government "gridlock" is overblown. Our constitutional system may make legislation hard to pass by creating multiple "veto points," but it also creates multiple "opportunity points" for innovation by judges, administrators, and state and local officials.[52] Congress has been only one contributor to the growth of the civil rights state, and often just a minor and reactive one.

On the other hand, the transformation of Title IX raises serious questions about political accountability. Should unelected judges and administrators have the power to impose on local schools and private universities rules that the elected legislators who voted for Title IX had never imagined? Should we trust those judges and administrators to update decades-old legislation to comport with their understanding of "progress"—even if many others see the changes they mandate as constituting retrogression or decay? This is a topic to which I will return in chapters 12 and 13.

Evaluating Policy and Process

Much of this book is devoted to describing the institutions of the American civil rights state and the unusual processes that produced current Title IX policies. I try to explain the evolution of policy on athletics, sexual harassment, and transgender rights in a way that both supporters and opponents of these policies will consider fair and accurate. That does not mean I am agnostic on the merits of these policies. As the reader will see, I consider many of OCR's rules—especially those on sexual harassment—badly flawed, and I trace those flaws to serious deficiencies in the process that produced them.

Most of the problems associated with the extensive regulations and guidelines generated under Title IX are a result of regulators' unwillingness to seek input from those most affected by and most knowledgeable about these issues, and their lack of interest in examining the long-term costs and unintended consequences of their actions. Convinced that they were on the side of the angels, they made little effort to hear dissenting voices or to temper their vast ambitions. By using Dear Colleague Letters rather than rules established through the process mandated by the Administrative Procedure Act, OCR avoided its obligation to justify its policies, collect relevant information, and respond to criticism. In order to do this, it had to conceal the novelty of its mandates. "Nothing new here," the agency repeated year after year as its demands on schools escalated. All too often federal judges did just the same, enabling and legitimizing such agency action and enforcing the resulting regulations. In 2017 Secretary of Education Betsy DeVos promised to end what she described as "rule by letter," and to employ Administrative Procedure Act rulemaking procedures for establishing new policies under civil rights laws.[53] Whether OCR will practice what Secretary DeVos has preached remains to be seen.

The connection between flawed policies and truncated procedures is clearest with sexual harassment rules. Surprising as it might seem, the due process and free speech issues that have featured so prominently in subsequent debate were never subjected to serious analysis by OCR before it issued its 2011 and 2014 guidelines. Nor was there any discussion of the substantial costs these requirements would impose on schools, or the way in which the new compliance offices mandated by the federal government would shift power within educational institutions. Instead of taking a hard look at the complicated evidence on the frequency and causes of sexual assault, the agency relied exclusively on a handful of studies, including one that even its authors described as unrepresentative of the diversity of American universities. None of the scores of agreements with individual schools were subject to public scrutiny before they were signed, sealed, and delivered. When criticism inevitably appeared, OCR's leadership responded primarily with invective, insisting that critics were trying to "roll back civil rights" because they did not understand the seriousness of the issue.[54]

As chapter 8 explains, a similar refusal to acknowledge the novelty of their guidelines or to explore their long-term implications characterized the athletics policies ever so slowly developed by the courts and OCR. Most disturbing was the potent combination of their focus on the most competitive level of college sports and their obliviousness to opportunity costs. Judges and administrators alike created strong incentives for schools to increase spending on intercollegiate athletics, despite the fact that at many colleges this benefited only a tiny fraction of "students-athletes" and reduced the resources available to those more serious about academic pursuits. How can it be, the president of Brown University asked, that the university can be "free to cut libraries and academic departments, but not athletics?"[55] The short answer is that neither the courts nor administrators gave any sustained attention to the central issue, namely, the relationship between sports and education. In a variety of ways described in chapter 8, it is likely that the unacknowledged costs of this interpretation of Title IX fall most heavily on women.

The transgender guidelines issued by OCR in 2016 (and revoked within a year) were in place for such a short time that it is impossible to evaluate their long-term consequences or their wisdom. What is notable about them, though, is that on the basis of a very shaky legal argument and with virtually no explanation or presentation of evidence, federal regulators laid down a rule for thousands of school districts that brooked no exceptions and left little room for school officials to consider the special circumstances of each case. The complex psychological issue of gender identity was addressed by applying an almost entirely inapt analogy, that of racial segregation. On transgender issues American culture is changing with remarkable rapidity, making it more likely that in most places school officials will treat students struggling with gender dysphoria with compassion and understanding. Curt dictates from inside the Beltway do more to stoke the culture wars than to help those on the receiving end deal with complicated, real-life problems.

Behind the debates over particular Title IX policies lies a broader issue: Who should decide? In the United States, decisionmaking on most educational policy is highly decentralized. State and local educational institutions bear most of the responsibility for elementary and secondary education. Our system of higher education includes schools public and private, large and small, religious and nonsectarian, liberal arts colleges and professional schools, brick-and-mortar and online—a remarkable variety that has helped make our colleges and universities the best in the world. On a few issues we have decided that some types of decisions cannot be left to the discretion of those running these thousands of schools. Most important, none of them can discriminate on the basis of race, and most of them cannot discriminate on the basis of sex. Some of these prohibitions have originated in the Supreme Court's interpretation of the Constitution. Most have come from Congress. But almost all the federal mandates examined in this book bear at best an attenuated relationship to what the Constitution or Congress commands. Consequently, the evolution of Title IX raises fundamental questions about control, accountability, and legitimacy within a constitutional democracy. While I make no secret of the fact that this worries me a great deal, I prefer not to preach, but to lay out the story as fairly as I can and let the reader judge.

Given the tenor of contemporary debate on these topics, it is important to emphasize that criticism of current policies does not imply disagreement with the original, underlying purpose of Title IX—promoting *educational* opportunity for women and girls—nor does it deny the remarkable achievements of female students over the past half century or the seriousness of problems they still confront. Those of us who have daughters should be thankful that they can now be student-athletes if they so choose. At the elementary and secondary levels, much remains to be done in many parts of the country to encourage athletic activity and physical fitness among girls. Despite the attention paid to the issue in recent years, sexual assault and other forms of sexual misconduct remain a serious problem on college campuses. Indeed, it is rare to talk to a female college graduate who does not have a disturbing story to tell. We have yet to get a firm handle on the extent of the problem, to say nothing of effective remedies for it. Transgender students face many serious personal and social challenges. Schools need to show compassion and flexibility in responding to their diverse needs.

Recognizing the *seriousness* of these *problems*, though, does not require us to accept the *adequacy* of the *solutions* offered by OCR and the courts. In the end, adequately understanding these issues requires us to descend from airy abstractions about rights, stereotypes, and equal opportunity into the sometimes confusing, often dreary weeds of statutory provisions, *Federal Register* notices, Dear Colleague Letters, judicial opinions, and settlement agreements. This is a world in which one finds many of the pathologies identified by serious students of regulation, including mission creep, goal displacement, bean counting, and unanticipated consequences. Regulating thousands of schools with millions of students and teachers is an enormously difficult task. It takes much more than good intentions. A first step for improving this regulatory regime is to learn from past mistakes.

TWO

The Civil Rights State

Compared with other advanced industrial democracies, the United States is usually considered the land of limited, decentralized government. Despite its growth over recent decades, our welfare state remains somewhat smaller and less nationally uniform than that of most European social democracies. In general we have less economic regulation, putting more trust in markets than in government. Our educational system remains remarkably decentralized, with most funding (in fact, 90 percent) and control in the hands of fifty state governments and 14,000 local school districts. Although these contrasts are not nearly as stark today as they were half a century ago, in many respects American government still reflects the distrust of centralized administrative authority that has long been a key element of our political culture.

Except when it comes to civil rights. Sexual harassment law offers a stark contrast between the United States and Europe, but not in the usual way. In her 2003 book *What Is Sexual Harassment? From Capitol Hill to the Sorbonne*, Abigail Saguy shows that in the employment context restrictions on sexual harassment are far stricter and more aggressively enforced in the United States than in France.[1] Kathrin Zippel makes a similar argument in her comparison of sexual harassment law in the United States, Germany, and the European Union. She notes that "the United States was the first country in the world to recognize sexual harassment as sex discrimination, and today probably has the most sophisticated legal and institutional apparatus to handle such complaints in the workplace and the legal system."[2]

Both Saguy and Zippel demonstrate that this was in large part a result of the interplay between federal judges and the U.S. Equal Employment Opportunity Commission (EEOC). According to Saguy, the American common-law system "provided American feminists a valuable entryway into the lawmaking process that their French counterparts did not enjoy."[3] Similarly, Zippel found that American law has been "deeply influenced by feminist legal arguments," largely because "U.S. courts have accepted a definition of sexual harassment from the victim's perspective."[4]

Zippel and Saguy completed their studies several years before the Office for Civil Rights (OCR) began its aggressive campaign to address sexual harassment on campus. For reasons explored in chapters 10 and 11, the EEOC's sexual harassment guidelines for employers are relatively mild in comparison with OCR's guidelines for schools. Consequently, in the education context the contrast between the United States and Europe is particularly pronounced. One can only imagine what the French have to say about the "affirmative consent" rules adopted by several states and many colleges!

The law on sexual harassment is no aberration. A number of recent works indicate that when it comes to civil rights, the usual transatlantic pattern is reversed: American government is more energetic and more efficacious than its European counterparts. In his comparison of race policy in the United States, Britain, and France, Robert Lieberman points out that "the 'weak' American state" has "not only produced more active and extensive enforcement of antidiscrimination law; it also managed to challenge the color-blind presumptions of its own law and to forge an extensive network of race-conscious policies and practices that have proven strikingly resilient in the face of political and legal challenges."[5] Erik Bleich shows how heavily—and consciously—Britain borrowed from the United States when it sought to strengthen its civil rights laws in the 1970s.[6] Sociologists who study employment discrimination policy have struggled to explain the paradox of our "weak state" producing such robust regulation.[7]

The key to unraveling this paradox, several scholars suggest, is understanding the synergistic relationship between courts and agencies that developed in the wake of the civil rights revolution of the 1960s.[8] As we will see throughout this book, federal administrators and judges have frequently engaged in a process of policy "leapfrog," with each institution incorporating and then adding to the regulatory initiatives of the other. Regulatory demands grow slowly, almost imperceptibly, with neither branch acknowledging the extent of its policy innovation.

From Extraordinary Measures to Ordinary Politics

In the summer of 1963 a quarter of a million people joined the March on Washington that culminated in Martin Luther King Jr.'s stirring "I Have a Dream" speech at the Lincoln Memorial. If anyone in that vast throng had thought to look around the District of Columbia for evidence of an American "civil rights state," they would have come up empty-handed. The few legal protections that remained in the federal statute books—largely a product of the Reconstruction era—had been reduced to nullities by decades of Supreme Court interpretation. The American party system that structured politics between Reconstruction and 1963 made it almost impossible for either Congress or the executive branch to take decisive action to attack the racial caste system of the South. The rules of Congress, especially those on seniority and the filibuster, gave southerners an effective veto over civil rights legislation. Since Democrats relied on the "solid South" to win presidential elections and to maintain control of Congress, even those presidents most sympathetic to the cause—Franklin Roosevelt, Harry Truman, and John Kennedy—were reluctant to push too hard on the issue. A serious attack on racial segregation and discrimination would require major changes in our party structure, core elements of our governing institutions, and our understanding of the constitutional powers of the national government.

The Policy "Breakthrough"

That transformation took place with startling rapidity in the mid-1960s. Congress enacted the Civil Rights Act of 1964, the Voting Rights Act of 1965, and the Fair Housing Act of 1968 (see table 2-1 for a list of the major provisions of these key laws). In 1965 President Johnson issued Executive Order 11246, prohibiting federal contractors from discriminating on the basis of race, color, religion, sex, or national origin, and requiring them to take "affirmative action" to ensure that all these groups are treated fairly. After a decade of inaction, the federal government finally began to enforce the Supreme Court's decision in *Brown v. Board of Education*. Within a few years it had achieved what Gary Orfield aptly called "the reconstruction of southern education."[9]

No change this significant has a single cause. Scholars and journalists have suggested a variety of factors that contributed to the civil rights revolution. The 1964 Civil Rights Act got an enormous boost from President Johnson's unparalleled legislative skill and his intense focus on passing landmark laws. The Voting Rights Act was enacted in the wake of the bloody (and televised) confrontation between peaceful demonstrators and club-wielding police at Edmund Pettus Bridge in Selma, Alabama. Housing legislation remained stalled in Congress until the assassination of Martin Luther King and the urban riots that followed convinced

Table 2-1   The Policy "Breakthrough" of the 1960s

Civil Rights Act of 1964
- Title II outlaws racial discrimination in commercial establishments open to the public
- Title IV authorizes the U.S. Department of Justice to file school desegregation suits
- Title VI requires federal agencies to terminate federal funding to subnational governments or private parties that engage in discrimination on the basis of race or national origin
- Title VII prohibits racial or sex discrimination by private employers

Voting Rights Act of 1965
- Bans the use of literacy tests in all "covered" jurisdictions, primarily the deep South
- Requires "covered" jurisdictions to "preclear" any changes in election law with either the Department of Justice or the federal district court in the District of Columbia before putting them into effect

Fair Housing Act of 1968
- Prohibits discrimination on the basis of race, religion, or national origin in the sale, rental, or financing of housing

---

a majority in the House and Senate that they needed to act quickly and forcefully. Suffice it to say here that civil rights protests stretching from the Montgomery bus boycott of 1955–56 to the 1963 March on Washington briefly made civil rights the most salient political issue in the nation, forcing citizens and politicians to choose between fidelity to the Constitution and the American creed on the one hand and more decades of hypocrisy and unrest on the other. The nobility of the protesters and their cause and the now visible hideousness of the southern response forced Americans outside the South to decide whose side they were on.

The danger remained that the seminal legislation passed in the 1960s would suffer the same fate as civil rights laws enacted during Reconstruction. Nearly a century earlier, federal efforts to ensure that the newly freed slaves would enjoy equal rights foundered on the fatal combination of the national government's lack of administrative capacity, Congress's abandonment of the project after 1876, and the Supreme Court's reluctance to extend federal authority. This time, in contrast, the federal government could build upon decades of expansion of federal constitutional authority and administrative power. Almost immediately the Voting Rights Act achieved its purpose of opening the electoral process to previously disenfranchised black voters, changing the political calculations of many politicians. The Supreme Court not only found the civil rights legislation passed by Congress constitutional, but adopted an expansive interpretation of many key provisions. Congress steadily expanded the authority of federal judges and administrators to enforce nondiscrimination mandates.

Moving beyond Jim Crow

This concerted attack on the racial caste system in the South had not initially been seen as the beginning of a wholesale effort to address inequality in its many forms, but only as a long overdue response to the unique problem of state-sponsored racial discrimination. In his opinion upholding Congress's authority to prohibit southern states from using literacy tests for voting and to require those states to preclear changes in their voting laws with federal officials, Chief Justice Earl Warren emphasized that the Voting Rights Act's "uncommon exercise of congressional power" was a legislative response to "unique circumstances," namely, an "insidious and pervasive evil which had been perpetuated in certain parts of our country through unremitting and ingenious defiance of the Constitution." According to the chief justice, "The Court has recognized that exceptional conditions can justify legislative measures not otherwise appropriate." He emphasized that Congress had built a "voluminous legislative history" supporting its unusually aggressive assertion of federal authority.[10]

Because the Voting Rights Act constituted such an unprecedented infringement upon the authority of state governments, Congress made some of its provisions temporary. But before these provisions expired in 1970, Congress extended them for another five years. In 1975 it added another seven years, in 1982 an additional twenty-five years, and in 2006 yet another twenty-five years. In the process, Congress extended the ban on literacy tests to the entire nation, provided protection to "linguistic minorities," and authorized legal challenges to redistricting plans that threaten to "dilute" the voting power of racial and linguistic minorities. Thus a temporary measure designed to protect African Americans against blatant disenfranchisement in the South became a permanent measure to enhance the political power of a wider array of groups everywhere in the country.[11]

The expansion of civil rights regulation proceeded along several dimensions. The first and most obvious was geographic. Initially school desegregation focused on de jure segregation in the South, but within a few years much of the attention was on de facto segregation in the North and West. Federal court litigation on prison conditions started in southern states with a long history of segregating and mistreating black inmates. Soon most northern and western prison systems were also under court orders.[12] The Equal Employment Opportunity Commission and the National Association for the Advancement of Colored People (NAACP) first targeted their Title VII efforts against southern employers that had previously made no secret of their discriminatory practices. By the early 1970s they were going after the more subtle hiring practices of employers in the Northeast and Midwest.[13]

Second, during the 1950s and early 1960s most of the emphasis was on chang-ing state and local laws and the behavior of public officials. Because the Civil War amendments to the Constitution apply only to "state action," not to private parties, prohibiting discrimination by private schools, employers, store owners, landlords, realtors, and bankers required congressional action under the Constitution's commerce clause. The 1964 Civil Rights Act, the 1968 Fair Housing Act, the Americans with Disabilities Act (ADA), and many other federal statutes—including Title IX—extend nondiscrimination mandates to private parties, vastly increasing the number of organizations subject to civil rights regulation.

Third, Congress steadily expanded the jurisdiction and enforcement powers of federal civil rights agencies and the federal courts (see table 2-2). For example, the 1972 Equal Employment Opportunity Act extended Title VII to educa-tional institutions and local, state, and federal employment. It also gave the EEOC authority to file suit to enforce Title VII. The 1976 Civil Rights Attorney's Fees Award Act authorized judges to award attorneys' fees and other costs to prevailing parties under a variety of civil rights laws. The 1988 Fair Housing Act Amend-ments and the 1991 Civil Rights Act further increased incentives for plaintiffs to file civil rights litigation by substantially increasing the damages courts can award. As we will see, the 1988 Civil Rights Restoration Act (commonly known as the "Grove City Bill"[14]) expanded federal jurisdiction under Title IX.

Fourth, in 1964 civil rights was almost entirely about race. But legislation and court decisions quickly brought other minorities and one majority (women) under the civil rights umbrella (see table 2-3). With little debate, the word "sex" was added to Title VII of the 1964 act. In the 1970s Congress enacted a series of what Hugh Davis Graham has called "Title VI clones,"[15] laws that prohibit discrimina-tion on the basis of sex, disability, or age by institutions receiving federal funds.

Fifth, civil rights regulation initially focused on banning and punishing overt and intentional discrimination. Before long, though, it had to address more subtle forms of discrimination. Thus began the lengthy and heated battle over "disparate impact" analysis. Federal courts and agencies interpreted civil rights statutes to require employers, schools, and other government bodies to justify practices that, based on statistical analysis, appear to have an adverse and dispro-portionate effect on legally protected groups. How one conducts these statistical studies, how employers and schools can defend themselves against accusations of discrimination, and the extent to which "disparate impact" analysis in effect cre-ate the very type of racial and gender quotas prohibited by federal law—these are questions that have roiled all forms of civil rights regulation for decades.[16]

Taken as a whole, this expansion of the civil rights state had two major po-litical consequences. First and most obviously, it changed the nature of opposi-tion to enforcement of the burgeoning set of regulations. No longer was civil rights a matter of "simple justice" (to use the title of a leading book on southern school desegregation); now it was about "complex justice" (to use the title of a

Table 2-2   Statutory Expansion of Regulatory Authority

Extensions of Voting Rights Act in 1970, 1975, 1982, and 2006
- Keeps the act's "temporary" provisions in effect through 2031
- Extends ban on literacy tests to the entire nation
- Covers more counties, including some in the North and West
- Addresses practices that inhibit voting by "language minority groups"; mandates bilingual ballots in districts with large numbers of non-English speakers
- Prohibits practices "which result in" abridgment of the right to vote

Equal Employment Opportunity Act of 1972
- Extends Title VII to schools and public employees
- Gives additional enforcement authority to EEOC

Equal Credit Opportunity Act of 1974
- Prohibits discrimination against credit applicants based on race, color, religion, national origin, sex, marital status, age, or source of income

Civil Rights Attorney's Fees Awards Act of 1976
- Authorizes federal courts to award attorneys' fees and other costs in all civil rights cases

Civil Service Reform Act of 1978
- Prohibits discrimination in federal employment on the basis of race, color, national origin, religion, sex, age, disability, marital status, or political affiliation

Fair Housing Amendments of 1988
- Prohibits discrimination on the basis of disability and family status
- Increases administrative enforcement power of HUD
- Authorizes federal judges to award punitive damages

Congressional Accountability Act of 1995
- Applies all civil rights laws to members of Congress and their staff
- Creates congressional Office of Compliance to enforce these prohibitions

---

study of the disastrous Kansas City desegregation litigation).[17] Many northerners, including some leading liberal Democrats (such as then-senator Joe Biden), opposed court-ordered busing to achieve racial balance. Affirmative action remains highly unpopular among the general public despite its wide support among educational and business elites.[18] Schools, businesses, and subnational governments frequently express frustration over the dense web of federal regulations and "unfunded mandates" with which they are expected to comply. Civil rights litigation constitutes a substantial proportion of the "litigation explosion" that has

Table 2-3   Federal Legislation Addressing Other Forms
of Discrimination

Sex Discrimination
   Equal Pay Act of 1963
   Title VII of the Civil Rights Act of 1964
   Title IX of the Education Amendments of 1972
   Pregnancy Discrimination Act of 1978
   Civil Rights Restoration Act of 1988 (the Grove City Bill)

Discrimination on Basis of Disability
   Architectural Barriers Act of 1968
   §§ 503 and 504 of the Rehabilitation Act of 1973
   Education for All Handicapped Children Act of 1975
   Developmental Disabilities Assistance and Bill of Rights Act of 1975
   Civil Rights of Institutionalized Persons Act of 1980
   Americans with Disabilities Act of 1990

Discrimination on Basis of Age
   Age Discrimination in Employment Act of 1967
   Age Discrimination Act of 1975
   Older Workers Benefits Protection Act (1990)

Additional Forms of Discrimination
   Indian Civil Rights Act (1968)
   Uniformed Services Employment and Reemployment Rights Act of 1994
   Religious Land Use and Institutionalized Persons Act (2000)
   Boy Scouts of America Equal Access Act (2001)
   Genetic Information Nondiscrimination Act of 2008

elicited so many complaints. The sexual harassment rules issued by OCR under Title IX have been roundly condemned by civil libertarians. In short, as the battlefield has expanded, so has the opposition.

Second, this expansion also brought new allies under the big tent of civil rights. Racial, ethnic, and language minorities; women; those with disabilities both physical and psychological, major and minor; the LGBT (lesbian, gay, bisexual, and transgender) community—together they make up a substantial majority of Americans. Each group has a number of well-organized advocacy groups claiming to speak for them. Although these groups sometimes compete for administrative resources and media attention, they have proved skillful at uniting to pass legislation and to defeat measures designed to roll back previous victories. (The 1988 Grove City Bill and the 1991 Civil Rights Act provide good examples of this.) The expanded civil rights coalition has lost very few legislative or administrative battles.

The Institutions of the Civil Rights State

Congress did not create a single, powerful agency to interpret and enforce civil rights laws. In typically American style, it distributed this authority to a patchwork of agencies and required them to share power with the federal courts. As a result, implementation of each law—and even individual titles within the same law—has taken a somewhat different form, producing a variety of patterns of division of labor between courts and agencies. To complicate matters further, some agencies are responsible for several different statutes. For example, the Office for Civil Rights in the Department of Education, the focus of this book, interprets and enforces not just Title IX, but also Title VI of the 1964 Act, section 504 of the Rehabilitation Act, the 1975 Age Discrimination Act, Title II of the Americans with Disabilities Act, the Individuals with Disabilities Education Act, and even the Boy Scouts of America Equal Access Act.

Of course, when most people think about civil rights, what comes to mind is not OCR or the EEOC, but Supreme Court decisions such as *Brown v. Board of Education*. Throughout this book we will see many examples of how court decisions have shaped Title IX policy and enforcement. The legal literature on the topic is vast. Entire casebooks, legal treatises, and law school courses are devoted to particular areas of civil rights law. As impressive and informative as this literature can be, it tends to overstate the role of courts and underestimate the importance of administrative agencies. Lawyers and law professors usually prefer to dissect appellate opinions rather than delve into the details of agency guidelines and standard operating procedures.

This book focuses not on courts or agencies in isolation, but on their complex interaction—on the intricacies of "separate institutions sharing powers," to use Richard Neustadt's apt phrase.[19] It attempts to provide for Title IX the type of interbranch analysis other scholars have applied to employment discrimination under Title VII,[20] access to public accommodations under the ADA,[21] transportation under section 504,[22] school desegregation,[23] and education for English-language learners.[24] The remainder of this chapter provides a context for this analysis by describing a few of the most important general features of civil rights agencies and jurisprudence.

Agencies

Pick up a good book on the American welfare state or on environmental regulation and you can find a useful overview of the variety of public programs and the agencies that carry them out.[25] But for some reason this is not true for civil rights. Because enforcement is dispersed among so many departments, agencies, and independent commissions, we do not even have a good estimate of how many federal employees work on civil rights. When the U.S. Commission on Civil

Table 2-4   Major Federal Civil Rights Agencies

Agency	Employees (approx.)	Enforcement actions/ year (approx.)
EEOC	2,200–2,500	Investigates 90,000–100,000 complaints
OFCCP	600–700	6,000–7,000 compliance reviews
OCR, Education	550–600	Investigates 10,000 complaints 30–50 compliance reviews
OCR, HHS	200–250	Complaints investigated exceeded 20,000 in 2016
HUD, Office of Fair Housing and Equal Opportunity	500–600	8,000–10,000 complaints (some investigations delegated to state and local agencies)
Civil Rights Division Department of Justice	700	NA

Sources: FY 2017 Congressional Budget Justifications; U.S. Commission on Civil Rights, *Funding Federal Civil Rights Enforcement: 2006* (September 2006).

Rights tried in 1996 to determine the size of the federal Title VI workforce, it discovered (much to the frustration of its staff) that many departments had no separate budget line for civil rights enforcement.[26] Hanes Walton found that not even the White House could put together a comprehensive list of civil rights compliance agencies.[27] The best we can do is provide current staffing levels for the largest components of the civil rights bureaucracy and a rough indication of their workload (see table 2-4). These figures do not include either civil rights offices in large departments (such as Defense and State) that do not provide separate budget figures or organizations such as the Civil Service Commission that combine enforcement of civil rights laws with their other duties.

How extensive are the rules and regulations promulgated by these agencies? That, too, is a hard question to answer because they can take so many different forms. As we will see, in recent years OCR has substituted unilateral Dear Colleague Letters for regulations published in the *Federal Register* after opportunity for public comment. In its investigations of complaints under the federal Individuals with Disabilities Education Act, OCR expects schools to follow the 320 pages of regulations promulgated by the Department of Education's Office of Special Education and Rehabilitative Services. Federal contractors must follow the guidelines established by the Office of Federal Contract Compliance Programs (OFCCP) in the Department of Labor. Its *Federal Contract Compliance Manual* covers more than 700 pages. The EEOC's rules run to almost 270 pages in the *Code of Federal Regulations* (*CFR*). (Since one page in the *CFR* has about twice as many words as the pages of this book, the EEOC's rules are about twice as long as this volume.) The rules established by the Civil Rights Division in the Department of Justice are even longer—more than 360 pages in the *CFR*. These figures do not include those agency guidelines, interpretations, compliance manuals, technical assistance documents, memorandums of understanding, and resolution agreements that are the daily fare of regulation. The bottom line is that the modern civil rights state has produced an intricate web of rules that apply to almost all businesses, educational institutions, government units, and non-profits in the country.

The legal authority of each civil rights agency reflects not just the special features of the particular problem it must tackle, but the composition of the congressional coalition required to enact authorizing legislation. The congressional politics of 1964 made the federal courts rather than the EEOC the primary forum for enforcement of Title VII.[28] At the other extreme lies the little known yet influential OFCCP, which must certify that business firms have complied with federal laws before these firms can receive lucrative government contracts. As Hugh Davis Graham explained, "Armed with the awesome power of the federal purse, the OFCC[P] stood between federal contractors and their livelihood. By finding, or threatening to find, contractors and bidders not 'in compliance' with agency criteria for workforce participation by minorities and women, the OFCC[P] held a mighty sword."[29]

The Department of Education's Office for Civil Rights lies between the extremes represented by the EEOC and OFCCP. Concern about possible abuses of administrative power led Congress to impose significant constraints both on the agency's rulemaking authority and on termination of federal funding. Although the original purpose of Title VI and Title IX was to empower administrative agencies to act quickly to cut off funding to those who discriminate, that sanction proved too draconian and administratively cumbersome in practice to use in any but the most extreme situations. In fact, the federal government has *never* terminated funding to educational institutions for violating Title IX. Private suits seeking injunctions and damages have replaced the funding cutoff as the primary enforcement tool for Titles VI and IX.

Courts

In 2016 nearly 38,000 civil rights cases were filed in federal district courts—13 percent of their total caseload.[30] More than 90 percent of these were brought by private parties who claimed that employers, commercial establishments, schools, or government bodies had deprived them of their statutory or constitutional rights. Those looking for detailed analysis of judicial opinions on Title IX will find much of it in the following chapters—probably too much for those not employed by law schools. For now, it will be useful to review four central aspects of the extensive jurisprudence on civil rights issues.

First, most civil rights decisions by the federal courts today focus on statutory rather than constitutional interpretation. That is not surprising since the civil rights statutes listed above are far more detailed than constitutional provisions. They cover private sector activity not subject to constitutional mandates, and they address types of discrimination such as age and disability that have never been recognized by the federal courts as violating the Equal Protection clause.

A crucial difference between constitutional and statutory decisions is that the latter can be overturned by Congress. As table 2-5 shows, this is a common occurrence. Congress has repeatedly revised federal laws to negate court decisions that have made it harder for civil rights litigants to file cases, to meet their burden of proof, and to seek judicial and administrative remedies. In other words, it has overturned many court rulings we would conventionally label as "conservative" (because they either reduce the power of the federal government or constrain its use of "disparate impact" analysis), but virtually none we would label "liberal" (because they either expand regulatory authority or endorse "disparate impact" analysis).

In addition, judges tend to be more adventuresome in their interpretation of statutes than in their interpretation of the Constitution. They can try to "update" or improve statutes without issuing sweeping constitutional pronouncements. They can assuage their concerns about unelected judges making public policy by arguing that if Congress does not like what they are doing, it can always change the law. As Donald Horowitz has put it, "Judges who recoil at innovation in constitutional lawmaking may not see the same dangers at all in the interpretation of statutes."[31] This approach to statutory interpretation was particularly apparent in the Burger Court, when pragmatic centrists held the balance of power.[32]

Second, from the 1960s through the late 1980s, federal courts generally leaned in a liberal direction, adopting an expansive meaning of civil rights mandates and of the enforcement authority of courts and agencies. For example, in 1979 the Supreme Court discovered an "implied private right of action" in Title IX, thus authorizing enforcement suits by private parties. By the mid-1990s, though, the tide had clearly shifted as a result of Ronald Reagan's and George H. W. Bush's appointments to the Supreme Court and the lower courts. For instance, in a 1999 decision interpreting Title IX, the Supreme Court defined school districts' liability for peer sexual harassment much more narrowly than had OCR. As Sean Farhang and Stephen Burbank have shown, the Rehnquist and Roberts Courts have issued many rulings that limited access to federal courts—decisions that attract little media attention but can have a significant influence on implementation of civil rights laws.[33]

Third, while federal agencies are generally preoccupied with the demands of their small sections of the civil rights landscape, federal judges hear all sorts of

Table 2-5   Laws Overturning Supreme Court Decisions

1978 Pregnancy Discrimination Act
- Amends Title VII to make it illegal to discriminate against a woman because of pregnancy, childbirth, or medical condition related to pregnancy or childbirth
- Overturns Court's decision in *General Electric v. Gilbert* (1976)

1982 Voting Rights Act Extension
- Prohibits practices that "result in" abridgment of the right to vote even if there is no finding of discriminatory intent
- Overturns Court's decision in *City of Mobile v. Bolden* (1980)

1988 Civil Rights Restoration Act
- Extends coverage of Title VI, Title IX, and section 504 to include all programs in an institution receiving federal funds
- Overturns Court's decision in *Grove City College v. Bell* (1984)

Civil Rights Act of 1991
- Revises evidentiary rules under Title VII to ease the burden on plaintiffs
- Authorizes judges to award compensatory and punitive damages
- Overturns Court's decision in *Wards Cove v. Atonio* (1989) and a number of other decisions

2006 Americans with Disabilities Act Amendments
- Significantly expands definition of "disability"
- Overturns Court's decisions in *Sutton v. UAL* (1999) and *Toyota v. Williams* (2002)

Lily Ledbetter Fair Pay Act of 2009
- Extends statute of limitations for Title VII
- Overturns Court's decision in *Ledbetter v. Goodyear Tire* (2007)

civil rights cases and, consequently, are more concerned with broader legal issues and with how all these pieces fit together. Who can file suit in federal court? When can states be sued? When can plaintiffs be awarded attorneys' fees? What is the burden of proof on claimants? What legal remedies are available to prevailing parties? How should damages be determined? These are the types of issues that most frequently arrive in appellate courts. Judges' preoccupation with these questions can be seen either as a valiant effort to increase uniformity in a regulatory area plagued by fragmentation and conflicting demands, or as a flight from the real world of regulation into the law school–dominated world of legal abstraction. Regardless of ideology, the contrasting experience and institutional position of judges and administrators often lead them to see the policy world differently.

Fourth and finally, it is important to realize that the Supreme Court simply does not decide many civil rights cases. Seldom does it accept more than two or three per term. Since 1972, the Court has handed down just eight Title IX decisions—less than two per decade.[34] Although Title IX rules on athletics have been controversial for over forty years, the Supreme Court has *never* addressed that topic. In 1998–99 the Court issued two Title IX decisions on sexual harassment in order to resolve conflicts among the circuit courts. It had never touched the issue before, nor has the Court revisited it since. Most questions about the proper interpretation of civil rights laws are left either to the lower courts or to administrative agencies. The fact that disagreements in the lower courts can persist for years or even decades without Supreme Court resolution increases the extent to which those subject to these laws look to federal agencies to explain what they must do. When the Supreme Court speaks clearly, people listen. But usually it remains silent.

Conclusion

Since 1964 the United States has built an extensive regulatory regime that addresses many forms of discrimination not through bureaucratic centralization, but through the form of governance that Robert Kagan has labeled "adversarial legalism."[35] Civil rights regulation is administratively fragmented, with authority to interpret and enforce statutory demands shared by federal judges and administrators in many different agencies. The structure of civil rights regulation reflects a number of key features of American politics, several of which remain in considerable tension with others: a new determination to dismantle the well-entrenched Jim Crow system in the South and the old distrust of centralized government; enthusiasm for applying the race discrimination model to sex, disability, age, sexual orientation, and gender identity and a tacit recognition of the many ways these forms of discrimination differ from one another; and heightened public expectation of the federal government in an era of chronic divided government and declining confidence in our political system. By dispersing federal authority, relying on a complex division of labor between courts and agencies, and mobilizing the language of individual rights, those who, by trial and error, constructed this regulatory regime were able to overcome traditional American opposition to a "strong state." The result, as Suzanne Mettler has suggested, is a "submerged state" whose size, scope, and omnipresence are rarely apparent to ordinary citizens.[36] Subsequent chapters of this book are designed to make the operation, the strength, and shortcomings of this portion of our "submerged state" more apparent to the reader.

THREE

Title IX: The Complexities
of a Simple Statute

Title IX is often described as a simple law—the historian Susan Ware has described it as "thirty-seven words that changed American sports."[1] But it is longer (nearly 1,500 words), more complex, and more ambiguous than this common description suggests. Like many statutes, it combines ill-defined substantive mandates with multiple constraints, exceptions, and procedures. These features have made interpretation of the law controversial and enforcement cumbersome. With only one exception (the 1988 Grove City Bill), Congress has failed to amend the law either to clarify its intent or to address the serious implementation problems that have arisen. Instead, this has been done by federal judges and administrators, who have not just filled in statutory gaps, but devised end runs around the constraints placed on them by the law's lesser known provisions.

Virtually all civil rights laws require judges and administrators to determine what constitutes adequate proof of discrimination. Must there be convincing evidence of differential treatment or intent to discriminate? Or is it enough to show that a particular practice has a "disparate impact" on a protected group? To this vexing problem Title IX adds two others. First, although Title IX was modeled on Title VI of the 1964 Civil Rights Act, it acknowledges that race and sex differ in important respects. That is why Title IX includes exemptions that no one but an unreconstructed segregationist would apply to Title VI. The most obvious example is separate male and female athletic teams. Second, Title IX's central enforcement mechanism, the termination of federal funds, has proved unworkable in practice. As this became evident, courts invented an alternative enforcement tool, the "implied private right of action." This means that when federal judges defer to OCR's interpretation of the statute, the agency can use the threat of legal action to negotiate agreements with educational institutions. When judges refuse to defer, though, OCR must scramble to devise new penalties short of termination of funding.

Three controversial legal issues have dogged implementation of Title IX from the start: (1) the meaning of the key term "discrimination" as it applies to sex; (2) the rulemaking authority of the Office for Civil Rights (OCR); and (3) the enforcement authority of OCR and the courts. One might think that, after forty-five years, most questions about how to interpret Title IX would have been resolved. As we will see, that is not the case. The resulting uncertainty adds yet another level of complexity to this allegedly simple statute.

A Mandate with Multiple Exceptions

Congresswoman Edith Green, the principal sponsor of Title IX, initially intended to address the problem of sex discrimination simply by adding the word "sex" to the nondiscrimination mandate contained in Title VI of the Civil Rights Act. That strategy had worked in 1964, when a House floor amendment added the word to Title VII, the employment discrimination section of that law. Southern opponents thought this "poison pill" might help them sink the entire legislation. Instead, prohibiting sex discrimination in employment gained widespread support. Adding "sex" to Title VI would have prohibited gender discrimination not just in educational programs, but in all activities funded in part by the federal government.

In 1970–71 Congresswoman Green shifted gears, largely because civil rights leaders did not dare open Title VI to amendment. Busing had become such a volatile political issue that they feared (with good reason) that opponents would use the opportunity to limit the federal government's authority to use busing to achieve racial balance in public schools. Green instead used her position on the House Committee on Education and Labor to add Title IX to an omnibus education bill then wending its way through Congress. Debate on the House provision was minimal. According to Bernice Sandler, who worked closely with Green on the legislation, "Mrs. Green's advice was 'Don't lobby for this bill.' She was absolutely right. She said, 'if you lobby, people are going to oppose it. Leave it. The opposition is not there right now so don't call attention to it.'"[2]

In the Senate this short section of the omnibus education bill did not go through the regular committee process, but was added on the floor by Senator

Birch Bayh. The chief Senate sponsor of the Equal Rights Amendment to the Constitution, Bayh had proposed a similar floor amendment the previous year only to see it ruled out of order. In 1972 he offered a brief defense of his amendment, assuring his colleagues that it would not require coed football or locker rooms. It passed by a voice vote. In both houses, Title IX's sponsors made the same basic argument: denying women and girls equal educational opportunity is no more acceptable than denying such opportunity to racial minorities. After a conference committee resolved differences between the House and Senate versions, the sprawling bill was signed by President Nixon. His signing statement made no mention of Title IX. As a result, Title IX's truncated legislative history provides little evidence of what members of Congress had in mind when they voted for it.[3]

Despite the extensive borrowing of language from Title VI, from the beginning it was clear that the race analogy was not always apposite. In the House, Congresswoman Green was forced to accept an exemption for the admissions policies of all private undergraduate schools as well as traditionally single-sex public undergraduate institutions. The latter provision was modified in conference, but the former remained. Title IX also grants a blanket exemption to religious schools and military academies. It gave schools that chose to shift from single-sex to coeducational seven years to comply with its requirements. It explained that "nothing contained herein shall be construed to prohibit" schools from "maintaining separate living facilities for the different sexes." In 1974 and 1976 Congress added exemptions for fraternities and sororities, the YMCA and YWCA, Girl Scouts and Boy Scouts, Boys State and Girls State, father–son and mother–daughter events, and scholarships for beauty pageants. Such provisions would have been unthinkable in a statute dealing with race. What was the rationale for deciding when the racial analogy should apply and when policymakers should acknowledge differences between race and sex? In 1972 no one in Congress made an effort to answer this pivotal question. Nor has Congress addressed the issue since.

That tricky task was left first to federal administrators, and then to judges. As John Skrentny has pointed out, "The similarities of race and sex discrimination had a compelling logic on the surface" that made Title IX "easy to pass." But administrators soon "discovered that women and blacks were not so similar after all." The "superficial" analogy between race and sex, Skrentny concludes, "made the *formal* inclusion of women easy. But getting the implementing regulations to make the right a reality was difficult."[4]

Nor did Congress provide much guidance on the key question of how to determine whether a school has engaged in sex discrimination. Just as Title VI explicitly stated that it should not be interpreted to require racial balance, Title IX provides that "nothing contained" in it should be interpreted to require schools "to grant preferential or disparate treatment to the members of one sex on account of an imbalance which may exist with respect to the total number or percentage of persons of that sex participating in or receiving the benefits of any federally supported program or activity, in comparison with the total number or percentage of persons of that sex in any community, State, section, or other area." On its face, this seems to prohibit the rules OCR later established for intercollegiate athletics. But Title IX also explains that this provision should "not be construed to prevent the consideration" of "statistical evidence tending to show that such an imbalance exists with respect to the participation" in federally funded programs "by the members of one sex." Thus, while OCR cannot demand that female students receive "preferential treatment" in order to create gender balance in athletic programs, it can use "statistical evidence" showing that "such an imbalance exists" to place a heavy burden of proof on schools to demonstrate that they have not shortchanged female athletes. In practice there is little difference between the two. What Title IX takes away with one hand, it arguably gives back with the other.

Administrative Rulemaking

Realizing that educational institutions would need far more guidance than Title IX itself provided, Congress granted rulemaking authority to federal agencies that dispense funds to educational institutions. Here, again, Title IX followed Title VI nearly word for word. All such agencies were "authorized and directed" to "issue rules, regulations, or orders of general applicability which shall be consistent with the achievement of the objectives" of Title IX. Like all other federal agencies, civil rights offices are subject to the Administrative Procedure Act (APA), which, as the name suggests, establishes procedures for rulemaking, adjudication, and judicial review.

Recognizing the politically sensitive nature of termination of federal funding, Congress added two unusual procedural demands. First, it insisted that the president take responsibility for all rules issued under Title IX: "No such rule, regulation, or order shall become effective unless and until approved by the President." The second unusual requirement was the congressional veto provision Congress added in 1974. Enacted at the height of Watergate, this empowered Congress to invalidate by concurrent resolution (which means without the approval of the president) any administrative regulation promulgated under an education statute.

Only once did OCR jump through all these hoops. That was in the initial Title IX rulemaking that stretched from 1972 to 1975. The agency issued a lengthy proposal with a detailed explanation; held hearings across the country; received and responded to 10,000 comments; negotiated with the Department of Health, Education, and Welfare (HEW) policy office and the White House staff; and made numerous changes in response to criticisms from all these sources. HEW secretary Weinberger made several additional alterations before sending the regulations to President Ford for his signature. In 1975 a bipartisan group of House members introduced a resolution of disapproval of the regulations, and the House held contentious hearings on intercollegiate athletics. Despite heavy lobbying by football coaches, the resolution never reached the floor. The regulations went into effect as written.

In 1983 the Supreme Court declared all legislative vetoes unconstitutional.[5] That did not end congressional efforts to block or modify Title IX rules. On several occasions, members of Congress have tried to use appropriations riders to block enforcement of Title IX rules. Although these riders were never enacted, they served as a reminder that Congress has a variety of ways to make administrators' lives difficult, and that executive branch officials ignore informal "signals from the Hill" at their peril.[6]

The year 1975 was also the last time OCR sent a major Title IX regulation to the president for his signature. None of the post-1975 rules on athletics, sexual harassment, or transgender rights discussed in subsequent chapters of this book were signed by the president. Few of those rules went through either the standard notice-and-comment rulemaking procedure outlined by the APA or interagency review.[7] OCR has evaded these requirements by labeling its commands "interpretations," "clarifications," and "guidance" rather than "rules," and denying—quite unconvincingly—that they add anything new. In recent years it has announced major policy decisions in Dear Colleague Letters (DCLs), inverting standard rulemaking procedures by asking for comments only after it has established its position.[8]

Soon after the Obama OCR issued its second set of guidelines on sexual harassment, Molly Corbett Broad, president of the American Council on Education, complained to a Senate committee about OCR's failure to follow APA procedures when it issues what it labels "significant guidance documents": "This means no affected party—advocacy groups, colleges and universities, civil liberties organizations, the public, policy makers, students and parents—has the opportunity to raise questions and ask for clarifications."[9] As a result, she warned, "Those who must comply with the law are far less likely to understand what they are expected to do." Her claim that "this serves no one's interest" was belied by OCR's adamant refusal to change its practices. Clearly, the agency believed that avoiding APA rulemaking served its bureaucratic interests in moving quickly before opponents can mobilize.

Are these "interpretations" and Dear Colleague Letters legally binding? During the Obama administration this became a contentious issue. Lawyers in the Department of Education and Department of Justice (DOJ) have been reluctant to give a definitive answer. On the one hand, DOJ lawyers insist that such "guidance documents" are "merely expressions of the agencies' views as to what the law requires," are "not legally binding," expose schools "to no new liability or legal requirements," and "do not create or confer any rights for or on any person."[10] Because these documents do not constitute "final agency action," DOJ has insisted that they should not be subject to judicial review. On the other hand, OCR officials have repeatedly warned schools that they will face serious sanctions if they fail to comply with the mandates contained in these documents.

In hearings before the Senate Committee on Health, Education, Labor, and Pensions (HELP), Senator Lamar Alexander (R-Tenn.) asked Catherine Lhamon, then the assistant secretary of education for civil rights, and two other Department of Education officials whether the standards announced in DCLs are legally binding. He received two answers: "yes" from Lhamon and "no" from Undersecretary Theodore Marshall and Deputy Assistant Secretary Amy McIntosh.[11] When asked why they are binding, Lhamon claimed it was because the Senate had confirmed her nomination. Senator Alexander obviously did not consider this an adequate response.[12]

Neither did Senators James Lankford (R-Okla.), chair of the HELP subcommittee on Regulatory Affairs and Federal Management. He wrote to Secretary John King to ask why the Department of Education regularly added important new regulatory requirements without following APA procedures. Perhaps, Lankford suggested, OCR has "sought to avoid notice-and-comment procedures, fearing that education officials and other interested groups would have voiced substantive objections to the letters' policies if given an opportunity." If so, he continued, "this fear would have been well-placed: Legal scholars and academics across the political spectrum have decried the Dear Colleague letters as offensive to First and Fourth Amendment protections."[13] Lhamon responded that her agency's DCLs on sexual harassment added nothing new to federal requirements, but "simply [serve] to advise the public of the construction of the regulations it administers and enforces."[14] This "failed to assuage" Lankford's concerns about the agency's "improper use of guidance documents that, while purporting to merely interpret existing law, fundamentally alters the regulatory landscape."[15]

A few months later the National Women's Law Center and eighty-five other advocacy organizations wrote to Secretary King defending OCR's practices, claiming that its 2011 and 2014 guidance documents are "simply clarifications of existing rights under Title IX" that "spurred schools to address cultures that for too long have contributed to hostile environments which deprive many students of equal educational opportunity."[16] Meanwhile, Lankford sent yet another letter to Secretary King complaining about OCR's failure to use notice-and-comment rulemaking for its controversial policy on the rights of transgender students.[17] In 2017 Secretary of Education Betsy DeVos announced that "the era of 'rule by letter' is over," and initiated a notice-and-comment rulemaking process to replace the Obama administration's sexual harassment guidance.[18] If the department carries through on this promise, it will constitute a major change in its regulatory practices.

As we will see in subsequent chapters, the argument that OCR's many interpretations and Dear Colleague Letters have added nothing new to Title IX regulation is, to put it mildly, unconvincing. Most of them announced substantial policy shifts. According to OCR, its policies have not changed for more than forty years—despite the fact that its 1975 regulations contain not one word about either sexual harassment or transgender issues. Nor did they include the "three-part test" that has become the centerpiece of its regulation of athletics. For years OCR has sought to obscure its innovations to avoid the procedural hurdles established by the APA and Title IX itself.[19]

Does this mean, then, that the agency's guidance documents are not legally binding? In practice, this comes down to two issues. First, will federal judges defer to these pronouncements as authoritative interpretations by an expert agency? Courts frequently do so—but not always. Second, will a school somehow put itself at risk by refusing to follow OCR's rules? Losing in court is only one form of risk that schools must consider. Going through a lengthy investigation can be costly to an institution both financially and in terms of its reputation. That is why many colleges have agreed to follow OCR sexual harassment guidance even when it differs substantially from the Supreme Court's interpretation of Title IX. In other words, the legal status of OCR's rules is closely connected to its enforcement authority, the topic to which we now turn.

The Enforcement Conundrum

Title IX states that compliance with its requirements "may be effected" either by "the termination of or refusal to grant or to continue" federal financial assistance or "by any other means authorized by law." The meaning of the latter phrase is unclear, but has generally been interpreted to mean enforcement through court suits brought by the Department of Justice under other jurisdictional statutes. OCR rarely refers Title IX cases to Justice, and Justice has almost never used such "other means" to enforce Title IX. From the beginning, termination of federal funding was designed to be the central enforcement mechanism for Title IX, much as it had been for Title VI. One of the most persuasive arguments put forth by the bill's sponsors was that the federal government should not be subsidizing educational institutions that engage in discrimination.

Terminators I: The Legal Hurdles

Congress is famous for protecting its "power of the purse," particularly when funding decisions affect the flow of federal dollars to members' states and districts. So it is not surprising that Congress imposed several constraints on agencies' power to cut off federal funds. First, termination must be based on an "express finding on the record, after opportunity for hearing, of a failure to comply" with Title IX's requirements. This means that OCR must present its evidence to an independent administrative law judge who will also hear the arguments presented by the educational institution and produce a written justification for her decision. This time-consuming hearing process is governed by the extensive case law developed by federal courts under the Administrative Procedure Act's provisions on adjudication.

Second, "no such action shall be taken until the department or agency concerned has advised the appropriate person or persons of the failure to comply with the requirement and has determined that compliance cannot be secured by voluntary means." In practice, this means that before federal administrators can initiate a termination hearing, they must enter into negotiations with the educational institution on how it might come into compliance. Such negotiations can last for months or even years.

Third, "any person aggrieved" by the termination can seek judicial review. Although the statute is silent on the issue, it is likely that a reviewing court will stay termination of funding while it is reviewing the federal agency's action. Fourth, before terminating funds, federal administrators must send to the House and Senate committees with jurisdiction over the program "a full written report of the circumstances and the grounds for such action," and "No such action shall become effective until thirty days have elapsed after the filing of such report." In other words, congressional committees must have sufficient time to complain and to convince the agency to reverse its position.

Finally, according to Title IX as enacted in 1972, any termination of funding "shall be limited in its effect to the particular program, or part thereof, in which such noncompliance has been so found." The "pinpoint" provision had been added to Title VI as part of the compromise engineered to produce a filibuster-proof majority for the 1964 Civil Rights Act. Assistant Attorney General Burke Marshall, the Johnson administration's lead negotiator, at the time wrote that this language "makes clear that any termination of federal payment must be limited precisely to the part of the program in which discrimination has been expressly found to be practiced."[20] It was carried over into Title IX without explanation.

What does "particular program, or part thereof" mean in practice? From the beginning, OCR and HEW insisted that it meant an entire school district or college. They had strong practical reasons for taking this position: not only does federal financial assistance to one part of an institution free up money for other parts, but tracing the flow of federal money within an institution can be difficult and time-consuming. But this interpretation seems to reduce the statutory language to a nullity. The issue came to a head when the Supreme Court issued its 1984 decision in *Grove City College v. Bell*. Writing for the majority, Justice Byron White maintained that federal agencies could terminate funding to an entire educational institution "only by ignoring Title IX's program-specific language." He found in the statute and its legislative history "no persuasive evidence suggesting that Congress intended that the Department's regulatory authority follow federally aided students from classroom to classroom, building to building, or activity to activity."[21]

Justice William Brennan's dissenting opinion pointed out that for nearly a decade Congress had expressed no opposition to OCR's broader definition. He argued that Title IX's enforcement provisions should be interpreted so as to further the "broad congressional purposes underlying enactment of the statute."[22] Although Brennan lost in the Supreme Court, his position eventually prevailed. After more than three years of fighting between the Reagan administration and congressional Democrats, Congress enacted, over the president's veto, the Grove City Bill, which stated that under Title IX "program or activity" shall include "all of the operations" of a college, university, corporation, or local educational agency that receives federal money.[23]

Terminators II: Practical Obstacles

Given the frequency with which OCR has threatened to revoke funding to schools that fail to comply with its guidelines, it is surprising to learn that the federal government has *never* cut off federal funding to punish an educational institution for violating Title IX. For a while, the mere threat of this draconian sanction might have been enough to induce schools to comply with OCR's demands. But eventually it became clear to almost everyone that the threat was an empty one. OCR desperately needed additional enforcement tools.

In the early days of southern school desegregation federal officials used Title VI's funding cutoff to force recalcitrant school districts to admit black students to previously all-white schools. Between 1964 and 1970, the period in which OCR was most aggressive and most successful in attacking southern school segregation, it initiated administrative proceedings against 600 of the more than 4,000 school districts in the South. Although funding was temporarily terminated in 200 of these schools, Beryl Radin found that "in all but four of these 200 districts, federal aid was subsequently restored, often without a change in local procedures."[24] And this was in circumstances most favorable to the use of the funding cutoff: those school districts had thumbed their nose at the Supreme Court and Constitution for years. Moreover, the federal funding in question was new, a product of the 1965 Elementary and Secondary Education Act; it had not yet become a virtual entitlement for school districts. The second half of the 1960s was the high-water mark for using the funding cutoff, but even then the water was barely ankle deep.

Why have federal administrators been so reluctant to terminate federal funding under either Title VI or Title IX? Most obviously, given the extent to which the colleges and local school districts have come to depend on federal money, termination is generally considered a "nuclear option": too extreme a sanction for a violation of an administrative guideline by one part of the school. HEW secretary Joseph Califano likened it to "opting for decapitation instead of plastic surgery to eliminate facial disfiguration."[25] To make matters worse, it would usually hurt the very students federal officials are trying to help. In a report critical of federal agencies' lax enforcement of Title VI, the U.S. Commission on Civil Rights identified the central dilemma: "Although funding termination may serve as an effective deterrent to recipients, it may leave the victim of discrimination without a remedy. Funding termination may eliminate the benefits sought by the victim."[26] On top of this, the funding cutoff threatens to damage relations between the federal agency and those state and local officials with whom they worked on a regular basis—not to mention antagonizing members of Congress upon whom administrators rely for appropriations.[27]

Originally sold as a swift administrative alternative to lengthy litigation, the funding cutoff proved much more time-consuming and troublesome in practice. As Judge John Sirica (of Watergate fame) explained in a 1978 decision: "The fund termination procedure involves a tedious series of notice, hearing and review steps at the various levels within HEW's hierarchy followed by separate review in the courts." Litigation, in contrast, "bypasses the most cumbersome of the administrative steps" and promises "greater promptness in limiting aid to deserving recipients."[28]

"Implied Private Rights of Action" to the Rescue

Federal administrators first confronted this enforcement problem when they used Title VI to attack southern school segregation. Here they had a crucial advantage: even without this law it was illegal to use federal money in a racially discriminatory manner. Moreover, racial discrimination by public schools violates the Equal Protection clause even when no federal money is involved. As a result, both the Department of Justice and private litigants had clear legal authority to file suit against public schools that engage in such discrimination or even against federal administrators who provide financial support to private schools. On the surface, Title VI added no new prohibitions, but only a new and possibly quicker enforcement process, one running parallel to litigation-based enforcement. But if that were so, what good was Title VI once funding termination had become a dead letter? This allegedly potent alternative to litigation seemed to offer no alternative in practice.

In fact, though, Title VI did add something of great significance: the authority of federal agencies to write rules that courts could then enforce. During the intense battle over the desegregation of southern schools, federal courts relied heavily on numerical guidelines issued by OCR. In a key case, Fifth Circuit judge John Minor Wisdom explained that HEW's desegregation guidelines "offer, for the first time, the prospect that the transition from a de jure segregated dual school system to a unitary integrated system may be carried out effectively, promptly, and in an orderly manner," thus rescuing the project from "the bog in which it had been trapped for ten years."[29] "Prepared in detail by experts in education and school administration," Judge Wisdom claimed, these guidelines were "intended by Congress and the executive to be part of a coordinated national program."[30] He promised that the Fifth Circuit would regularly update its requirements to match those of HEW. His colleague (and future U.S. attorney general) Judge Griffin Bell noted that since "HEW has the carrot in the form of federal funds but no stick," the Fifth Circuit aimed "to make a stick out of the federal courts." He questioned whether the federal courts should be willing to wield "any stick that HEW may formulate" in the future.[31] But he lost; Judge Wisdom's approach prevailed.

The rulemaking authority of federal administrators under Title VI took on even more significance a few years later when, in *Lau v. Nichols*, the Supreme Court recognized as legally binding—and enforceable by private suit—guidelines on bilingual education announced in an OCR memo.[32] No one claimed that this was a constitutional requirement; it was based solely on the statute, not the Equal Protection clause. Nor had there been any effort to use the rulemaking procedures mandated by the APA and Title VI itself. Originally seen as a way to enforce constitutional norms without litigation, Title VI had been transformed, with virtually no explanation, into a generator of judicially enforceable federal guidelines that reach far beyond constitutional mandates.[33]

Would the federal courts recognize a similar "implied private right of action" under Title IX and thus transform it, too, into a font of administrative guidelines enforced by federal judges? Although the Supreme Court was inclined to apply the same rules to Title IX that it had applied to Title VI, there were two competing considerations. First and most important, under the Equal Protection clause, race is a "suspect classification," which means that racial discrimination is almost always unconstitutional. Sex, in contrast, is *not* a suspect classification. In the early 1970s the Court had begun to invalidate some sex classifications, but regulations issued under Title IX simply could not claim the same constitutional status as the desegregation guidelines issued by OCR a decade earlier.

Second, when Title IX cases first came before federal judges in the late 1970s, the Supreme Court was shifting its position on when to recognize "implied private rights of action" in federal statutes. During its heyday, the Warren Court had created a strong presumption in favor of judicial enforcement of federal laws, even if Congress had vested enforcement authority in a federal agency and made no provision for enforcement through private suits.[34] The Burger Court began to reverse that presumption: private litigation could supplement administrative action only if Congress had explicitly authorized such suits or very strongly hinted that it had intended to do so.[35]

The Supreme Court resolved this tangled legal issue with its 1979 ruling in *Cannon v. University of Chicago*, the most important decision it has ever handed down on Title IX.[36] Justice John Paul Stevens's opinion for the six-member majority argued that since Congress had modeled Title IX on Title VI and since in 1972 many lower courts had recognized a private right of action to enforce Title VI, Congress must have intended that enforcement option to be available under Title IX as well.

Stevens added a practical reason: because the funding cutoff is so "severe" a punishment, it "may not provide an appropriate means" for protecting individuals from "isolated" incidents of discrimination. When a court finds that the recipient of federal funds has discriminated against a particular individual—for example, an applicant denied admission, as was the case in *Cannon*—"the violation might be remedied more efficiently by an order requiring an institution to accept an applicant who has been improperly excluded." According to Justice Stevens, "It makes little sense to impose on an individual, whose only interest is in obtaining a benefit for herself, or on HEW, the burden of demonstrating that an institution's practices are so pervasively discriminatory that a complete cutoff of federal funding is appropriate." Injunctive relief that offers a plaintiff admission to an educational program (or the opportunity to play on a volleyball team) "is not only sensible but is also fully consistent with—and in some cases even necessary to—the orderly enforcement of the statute."[37] In other words, Title IX should be interpreted to provide judicially crafted remedies for those individuals harmed by particular instances of discrimination, not just blunt administrative remedies for systematic discrimination.

The three dissenters, in contrast, argued that the Court had not only ignored its recent jurisprudence on private rights of action, but distorted the regulatory scheme created by Congress. When Congress creates an explicit enforcement mechanism in a statute, the dissenters argued, that should remain the only one available. Listing a number of cases in which lower courts had discovered "implied" private rights of action in federal statutes, Justice Lewis Powell wrote sarcastically, "It defies reason to believe that in each of these statutes Congress absentmindedly forgot to mention an intended private action." To the argument that Title IX should follow Title VI, the dissenters responded, "An erroneous interpretation of Title VI should not be compounded through importation into Title IX under the guise of effectuating legislative intent." According to Justice White's dissenting opinion, "There is not one statement in the legislative history indicating that the Congress that enacted Title IX was aware" of the Title VI case law that the majority claimed it had tacitly incorporated into Title IX.[38] Justice Powell warned that this "self-aggrandizement" by the judiciary would lead to a flood of litigation and unnecessarily limit "the authority of the academic community to govern itself."[39] On this score, he was clearly prophetic.

Although the Court continued its assault on "implied private rights of action" in the 1980s and 1990s, it never reconsidered its decision in *Cannon*.[40]

In fact, thirteen years later, the Court unexpectedly expanded the enforcement authority of federal judges and increased plaintiffs' incentives to file suit under Title IX. In *Franklin v. Gwinnett County Public Schools* (1992), it ruled that in private Title IX suits, judges could not only issue injunctions but also award monetary damages to successful plaintiffs. Over the objection of the solicitor general (and the deputy solicitor general who handled the case, John Roberts, the future chief justice), a unanimous Court held that a student who had been subjected to serious and repeated sexual misconduct by a teacher deserved compensation from the school district that had done nothing to prevent it. Oddly enough, the Court's opinion was written by Justice White, a dissenter in *Cannon*. He maintained that whenever the judiciary finds an "implied" private right of action, it must infer that Congress intended to create an effective judicial remedy. If Congress had meant to prohibit monetary damages, it could have said so. As Justice Antonin Scalia pointed out, "To require, with respect to a right that is not consciously and intentionally created, that any limitation of remedy not be expressed, is to provide, in effect that the most questionable private rights will also be the most expansively remediable."[41] Yet he concurred in the judgment.[42]

The End of the Ancien Régime?

For private suits to provide federal administrators with the enforcement sanctions they otherwise lack, judges must defer to their regulations, guidelines, and Dear Colleague Letters. In *Lau v. Nichols*, the Supreme Court had rather cavalierly endorsed judicial enforcement of an OCR memo issued without regard for any of the procedures described above.[43] Almost all circuit court judges have followed OCR's various "interpretations" and "clarifications" of Title IX's requirements on athletics (see chapter 7). But judges do not always accept OCR's reading of the act (see chapters 10 and 12).

In 2001 the Supreme Court heard a case very similar to *Lau v. Nichols*, and came to a much different conclusion. In *Alexander v. Sandoval*, a closely divided Court ruled that although private suits can be used to enforce the statutory language of Titles VI and IX, they cannot be used to enforce the *administrative regulation* issued under them. Unless federal administrators can demonstrate that their guidelines are very closely linked to the explicit nondiscrimination mandates of those statutes, they cannot expect judges to enforce them. In effect, this means no deference to agency rules, even if the agency has followed all the procedural requirements contained in those laws. Justice Scalia's majority opinion acknowledged that this undermined practices first established in the 1960s and 1970s. But he described those practices as part of an "ancien régime" subsequently abandoned by the

Supreme Court: "Having sworn off the habit of venturing beyond Congress's intent, we will not accept respondents' invitation to have one last drink."[44]

This drew an impassioned defense of this "ancien régime" from Justice Stevens. He argued that the "integrated remedial scheme" that had emerged under Title VI and Title IX constituted "a reasonable—indeed inspired—model for attacking the often-intractable problem" of discrimination. To address "subtle forms of discrimination" such as "ostensibly race-neutral" rules that "have the predictable and perhaps intended consequence of materially benefiting some races at the expense of others," judges should eschew a "static approach" and instead empower civil rights agencies to "evaluate social circumstances to determine whether there is a need for stronger measures." This institutional arrangement "builds into the law flexibility, an ability to make nuanced assessments of complex social realities, and an admirable willingness to credit the possibility of progress."[45] In short, private rights of action combined with judicial deference to administrative rules are essential for producing aggressive regulation that goes beyond prohibiting intentional discrimination to address subtle forms of bias not contemplated by the enacting Congress.

As applied to Title IX, the Court's decision in *Alexander v. Sandoval* could be interpreted in either of two ways. It could be read broadly to mean that private rights of action can be used only to enforce prohibitions clearly laid out in the text of that statute. Since the text says so little, under this interpretation, private rights of action would be of little use to plaintiffs. Alternatively, it might mean only that the Supreme Court looks upon disparate-impact rules with a jaundiced eye, and will limit private rights of action to cases of intentional discrimination.

Four years later the second interpretation prevailed. In *Jackson v. Birmingham Board of Education*, a closely divided Court held that a male coach of a girls' team who had been penalized for complaining about unequal treatment of female athletes could sue the school district for damages. The circuit courts had split over whether Title IX's implied private right of action extends to such retaliation suits. Some followed the broader interpretation of *Sandoval*, ruling that because the statute itself fails to mention retaliation, such private rights of action are not permitted. Others followed the narrower interpretation, arguing that retaliation is an intentional action designed to undermine rights established by Title IX. Justice Sandra Day O'Connor's majority opinion sided with the latter: "Retaliation against a person . . . [who] has complained of sexual discrimination is another form of intentional sex discrimination encompassed by Title IX's private right of action."[46] Although retaliation is not mentioned in the statute, "Reporting incidents of discrimination is integral to Title IX enforcement." "Indeed, if retaliation were not prohibited," Justice O'Connor warned, "Title IX's enforcement scheme would unravel."[47]

Justice Clarence Thomas's dissenting opinion charged that this constituted a rejection of the main holding of *Sandoval*: "By crafting its own additional enforcement mechanism, the majority returns this Court to the days in which it created remedies out of whole cloth to effectuate its vision of congressional purpose. In doing so, the majority substitutes its policy judgments for the bargains struck by Congress, as reflected in the statute's text." The only question the Court should have addressed, the four dissenters insisted, is "whether Title IX prohibits retaliation, not whether prohibiting it is good policy."[48]

The *Jackson* decision made it clear that the Court would not limit the federal judiciary to enforcing the bare words of Title IX. But on the crucial question of how much deference judges should pay to administrative guidelines, the Court remained noticeably silent. In arriving at its decision, the majority explained, it "did not rely on the Department of Education's regulation at all, because the statute itself contains the necessary prohibition."[49] Yet once the courts take on the task of determining what is required to create an *effective* regulatory structure, it is hard to see how they can avoid seeking guidance from the agency that deals with these issues on a daily basis.

Conclusion

When a statute's substantive mandates are ambiguous—as is certainly the case with Title IX—the institutional arrangements established to interpret and enforce the law become especially important. Who establishes the authority of judges and agencies? To some extent that is done by Congress. But with Title IX the central enforcement mechanism created by Congress, the funding cutoff, proved unworkable in practice. Moreover, the rulemaking process established in the law has long been evaded by OCR. The federal judiciary responded to the former by inventing an alternative enforcement practice. The latter met with virtually no protest from the courts.

Justices on the U.S. Supreme Court have disagreed not just about the meaning of the word "discrimination" but also about the legitimacy of the regulatory regime that evolved after 1972. To Justice Stevens and his allies, this "integrated remedial scheme" constitutes an "inspired model" that "builds into the law flexibility, an ability to make nuanced assessments of complex social realities, and an admirable willingness to credit the possibility of progress." For Justices Scalia and Thomas and their allies, when the judiciary creates "remedies out of whole cloth to effectuate its vision of congressional purpose," it usurps the authority of Congress to make the law. Thus, behind judicial interpretations of Title IX lie competing understandings not just of equality, but of the proper operation of the separation of powers under our Constitution.

FOUR

The Enigmatic OCR

The Office for Civil Rights (OCR) in the Department of Education is a small agency with a very big job. It is responsible for ensuring that the more than 18,000 local educational agencies and 7,200 postsecondary educational institutions that enroll nearly 80 million students comply with multiple nondiscrimination mandates.[1] These include not just Title IX, but Title VI of the Civil Rights Act (race and language), section 504 of the Rehabilitation Act (disability), the Age Discrimination Act, and Title II of the Americans with Disabilities Act. Over the eight years of the Obama administration, OCR received 76,000 complaints, resolved 66,000 of these, negotiated 5,400 resolution agreements, and issued 34 major policy guidance documents.[2] Investigation of some complaints requires on-site visits, interviews with students and school officials, extended negotiations, detailed "letters of finding," and monitoring of compliance. OCR does all this with only about 550 employees. As a result, investigations can drag on for months, even years

Most federal agencies, especially those as small as OCR, become contentious only on rare occasion. OCR, in contrast, has seldom escaped political and legal controversy. In the 1960s it became the bête noir of southern leaders seeking to slow the pace of school desegregation. Soon thereafter it drew the wrath of northern opponents of busing. In the 1970s and again in the 1990s, it aggressively promoted bilingual education, provoking intense opposition each time. Throughout the 1970s and 1980s OCR was essentially placed in judicial receivership as a result of *Adams v. Richardson*, an extraordinary case brought by civil rights groups who convinced the court that OCR had not been sufficiently aggressive in enforcing federal antidiscrimination law.[3] For decades, OCR has been attacked from the left for insufficient vigor and from the right for exceeding its statutory mandate.

Although Title IX was only a secondary or even tertiary concern of the agency during the two decades that followed its enactment, under both President Clinton and President Obama OCR issued controversial guidelines and launched extensive investigations on athletics, sexual harassment, and schools' treatment of transgender students. These were not OCR's only controversial initiatives during the Obama years: it issued detailed guidance documents on bullying, racial disparities in school discipline, allocation of school resources, instruction of English-language learners, and affirmative action as well.[4]

This chapter provides the context for the detailed policy stories that follow by looking at OCR from two perspectives. The first is top-down: Who has led the agency and what difference has this made? How do those appointed by Republican presidents differ from those appointed by Democrats? The second is bottom-up: How does OCR define and structure its basic tasks? Why has investigating and promptly resolving every complaint that comes in the door become such a crucial measure of its performance? How has this emphasis on processing complaints affected the way it develops and enforces its policies?

The agency does not make it easy for outsiders to examine its internal operations. As we will see, most of its work involves investigating complaints and negotiating compliance agreements. Seldom does it make its findings public. When a reporter for the *Chronicle of Higher Education* filed a Freedom of Information Act request on OCR's handling of one investigation, the documents he received were "almost entirely redacted." The conduct of OCR's investigations, he noted, "are notoriously opaque."[5] In her extensive examination of OCR's use of rulemaking and enforcement discretion, law professor Catherine Kim found that the agency not only "implement[s] contentious policy initiatives through guidance documents to evade the more onerous constraints imposed on rulemaking," but, "more alarmingly," also "circumvent[s] even the modest checks on guidance documents by channeling policy initiatives through the strategic exercise of enforcement discretion." "OCR enforcement proceedings," she found, "do not *usually* result in settlement, but rather they *always* do." As a result, "There has not been a single instance over the past quarter century in which enforcement decisions resulted in the final agency action necessary for judicial review." In short, Kim writes, "The limited disclosure of OCR enforcement decisions has precluded the public's ability to exercise meaningful checks on them."[6]

In the 1960s and 1970s OCR was an unusually transparent organization, the subject of lively oral histories, extensive documentation (much of it brought to light through litigation), and detailed studies by Jeremy Rabkin, Gary Orfield, Stephen Halpern, Beryl Radin, Rosemary Salomone, and Michael Rebell and Arthur Block.[7] During the next decade and a half investigations by congressional committees and the U.S. Commission on Civil Rights shed some light on its standard operating procedures.[8] Since then, studies of OCR's internal dynamics have disappeared.

To its credit, the Obama OCR made more compliance agreements available to the public than had its predecessor. Its primary purpose in doing so was to provide schools with more specific guidance on what was expected of them; it described some of these agreements as "blueprints" that other schools should follow.[9] For one category of cases—sexual assault—OCR in 2014 reversed its previous practice, and began to announce its investigations at the outset rather than waiting for a final resolution. Although defended in the name of transparency, this strategy has been used selectively to increase pressure on universities to agree to OCR's demands. When it came to encouraging public participation in rulemaking, in contrast, the agency continued to demur, falling back on the fiction that its innovative policies were merely continuations of prior practices. In 2017 Secretary of Education Betsy DeVos promised to end what she described as "rule by letter" and to use the Administrative Procedure Act's notice-and-comment rulemaking process for establishing major policies.[10] This would represent a major change in OCR's method of operation.

In short, the agency, once an open book, has become a black box. Since recent OCR leadership has refused to allow scholars to interview agency staff, this book relies primarily on publicly available documents, supplemented by a handful of personal interviews with former OCR officials, to describe the development of its Title IX rules and enforcement practices.[11] Fortunately (as the footnotes to these chapters indicate), that public record is extensive enough to reveal the main features of policymaking within the organization.

Politics and Executives

OCR began life as a small unit in the Department of Health, Education, and Welfare (HEW) devoted entirely to school desegregation.[12] When the Department of Education was spun off from HEW in 1980, most of the agency's personnel were transferred to the new department. It became a bigger fish in this smaller pond, with its director now elevated to the position of assistant secretary for civil rights. By then its regulatory portfolio and constituency had expanded significantly. Yet, starting in 1981, its staff began to shrink (see figure 4-1). As a result, the priorities and enforcement strategy established by OCR's handful of political appointees have had important consequences for agency performance.

Figure 4-1   OCR Staff Levels, 1981–2016

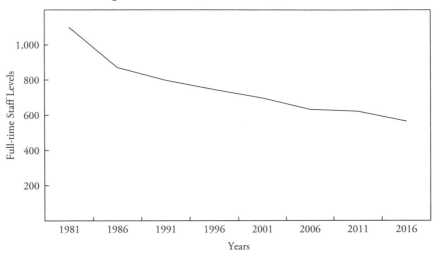

Source: OCR, *Securing Equal Educational Opportunity: Report to the President and Secretary of Education, FY 2016*, p. 9.

During OCR's early years, presidents learned that it could produce plenty of political trouble. It was frequently at loggerheads with the White House and HEW secretaries. In 1965 the young agency infuriated the Johnson White House by threatening to cut off federal funds to public schools in Chicago, home of its powerful mayor, Richard Daley. By the end of what came to be known as "the Chicago fiasco," the city had retained its money, but Commissioner of Education Francis Keppel had lost his job. A few years later President Nixon abruptly fired OCR director Leon Panetta for failing to heed his instructions to go slow on southern school desegregation. Two thousand employees at HEW protested the president's decision. The confrontation did more to tarnish the reputation of Nixon than of Panetta, who went on to a long and distinguished career of public service.[13]

The Panetta affair and resulting animosity between OCR personnel and the Nixon administration convinced civil rights lawyers to initiate *Adams v. Richardson*. From the early 1970s through 1990, responding to court orders became OCR's top priority. This was a major source of irritation for the Ford and Carter administrations. As he was leaving office in 1976, HEW secretary David Matthews told his successor, Joseph Califano, "That place is a law unto itself. You will find OCR takes major actions without informing you. It even attacks you in the press, attacks the Secretary." Califano subsequently complained that OCR had "no sense of identification with the political leadership of the administration, or loyalty to it." Its loyalty, he concluded, lay with the federal courts to which it reported on a regular basis and with the civil rights groups that had brought the litigation and continued to drag it back into court.[14]

By the end of the 1970s this tension had begun to fade. Once moved to the smaller Department of Education, each assistant secretary for civil rights developed good working relations with the secretary of education. As the *Adams v. Richardson* litigation slowly wound down, agency personnel could not so easily insulate themselves from demands from the top. More important, though, was the broader change in the political parties' positions on civil rights.

When OCR was first created, both the Republican and Democratic parties were internally divided on the central civil rights issue of the day, racial segregation. Most of the votes against the Civil Rights Act of 1964 came from the southern wing of the Democratic Party. Despite the strong support for civil rights legislation among Republican members of Congress, the GOP standard bearer in 1964, Barry Goldwater, was one of the handful of non-southern "no" votes. By 1980, partisan sorting had dampened these internal schisms and increased the differences between the parties on a growing array of civil rights issues.

Increasingly the parties saw these issues through different lenses. For Democrats they involved matters of fundamental justice and equality—and of great consequence to their most loyal constituencies. This meant OCR should not only enforce civil rights laws aggressively, but should view racism and sexism as systemic and deeply rooted. Racial and gender imbalance should be seen as prima facie evidence of discrimination. Republicans, in contrast, viewed Democrats' interpretation of civil rights law as a form of regulatory overreach, a prime example of how the other party had distorted statutory language to extend federal power and create unconstitutional racial and gender quotas. Republicans insisted that OCR focus on "disparate treatment," and not assume that any finding of "disparate impact" constitutes a civil rights violation. Democrats countered that this approach ignored institutional racial and sex discrimination and substantially reduced the effectiveness of federal regulation for promoting equality.

Opposition to the aggressiveness of OCR under Presidents Carter and Clinton fueled the promises in the GOP's 1980 and 1996 platform to abolish the Department of Education. The Reagan administration entered office vowing to overturn federal regulations on bilingual education, sexual harassment in the workplace, intercollegiate athletics, and affirmative action. The George W. Bush administration raised doubts about the legality of OCR's sexual harassment guidelines, and tried to make it easier for colleges to comply with Title IX rules on athletics. The 2016 Republican platform charged that the original purpose of Title IX had been perverted "by bureaucrats—and by the current President of the United States—to impose a social and cultural revolution upon the American people."[15] The Trump administration quickly withdrew OCR's guidelines on transgender rights. Soon thereafter, it announced it would reevaluate the Obama administration's sexual harassment guidelines and enforcement practices.

Democrats have responded in kind. During the Clinton administration, OCR's leaders decried the fact that they had "inherited a reactive approach to civil rights enforcement" that had failed "to protect students from egregious cases of discrimination." "Because the vast majority of the agency's resources were spent reacting to complaints that arrived in the morning mail," OCR charged in its 1995 report to Congress, "Glaring instances of long-standing discrimination went unredressed."[16] Fifteen years later Secretary of Education Arne Duncan traveled to Selma, Alabama, to charge the Bush administration with similarly failing to enforce civil rights in education: "The hard truth is that, in the last decade, the Office for Civil Rights has not been as vigilant as it should have been in combating gender and racial discrimination and protecting the rights of individuals with disabilities. But that is about to change."[17]

For half a century, divided government has been the norm in American politics. From 1968 to 2018 one party has controlled the House, the Senate, and the White House for only fifteen years. This means that OCR can usually expect criticism from at least one house of Congress. During the administrations of Ronald Reagan and George H. W. Bush, Democrats in the House launched several investigations of OCR. A 1988 congressional report encapsulated their conclusions: "The history of the Office for Civil Rights is a history of lethargy, defiance, and unwillingness to enforce the law according to its mandates."[18] When Republicans captured both the House and the Senate in 1994, OCR faced not just contentious hearings, but the threat of appropriations riders designed to prevent enforcement of guidelines issued under Titles VI and IX. Rarely has Congress amended these two laws. Yet its members frequently express strong opinions on how they should be interpreted.

Of the several hundred people who work at OCR, only a handful are appointed by the president. The others—including every employee in OCR's twelve regional and field offices—are civil servants. Nonetheless, these political appointees, especially the assistant secretary for civil rights, have significant control over the policy guidelines issued by the agency and its enforcement strategies. Since 1976, these appointments have followed a predictable pattern: Democratic presidents appoint people with close ties to civil rights organizations; Republicans appoint lawyers who have worked for Republican members of Congress or held previous positions within the administration (see table 4-1). Democratic appointees stay longer than Republican appointees. Norma Cantú was assistant secretary during the entire Clinton administration; Russlynn Ali and Catherine Lhamon served for a combined eight years during the Obama administration. The names of these three assistant secretaries will feature more prominently in the coming chapters than those of Republican appointees.

Table 4-1   OCR's Chief Executives

Years	Head	Previous Position
1969–70	Leon Panetta	Legislative assistant to Senator Thomas Kuchel (R-Calif.)
1970–73	Stanley Pottinger	Deputy to Leon Panetta; left to become assistant attorney general
1973–75	Peter Holmes	OCR
1975–76	Martin Gerry	OCR
1977–79	David Tatel	National director, Lawyers Committee for Civil Rights under Law; later appointed to D.C. Circuit court by President Clinton
1979–80	Roma Stewart	Employment discrimination attorney; later appointed Illinois solicitor general
1981–82	Clarence Thomas	Legislative assistant to John Danforth; left to become chair of EEOC
1982–85	Harry M. Singleton	Deputy assistant secretary for congressional affairs, Department of Commerce; staff member, House Committee on the District of Columbia
1987–89	LeGree S. Daniels	Deputy secretary of Pennsylvania; cochair, National Black Republican Council
1990–92	Michael L. Williams	Deputy assistant secretary, Department of the Treasury; special assistant to Attorney General Thornburg
1993–2000	Norma V. Cantú	Attorney, Mexican American Legal Defense and Education Fund
2002–03	Gerald A. Reynolds	President, Center for New Black Leadership; left to become deputy assistant attorney general; later named chair, U.S. Commission on Civil Rights
2005–08	Stephanie J. Monroe	Chief counsel, Senate Committee on Health, Education, Labor, and Pensions
2009–12	Russlynn Ali	Vice president of Education Trust; before that, Children's Defense Fund
2012–17	Catherine Lhamon	American Civil Liberties Union; before that, director of impact litigation at Public Citizen; appointed chair of U.S. Commission on Civil Rights shortly after leaving OCR

Note: This list does not include acting officials.

Not surprisingly, Democratic appointees tend to be greeted with more enthusiasm from the rank and file at OCR than their Republican counterparts. Congressional investigations of OCR in the 1980s discovered widespread dissatisfaction with the agency's Republican leadership. George W. Bush's appointees took steps to curb the enthusiasm of bilingual education advocates placed in the regional offices by Assistant Secretary Cantú. Not long after the Trump administration appointed an acting head of OCR, internal memos began to be leaked to the press—something that had not happened during the preceding eight years. Democratic administrations face a different problem: how to wean lower-level officials from routines honed under Republicans and how to free up resources for new initiatives. In short, the policy preferences of political appointees are always filtered through existing bureaucratic routines and lower-level administrators' understanding of their jobs. To appreciate political appointees' strategies and their effectiveness, it is therefore necessary to explore the nature and structure of OCR's administrative tasks.

Bureaucratic Tasks

Every government agency faces the challenge of turning the vague goals announced in its authorizing statutes into specific, routinizable tasks that can be performed on a daily basis by "street-level bureaucrats." Those at the bottom need to know what is expected of them; those at the top need to show Congress and the public that the organization is accomplishing something; those in the middle need some way to measure what their subordinates are doing all day. As James Q. Wilson has explained, many factors influence the way these bureaucratic tasks come to be defined. History, circumstances, and chance often play a larger role than conscious policy choice.[19]

Problems

As OCR struggled to define its role and the activities of its rapidly growing workforce in the late 1960s and the 1970s, it faced three fundamental problems. The first was the ambiguity of its central mandate, namely, to rout out various forms of discrimination. Here it faced a dilemma. If it equates "discrimination" only with intentional discrimination or with obvious "disparate treatment," then enforcement will be quite limited. Intentions are hard to determine, especially once it has become clear that overt discrimination is illegal. Proving "disparate treatment" requires intensive investigation of how a school has treated similarly situated students of different races or genders.

In light of these difficulties, administrators in civil rights agencies often resort to "disparate-impact analysis," using statistics to highlight areas of possible discrimination and requiring schools and businesses to justify the practices that contribute to these imbalances. This approach has the great advantage of simplifying regulators' task while allowing them to leave a deeper imprint on the practices of schools or employers. The problem is that both Title IX and Title VII explicitly state that they should not be interpreted to require racial or gender balance in educational programs. Moreover, the Rehnquist and Roberts Courts have frequently (if not consistently) disfavored use of disparate-impact analysis under civil rights laws. To the extent that OCR embraces disparate-impact analysis, it invites charges that the government is imposing gender and racial quotas. But when it fails to do so and focuses instead on intentional discrimination or "disparate treatment," it incurs the wrath of civil rights organizations that charge it with ineffectiveness and willful blindness to systemic discrimination.

Second, OCR's enforcement powers are weak. It can threaten to revoke federal funds, but its long history of never doing so undermines its credibility (see chapter 3). For decades, private rights of action—that is, lawsuits filed by private parties seeking injunctions or monetary damages—have provided the primary enforcement teeth for Titles IX and VI. This has two important implications: first, private groups will play a major role in setting the agency's enforcement priorities; and second, OCR will need to stay close to the courts' interpretation of civil rights statutes. If OCR allows its policy to diverge from judicial interpretations, it will be forced to invent new methods for putting pressure on schools to comply with its mandates. This requires the expenditure of significant agency resources and a more adversarial stance toward the institutions whose cooperation it desperately needs. This was particularly evident between 2014 and 2016, when OCR used lengthy, institution-wide investigations to pressure schools to comply with its sexual assault guidelines (see chapter 11). In short, relying on judicial enforcement reduces the agency's autonomy. But setting off on its own is expensive and risky.

The third problem is administrative and political overload. During the 1970s, Congress piled new jobs on OCR just as the agency itself was initiating ambitious regulatory campaigns. The combination of Panetta's abrupt dismissal and appropriations riders passed by Congress took OCR out of the school busing quagmire. But Panetta's replacements remained committed to promoting equal educational opportunity. Looking "for other problems to solve," OCR's incoming director, Stanley Pottinger, issued a memo to school districts announcing that the failure to provide special assistance to English-language learners constitutes discrimination on the basis of "national origin" and therefore violates Title VI.[20] While engaged in this ambitious effort to require schools to institute bilingual/bicultural programs, OCR also launched a resource-intensive review of the treatment of minority students in large northern cities, starting with New York. It soon became clear that this Big City Review would require far more personnel than anyone had expected. Meanwhile advocacy groups and the federal courts insisted that the agency devote more attention to rulemaking and enforcement under Title IX and section 504. OCR, Gary Orfield notes, "searched for and found enthusiastic new constituencies with real need and with intellectuals who had a vision of educational change."[21] Juggling these multiple tasks and constituencies became OCR's biggest challenge.

For a decade and a half after its creation, OCR fumbled around, trying to find a workable administrative strategy. According to Wilbur Cohen, the wily veteran who served as undersecretary and acting secretary of HEW during the late 1960s, the office was filled with "young lawyers who had good ideas, but their concept of enforcement and administration was juvenile." They were "just a bunch of amateurs with real good ideas and very socially minded, wandering around in the desert of Sinai."[22] Its first director later conceded that his young staff lacked an "appreciation of the monstrousness of the task before us."[23] The leaders of OCR during the Nixon and Ford administrations were more experienced and politically realistic (nothing like a good firing to increase attentiveness to politics), but they, too, struck off in many directions with little appreciation for the difficulty of OCR's new tasks.

The Carter administration soon learned that OCR was incapable of carrying all these projects to fruition. In their detailed history of the Big City Review, Michael Rebell and Arthur Block applaud its egalitarian objectives, but conclude that in the end it produced only an "eclectic package of standards and methods" that "did not prove viable in practice."[24] By 1980, OCR's bilingual education project had collapsed under the combined weight of disheartening research findings, adverse court decisions, opposition from other offices within the Department of Education, growing criticism from Congress, and bad press.[25] Women's groups and organizations representing the disabled protested that they were being ignored. OCR's new director, David Tatel, was frustrated by OCR's inability to focus on the issues he cared most about, especially desegregation of higher education. OCR was still careening from one ambitious enterprise to another without demonstrating a capacity to bring about the changes in educational practices that it had promised.

Order from the Courts

During the 1970s and 1980s, the most consequential criticism of OCR came from federal judges in the District of Columbia. In 1972, D.C. district court judge John Pratt accused the agency of systematic nonenforcement of Title VI. He issued an injunction requiring OCR to begin formal enforcement proceedings against more than two hundred school districts in seventeen southern and border states, and to terminate federal funding of those found to be out of compliance with Title VI.[26] Subsequent judicial orders extended judicial supervision to enforcement of Title IX and section 504 as well as the agency's investigation of racial discrimination complaints in northern and western cities.

In a 1990 decision that marked the end of the *Adams* litigation, Ruth Bader Ginsburg, then a judge on the D.C. Circuit, complained that the *Adams* litigation had "grown ever larger in the two decades since its initiation," turning the district court judge into an "overseer or pacer of procedures government agencies use to enforce civil rights prescriptions." "Over the past two decades," Judge Ginsburg wrote, "the once contained action expanded to colossal proportions: the litigation came to encompass enforcement by units of the Department of Education and the Department of Labor of four civil rights measures as they pertain to the education systems of all fifty states."[27] Born out of deep distrust of the Nixon administration's "southern strategy," the *Adams* litigation dragged on for years, only to be dismissed when Judge Pratt made the astounding finding that the original plaintiffs lacked standing to bring the case. One circuit court judge explained this strange turn of events by claiming that "what really happened is that Judge Pratt just got tired of being the Czar of civil rights enforcement."[28]

In a way that no one anticipated, it was the *Adams v. Richardson* litigation rather than Congress or agency leaders that eventually established the task structure of OCR, elevating prompt investigation of all complaints filed by private parties to OCR's most important task. Nothing in the statutes that OCR administers requires it to investigate all of the thousands of complaints it receives each year. During the battle over southern school desegregation, OCR did not wait for private citizens to file complaints: it demanded that each school that had engaged in de jure segregation in the past demonstrate that it was meeting benchmarks established by the agency.

On the final page of his detailed 1975 "Supplemental Order" in the *Adams* case—under the bland, bureaucratic heading "Appendix F"—Judge Pratt not only took the novel step of requiring the agency to investigate all complaints submitted to it, but also established deadlines for each phase of OCR's investigations. His order gave OCR ninety days from the receipt of a complaint to determine whether an educational institution had complied with Title VI; if it found a violation, it had an additional ninety days to seek compliance through negotiations; if voluntary compliance was not forthcoming, it had another thirty days to initiate formal enforcement proceedings. Judge Pratt soon applied this rigid (and wholly unrealistic) formula to complaints brought under Title IX and section 504. His only explanation was that "HEW has often delayed too long in ascertaining whether a complaint or other information of racial discrimination constitutes a violation of Title VI."[29]

The procedures mandated by the court in *Adams* produced heated debate, unusual schisms, and unexpected consequences. The civil rights lawyers who brought the case viewed the "Appendix F" framework as essential for forcing

OCR to take aggressive action—including termination of federal funding—to desegregate public schools. In contrast, OCR's leaders in both the Ford and Carter administrations saw mandatory investigations as a serious drain on agency resources, one that forced them to curtail more systematic compliance reviews. In 1975 HEW maintained that "complaints received by the Department over the last few years have not been broadly representative of the spectrum of the Department's civil rights enforcement program," and that "investigations, negotiations, and enforcement action concerning isolated incidents of discrimination by a grantee can consume as much staff time as monitoring the operation of, for example, some entire school systems." It sought to develop "a methodical approach geared toward identifying and eliminating systemic discrimination" rather than follow the court-mandated "reactive or complaint-oriented approach."[30] Having little trust in OCR, HEW, or the Ford administration, civil rights groups went back to court and forced the department to back down.

The same argument soon broke out during the Carter administration despite the fact that OCR's new leadership had close ties to those advocacy groups. David Tatel told the court that OCR could not "plan systematically if we must respond to each group's attempts to compel OCR to commit the bulk of its resources to enforcement of a particular law, or to enforcement in a particular set of institutions in a particular manner."[31] Stephen Halpern reports that OCR's petition to loosen the deadlines led to "a bitter fight between civil rights lawyers who remained on the outside and those who had joined the new administration." Carter appointees "spent many a difficult evening and weekend in heated sessions with the opposing civil rights lawyers—their former compatriots. There was much finger pointing and hostility."[32] Judge Pratt would agree only to marginal changes in "Appendix F." OCR did manage to use the court order to its advantage in one way: the judge ordered it to ask Congress for several hundred more staff positions than OMB and HEW had previously requested. OCR did not object to being thrown into that budgetary briar patch. Congress went along, and OCR reached its peak size. For OCR's leaders the court was sometimes a useful ally, sometimes a thorn in their side, but always the dominant force in their political environment.

From Judicial Mandate to Bureaucratic Routine

After nearly two decades of court-imposed deadlines, the focus on investigating and resolving individual complaints became deeply ingrained in the agency's standard operating procedures. Although Titles VI and IX are silent on the topic, no one any longer questioned the assumption that OCR must process every complaint it receives. As the agency blandly stated in its FY 2018 budget request, "OCR's performance measures are based on the percentage of complaints resolved within 180 days and the percentage of complaints pending after 180 days."[33] In

1988 the head of OCR responded to the looming dismissal of the *Adams* litigation by distributing a memorandum explaining that the procedures and deadlines mandated by *Adams* would remain in effect until OCR reassesses the complaint processing procedures imposed by the court.[34] No such reassessment ever took place.

Stephen Halpern has noted the irony that an agency that only a few years earlier had "led a social revolution" in the segregated South, became "preoccupied with management efficiency in the processing of complaints." This became "the primary organizational objective."[35] As Jeremy Rabkin put it, "The litigation forced OCR to become a complaint processing agency, a sort of small claims court for civil rights disputes."[36] "The great catch phrase in OCR operations in the late 1970s and into the 1980s," he writes, was "productivity," with "an endless stream of memos harping on the need to improve the productivity of regional offices and individual agency investigators." Unfortunately, this "did not refer to any measure of real-world benefits per man-hour of effort, but simply to the number of complaints that were processed—with whatever outcome—per investigator per month." With good reason, Rabkin describes this as "a classic example of bureaucratic goal displacement."[37] Secretary Califano speculated that it was easier for OCR to fall back on this immediate, routinizable task than to confront more challenging and controversial issues: "At times it seemed as though OCR sought in its forms and bureaucratic cant refuge from the extraordinary subtleties the second generation of civil rights issues presented."[38]

This changed little over time. By 1993, OCR itself reported that "nearly 90 percent of OCR resources were spent in a complaint mode." This despite the fact that such an approach does not, according to the agency, "adequately address the variety of civil rights problems faced by vulnerable groups in the U.S. unable or afraid to complain."[39]

OCR's focus on complaint processing may have had its origin in a quirky appendix to a court order, but it took root and continued long after the *Adams* litigation ended because it served a number of bureaucratic purposes. It structured the work of OCR's regional offices, giving managers a method for gauging productivity. It offered the agency a way to demonstrate that it was responding to public concerns and achieving concrete results. When the number of complaints increased, agency leaders could ask for more money from Congress. For Republicans, complaint processing offered the opportunity to focus on individual accusations of discriminatory treatment rather than undertake systemic investigations based on disparate-impact analysis. They could deflect Democrats' charge that they were hostile to civil rights by touting their efficiency in resolving complaints. Democratic administrations could hide the novelty of their initiatives by first embedding them in settlement agreements negotiated in private, then using these agreements to bolster their claim that they were merely following long-established policies. Originally imposed on a resistant agency, the emphasis on prompt processing of complaints has created a stable, politically useful routine for an agency often beset by controversy.

Who Complains?

An important implication of this understanding of OCR's job is that the array of complaints filed by private citizens has major consequences for the allocation of agency resources. The pie charts in figure 4-2 provide a rough look at how OCR's caseload has changed over time. (OCR's inconsistent reporting of data makes precise over-time comparisons difficult. For some years we have a breakdown by race/national origin, sex, age, and disability. For others years it includes the categories "multiple" and "other." For some years we have no data at all.)

Three features of these charts bear noting. First is the large percentage of disability complaints. The majority of these involve parents' disagreement with the details of the individualized education plans prepared by school districts for their children under the Individuals with Disabilities Education Act. Second, Title IX sex discrimination cases have now overtaken Title VI race discrimination cases as the second biggest category. Most of these involve either athletics (the subject of part II of this book) or sexual harassment (the subject of part III). For example, in 2013 and 2014 OCR received 5,845 Title IX complaints. Of these, 3,609 were on athletics and 854 on sexual harassment. The third largest category of Title IX complaints, retaliation (652 complaints), mainly involved athletic and harassment issues as well.[40]

Third and less obviously, the number of complaints filed each year is not entirely exogenous (see figure 4-3). OCR can encourage certain types of complaints by issuing new rules, by publicizing an issue, and by allowing an individual or organization to file multiple complaints. The number of sexual harassment complaints filed against universities escalated rapidly after OCR issued its 2011 and 2014 guidance documents and initiated well-publicized investigations. During President Obama's first term, the average number of sexual harassment complaints against colleges was 14 per year. That rose to 106 in 2014, 165 in 2015, and 177 in 2016.[41] The sharp increase in the total number of complaints in 2016—which OCR claimed justified a significant budget increase for the agency—was almost entirely the consequence of 6,157 Title IX athletics complaints filed *by a single unnamed individual*. Similarly, in 2014 two unidentified individuals filed more than 1,700 Title IX complaints.[42] OCR's novel policy of entertaining such mass complaints has increased the power of advocacy groups that can now serve as complaint "bundlers" (to adapt a term from campaign finance)—or at least those filed by groups viewed favorably by agency leadership.

Figure 4-2   Distribution of Complaints over Time

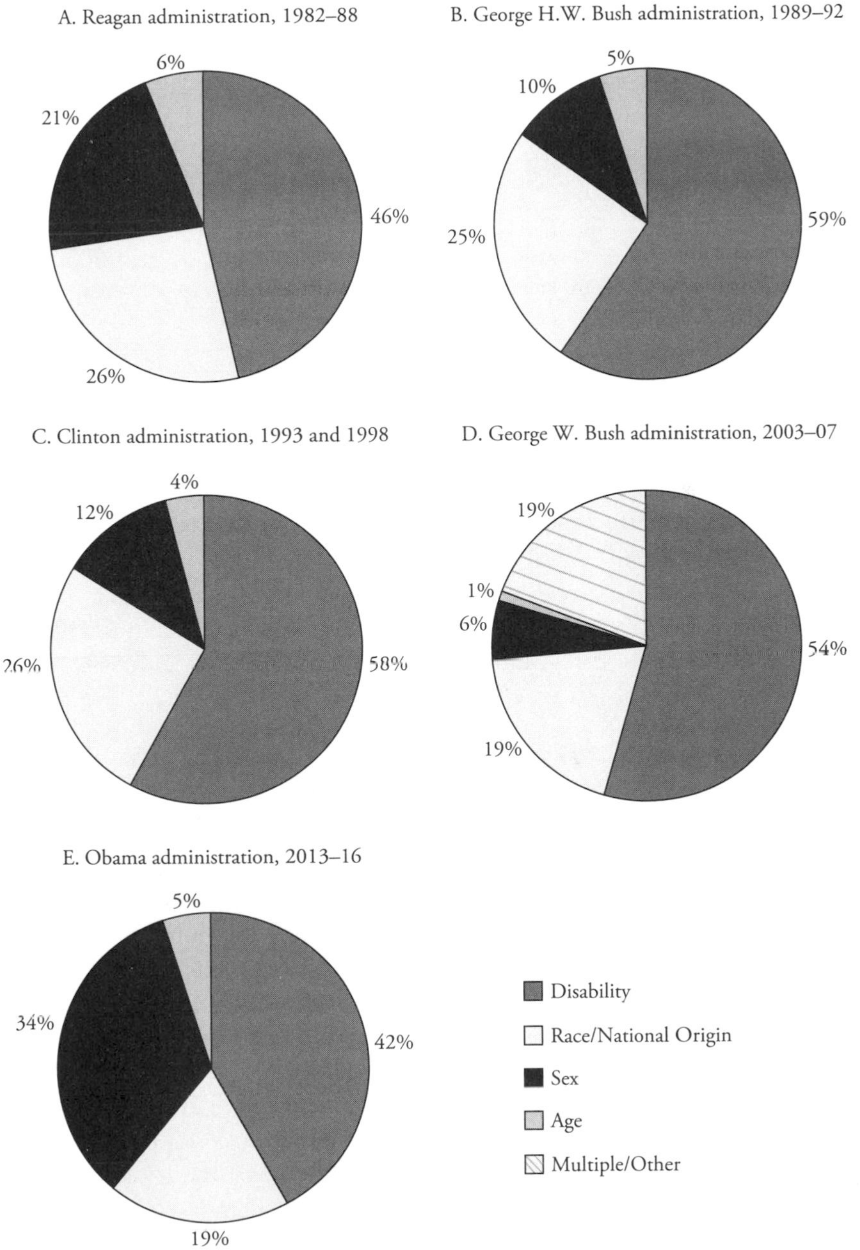

A. Reagan administration, 1982–88

6%
21%
46%
26%

B. George H.W. Bush administration, 1989–92

5%
10%
25%
59%

C. Clinton administration, 1993 and 1998

4%
12%
26%
58%

D. George W. Bush administration, 2003–07

19%
1%
6%
19%
54%

E. Obama administration, 2013–16

5%
34%
42%
19%

- Disability
- Race/National Origin
- Sex
- Age
- Multiple/Other

Sources: (A–B) U. S. Commission on Civil Rights, *Equal Educational Opportunity Project Series*, vol. 1 (December 1996), p. 224, Table 5.4; (C) *Equal Educational Opportunity Project Series*, vol. 1, p. 224, Table 5.4, and OCR, *Annual Report to Congress, FY 1998*; (D) OCR, *Annual Report to Congress, FY 2003–2007*; (E) OCR, *Protecting Civil Rights, Advancing Equity, Report to the President and Secretary of Education, FY 2013–14, Delivering Justice: Report to the President and Secretary of Education, FY 2015*, and *Securing Equal Educational Opportunity: Report to the President and Secretary of Education, FY 2016*.

Figure 4-3   Complaints Received by OCR, 1981–2016

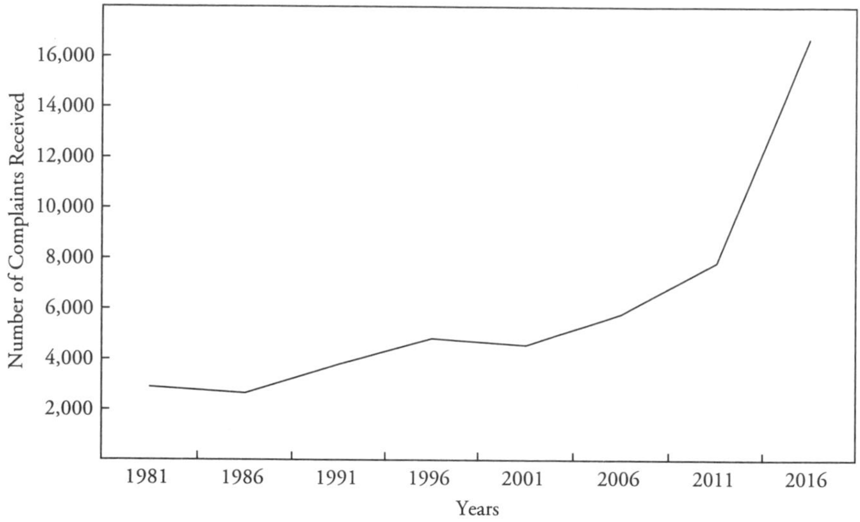

Source: OCR, *Securing Equal Educational Opportunity: Report to the President and Secretary of Education, FY 2016*, p. 9

Complaint Processing and Partisan Priorities

Ironically, the civil rights lawyers' enemies in the Reagan administration turned out to be more satisfied with Judge Pratt's framework than their friends in the Carter administration had been. Although the Reagan administration's Department of Justice repeatedly called upon the federal courts to end their supervision of OCR, its appointees to OCR discovered that the procedures mandated by *Adams* served their purposes relatively well. Not only was the focus on processing individual complaints consistent with their emphasis on "disparate treatment" rather than "disparate impact," but the court's insistence on prompt resolution of complaints created pressure for constricting the scope of OCR's investigation and reaching quick settlements. According to procedures adopted during the Reagan administration, when a regional office found that a legal violation had occurred, its "letter of finding" was subject to lengthy headquarters review. This lowered the regional office's closure rate. As a result, a congressional staff report charged, "The agency severely increased pressure upon enforcement staff to accept a settlement prior to issuing the letter of findings."[43] This almost always meant a settlement more favorable to the educational institution. Moreover, OCR devoted few resources to monitoring compliance with the settlements it helped negotiate, relying instead on schools' promises to change their practices. Since the *Adams* framework did not include monitoring of settlements, little of it took place.[44]

This administrative strategy allowed the Reagan administration to reduce significantly the number of missed *Adams* deadlines, by then the standard measures for judging the agency's performance. For example, between 1982 and 1984 the average time for processing a complaint plummeted from 1,300 days to 230.[45] The number of complaints missing at least one *Adams* deadline declined from 500 in 1984 to only 100 in 1988.[46] During those years OCR absorbed a reduction in its appropriation, and even returned money to the Treasury at the end of several fiscal years.

When Norma Cantú became assistant secretary in 1993, she echoed the Carter administration's preference for shifting more resources to systematic reviews. In the Clinton years the number of compliance reviews conducted by the agency increased substantially, averaging 112 per year—almost three times as many as in the Reagan and Bush years.[47] The fact that the Reagan administration had eliminated OCR's huge backlog made this possible, as did the regional offices' growing familiarity with the issues commonly raised. During the George W. Bush administration, in contrast, the number of compliance reviews fell back down to 39 per year, one-third of which were closed due to insufficient evidence.[48]

Surprisingly, the Obama administration initiated even fewer compliance reviews than the Bush administration. In 2013 and 2014, for example, the average was only thirty-four.[49] In 2016 it conducted only seven compliance reviews under Title VI and four under Title IX.[50] The main reason for this was that agency officials had learned an important lesson from the experience of the 1990s: an investigation of an individual complaint can easily be turned into a systematic review of an entire institution without calling it a "compliance review."

This strategy lay at the heart of the Obama administration's enforcement of its sexual harassment rules. In 2015 Assistant Secretary Lhamon told a *New York Times* reporter that rather than focusing on the facts presented by an individual sexual harassment complainant, "It's better to look at a school's policies, and other case files, to see if what happened to that student is an aberration." She explained, "We are more systemic in the way we evaluate because I think that's the way to get at civil rights compliance more effectively."[51] Lhamon conceded that such reviews can take years to complete. This means, she told congressional appropriations committees, that the agency needs more money to hire more investigators.

The Trump administration's first move on the sexual harassment front was to reverse this investigative strategy. In a memo circulated to regional offices in June 2017, Candice Jackson, the acting assistant secretary, emphasized the importance of prompt resolution of individual complaints.[52] This vividly illustrates the difference between Republican and Democratic leadership at OCR: the former views resolution of individual complaints as the agency's core mission; the latter views investigation of individual complaints as a point of entry for more sweeping institutional reform.

Policymaking Style: The Allure of Opacity

OCR's bureaucratic emphasis on complaint investigation has produced a distinctive policymaking style. Rather than developing regulations through the Administrative Procedure Act's rulemaking process and then applying these regulations to particular cases, OCR's policies have been developed in an ad hoc—and often inconsistent—manner through its investigation and negotiation of disputes that come through the door. These proceedings usually take place in private. Until recently, few of the resulting agreements have been made available to the public. Because its guidelines are allegedly advisory rather than mandatory, and because these agreements are allegedly voluntary, few of OCR's actions are subject to judicial review.[53] Despite the fact that in the aggregate these agreements constitute federal policy, the "letters of finding" issued by the agency at the conclusion of its investigations and negotiations always include this proviso: "This letter sets forth OCR's determination in an individual case. This letter is not a formal statement of OCR policy and should not be relied upon, cited, or construed as such."[54] Nonetheless, OCR frequently relies on these agreements in subsequent negotiations and to justify the general policy statements it later announces. For an agency subject to strenuous criticism for whatever position it takes, policymaking through below-the-radar negotiations is an attractive way to proceed.

For years one of the most common complaints lodged against OCR has been that it fails to give educational institutions a clear idea of what they must do to comply with federal mandates. The General Accounting Office offered this criticism in 1977.[55] A few years later Jeremy Rabkin described OCR's leadership as "almost pathologically cautious about clarifying particular requirements."[56] In the final year of the Reagan administration a House staff report faulted OCR for the "dearth of written substantive enforcement policy."[57] This did not change during the Clinton administration. After conducting a comprehensive review of OCR's records in 1996, the U.S. Commission on Civil Rights concluded that its "restrained approach to issuing policy" failed to provide "definite policy guidance for school districts detailing the various program requirements they must address in ensuring equal educational opportunity for all students."[58] Three years later, another report of the Commission on Civil Rights found that although "OCR has placed a high priority on issues related to ability grouping practices," it "has not issued a single, coherent, and cohesive policy guidance document or investigative manual" on the topic.[59] A 2004 report by the commission repeated this complaint, noting that OCR had announced that "girls' access to advanced mathematics and science education" should be a "high priority," but still had "not finalized the draft investigative manual" on the subject.[60] Subsequent chapters of this book provide multiple examples of the agency's reluctance either to issue clear policy statements or to employ standard rulemaking practices.

To some extent the Obama administration represented a break from this pattern. Most important, it issued an unusually large number of Dear Colleague Letters—thirty-four in all, more than all previous administrations combined. Many of these letters spelled out in great detail how OCR interprets Title IX and Title VI. It also made public many of the agreements it had signed with public schools (especially on athletics and English-language learners) and with colleges (especially on sexual harassment). The Obama administration's strategy of selective transparency was a product of its ambitious goals and, in the case of sexual harassment, its determination to go well beyond what the federal courts have mandated (see chapter 11). Without being able to rely on judicial enforcement, OCR used the threat of bad publicity to induce schools to sign detailed resolution agreements. That is why advocacy organizations such as Know Your IX objected so strenuously to the Trump administration's policy of refocusing sexual harassment investigations on individual complainants.

Conclusion

Like most federal agencies, OCR is neither a pliant tool available to every new presidential administration nor an autonomous unit of a politically unaccountable "administrative state." Political appointees can have a great deal of influence not only over the regulations and guidance announced by the agency, but also over its enforcement strategies and priorities. They are constrained, though, by the accumulation of policies over time (especially when educational institutions have devoted resources to complying with those regulations) and by the complaint-processing routine that defines its bureaucratic task structure. Much of the agency's work is devoted to relatively small-bore investigations of such matters as the adequacy of an individualized education plan for a child with disabilities or the condition of the girls' softball field. Though not required by statute, these routines are deeply embedded in the agency's understanding of its job. For reasons explained above, in different ways they serve the purposes of both Republican and Democratic administrations.

OCR and its leaders are also constrained by the courts. That is not because they must contend with judicial review of the agency's rules and regulations. By relying almost entirely on legally ambiguous "guidance" rather than on legally binding regulations, the agency's general policy pronouncements are almost never challenged in court. But the weakness of OCR's enforcement authority means that in most circumstances it will rely on court suits brought by private individuals to impose sanctions on institutions that fail to comply with its demands. If, on the one hand, agency leaders want to go beyond what courts have required (as with sexual harassment), they must devise an alternative enforcement strategy, which is likely to be resource-intensive and thus hard to sustain. If, on the other hand, agency leaders want to dial back regulatory demands, those who believe their civil rights have been violated can take their case to court—as lawyers representing female athletes frequently did in the early 1990s.

Together these three factors—OCR's reluctance to use standard rulemaking, the centrality of its complaint-processing routines, and the crucial enforcement role played by courts—often make it difficult to get a handle on what the federal government actually requires of educational institutions and how it arrived at these policies. The remainder of this book delves into the details of three policy issues to paint a fuller picture of Title IX regulation in action. If the twists and turns of policymaking by courts and agencies at times seem hard to follow, keep in mind that this complexity is an essential part of the politics of Title IX regulation: the harder these issues are for most people to understand, the easier it is for those who devote themselves wholeheartedly to them to influence the evolution of federal regulation.

Part II

Athletics

FIVE

The Troubled Return of "Separate but Equal"

When Title IX was before Congress in 1971–72, athletics received virtually no attention. According to Representative Patsy Mink (D-Hawaii), an avid supporter for whom the law was later named, "When it was proposed, we had no idea that the most visible impact would be in athletics. I had been paying attention to the academic issue."[1] During the brief floor debate on Title IX, the only mention of sports came from Birch Bayh, the amendment's main Senate sponsor, who assured his colleagues: "We are not requiring that intercollegiate football be desegregated, nor that the men's locker room be desegregated."[2]

Yet athletics—especially college football—soon dominated the intense controversy over how to interpret Title IX. Defending the Department of Health, Education, and Welfare's 1975 regulations before Congress, Secretary Caspar Weinberger noted with exasperation, "I had not realized until the comment period closed that the most important issue in the United States today is intercollegiate athletics."[3] Until the Obama administration launched its sexual harassment initiative in 2011, no Title IX issue received nearly as much attention as college sports. Indeed, so closely is the law associated in the public mind with athletics that a glossy catalog for women's sports apparel is called *Title Nine*—making it the only line of clothing named after a section of the U.S. code.

The 1975 regulations defended by Secretary Weinberger were only the beginning. Decades of Office for Civil Rights (OCR) "interpretations" and "clarifications" of those rules along with numerous federal court decisions kept the issue in the news and pushed colleges to increase the number of varsity teams for women. Title IX obviously did not—as many prominent football coaches had predicted—kill big-time football. In fact, college football revenues (and expenses) grew exponentially in subsequent years. Advocates for the expansion of women's intercollegiate sports eventually reached a tacit accord with the so-called revenue-generating men's sports—football and basketball. Universities would devote more resources to women's varsity sports, either by increasing colleges' athletic budget (the option favored by the National Collegiate Athletic Association [NCAA], most women's groups, and OCR) or by eliminating "minor" men's teams such as wrestling, gymnastics, and diving. Since these "minor" sports had influential defenders (most notably, former wrestling coach Speaker Dennis Hastert and former college grapplers Senator Paul Wellstone and Secretary Donald Rumsfeld), the array of varsity teams offered by colleges became a national political issue. Regulation of college sports combined potent political symbolism—advocates of new role models for women vs. defenders of the "manly" sport of football—with traditional interest-group politics, as each sport fought for a bigger slice of the college athletic budget.

We have become so accustomed to equating Title IX with athletics that we often forget just how odd it is that a law aimed at increasing *educational* opportunities for women has focused so intensely on athletics. After all, athletics is just one of many extracurricular activities offered by colleges and other schools. The fact that female students now outnumber males in student government, student newspapers, drama, debate, music, and almost every other form of extracurricular activity does not lead the federal government to push for more opportunities for guys.[4] Moreover, while athletics can in some circumstances contribute to a well-rounded education, in practice, college varsity athletics is often antithetical to the central mission of higher education. All too often it brings to campus unqualified "student athletes," creates an anti-intellectual subculture, and leads to subtle as well as overt forms of corruption. Nearly eighty years ago Robert Maynard Hutchins warned that of all the "crimes committed" by highly competitive college sports, "the most heinous is the confusion of the country about the primary purpose of higher education."[5] If the goal of Title IX is to improve the educational opportunities available to women, why have college sports taken center stage?

The answer lies in a peculiar feature of intercollegiate and interscholastic (that is, varsity competition at the high school level) sports: they are almost always segregated by sex. In all areas of education except sports, "leveling the playing field" means removing artificial barriers to women's participation and allowing them to compete with men. In the early days of Title IX, some men's coaches claimed that they would comply with the new law by letting female undergraduates try out for the football team. Not surprisingly, the prospect of an occasional female placekicker on the men's football team did not satisfy the women's organizations monitoring compliance with Title IX. They demanded separate teams with equal treatment—in short, "separate but equal."

Athletics is the most important area where the analogy between racial discrimination and sex discrimination breaks down. Racial segregation was long used to stigmatize and disadvantage racial minorities. Sex discrimination in sports neither stigmatizes nor disadvantages, but recognizes undeniable biological differences between male and female athletes. By the time they reach high school, the best male athletes are bigger and stronger than the best female athletes. Few people would think it fair to tell a female sprinter, "You have run the race and lost to the guys, so don't complain when you don't make the team."

But how do we know when "separate" becomes "equal"? That is the question that has bedeviled regulation for nearly half a century. Since the 1990s the debate has pitted those who believe that the number of male and female varsity athletes should mirror the undergraduate population of the school (the "parity" argument) against those who believe that the number of male and female varsity athletes should reflect the proportion of male and female students with an interest in playing varsity-level sports (the "relative interest" argument).[6] Chapter 7 describes the triumph of the parity argument in the 1990s and thereafter.

But why, one should ask, do we focus so intently on *varsity* sports instead of jayvee, club, intramural, and recreational sports or the many varieties of fitness activities? Why define "sports" so narrowly? To put it another way, why has there been so much attention paid to the *denominators* in the equations listed in table 5-1, and so little to the *numerators*? The answer lies both in regulatory agencies' need for easily quantified measures and in the political clout of those with the most intense interest (varsity athletes) and most extensive organizations (coaches' associations, athletic conferences, and above all the NCAA). How regulation came to focus so narrowly on varsity sports is the principal topic of chapters 6 and 7. The remainder of this chapter provides the foundation for that story by explaining the peculiarities of intercollegiate athletics and the options available to regulators seeking to define "separate but equal."

The Athletic Anomaly and the Search for Equality

Sports is the only part of our society that is sex segregated. . . . That's why there is a lot of misunderstanding around Title IX. People don't have any other frame of reference to think about a sex-segregated part of education.

—Nancy Hogshead-Makar, former president
of the Women's Sports Foundation[7]

Football is the fat man tipping the canoe of Title IX.

—Jessica Gavora, *Tilting the Playing Field*[8]

No other country has anything resembling America's college sports programs.

—James Shulman and William Bowen, *The Game of Life*[9]

How does one measure the extent to which a college or a high school provides "equal athletic opportunity" to female students? One might start by looking at the full array of athletic activities that schools offer, ranging from varsity and jayvee teams to club and intramural sports to recreational and fitness programs. This was the approach initially adopted by OCR and the Department of Health, Education, and Welfare (HEW) in 1975. One advantage of examining the full panoply of opportunities is that male and female students might have a different array of athletic interests. For example, female students might be more interested in athletic activities that they can continue to enjoy for many decades, while male students might focus on team sports that few will be able to play after graduation. (Chalk that up to an excess of testosterone.)

This understanding of equality soon evaporated. From a regulatory point of view this approach has a major drawback: how can one compare participation in yoga, intramural ultimate Frisbee, club lacrosse, and varsity hockey? Does one predominantly female yoga class counterbalance the men's varsity hockey team? Does a women's club volleyball team equal a men's varsity basketball team? By 1979 the focus of regulation had subtly shifted to equal opportunities within each "level of competition." And in practice that meant looking at varsity teams and little else. To the extent that regulators have paid any attention at all to club or intramural teams, it has only been to gauge and increase women's interest in varsity sports.

Once the issue had been narrowed in this way, regulators faced another major question, one that has dominated Title IX politics for years: How does one measure equality at the varsity level? One could start with the presumption that for every men's team there should be an identical or equivalent women's team: basketball, track, hockey, lacrosse, tennis, swimming, gymnastics, and soccer for both men and women; men's baseball and women's softball; and perhaps football for men and field hockey for women. As reasonable as this might seem, this approach raises one very big question and several smaller yet persistently knotty ones.

The big question is this: What do we do about football? It is not sufficient simply to add a cognate women's team such as field hockey or even flag football. The reason is that football dwarfs all other sports—male or female—in its number of roster slots and its expense. College football teams usually carry 100–120 players, the equivalent of five or six regular varsity teams. They have offensive units, defensive units, special teams, and multiple reserves to replace the large number of players injured during the season. At many schools, football teams play in huge stadiums, use expensive equipment, command large, specialized coaching and training staffs, and pay head coaches more than any other school or even state employee. For example, in 2017 the University of Michigan made history by employing not only a head coach with a multimillion-dollar salary, but three assistant coaches who each make over a million dollars a year.[10] At the Division I and II levels, football offers more athletic scholarships than any other sport. Indeed, at many schools football costs more than all women's sports combined.[11] This led *Sports Illustrated* to describe college sports as divided into three parts: male, female, and football—"the overfed sacred cow."[12] As law professors Earl Dudley and George Rutherglen observe, football "creates a nightmare in a world driven by the superficial statistics of parity with enrollment."[13]

If the football problem means that one cannot ensure equality just by creating an equal number of teams, then should regulators focus on expenditures? In the 1970s some advocates for women's sports argued for a 50/50 split of athletic resources. This would not only provide an easy measure of equality (equal money), but would also permit women to run their own programs and respond to the distinctive interests of female students. But this proposal ran into an insurmountable problem: "revenue-generating sports," which means football, men's basketball, and, at a few schools, men's hockey. In the years following the enactment of Title IX, college football and basketball became very big business indeed, thanks in large part to the expansion of cable TV networks. The Department of Education reports that in 2015, the 2,075 schools from which it collected data reaped revenues of $12.6 billion from their athletic programs.[14] Football and basketball coaches tried to convince Congress and HEW to exempt these sports from Title IX. But they failed. At the small—indeed tiny—number of colleges that generate net profits from football and basketball, these proceeds are now used to subsidize women's sports, creating an unlikely alliance between supporters of women's varsity teams and the "major" men's sports. Given the political clout of revenue-generating sports and the ease with which schools can manipulate budget figures (they routinely hide many of the costs of running a competitive football program), federal regulators decline to require equal spending on men's and women's sports.

This left only one alternative: counting the number of athletes on varsity teams or, as the courts have misleadingly put it, "genuine athletic participation opportunities."[15] This is the formula that lies at the heart of OCR's pivotal Three-Part Test, which first appeared in the agency's 1979 "interpretation" of its 1975 regulations. As simple as this might seem, counting the number of varsity athletes raises all the questions Judge Underhill confronted in the Quinnipiac case described in chapter 1. What qualifies as a "varsity sport"? Are competitive cheer and tumbling, flag football, or synchronized swimming "real" sports? Who counts as a varsity athlete? A male "walk-on" football player who practices with the team but never makes it into a game? A female benchwarmer who quits soon after the season starts? An injured player who sits out most of the season? The inexperienced and uncompetitive rowers in an eight-person crew who have been added simply to increase the number of female athletes? Does a cross-country runner who also participates in indoor and spring track count as one, two, or three? If a women's team does not fill all the available roster slots, should these still be counted as athletic "opportunities" or is the word "opportunities" simply a euphemism for "actual varsity athletes"? To all these difficulties one must add the inescapable consequence of football: to counterbalance its huge roster requirements, schools must create four, five, or even six women's teams with no male equivalent. In other words, schools must either have many more women's teams than men's teams or invent a sport with a roster equivalent to football.

Compared to What? Parity versus Relative Interest

Once regulators narrowed their focus to the number of male and female varsity athletes, they faced yet another difficult question: To what does one compare these numbers? The 50/50 split advocated by some women's groups in the 1970s now seems anachronistic: female enrollments have reached 55–65 percent at most undergraduate schools. Does this mean that 55–65 percent of varsity athletes must be women? According to the OCR and federal judges, the answer to this question is "Yes."

The major alternative to "parity" is the "relative interest and ability" standard originally invoked by HEW in 1975 and later favored by the George W. Bush administration (see table 5-1). To compare the "athletic opportunities" offered to male and female students at a school, the 1975 regulations explained that regulators would consider "whether the selection of sports and levels of competition effectively accommodate the interests and abilities of members of both sexes." If a smaller percentage of female students have an interest in and ability to play varsity sports than do their male counterparts, then the school need not provide as many varsity slots. In 1975, HEW suggested that schools might use annual surveys to estimate the "interests and abilities" of its male and female students. Thirty years later the Bush administration provided schools with a model survey that nudged federal policy in that direction. Although the "interest and ability" approach provoked little controversy in the 1970s, it was later vehemently attacked by women's groups, by many Democrats in Congress, and, in an important twist, by the NCAA.

The seemingly technical issue of the proper denominator—that is, whether one should compare the number of male and female athletes with the total number of male and female students or with the number of male and female athletes interested in varsity athletics—inevitably raises the question of whether sex differences in athletic interest are entirely "socially constructed" or reflect more basic differences between the sexes. Most women's groups and federal judges

Table 5-1   The Factions' Preferred Fractions

"Parity"

$$\frac{\text{Number of Male Varsity Athletes}}{\text{Males in Student Body}} = \frac{\text{Number of Female Varsity Athletes}}{\text{Females in Student Body}}$$

"Relative Interest"

$$\frac{\text{Number of Male Varsity Athletes}}{\substack{\text{Males in Student Body with} \\ \text{Interest in Varsity Sports}}} = \frac{\text{Number of Female Varsity Athletes}}{\substack{\text{Females in Student Body with} \\ \text{Interest in Varsity Sports}}}$$

have insisted that any gap between male and female interest in competitive sports reflects "past bias against women's participation in sports" and the "lingering lack of exposure and the second-class status of opportunities for women."[16]

When Brown University argued that its 60/40 split between male and female athletes reflected student interest, the First Circuit emphatically rejected the school's "unproven assertion" that male and female students might differ in their commitment to varsity sports. In the most important federal court decision on Title IX and athletics, the court insisted that "women's lower rate of participation in athletics reflects women's historical lack of opportunities to participate in sports."[17] Women show less interest in sports only because they have been offered fewer opportunities and have been expected to conform to female stereotypes that discourage competitiveness, assertiveness, and physical vigor. Providing equivalent opportunities will counteract those stereotypes, and eventually lead them to demonstrate the same level of interest as men. Borrowing from the movie *Field of Dreams*, advocates of the parity standard have adopted the slogan, "Build it and they will come."[18] From concrete opportunities will come new attitudes about sports, undermining old stereotypes about women.

Those who support the use of surveys to judge student interest in varsity sports argue that OCR's parity standard substitutes an abstract, dogmatic understanding of sex differences for the actual interests and abilities of real students. At a 2007 hearing on the topic, Abigail Thernstrom, vice chair of the U.S. Commission on Civil Rights, argued that opposition to the use of surveys is "premised on the condescending assumption that women are incapable of articulating their interest in participating in college sports." After years of progress, "Now women have the power to make their own determination of their interest in collegiate athletics as well as virtually all other areas of endeavor in our society."[19]

To a large extent this is the old nature/nurture debate applied to a concrete public policy issue. But for colleges—as opposed to public elementary and high schools—there is an important twist. For better or for worse, colleges consider athletic interest and ability when they admit students and award scholarships. Most colleges actively recruit athletes, and selective schools give them large admissions advantages. Creating a new team can make a school more attractive to high school students with those special skills. Eliminating a team will lead those high school athletes to look elsewhere. In this sense "build it and they will come" is not just a debatable assertion about the socially constructed nature of male and female differences, but an accurate description of how colleges attract, recruit, admit, and retain undergraduates. A college that wants to promote varsity sports for women can do so by devoting two forms of scarce resources to that endeavor: money (for coaches, scholarships, equipment, playing fields, and travel) and admissions slots, by far the scarcest resource at selective colleges.

For selective undergraduate schools, the flip side of the "build it and they will come" argument is "build more sports teams, and more nonathletes will be turned away." More money for athletic scholarships means fewer scholarships for those who shine academically and for those in financial need. More slots for athletes means fewer for musicians, social entrepreneurs, and the most serious and gifted scholars.

The expansion of intercollegiate women's athletics has sometimes come at the expense of "minor" men's sports such as wrestling, gymnastics, and diving. How often this happens has been the subject of fierce debate. Both OCR and women's groups have condemned the practice of robbing male wrestlers to pay women volleyball players. Cutting men's teams, OCR has frequently stated, is a "disfavored practice."[20] This might be good politics, but it is obviously flawed policy analysis. If male athletes do not pay the price, someone else will—and given female students' superior academic performance, it is likely to be nonathlete female undergraduates and applicants.[21]

To the three peculiar features of college athletics described above—sex segregation, the football behemoth, and colleges' control over admissions—we must add a fourth: the remarkable visibility and popularity of intercollegiate athletics. The United States may not be the only country where universities sponsor sports teams, but nowhere else is the reputation and popularity of a school so closely tied to its success on the playing field. Nowhere else in the world is intercollegiate sports such a big part of college life, and nowhere else is it a multibillion-dollar business with unpaid labor. Nowhere else do colleges run farm teams for professional sports leagues and bestow special scholarships and huge admissions boosts on middle linebackers, point guards, and goalies. And nowhere else has college sports engendered so many forms of corruption.[22]

For Title IX, this cuts in two directions. First and most obviously, it creates a powerful constituency for protecting the most popular and lucrative sports, which almost always means football and men's basketball. Many colleges, particularly those in the NCAA's elite Football Bowl Subdivision, are engaged in an expensive arms race with other football and basketball teams. Efforts to shrink the budgets of these teams and their influence within the university have almost always failed. This represents a huge challenge not just for advocates of women's athletics, but for the future of American higher education in general.[23]

Second, the visibility of college sports offers an opportunity to change public expectations about women's athletic interests and to change girls' understanding of how to succeed. Creating more college teams for women—especially when they come with athletic scholarships and significant admission boosts—creates strong incentives for high school girls to join a team, to specialize, and to apply themselves wholeheartedly to that activity. It encourages them to become fierce competitors rather than mere cheerleaders for the guys. (The cheerleader stereotype helps explain many feminists' hostility to "competitive cheer and tumbling.") College teams also prepare women for competition in Olympic sports and professional sports leagues. Among the biggest boosters of aggressive interpretation and enforcement of Title IX is the Women's Sports Foundation (WSF), founded by tennis star Billie Jean King in 1974. Led by professional athletes, it promotes college athletics as a pipeline to professional sports. Perhaps the strongest political argument for the parity standard is that the heightened visibility of women's sports produces stars such as soccer players Mia Hamm and Hope Solo, skier Lindsay Vonn, and tennis stars Venus and Serena Williams, all of whom have become role models for girls across the country.

When Title IX was enacted in 1972, the Association for Intercollegiate Athletics for Women (AIAW) was fast becoming the women's counterpart to the NCAA, which at the time handled only men's sports. The AIAW was run by women's coaches and physical education administrators who adamantly rejected the NCAA model of competition. The founders of the organization "shared a commitment to a more participation-oriented, less elitist approach to sports that differed fundamentally from the reigning model of sports which intertwined competition, winning, and commercialization."[24] This commitment was embedded in AIAW policy: member schools could not offer athletic scholarships; they could engage in very little recruiting; they were expected to schedule games in a way that did not interfere with studying; and they favored tournaments open to a large number of schools rather than championship playoffs limited to schools with the best regular season records.[25]

Ironically, the AIAW was an early victim of Title IX. Its opposition to athletic scholarships conflicted with regulators' demand that male and female athletes be treated equally. With scholarships came recruitment, and with recruitment and scholarships came an emphasis on building winning teams. In the early 1980s the NCAA lured away most of the AIAW's members by offering subsidies and publicity for national championship games. The AIAW went out of business, taking with it the alternative model of women's sports.[26]

Since then, the two organizations most vocal on women's athletic issues, the Women's Sports Foundation and the National Women's Law Center (NWLC), have taken the opposite position, emphasizing highly competitive sports. For example, the NWLC brought a Title IX lawsuit against the state of Florida, challenging its decision to count high school flag football (an increasingly popular sport for high school girls) as a varsity sport. It has also objected to schools listing competitive cheer and tumbling as varsity sports. "These activities," the organization explained, "do not provide female students with the same type of competitive opportunities that male students receive and therefore raise Title IX concerns." Girls who play flag football in high school will not have "opportunities to play at the college level and earn athletic scholarships."[27] According to this understanding, high school sports should prepare female athletes for college sports, which should prepare them for professional or Olympic sports. At each stage the number of participants declines precipitously, with more and more resources lavished on fewer and fewer athletes.

Progress and Proportionality

How have athletic opportunities for women and girls changed since 1972? Two things are certain. First, the number of girls playing interscholastic sports and women playing intercollegiate sports has grown dramatically over the past half century. Second, at neither the high school nor college level does the proportion of female athletes mirror the proportion of female students. To some observers this indicates that schools simply have not been aggressive enough in creating and promoting teams for women and girls; to others it indicates that female students are just not as interested in sports as guys are. Both sides have their story and are sticking to it. What both sides seem to accept, though, is the dubious assumption that the best way to measure "athletic opportunity" is to look at the number of varsity athletes.

Tables 5-2 and 5-3 summarize the growth of female varsity athletes at the college level. In the mid-1960s, only 15,000 women were involved in intercollegiate sports—as compared to 152,000 men. By 1972 the number of female college athletes had doubled to 30,000. Over the next five years, this doubled again, to 63,000. By 1991 it reached 96,000, and by 2001, 156,000. In 2014–15 there were well over 200,000 female intercollegiate athletes, 43 percent of the total.

As table 5-3 shows, over the past quarter century colleges have added more than three times as many women's teams as men's teams. By the end of the century, NCAA schools offered more teams for women than for men.[28] In 1970 colleges offered, on average, only 2.5 varsity teams for women. Today the average is almost 9.[29] In 1970, almost all athletic scholarships went to male students; today over 40 percent go to females.

Despite the fact that until recently federal regulators have devoted little attention to high school sports, the increase in girls' participation in interscholas-

Table 5-2   College Varsity Athletes, 1966–2015

Academic Year	Male varsity athletes (approx., in thousands)	Female varsity athletes (approx., in thousands)	Percent female
1966–67	152	15	9
1971–72	170	30	15
1976–77	168	63	27
1981–82	170	74	30
1991–92	186	96	34
2001–02	212	156	42
2015–16	278	214	43

Sources: Susan Ware, *Title IX: A Brief History with Documents*, p. 20 (for years 1966 to 1977); NCAA, *Student-Athlete Participation, 1981–82—2015–16* (October 2016), pp. 11–80 (for years 1981 to 2016).

Table 5-3   Changes in Number of Men's and Women's College Varsity Teams, 1988–2016

	Division 1	Division 2	Division 3	Total
Men's teams added	658	1,378	2,009	
Men's teams eliminated	986	783	1,249	
Net change, men	−330	+594	+751	+1,015
Women's teams added	1,268	1,836	2,502	
Women's teams eliminated	468	589	1,125	
Net change, women	+803	+1,253	+1,379	+3,435

Source: NCAA, *Student-Athlete Participation, 1981–82—2015–16* (October 2016), pp. 183–84, 261–62, 272–73. I have not attempted to correct small discrepancies in the NCAA's calculations.

tic sports has been equally dramatic (see table 5-4). In 1971, only 7 percent of high school athletes were female: boys outnumbered girls 3.7 million to 294,000. A decade later almost 2 million high school girls were on sports teams, constituting 35 percent of the total. By 2010 that number reached 3.2 million, about 41 percent of the total. Thereafter, the number of girls on interscholastic teams increased somewhat, but their percentage of the total plateaued. (Girls constitute 49 percent of the high school population.)

In short, in the four decades from 1972 to 2012 the number of high school girls playing interscholastic sports increased tenfold. The number of college women playing intercollegiate sports increased sevenfold. Those are big increases by almost any measure.

Table 5-4   High School Varsity Athletes, 1971–2010

Academic Year	Male varsity athletes (approx. in millions)	Female varsity athletes (approx. in millions)	Percent female
1971–72	3.7	<0.3	7
1975–76	4.1	1.6	29
1980–81	3.5	1.9	35
1985–86	3.3	1.8	35
1990–91	3.4	1.9	36
1995–96	3.6	2.4	39
2000–01	3.9	2.8	42
2005–06	4.2	3.0	41
2010–11	4.5	3.2	41
2015–16	4.5	3.3	42

Source: National Federation of State High School Associations, Participation Statistics (www.nfhs.org/ParticipationStatistics), p. 55.

Two features of the timing of this expansion bear noting. First, the expansion of women's sports began before the enactment of Title IX, accelerated before OCR had provided guidelines for athletics, and continued during the 1980s, when the Supreme Court's decision in the *Grove City* case halted federal enforcement of Title IX in athletics. During the Reagan administration, when federal regulation was moribund, the number of women's college varsity teams grew by 20 percent.[30]

Second, at the college level, the number of women's teams grew most rapidly in the 1990s and early 2000s, the time of greatest pressure from the federal government. During those years the number of men's teams declined, especially at Division I schools. This suggests that both cultural change and federal regulatory demands contributed to the expansion of women's sports, with the relative importance of the two factors nearly impossible to establish with certainty.

The Slow Evolution of Federal Regulation

The history of Title IX regulations on athletics offers a glimpse at the civil rights state in operation. Seldom in this saga does one find sustained debate over the meaning of equality or the purpose of athletics in the educational setting. Instead, one finds incremental expansion of federal regulation by administrators and judges who almost always claim they are just following previously established policy. In their efforts to shield their innovations from political attack, they hid, even from themselves, the long-term consequences of their rules.

Understanding how federal regulation first came to focus almost exclusively on varsity athletes and then established "parity" as the only "safe harbor" for schools' athletic programs requires us to descend into the weeds of administrative rules and guidelines. Regulatory policy evolved in nine stages:

1. Between 1972 and 1975, OCR engaged in the most comprehensive rule-making in the history of Title IX. Athletics proved to be the most contentious issue. The final rules stated that schools must "effectively accommodate the interests and abilities of both sexes," but remained vague on what this would mean in practice.

2. Flooded with requests from colleges to explain in more detail what was expected of them, in 1979 OCR announced the Three-Part Test, which eventually became the cornerstone of federal regulation. Neither the Carter administration nor the Reagan administration made any effort to enforce this interpretation.

3. The Supreme Court's 1984 decision in *Grove City College v. Bell* temporarily ended enforcement of Title IX rules on athletics. The 1988 Civil Rights Restoration Act (usually known as the Grove City Bill) overturned that opinion, opening the door to renewed enforcement.

4. The combination of the 1988 law and a 1992 Supreme Court decision allowing federal courts to award monetary damages in Title IX suits (*Franklin v. Gwinnett County Public Schools*) led to a surge in lawsuits against college athletic programs. This, in turn, led colleges to demand more guidance from OCR. In most of these cases colleges agreed to expand the number of women's teams.

5. In 1993 and 1996 the First Circuit issued two lengthy opinions in *Cohen v. Brown*, endorsing and strengthening OCR's 1979 Three-Part Test. Under its interpretation, schools would be hard pressed to comply with Title IX until the number of male and female varsity athletes mirrors the gender distribution of the undergraduate student body as a whole. Every federal court that heard a Title IX case followed the First Circuit. When the Supreme Court denied certiorari in that case, the First Circuit's ruling became the definitive legal precedent

6. In 1996, OCR announced a "clarification" of its 1979 "interpretation" that made proportionality the only "safe harbor" for college athletic programs. It later required athletic scholarships to reflect the proportion of male and female varsity athletes, and significantly increased the resources it devoted to investigating athletic programs.

7. A counterattack against this regulatory surge began when Republicans took control of Congress in 1995. Buoyed by the First Circuit's decision, the Clinton OCR stood its ground.

8. The George W. Bush administration tried to make it easier for schools to use surveys to show that they had "accommodated the interests and abilities" of female athletes. Its effort to modify the Three-Part Test ultimately failed, in large part due to opposition from the NCAA.

9. In 2010 the Obama administration rescinded the Bush administration's "Additional Clarification," replacing it with a Dear Colleague Letter that made it much harder for schools to evade the proportionality standard. A number of OCR investigations culminated in agreements with individual schools (such as Quinnipiac) to increase substantially their spending on women's sports programs. The Obama OCR also focused more attention on interscholastic athletics.

The first four stages are described in chapter 6, the final five in chapter 7.

Conclusion

These events illustrate not only the institutional "leapfrogging" so common in the American civil rights state but also the subtle interaction of ideology and organized interests. At one level this was a battle between those who expect males and females to have different levels of interest in competitive sports and those who insist that any such difference we observe today is "socially constructed," the consequence of outmoded stereotypes and unequal opportunity. For the former, "equal opportunity" means responding to different preferences. For the latter it requires reshaping public attitudes.

At the same time, though, this debate was narrowed to focus on one tiny segment of athletics, varsity sports, especially at Division I colleges. Varsity athletes, prospective varsity athletes, and, most important, their coaches, have the personal interest and organizational bonds needed to pursue these cases in OCR and the courts. The Women's Sports Foundation was founded by successful professional athletes to promote women's athletics at the most competitive levels. Once the NCAA changed its strategy in 1981, it too had a strong organizational interest in promoting highly competitive women's college sports. Ultimate Frisbee teams and yoga instructors could not match this combined organizational clout. The story told in the following two chapters thus reveals a complex combination of ideology, interests, and institutional interaction.

SIX

Regulation in Fits and Starts, 1972–95

Title IX's first two decades were filled with heated debates over intercollegiate athletics, but little specific regulatory guidance and virtually no enforcement. It took the Department of Health, Education, and Welfare (HEW) three years to write its first Title IX regulations. Not only were those rules vague on key points, but they gave colleges an additional three years to "adjust their athletics offerings" to comply with the new rules.[1] At the end of that grace period, the Carter administration proposed further guidance, but quickly backed away in the face of criticism from all sides. Not until the end of 1979 did it offer an "interpretation" on athletics. Before any serious enforcement could begin, though, President Carter suffered a stunning defeat by Ronald Reagan, who vowed to slash federal regulation of educational institutions. In the early 1980s the federal courts adopted an interpretation of Title IX's "pinpoint" provision that in effect removed colleges' athletic programs from the Office for Civil Rights' (OCR) jurisdiction.

Federal regulation of athletics did not come back to life until 1988, after Congress enacted the Grove City Bill over President Reagan's veto. By the early 1990s a number of factors, including a Supreme Court decision allowing judges to award monetary damages in Title IX suits, produced a surge of court cases, OCR investigations, and settlement agreements with colleges. The Three-Part Test, previously a minor, barely noted provision of the 1979 OCR "interpretation,"

Table 6-1   Title IX Athletics Chronology, 1972–95

1972	OCR begins work on Title IX regulations
1974	Congress fails to pass the Tower Amendment exempting revenue-producing sports from coverage; instead it passes the Javits Amendment directing HEW to issue regulations that provide for "reasonable provisions considering the nature of particular sports"
	After extensive debate within HEW and the Ford administration, OCR proposes a comprehensive set of Title IX regulations and asks for comments
1975	President Ford signs HEW's comprehensive Title IX regulations; colleges are given three years to comply with provisions on athletics
1978	With the deadline for compliance nearing, OCR proposes a more detailed "interpretation" of rules on college sports; HEW secretary Califano puts a hold on promulgation
1979	After a shake-up at HEW, OCR announces a significantly different "interpretation" of athletic rules
1981	Vice President Bush's Task Force on Regulatory Relief includes Title IX regulations among those slated for reexamination
1982	Association for Intercollegiate Athletics for Women disbands; NCAA completes its takeover of women's sports
1984	Supreme Court's *Grove City College v. Bell* decision removes college sports from Title IX coverage; OCR closes all its athletic investigations
1988	Congress passes Civil Rights Restoration Act, reasserting Title IX jurisdiction over athletics
1990	The Bush OCR issues a new Title IX enforcement manual and opens investigations of several college programs
1992	The Supreme Court issues its decision in *Franklin v. Gwinnett County Public Schools*, authorizing federal judges to award monetary damages in Title IX suits; the number of Title IX suits shoots up
1993	The First Circuit issues its first decision in *Cohen v. Brown University*, relying primarily on the 1979 Three-Part Test; other courts agree with the First Circuit
1995	Republicans take control of Congress; Republican leaders urge OCR to relax Title IX rules; football coaches renew their efforts to exempt "revenue" sports from Title IX

suddenly emerged as the linchpin of the federal regulatory effort. Ripped from its original context, that test became the principal legal legacy of the first twenty years of Title IX (for a detailed chronology, see table 6-1).

The 1975 Regulations and the Art of Ambiguity

Between 1972 and 1975, OCR and its then parent department HEW undertook an unusually lengthy, participatory, and wide-ranging review of how to interpret Title IX. They held hearings across the country, met with leaders of universities and advocacy groups, and received nearly 10,000 comments on their initial proposal. HEW issued its final rule along with a detailed justification in 1975. Although OCR spearheaded the effort, HEW secretary Caspar Weinberger and his immediate staff made a number of changes in the regulation. The White House staff also examined the regulations closely, and asked for a few modifications. Since OCR's rules were at the time subject to a legislative veto, the likely congressional reaction was very much on administrators' minds.[2]

The process dragged on for nearly three years, in part because OCR was overwhelmed by other tasks and hamstrung by Judge John Pratt's mandates in *Adams v. Richardson*.[3] But it was also true, as women's advocacy groups charged, that many people within OCR did not consider sex discrimination nearly as pressing a national problem as racial discrimination. Most important, Title IX presented a plethora of unanticipated and thorny policy questions.

From its inception, Title IX was based on the assumption that sex discrimination is no different from racial discrimination, and therefore should be governed by the same rules. But exceptions kept popping up. Some seemed trivial: Are mother–daughter elementary school events allowed? Girls' choirs? Others were more important: Can schools participate in the selection of recipients of scholarships that are limited to one sex (for example, the Rhodes)? What about bequests that benefit only one sex? Must physical education classes at the elementary and high school levels be coed? How about sex education courses? Title IX covers admissions to all schools granting professional degrees, but exempts admissions to private undergraduate schools. What about the handful of private undergraduate schools that also grant professional degrees? Women's groups opposed a provision in the proposed plan requiring those alleging Title IX violations to take their claims to the school before filing a complaint with OCR. Some of these advocacy organizations also insisted that the federal government inspect all school textbooks to be sure they do not include stereotypical views of women. They won on the former, but not on the latter. Secretary Weinberger adamantly opposed federal review of textbooks, which he considered both politically imprudent and a threat to freedom of speech. As early as 1973–74, it was clear that defining sex discrimination would be a

contentious job, a far cry from the consensus that surrounded the enactment
of Title IX.

Nothing matched the intensity of the controversy over athletics, which dominated congressional hearings and debate. The National Collegiate Athletic Association (NCAA) and prominent football coaches such as Darrell Royal at the
University of Texas pushed so hard that they earned the scorn and enmity of
Secretary Weinberger, who was hardly a crusading feminist.[4] While HEW was
working on its regulation, the NCAA and other football boosters came close to
passing an amendment sponsored by Senator John Tower (R-Tex.) that would
exempt "revenue-generating" sports from Title IX regulation. That legislative
strategy ultimately backfired. When the conference committee met to consider
the education legislation to which Tower had attached his amendment, it substituted an amendment sponsored by Senator Jacob Javits (R-N.Y.) specifying that
HEW's Title IX regulations "shall include with respect to intercollegiate athletic
activities reasonable provisions considering the nature of particular sports." On
the one hand, this seemed to require HEW to acknowledge the special features
of football. On the other hand, it established without a doubt the federal government's authority to regulate athletics under Title IX—exactly what the NCAA
had so vigorously contested. The possibility that the NCAA and HEW would
agree on what constitutes "reasonableness" on intercollegiate sports was slim.

Secretary Weinberger complained that although HEW had tried "to reach a
middle ground" with its regulation, it had discovered that it is "impossible to
please everyone in these controversial fields."[5] The NCAA was angry that football remained covered, and women's groups were angry that after three years of
waiting for regulations, HEW had given athletic programs another three years
to come into compliance. The hard truth was that Weinberger's "middle ground"
on athletics rested on a foundation of ambiguity. The 1975 rules laid out a basic
framework for assessing equity in athletics, but were very short on specifics.

Those rules established four regulatory principles that remain in effect to this
day. First, Title IX applies to "interscholastic, intercollegiate, club, or intramural
athletics offered by a recipient."[6] HEW explained that it had added the word
"intramural" to emphasize that it would examine a school's entire athletic program, not just intercollegiate sports.[7]

Second, the regulations provided that schools may "sponsor separate teams
for members of each sex where selection for such teams is based upon competitive skills or the activity involved is a contact sport." Rare is the varsity team (or
club team) that does not base selection on "competitive skills." This means that
beyond intramural ultimate Frisbee, single-sex teams are permitted. The regulations do allow girls to try out for boys' teams in noncontact sports if no comparable girls' team is offered, and vice versa. But this seldom happens.

This left the big question: How would OCR determine whether a school had
provided "equal athletic opportunities for members of both sexes"? Here the reg-

ulations became hopelessly fuzzy. The third important section of the regulations announced that to assess whether members of each team were afforded equal athletic opportunity, OCR would "consider, among other factors" ten listed items. Nine of these were resources that should be made available to male and female teams playing the same sport or similar sports: equipment, practice fields, locker rooms, coaching, medical treatment, travel funds, and the like.

Only one of these items alluded to the pivotal question of *which* sports a school must offer. Here HEW introduced its fourth requirement: schools must offer a "selection of sports and levels of competition" that "effectively accommodate the interests and abilities of members of both sexes." The latter phrase would echo through the Title IX debate for decades.

The first draft of HEW's regulations had required schools to conduct annual surveys of undergraduates to ascertain their "interests and abilities." This was eventually dropped for impinging too much on schools' institutional autonomy. The "interests and abilities of both sexes" could be determined by any "reasonable method" that the school "deems appropriate." A subsequent letter from the head of OCR required all schools to conduct such a "self-assessment" by July 1976 in order to take advantage of the three-year grace period offered by the 1975 regulations.[8]

On the hot-button issue of relative spending on male and female teams, ambiguity reigned. The regulations themselves and Secretary Weinberger's statement to Congress emphasized that "unequal aggregate expenditures for members of each sex" or even "unequal expenditures for male and female teams" playing the same sport would "not constitute noncompliance" with Title IX. Yet the regulations also stated that OCR would "consider the failure to provide necessary funds" for women's teams in its assessment of whether "equality of opportunity" had in fact been achieved.[9] Would this require an equal number of athletic scholarships for male and female teams, or would that depend on the market for competitive athletes? How does one compare the expenditures of a women's field hockey team with those of a men's ice hockey team? If the latter will cost more due to the nature of the sport, how much more? What if men's basketball coaches are in higher demand and thus more expensive than women's? What if a women's team plays only local rivals but the men's team travels to away games all over the country? The 1975 regulations raised more questions than they answered.

Like Secretary Weinberger, Title IX's chief sponsor and defender in the Senate, Birch Bayh (D-Ind.), emphasized what the regulations did *not* do:

Do the guidelines require equal aggregate expenditures for either male or female teams or individual male and female players? The answer is no. . . .

Do the guidelines require that equal athletic scholarships be given to male and female athletes? The answer is no.

Do the guidelines require that certain sports must be offered for women?
Again, the answer is no.[10]

All they require, Bayh claimed, is "equal opportunity for women athletes." The
three-year grace period granted to colleges by the 1975 regulations allowed the
leaders of HEW and OCR to pass along the most difficult issues to their succes-
sors in the Carter administration.

The Immaculate Birth of the Three-Part Test, 1978–79

The Carter administration, like the president himself, was a jumble of contradic-
tions. To lead many regulatory bodies, Carter appointed staffers from the liberal
advocacy groups that had criticized and sued these agencies during the preceding decade. As *Fortune* magazine noted, "Nader's Invaders" were now "Inside the
Gates."[11] Carter's nominee to head OCR, David Tatel, had worked closely with
civil rights organizations, and was intensely committed to school desegregation.
But President Carter also appointed a number of Washington "insiders" such as
HEW secretary Joseph Califano, and he sometimes sounded like a traditional
conservative attacking excessive federal regulation. For example, when Califano
recommended that OCR remove provisions on school dress codes from its Title
IX regulations, Carter agreed, writing, "Let's do more of this."[12]

Secretary Califano was no more eager to wade into the political swamp of
college athletics than his Republican predecessors had been. Annoyed by decisions he viewed as excessive and politically obtuse (such as prohibiting father–
daughter dinners and half-court girls' basketball), Califano required OCR to
clear all such determinations with his office. He also insisted that "HEW should
not get involved in prescribing specific sports."[13]

By November 1978, OCR had received nearly a hundred complaints about
inequities in athletic programs at particular colleges. With the end of the grace
period fast approaching, colleges begged OCR for more specific guidance. According to the "Proposed Policy Interpretation" that the agency circulated in
December 1978, OCR's evaluation of college programs would come in two
phases.[14] During the first, OCR would examine existing teams. Title IX, it explained, requires "the immediate elimination of discrepancies in average per
capita expenditures for financially measurable benefits and opportunities"
unless the school could "demonstrate that the discrepancies are based on differences in the cost of particular sports (e.g. equipment), their scope of competition (for example, national, regional or local), or other non-discriminatory factors."
Benefits and services that are "not readily financially measureable" must also
pass a "comparability" test. Although this seemed to be a departure from previous
policy, the proposal emphasized that equal aggregate expenditures on male and

female sports are *not* required, largely because the "unique size and cost of football programs" distinguish it "from other sports, both men's and women's." Unequal spending levels simply shift the burden to the school to identify "nondiscriminatory" reasons for the disparity. Of course, OCR would wield significant discretion in determining what is "nondiscriminatory" and what constitutes "comparability."

During the second phase, OCR would examine the array of sports offered to men and women. It gave schools a "longer period of time" to eliminate "the discriminatory effects of the historic emphasis on men's intercollegiate sports, and to facilitate the continued growth of women's athletics." Colleges must propose plans that "encourage an increase in the number of women participants at the club, intramural and intercollegiate level" and "elevate the scope of women's intercollegiate competition (for example, from local to State, State to regional, and from regional to national)." The requirements of the second phase remained fuzzy, reflecting OCR's "desire to allow for maximum institutional flexibility and minimal Federal intrusion into the operation of intercollegiate athletic programs."[15]

The proposal pleased almost no one. According to Califano, "Walking the policy down the middle of the street, we were ambushed from both sides. Women's groups thought we allowed too big an exemption for football, male coaches charged that the guidelines would kill big-time football." Califano was surprised to hear from OCR director David Tatel that some civil rights leaders feared that increasing spending on women's athletics would reduce the number of scholarships available to African American men.[16] Califano initially planned to submit the guidelines to Congress under the congressional veto process created in 1974. But he ran into serious opposition from his usual allies in Congress, including heavyweights such as House Speaker Tip O'Neill (who was worried about football at Boston College), House subcommittee chair John Brademas (whose district included South Bend, Indiana, and thus Notre Dame), and House majority leader Jim Wright ("representing big-time Texas college football"). Liberal Democratic Senator Dick Clark angrily told Califano that HEW should "get the hell out of girls' basketball" because it was hurting Democrats in Iowa. Brademas warned Califano, "Whatever you do, you can't send these guidelines to the House. All hell will break loose on the floor." Convinced that Congress would pass an appropriations rider barring all enforcement of Title IX athletics rules if he endorsed the proposed rules, Califano put the proposed interpretation on hold. Representatives from women's groups reluctantly agreed. OCR went back to the drawing board, meeting with college presidents and athletic directors, and visiting several campuses to gain a clearer understanding of their athletic programs.[17]

The ensuing months were not kind to the Carter administration. The second oil embargo, long gas lines, the hostage crisis in Iran, and high inflation all led to a sharp decline in the president's popularity. In the summer of 1979 Carter responded by going to the mountain top, delivering his infamous "malaise" speech, and firing about half his cabinet. That included Joseph Califano, who was replaced by the more liberal and less politically astute former secretary of the Department of Housing and Urban Development, Patricia Harris. In his memoirs, Califano complained that after the Carter administration's dramatic shakeup in the summer of 1979, the president reversed himself on Title IX issues, "apparently in response to the pleas of Washington-based women's groups that had supported his successful effort to pass legislation establishing the Department of Education."[18]

A few months later OCR announced its final "interpretation" of its athletic rules. This lengthier version was "designed specifically for intercollegiate athletics."[19] In several important respects, the final guidelines were more demanding than those proposed a year earlier. They placed more emphasis on equal per capita spending for male and female sports, especially for athletic scholarships. They provided long lists of services and facilities that must be comparable. And they replaced the two-phase scheme with the expectation that colleges would begin immediately to "substantially expand opportunities for women to participate and compete at all levels." By insisting that this was just an "interpretation" rather than a rule, the department avoided the politically risky step of submitting the guidelines to Congress or the president.

Key sections of the agency's guidance remained maddeningly ambiguous. For example, despite the new emphasis on per capita spending, "purely financial measures" do not in themselves constitute conclusive evidence of discrimination, "except where the benefit or opportunity under review, like a scholarship, is itself financial in nature." "Failure to provide compelling justifications for disparities in per capita expenditures," it explained, would *not* "automatically result" in "a finding of noncompliance," but only deprive the school "of the benefit of the presumption that it was in compliance with the law." Federal administrators "would still have the burden of demonstrating that the institution was actually engaged in unlawful discrimination."[20] College officials were hard-pressed to predict what this bureaucratic double-talk would mean in practice. To some it looked like a gender quota in nonthreatening legal clothing. To others it looked like an extensive paperwork exercise.

Replacing the 1978 proposal's "Phase Two" was a subsection of the 1979 interpretation titled "C. Effective Accommodation of Student Interests and Abilities." Under this heading came a few vague suggestions about how schools can gauge the "interests and abilities" of their "male and female athletes." Buried in subsection C(5)(a) was a one-sentence explanation of how regulators would determine whether a school had provided "opportunity for individuals of each sex to participate in intercollegiate competition."[21] This was the Three-Part Test that after 1990 became the linchpin of Title IX regulation (see table 6-2).

Table 6-2   The Three-Part Test

C. **Effective Accommodation of Student Interests and Abilities.**

. . .

5. **Application of the Policy—Levels of Competition.**
In effectively accommodating the interests and abilities of male and female athletes, institutions must provide both the opportunity for individuals of each sex to participate in intercollegiate competition, and for athletes of each sex to have competitive team schedules which equally reflect their abilities.

a. **Compliance will be assessed in any one of the following ways:**

(1) Whether the intercollegiate level participation opportunities for male and female students are *provided in numbers substantially proportionate to their respective enrollments*; or

(2) Where the members of one sex have been and are underrepresented among intercollegiate athletes, whether the institution can show a *history and continuing practice of program expansion* which is demonstrably responsive to the developing interest and abilities of the members of that sex; or

(3) Where the members of one sex are underrepresented among intercollegiate athletes or the institution cannot show a continuing practice of program expansion such as that cited above, whether it can be demonstrated that the *interests and abilities of the members of that sex have been fully and effectively accommodated* by the present program

---

Source: "Title IX of the Education Amendments of 1972; a Policy Interpretation; Title IX and Intercollegiate Athletics," 44 *Federal Register* 71418 (December 11, 1979) (emphasis added).

On its surface, this crucial section of the "Interpretation" offered three separate paths to compliance. Prong One—providing intercollegiate participation opportunities "substantially proportionate" to male and female enrollments—is the easiest to measure and therefore the surest route to compliance. In 1996, OCR described it as the only "safe harbor" for complying with Title IX.[22] Prong Two requires schools that have not yet achieved proportionality to demonstrate that they are steadily moving in that direction by adding new women's teams. The meaning of "continuing practice of program expansion" later became a bone of contention. How recent and how large must the expansion be to allow the school to pass this part of the test?

Prong Three requires schools that have neither achieved proportionality nor recently added women's teams to "demonstrate that the interests and abilities" of the underrepresented sex have been "fully and effectively accommodated." For the past two and a half decades the debate over Title IX policy on athletics has focused on how to interpret this phrase.

According to one view, the Three-Part Test must be read in context, which means as just one subsection of the part of the 1979 "interpretation" labeled "Effective Accommodation of Student Interests and Abilities." This section opens by stating: "The regulations require institutions to accommodate effectively the interests and abilities of students to the extent necessary to provide equal opportunity in the selection of sports and levels of competition available to members of both sexes." This would mean that a school can satisfy Prong Three by demonstrating that they have accommodated the "interests and abilities" of female students as "fully and effectively" as they have accommodated the "interests and abilities" of male students.

That was the understanding adopted by OCR the next year in its first *Title IX Intercollegiate Athletics Investigator's Manual.* The 1980 manual explained that colleges are required "to meet the interests and abilities of women to the same degree as they meet the interests and abilities of men."[23] A revised version of the manual put together by two OCR veterans a decade later similarly stated that under Prong Three, investigators must determine "if the interests and abilities of both sexes are accommodated equally effectively." The 1990 version also noted that while student surveys are not required for determining "interests and abilities," they remain "the simplest method for institutions and OCR to determine interests and abilities."[24]

According to an alternative interpretation of Prong Three—the interpretation adopted by OCR and the courts in the mid-1990s, and the foundation of federal Title IX policy ever since—schools that fail to meet Prongs One and Two must demonstrate that they have *fully* accommodated the "interests and abilities" of female athletes, even if they do not do the same for male students. This literal interpretation implies that whenever there are enough women at a school with the interest and ability to form a varsity team, the school is obliged to fund it, even if that means disbanding existing men's teams to come up with the cash. How well the school accommodates the interests and abilities of *male* students becomes irrelevant. The only question is whether more women's teams can be created in order to move closer to the parity standard announced in Prong One. Under this reading of Prong Three, eliminating or downgrading women's sports teams will almost always be deemed a violation of federal law, even if such budget cuts are packaged with greater cuts for men's teams.

As many commentators have pointed out, over the long run the latter interpretation of Prong Three in effect turns the Three-Part Test into a one-part test.[25] Colleges must either offer athletic participation opportunities proportional to undergraduate enrollments (Prong One) or steadily move in that direction by adding more women's teams (Prongs Two and Three). Surveys showing that more men than women are interested in varsity sports become irrelevant. Parity becomes the only "safe harbor."

OCR's lengthy *Federal Register* notice on the 1979 interpretation did not contain a single word of explanation for this subsection of the new guidelines. How and why it was inserted remains unclear. We do know that women's groups and their allies within the Carter administration had been pushing for a mandated 50/50 split in varsity sports and were unhappy with the administration's willingness to give colleges more time to expand women's teams. It is possible that they viewed the Three-Part Test as a subtle, initially uncontroversial way to nudge schools along.

For nearly a decade and a half, no one paid much attention to the dry bureaucratic language of section C(5)(a).[26] Almost no school could meet the proportionality standard of Prong One, but most were expanding women's intercollegiate programs and thus could meet Prong Two. In the late 1980s and early 1990s, though, many colleges faced serious financial difficulties and began to cut a variety of programs, including sports. Often it was the schools that had previously expanded women's teams most rapidly that decided to eliminate some male and female teams. These colleges—like Brown, which stated its position most forcefully and lost the most important court decision interpreting the Three-Part Test—argued that as long as they cut men's teams more steeply than women's teams and thus continued to expand the relative proportion of women's sports in their athletic portfolio, they were complying with Title IX.

OCR and the courts disagreed. If Brown had a women's volleyball team in 1990, but eliminated it in 1991, it was not "fully accommodating" the interests and abilities of the former players still in school. In effect, any college that eliminated a women's team—and there were many of these in the late 1980s and early 1990s—would flunk this version of Prong Three no matter how sharply it cut men's teams.

The 1980s: Regulatory Pause, Athletic Shift

If the Carter administration had been ambivalent about Title IX, the Reagan administration was uniformly hostile. Reducing federal regulation had been a principal theme of the Reagan campaign. Vice President Bush's Task Force on Regulatory Relief targeted OCR's Title IX athletic rules, stating in 1982, "We anticipate making amendments to the regulation that will reduce fiscal and administrative burdens" on recipients of federal funds.[27] The incoming head of the Education Department, Terrill Bell, told the Senate Budget Committee, "It is not the policy of the Education Department to specify what sports you have to offer."[28] President Reagan's appointment to head OCR was Clarence Thomas, no fan of government-mandated proportional representation in any of its guises.

Before long, though, court action obviated the need for administrative revision. A federal district court in Virginia ruled that OCR could not enforce its Title IX athletic regulations because the law limits termination of funds to the "particular program or part thereof" in which "noncompliance has been found."[29] Since athletic programs do not receive federal funds, they remain outside the purview of Title IX. Over the protest of Secretary Bell, the Reagan Justice Department declined to appeal the ruling of the Virginia court. When the circuit courts of appeal split on the issue, Solicitor General Rex Lee recommended that the Supreme Court review a case raising the issue in a non-athletic context, *Grove City College v. Bell.* After the Court agreed to hear the case, the solicitor general argued for a narrow interpretation of Title IX's reach. By a 6 to 3 vote the Supreme Court agreed.[30] Immediately thereafter, OCR closed twenty-three investigations of athletic programs, including complaints against the University of Maryland, Penn State, Alabama, Auburn, Duke, Idaho State, the University of Washington, and the New York City public schools.[31] A similar fate befell Title IX court suits filed by private parties.

It took almost four years, but Congress eventually overrode President Reagan's veto and overturned the Supreme Court's interpretation of Title IX. A curious feature of the politics of the Grove City Bill is how little effort universities made to limit federal regulation of their activities. Although many schools opposed OCR's rules on athletics, almost none came to the defense of tiny, iconoclastic Grove City College. In contrast, the Leadership Conference on Civil Rights put together an impressive coalition of 165 member organizations to overturn the decision. Liberal and moderate Republicans (not yet an extinct species in Congress) voted with Democrats to hand the Reagan administration an embarrassing defeat. With those subject to regulation remaining silent, the debate proved one-sided.[32]

Despite the pause in federal regulation, the number of women and girls participating in intercollegiate and interscholastic sports continued to climb. Revenues generated by college football and men's basketball grew even faster—as did the expenses of these teams. Competition for lucrative TV deals and for playoffs and bowl game selection grew fiercer, which in turn increased competition for the top high school athletes. Specialization and year-round practice became essential for success at the college level, and consequently the number of two-sport athletes dropped. The admissions boost received by college athletes—male and female alike—increased, and their grades and attention to course work dropped (see chapter 8).

Given all these changes in college athletics, the revival of regulation after passage of the Grove City Bill might have spurred a reevaluation of federal policy. But that was not to be. OCR remained mum as activity shifted to the courts. The courts then fastened on a literal reading of Prong Three, which proved to be a potent legal weapon in a time of budget cuts.

The Revival of Regulation, 1990–95

In 1990 federal regulation of intercollegiate sports suddenly awoke from its decade-long slumber. A number of factors contributed to this shift. First and most obvious, the Grove City Bill restored federal jurisdiction over college sports. A second factor was the termination of the long-running *Adams v. Richardson* case. The end of judicial supervision gave OCR the opportunity to set its own priorities. No longer would it be evaluated solely on how quickly it resolved the individual complaints that came in the door. Now it could devote more resources to systematic compliance reviews of the sort needed to evaluate colleges' athletic programs.

Third, President George H. W. Bush took office in January 1989, intent upon showing that he was not merely a Reagan clone, but an advocate for a "kinder, gentler" nation. In part that meant an administration more attuned to the interests of women voters. In 1991 OCR announced that it would make enforcement of Title IX one of its top priorities.[33] It backed its words with action, revising its Title IX compliance manual, increasing the number of compliance reviews, and sending a letter to college presidents warning them not to reduce opportunities for women when they cut their athletic budgets.[34] In 1992, OCR found the athletic programs at the University of Maryland and Brooklyn College out of compliance with Title IX. Maryland responded by expanding its women's program; Brooklyn by eliminating all its varsity teams.[35] According to a lawyer for the National Women's Law Center (NWLC), OCR had "finally moved out of its enforcement black hole."[36] One advocate for women's sports described OCR's effort as "not bad, especially considering that they haven't done a damn thing for the last 10 years."[37]

A fourth factor was the formation of a loose network of lawyers and advocates who helped students file administrative complaints and lawsuits. Arthur Bryant, executive director of a Texas-based advocacy group, Trial Lawyers for Public Justice (TLPJ), represented female students at William and Mary, Brown, the University of Oklahoma, Colgate, the University of New Hampshire, Northeastern University, the University of Massachusetts, and Indiana University of Pennsylvania, among others. In early 1992, representatives of a number of advocacy groups met in New York to map out "a national campaign of litigation and lobbying to force colleges to comply with laws barring sexual discrimination." According to the *Chronicle of Higher Education,* their message was clear: "Comply with the law now, or we'll see you in court later."[38]

Fifth, new sources of information on college athletic programs made it easier for these lawyers to identify inviting targets and to support their claims. In 1991 the NCAA conducted a survey of its members, and found that men still commanded far more athletic resources than women: women constituted 30 percent of varsity athletes at these schools, received 23 percent of the overall athletic budget, and only 17 percent of the recruiting budget.[39] The next year the NCAA created a Gender Equity Task Force that reports regularly on colleges' distribution of money and roster slots. In 1994 Congress enacted the Equity in Athletics Disclosure Act (EADA), which requires colleges to report the number of male and female athletes and coaches, as well as the money spent on all aspects of athletic programs. As Jessica Gavora has pointed out, "The EADA created a ready-made client shopping list for trial lawyers. One glance at a school's EADA submission shows a would-be plaintiff's attorney whether or not a school is vulnerable to a Title IX lawsuit."[40]

Sixth, in 1992 the Supreme Court handed a powerful new weapon to those filing Title IX suits: it authorized federal judges to award monetary damages in Title IX cases. Although that decision, *Franklin v. Gwinnett County Public Schools*,[41] involved sexual harassment rather than athletics, it raised the prospects of large monetary judgments against schools found to have denied female students equal athletic opportunity. This in turn meant that attorneys could take Title IX cases on a contingency fee basis. Advocacy lawyers like the TLPJ's Arthur Bryant could use fees collected in one case to subsidize work on another. Lawyers not so devoted to the cause could now hope to be compensated for representing female athletes.[42] Conversely, schools now had stronger incentives to settle cases. After *Franklin*, Susan Ware writes, "Lawsuits rather than complaints to enforcement agencies" became "the main avenue for raising and resolving Title IX disputes." "As the stakes got higher," Ware notes, "the level of acrimony surrounding implementation of the law increased dramatically."[43]

Almost all these cases were filed on behalf of female students whose teams had been cut or demoted to nonvarsity status in universities' austerity moves. The main legal issue was whether Prong Three allowed schools to cut women's teams as long as they cut as many or more men's teams. Most were settled before going to trial. When judges did issue decisions, they almost always read Prong Three to prohibit *any* cuts to women's teams until the number of women athletes mirrored their proportion of the undergraduate population.

Nearly twenty schools faced court suits in the early 1990s. As a result of this litigation, Auburn upgraded its women's soccer team to varsity, increased scholarships for female athletes, and paid the plaintiffs' legal expenses. The University of New Hampshire not only reinstated the women's tennis team, but added four new women's sports and increased its overall support for the women's athletics program. Colgate upgraded its women's hockey team. Colorado State reinstated its women's varsity softball team. Cornell reinstituted its women's gymnastics and fencing teams. The University of Massachusetts restored women's lacrosse, tennis, and volleyball. Indiana University of Pennsylvania reinstated its gymnastics and field hockey teams. A suit brought by the California chapter of the National Organization for Women induced the California State University system to agree to increase the number of women's teams at all of its nineteen campuses until the percentage of female athletes was within 15 percent of the female share of the undergraduate population. The University of Texas at Austin, known to have one of the best women's athletic programs before 1990, agreed to devote an additional million dollars to the women's program and to double the number of female varsity athletes. The Southeastern Conference promised to require its members to sponsor two more teams for women than for men.[44]

Seventh and finally, the incoming Clinton administration promised to enforce civil rights laws more vigorously than had the Reagan and Bush administrations. The new head of OCR, Norma Cantú, had previously been a litigator for the Mexican American Legal Defense and Education Fund, and promised to bring a more aggressive enforcement approach to OCR. No sooner had she arrived than the agency was hit by a critical report published by the Lyndon B. Johnson School of Public Affairs at the University of Texas. It charged that OCR had failed "to capture the spirit of Title IX" or "to provide effective and adequate enforcement." As a result it had "become an impediment to gender equality rather than a facilitator or enforcer."[45] Women's groups needed to be convinced that things would be different in a Democratic administration. In late 1993, the senior counsel for the National Women's Law Center complained, "There's little to no faith that going to OCR with a complaint will get anything accomplished."[46]

Although Cantú had previously shown little interest in Title IX or athletics, she took a number of steps to respond to the skeptics. She hired the author of the critical University of Texas report to advise her on Title IX issues. She appointed a national Title IX coordinator. She promised to revise the Title IX compliance handbook, to make greater use of the funding cutoff, and to refer more cases of noncompliance to the Department of Justice.[47] She met regularly with representatives of the Women's Sports Foundation and other groups dedicated to increasing the number of female athletes. She initiated investigations of seventeen colleges, including several large state universities and Brigham Young University. Over the next few years OCR would devote nearly three-quarters of its compliance reviews to Title IX athletics even though less than 10 percent of individual complaints focused on that topic.[48]

Despite this new commitment, OCR's investigations and negotiations proceeded slowly. By the fall of 1993 it had signed only two "letters of finding" with the colleges it had targeted. The new leaders of OCR were discovering what their predecessors had learned: the agency has few sanctions to impose when schools dig in their heels. Moreover, OCR proved incapable of providing colleges with the "clear, bright" rules that Cantú had promised. The revised compliance manual never materialized. On the crucial question of the meaning of Prong Three, Cantú equivocated, denying that the Three-Part Test requires that male and female athletes mirror the student body, but at the same time demanding that schools reinstate women's teams eliminated for budgetary reasons.[49]

When Republicans took control of Congress in 1995, Cantú and her boss, Secretary of Education Richard Riley, were suddenly thrown on the defensive. Football coaches claimed that OCR was ignoring the Javits amendment, and they urged the Republican majority to amend Title IX to protect their sport. Advocates for "minor" men's sports—especially wrestling, which not only was the target of the biggest cuts but also had the enthusiastic support of Dennis Hastert, who was soon to become Speaker of the House—demanded a commitment from either OCR or Congress that eliminating men's teams would not be considered an acceptable means of complying with Title IX. At first Cantú and Riley seemed receptive to a more "flexible" approach to enforcement.[50] Cantú repeatedly denied imposing a proportionality test, and she promised to provide colleges with "objective criteria" for compliance.

Soon, though, the two sides reached an impasse. When OCR failed to clarify its Title IX rules, the House Appropriations Committee threatened to cut the agency's funding until it produced the promised "objective criteria."[51] Meanwhile, Representative Hastert circulated a letter urging OCR to find that a college has complied with Title IX if it has added an average of one women's sport every three years since 1972. A total of 134 members of Congress signed the letter. Meanwhile Representative Patsy Mink convinced 96 House members to sign a letter encouraging OCR to keep its current interpretation of the Three-Part Test. The letter argued that it would be a "tragedy" to change current policy, which had been "well-settled" in court.[52]

In the fall of 1995, OCR produced a draft "clarification" of its 1979 "interpretation" that pleased almost no one. After reviewing hundreds of critical comments, the agency went back to the drawing board. At the time, it looked like 1978 all over again: a cautious OCR stymied by opposition from an increasingly conservative Congress. Nearly a quarter of a century after the enactment of Title IX, federal policy on intercollegiate sports remained unclear and unsettled.

The Critical Juncture

In the long run, the brief Three-Part Test quietly tacked onto OCR's 1979 interpretation proved to be a godsend to female athletes whose varsity sports had been cut and to the lawyers allied with women's advocacy groups. If judges adopted a literal interpretation of that test, all a lawyer needed to do to win a Title IX case was produce current or admitted students who wanted to play that sport. No further evidence would be needed.

But the foundations for this strategy seemed ready to crumble at any time. No one could be sure whether the courts would rely on an "interpretation" that had not gone through the Administrative Procedure Act's notice-and-comment rulemaking, or that they would adopt a literal reading of Prong Three—

especially since the Supreme Court had recently adopted a narrow interpretation of several other civil rights laws. OCR faced strong opposition in the aggressively antiregulation Republican Congress. When the agency had encountered similar criticism from Congress in the late 1970s, it had delayed announcing any guidelines for over a year and placed enforcement on the back burner.

As we will see in the next chapter, what made the story different this time around was the activities of the federal courts. Instead of undercutting enforcement (as the Supreme Court had done in the early 1980s), federal appellate courts provided a ringing endorsement of a strict reading of Prong Three. In *Cohen v. Brown*, the First Circuit based its reading of Prong Three on the "build it and they will come" understanding of the role of Title IX. By that time the Clinton administration had shifted out of its defensive crouch, realizing—after two long and unpopular government shut-downs commonly blamed on the Republican Congress—that confronting Speaker Newt Gingrich and House Republicans was good politics after all. OCR hitched its wagon to the courts. As Cantú's deputy Jeannette Lin put it, "the courts have been very active. We want to reflect that."[53] The game of policy leapfrog—with the courts interpreting an agency interpretation and the agency incorporating those decisions into its guidelines—had begun in earnest.

SEVEN

The Triumph of Parity, 1995–2016

During the first three years of the Clinton administration, the Office for Civil Rights (OCR) equivocated on the meaning of the Three-Part Test. Publicly it denied that it required schools to keep expanding varsity teams for women until they reached parity—that is, until the percentage of female varsity athletes mirrored the percentage of women in the undergraduate student body. Informally it told schools to do just that. Advocates for women's sports expected the administration to push colleges still harder. Republicans in Congress demanded that they ease up.

While OCR fiddled, federal judges acted decisively, reading Prong Three of the Three-Part Test to require schools to "fully" accommodate women athletes until they achieved numerical parity. The key decision was *Cohen v. Brown University*, a bitterly fought case that stretched on for six years, culminating in an expensive loss for Brown.[1] All seven of the other circuit courts that heard similar cases eventually agreed with the First Circuit.[2] OCR incorporated the courts' understanding of the Three-Part Test into the guidelines it issued in 1996—its first major statement on athletics in seventeen years—and then further tightened its requirements on athletic scholarships. Although the George W. Bush administration tried to make it somewhat easier for colleges to comply with Prong Three, this effort ended in failure. In 2010 the Obama administration issued a

Dear Colleague Letter (DCL) that made the Three-Part Test even harder to pass (for the chronology, see table 7-1).

The Other *Brown* Case

Cohen v. Brown University became the leading case on Title IX athletics not just because it was first, but also because of Brown's unusual status and the extraordinary determination of its president, Vartan Gregorian. For decades Brown had been the epitome of a prestigious, proudly progressive college. It was widely acknowledged to be the most liberal of the Ivy League schools, known for its lax curricular requirements and high proportion of minority students. Gregorian, a respected scholar with "impeccable liberal and academic credentials," was hired in 1988 "to substantially improve Brown's academic and fiscal standing."[3] During his tenure Brown became one of the most selective colleges in the country.

Brown was also a leader in offering athletic opportunities to its female undergraduates. During the 1970s it had greatly expanded the number of women's teams. By the time the litigation began, it fielded eighteen varsity teams for women, more than twice the national average and more than it offered its male students. Only one school in the country (Harvard) offered more women's teams. Twelve percent of undergraduate women played varsity sports, almost three times the national average. Since 43 percent of its varsity athletes were female, Brown was well above the average for Division I schools. As Judge Bruce Selya noted in his 1993 opinion for the First Circuit, "Brown will never be confused with Notre Dame or the more muscular members of the Big Ten."[4] Its football team usually resided in the Ivy League cellar, a fact that bothered almost no one in Providence (if they even noticed). Like the other Ivies, it offered no athletic scholarships. Brown prided itself both on keeping athletics and academics in proper balance and in treating its female students fairly. In short, if Brown could not stay on what Judge Selya called "the sunny side of Title IX," it was hard to imagine what school could.

The controversy that became *Cohen v. Brown* began in 1991, when a looming budget deficit led Gregorian to order a 5 percent cut in the operating budget of each unit within the university. To comply, the athletic department demoted two men's teams (golf and water polo) and two women's teams (volleyball and gymnastics) from varsity to club status. That did not change their competitive schedule, but did require them to raise most of their money from private sources rather than from the university. Although all four teams managed to do so, some members of the women's teams and their coaches were unhappy with their new status. The coaches lost not only their university offices and telephones, but also their ability to recruit athletes and secure admissions boosts for them. A Brown alumna at the Women's Sports Foundation put disgruntled gymnasts and

Table 7-1 Title IX Athletics Chronology, 1993–2011

1993	First Circuit issues initial decision in *Cohen v. Brown*
1994	Republicans win control of House and Senate in November elections
1995	OCR proposes a "clarification" of its 1979 "interpretation," following the First Circuit's reading of the Three-Part Test and describing Prong One as a "safe harbor"
1996	Despite congressional criticism, OCR issues its "Clarification of Intercollegiate Athletics Policy Guidance: The Three-Part Test" with few changes
	First Circuit issues its second decision in *Cohen v. Brown University*, reaffirming and strengthening its reading of the Three-Part Test
1997	The Supreme Court denies certiorari in *Cohen v. Brown*
1998	OCR issues Dear Colleague Letter stating that to comply with Title IX the percentage of athletic scholarship money given to women must be within 1 percent of the proportion of female varsity athletes
2002	Secretary of Education Rod Paige establishes the Commission on Opportunity in Athletics, charging it with recommending improvements for Title IX; the commission provokes controversy but produced few major recommendations
2003	OCR issues a "Further Clarification of Intercollegiate Athletics Policy Guidance regarding Title IX Compliance" that reaffirms its commitment to existing policies
2005	OCR issues Dear Colleague Letter, "Additional Clarification of Intercollegiate Athletics Policy: Three-Part Test, Part Three," encouraging schools to use student surveys to comply with Part Three
	The NCAA discourages schools from using surveys to comply with the Three-Part Test, and criticizes the Bush administration for weakening regulation
2007	U.S. Commission on Civil Rights holds contentious hearings on "Title IX Athletics"; its final report supports the Bush administration's recommendation on surveys, drawing a sharp dissent from some commission members
2010	OCR rescinds the 2005 "Additional Clarification," discourages use of surveys, and makes it more difficult for schools to pass the Three-Part Test
2011	National Women's Law Center files suit against twenty-five public school systems, arguing that OCR rules should apply to interscholastic as well as intercollegiate sports

volleyball players in touch with Arthur Bryant of Trial Lawyers for Public Justice (TLPJ).[5]

The same scenario was playing out at colleges throughout the country: financially strapped schools reduced spending on athletic programs by cutting or downgrading both male and female teams, with the men taking a bigger hit. Attorneys for the TLPJ and other advocacy organizations filed suit on behalf of disappointed female athletes and their coaches, arguing that any cuts in women's teams would prevent a college from meeting Prong Two or Prong Three. Most schools capitulated either to avoid litigation or after losing in federal district court.

Not so at Brown. Gregorian was infuriated by what he saw as excessive government intrusion into the internal affairs of universities. He hired aggressive and well-connected attorneys to pursue the case. Twice Brown appealed the district court's decisions to the First Circuit. When the school lost, it appealed to the Supreme Court, putting together an impressive list of allies. Gregorian also argued his case before Congress, telling an oversight committee, "I am a frustrated university administrator who does not like bureaucracy and who does not like to be intimidated by lawyers." He accused OCR and the courts of imposing arbitrary numerical quotas. How can it be, he asked, that the university can be "free to cut libraries and academic departments, but not athletics"?[6]

The entire *Brown* case hinged on the meaning of Prong Three. Simply put, Brown could not meet Prong One because at the time women made up 49 percent of the undergraduate population but only 39 percent of varsity athletes. While recognizing that Brown was well ahead of most schools, the judges saw no evidence of the "continuous improvement" required by Prong Two. Brown had not added a single women's varsity team over the previous decade. So everything came down to the question of whether Brown was "fully and effectively" accommodating the "interests and abilities" of the "underrepresented sex," namely, women.

Brown emphasized that the 1975 regulations required schools to offer athletic opportunities that reflect the "interests and capacities" of *both* sexes, and that according to OCR's 1979 interpretation, "The governing principle in this area is that the athletic interests and abilities of male and female students be *equally* effectively accommodated."[7] If male students are more interested in varsity sports than are women, then the distribution of varsity slots can—indeed must—reflect that disparity. That is why the Department of Health, Education, and Welfare (HEW) had originally encouraged schools to conduct surveys of undergraduate interest. Brown further argued that if the courts accepted the plaintiff's interpretation of Prong Three, schools would be forced to increase the number of women's slots until they reached parity with enrollment. As a result, the "interests and abilities" of many male students would remain only partially accommodated when those of women were "fully accommodated." This would create the type of sex-based quota explicitly prohibited by Title IX, and constitute illegal discrimination against men. While the case was before the First Circuit, Brown's lawyers emphasized, the Supreme Court had warned lower courts not to turn nondiscrimination statutes into affirmative action laws.[8]

Twice the First Circuit rejected Brown's "relative interest" interpretation of Title IX. Six of the seven federal judges to hear the case (the district court judge and two three-judge appellate panels) first held that they were required to defer to OCR's 1979 "Interpretation," and then adopted a literal reading of Prong Three. They paid no attention to OCR's much different reading of the "Interpretation" in its 1980 and 1990 compliance manuals. Nor did they seek OCR's advice on the case. Despite the publicity generated by the case, OCR never attempted to intervene, preferring to leave this hot potato to the courts.

Why did the judges who heard this case lean so heavily on a few unexplained phrases in OCR's 1979 "Interpretation" while placing so little importance on the language of the underlying statute itself or on the only regulations promulgated according to procedures mandated by the statute? Appellate judges gave two answers to this question. The first was regulatory simplicity. The "relative interest" test championed by Brown would "aggravate the quantification problems that are inevitably bound up with Title IX" and "overcomplicate an already complex equation." Plaintiffs who challenge a school's practices "would be required to assess the level of interest in both the male and female student populations and determine comparatively how completely the university was serving the interests of each sex." This would raise "thorny questions as to the appropriate survey population, whether from the university, typical feeder schools, or the regional community." The court's reading of Prong Three, in contrast, "requires a relatively simple assessment of whether there is unmet need . . . sufficient to warrant a new team or the upgrading of an existing team." The First Circuit concluded that "the simpler reading is far more serviceable."[9]

The court's second, more frequently and passionately stated argument was that Brown had mistakenly assumed that male and female students differ in their attraction to highly competitive sports. If this is true of students at Brown, the judges argued, that is either because women's interest in sports had been suppressed by now-discredited stereotypes, or because Brown's recruitment policies reflected and reinforced those stereotypes. "To assert that Title IX permits institutions to provide fewer athletics participation opportunities for women than for men," based upon the premise that women are less interested in sports than are men," Judge Hugh Bownes wrote in the 1996 opinion, "is (among other things) to ignore the fact that Title IX was enacted in order to remedy discrimination that results from stereotyped notions of women's interests and abilities." Brown's approach "undermines the remedial purposes of Title IX by limiting required program expansion for the underrepresented sex to the status quo level of relative interests."[10]

Brown presented evidence indicating not only that women currently enrolled at Brown were less interested in varsity sports than currently enrolled men, but also that the same gap appeared among those who had applied to Brown but had not been accepted. To this the judges replied, "Because recruitment of interested athletes is at the discretion of the institution, there is a risk that the institution will recruit only enough women to fill positions in a program that already underrepresents women, and that the smaller size of the women's program will have the effect of discouraging women's participation."[11] To Brown's claim that female athletes were less likely to apply to Brown than to other comparable schools, the court replied, in effect, that is because the school does not devote enough resources to women's sports. First make the school more attractive to female athletes, then aggressively recruit them, and eventually they will come.

This argument particularly incensed President Gregorian, who wondered why the federal government was pushing Brown to spend more money attracting athletes rather than budding musicians, mathematicians, physicists, classicists, or political scientists. The court's answer was that since "interest and ability rarely develop in a vacuum" but rather "evolve as a function of opportunity and experience," Title IX obligates colleges to take all feasible steps to change gender stereotypes in the larger society. OCR's 1979 policy interpretation "recognize[d] that women's lower rate of participation in athletics reflects women's historical lack of opportunities to participate in sports." Consequently, "statistical evidence purporting to reflect women's interest instead provides only a measure of the very discrimination that is and has been the basis for women's lack of opportunity to participate in sports." Therefore, "even if it can be empirically demonstrated that, at a particular time, women have less interest in sports than do men, such evidence, standing alone, cannot justify providing fewer athletics opportunities for women than for men." Citing a recent article in *U.S. News and World Report*, Judge Bownes found that "the tremendous growth in women's participation in sports since Title IX was enacted disproves Brown's argument that women are less interested in sports for reasons unrelated to lack of opportunity." According to the judge, "Had Congress intended to entrench, rather than change, the status quo—with its historical emphasis on men's participation opportunities to the detriment of women's opportunities—it need not have gone to all the trouble of enacting Title IX."[12] Changing public attitudes "is not sport for the short-winded: the institution must remain vigilant, upgrading the competitive opportunities available to the historically disadvantaged sex as warranted by developing abilities among the athletes of that sex, until the opportunities for, and levels of competition are equivalent by gender."[13] This was the fullest and most explicit defense of the parity standard ever provided by federal officials.

One First Circuit judge, Juan Torruella, dissented, agreeing with the university that "the three prong test, as the district court interprets it, is a quota" that violates Title IX by discriminating against male students. Title IX regulations, he wrote, are "intended to protect against discrimination, not to promote athletics on campuses."[14] In a case against Louisiana State University, a federal district court judge held that the 1979 "interpretation" does not have "binding effect" because it had not been signed by the president and was "distinctly at odds with the statutory language." To accept the interpretation of the First Circuit, Judge Rebecca Doherty argued, "One must assume that interest and ability to participate in sports is equal as between all men and women on all campuses." "It seems much more logical," she claimed, "that interest in participation and levels of ability to participate as percentages of the male and female population will vary from campus to campus and from region to region and will change with time." Title IX, she argued, "does not mandate equal numbers of participants," but only "prohibits exclusion based on sex and requires equal opportunity to participate for both sexes."[15] But Judge Torruella was outvoted and Judge Doherty overruled by the Fifth Circuit.

Eventually the Third, Fifth, Sixth, Seventh, Eighth, Ninth, and Tenth Circuits all agreed with the First Circuit's *Brown* ruling.[16] Writing for a panel of the Ninth Circuit, Judge Cynthia Holcomb Hall explained that Title IX "recognizes that, where society has conditioned women to expect less than their fair share of the athletic opportunities, women's interest in participating in sports will not rise to a par with men's overnight." Already Title IX has "altered women's preferences, making them more interested in sports, and more likely to become student athletes. Adopting Appellees' interest-based test for Title IX compliance would hinder, and quite possibly reverse, the steady increase in women's participation and interest in sports that have followed from Title IX's enactment." Citing a *Harvard Law Review* article with the subtitle "Using Title IX to Fight Gender Role Oppression," Judge Hall explained that the approach of the circuit courts "recognizes that women's attitudes toward sports are socially constructed and have been limited by discrimination and gender stereotypes. Congress passed Title IX to combat such discrimination and stereotypes, thereby changing the social environment in which girls and women develop, or do not develop, interests in sports."[17]

Gregorian reacted angrily to Brown's repeated losses in court. "By judicial fiat," he declared, women's sports "have risen past all other priorities including undergraduate scholarships, faculty salaries, and libraries."[18] "Where Congress once sought to ensure equality of opportunity," he charged, a federal judge "is now requiring an unwarranted numerical conformity and is intruding upon the legitimate administrative autonomy of colleges and universities. Colleges and universities are facing very hard choices today. They cannot allow their decision-making to be needlessly compromised."[19]

Gregorian's fury led him to build a broad coalition to convince the Supreme Court to hear the case. Sixty universities joined a brief arguing that courts should not "become embroiled in reviewing what are essential educational decisions, i.e. what programs to offer."[20] Additional briefs supporting Brown were filed by the American Council on Education, the Association of American Universities, the American Association of State Colleges and Universities, the National Association of Independent Colleges and Universities, and a number of coaches' associations. Former HEW secretary Caspar Weinberger submitted a brief claiming that the First Circuit's decision "is flatly contrary to the H.E.W. regulations" that he had signed two decades before. Forty-nine members of Congress signed a brief complaining that the courts and OCR had distorted congressional intent.[21]

Despite this impressive coalition, the Supreme Court announced in April 1997 that it would not review Brown's case. Although one never knows why the Court has declined to review a particular case, Gregorian and his allies lacked two things that are usually necessary for attracting the Court's attention: a split within the circuits and support from the solicitor general. The fact that no circuit court had disagreed with the First Circuit made it easier for the Supreme Court to duck the contentious issue. The Department of Justice submitted a brief written by Deval Patrick, then head of its Civil Rights Division, arguing both that the lower courts were right to defer to OCR's guidelines and that in college sports "team size is largely predetermined by the institution's own recruiting practices."[22] According to Andrew Zimbalist, "U.S. colleges and universities took the April, 1997 decision as a clear message that they must act decisively to support gender equality."[23] They were receiving that same message from OCR, which quickly fell in line with the federal courts.

What did the attack on sexual stereotypes mandated by the courts look like in practice? In his preliminary order in 1992, district court judge Raymond Pettine had ordered Brown to restore to varsity status the women's gymnastics and volleyball teams, and he prohibited it from reducing the status of or funding for any women's varsity team until the case was fully resolved. Later Brown agreed to upgrade facilities and improve the schedule for a variety of women's teams. Eventually the district court ordered Brown to grant varsity status to women's fencing, ski, and water polo teams as well. The final agreement reached after the Supreme Court denied certiorari committed the school to keeping the share of female varsity athletes within 3.5 percent of the proportion of female undergraduates. Before it could add a men's team or drop a women's team it would need to reduce that gap to 2.25 percent.[24] Brown was also required to pay $1 million in attorneys' fees to the plaintiffs' lawyers, not to mention its own substantial legal costs.[25]

In subsequent years Brown found it difficult to fill all the slots on women's teams that had been created in the wake of the litigation. This included the women's volleyball team saved by the court. A captain of that team told the *Chronicle of Higher Education*, "Last year we had to add players—walk-ons— just to fill slots, while the men's lacrosse team had to cut players to make up for it. That's completely unfair."[26] Apparently, even after you build it, they don't always come. Or maybe they develop other interests after getting there. Most people fortunate enough to get into Brown do not go there to play varsity sports.

OCR Ups the Ante

In early 1995 OCR was on the defensive, fearful of congressional attacks on its Title IX policies, and apparently willing to pull back on enforcement to appease Republican critics. A year later, just before the First Circuit's second decision, it reversed direction by issuing a "clarification" of the Three-Part Test that incorporated the First Circuit's understanding of Prong Three. When the First Circuit handed down its second ruling a few months later, it in turn leaned heavily on this OCR "clarification." This was a vivid illustration of the policy of "leapfrogging" so common in the American civil rights state: the courts defer to agency guidelines while incrementally expanding upon them; the agency then argues that the judiciary has endorsed its reading of the statute, emboldening it to be a little more aggressive; and the court then incorporates this administrative iteration into its interpretation of the law. Each denies adding anything new while together they build a more demanding regulatory program.

OCR's blandly titled "Clarification of Intercollegiate Athletics Policy Guidance: The Three-Part Test" was announced in a 1996 Dear Colleague Letter sent to schools by Assistant Secretary Norma Cantú—the first of many Title IX DCLs. OCR made it clear that this little-noted subsection of its previous "interpretation" had become the centerpiece of federal regulation of athletics. That "interpretation," Secretary Cantú wrote, had enjoyed not only "the bipartisan support of Congress" but also "the support of every court that has addressed issues of Title IX athletics."[27] No longer would the Three-Part Test be but one part of the "holistic" review promised by the 1975 regulations. A school that flunked this test would violate Title IX.

The most controversial feature of the 1996 DCL was its description of Prong One as a "safe harbor" that would protect schools from further investigation. This seemed to indicate that achieving parity was the only sure way to comply with Title IX. OCR refused to define "substantial proportionality," explaining that it "makes the determination on a case-by-case basis, rather than through use of a statistical test." But its examples showed that it would tolerate little deviation from complete parity: the shortfall for women can be no greater than the number needed to sustain a "viable" team, which means around ten to fifteen students. OCR also explained that in counting "athletic opportunities," it would *not* include "unfilled slots." It would only "count actual athletes because participation opportunities must be real, not illusory." Behind this Orwellian use of the term "opportunity" lay OCR's determination to prevent schools from fiddling with the numbers. In practice it meant that if not enough females signed up for a team (or if some dropped out), the number of male athletes would need to be reduced proportionally.

The "clarification" also tightened Prong Two by requiring "actual program expansion," that is, adding more women's teams. It would not find "a history and continuing practice of program expansion" if a school increased the percentage of female athletes by reducing the number of male athletes. Nor would it give schools credit for major expansions that occurred more than a few years in the past. The key question became: What have you done for women athletes lately?

For Prong Three, the "Clarification" endorsed the position of the First Circuit: to determine whether a school has "fully and effectively accommodated [the] interests and abilities [of the] underrepresented sex," OCR will *not* look at the overall distribution of varsity slots compared to the overall distribution of "interests and abilities" among male and female undergraduates, but *only* at the underrepresented sex's "unmet interest in a particular sport" and the extent to which female athletes can "sustain a team" and find suitable competition in that sport. To determine "unmet interest," schools must look beyond basic statistics to consider requests from current and admitted students, interviews with coaches and undergraduates participating in club and intramural sports, and participation levels at local high schools. For example, if OCR finds that a particular sport is played by high school girls in the region, the burden shifts to the college to explain why it does not offer that sport. If a school recruits men for a particular sport, it must also recruit women for that sport. OCR set a low bar for determining whether there is "sufficient interest and ability" among female students to sustain an intercollegiate team: "Neither a poor competitive record nor the inability of interested students or admitted students to play at the same level of competition engaged in by the institution's other athletes is conclusive evidence of lack of ability." Colleges bear responsibility for developing this "potential" by providing training and playing opportunities. Although these "general principles" were "designed for intercollegiate athletics," they "often will apply to elementary and secondary interscholastic athletic programs" as well.[28]

The charge that this policy "improperly establishes arbitrary quotas," OCR confidently asserted, "is wrong." Although "quotas are impermissible" in most areas of education, using numerical targets is "a legitimate measure of unequal opportunity" in the context of sex-segregated sports. Under OCR's new policy, the ship of college athletics must keep moving toward a higher percentage of female athletes until it reaches that one true "safe harbor." Unlike the First Circuit, OCR never explained why this "safe harbor" should be based on the total number of male and female students rather than on the percentage of students interested in varsity athletics. It was long on requirements but short on justification.

Two years later OCR issued another DCL, further ratcheting up its rules on athletic scholarships. In negotiations with twenty-five universities that had been sued by the National Women's Law Center, OCR's national coordinator for Title IX athletics demanded that scholarship money awarded to male and female athletes be within 1 percent of the proportion of male and female varsity athletes at the school. That is, if men constitute 60 percent of varsity athletes, they can receive no more than 61 percent of scholarship grants. When those schools complained that this was not required by OCR's guidelines, Assistant Secretary Cantú circulated to all schools a letter explaining that this now constituted OCR policy. The letter claimed this was a "longstanding" standard implicit in OCR's 1979 "substantial proportionality" test.[29] This came as a surprise to the coauthor of OCR's 1990 compliance manual for Title IX, Valerie Bonnette, who saw the letter as a rewriting of the rules: "If OCR is attempting to enforce a narrower standard, then what they are doing is enforcing a policy that is counter to their written policy, and I believe it is of questionable legality for them to do so."[30] These guidelines on scholarships were announced with no opportunity for public comment. Once again OCR avoided political debate by denying, unconvincingly, that it was doing anything new.

The combination of the regulatory demand for more women's teams and the continuing arms race in college football put enormous pressure on colleges' athletic budgets, even as the economy improved over the course of the 1990s. As a result, many schools dropped "minor" men's teams. A General Accounting Office (GAO) report found that in the 1980s and 1990s colleges discontinued 171 men's wrestling teams, 84 men's tennis teams, 56 men's gymnastics teams, 42 men's fencing teams, 27 men's track teams, and 25 men's swim teams. From 1992 to 1997 alone, National Collegiate Athletic Association (NCAA) schools lost 200 men's teams and as many as 20,000 male athletes, primarily in Division I programs. By 2000, there were 330 more women's varsity teams than men's teams competing in intercollegiate sports.[31]

These cuts produced reverse discrimination suits by male athletes. Swimmers sued the University of Illinois at Urbana-Champaign, Kansas State University, and the State University of New York. Soccer players sued Illinois State. Wrestlers sued the University of North Dakota. The National Wrestling Coaches Association sued OCR. In the most highly publicized case, national wrestling champion Stephen Neal sued California State University, Bakersfield, which had disbanded his team to comply with the school's agreement with the California branch of the National Organization for Women. They all lost. Overall, eight circuit courts dismissed the reverse discrimination cases brought by male athletes.[32]

By 2000 the courts and OCR were united in their determination to increase the number of intercollegiate women athletes, even if this meant cutting men's teams. Advocates for women's sports argued that male wrestlers and swimmers need not bear the brunt of this shift in resources: a better strategy would be to restrict the size of football squads and the large number of football scholarships. But only a few schools were willing to consider this option, and the NCAA refused to change its own rules on the subject.

Congressional efforts to rewrite Title IX to reverse OCR and the courts got nowhere. Not only did those who sought to change existing policy face stiff opposition from women's groups, but they could muster little public support. A 2000 *Wall Street Journal*/NBC poll found that 70 percent of Republicans and 79 percent of Democrats approved of "cutting back on men's athletics to ensure equivalent athletic opportunity for women." Almost as many men agreed with this policy (73 percent) as women (79 percent).[33] During the 2000 Iowa caucuses a group called "Iowans against Quotas" tried to get all the presidential candidates to sign a pledge to change enforcement of Title IX. Only a few minor Republican candidates did so. The Democratic candidates used the occasion to reiterate their strong support for Title IX. George W. Bush said only that he opposed the use of quotas.[34] When he got into office, his administration did try to modify the Title IX policies established in the 1990s. But it failed. The court–agency alliance and the policies it established in the 1990s prevailed.

The Failed Counterattack, 2001–08

Critics of OCR's athletics policy had reason to hope the Bush administration would pull back from the demand for parity. The Republican Party had a long history of opposing federal mandates in education, and its 2000 platform called for "a reasonable approach to Title IX that seeks to expand opportunities for women without adversely affecting men's teams."[35] President Bush's choice for secretary of education was Roderick Paige, a former football coach who wrote his dissertation on the response time of football linemen.[36] With Bush's nominee for head of OCR, Gerald Reynolds, stalled for months in the Senate, Paige took the lead on Title IX. Meanwhile, the leading critic of the Three-Part Test, Dennis Hastert, had become speaker of the House. With only a bare majority of Republicans in the House, President Bush relied heavily on the House leadership to pass his tax bill and other legislative initiatives. That gave Hastert significant leverage with the administration.

To cope with this controversy, Secretary Paige and the White House relied on the time-honored strategy of appointing a commission to examine the problem and suggest alternative solutions. Paige asked the new Commission on Opportunity in Athletics to address a variety of issues, ranging from the merits of the Three-Part Test to whether bowling and cheerleading should be considered intercollegiate sports. The commission was dominated by athletic administrators at big-time sports schools and by women athletes, including cochair Cynthia Cooper-Dyke (basketball), Donna de Varona (swimming), and Julie Foudy (soccer). De Varona and Foudy had both served as president of the Women's Sports Foundation (WSF), and became harsh critics of the commission's final recommendations. The National Women's Law Center (NWLC) opposed the commission from the start, issuing a press release titled, "NWLC to Bush Administration: Hands Off Title IX."[37]

The commission held animated hearings in four cities. It did not take long for major disagreements to emerge. As the commission held its final meeting, both the Women's Sports Foundation and the College Sports Council (a group representing wrestlers and other "minor" men's sports) issued warnings about the dangers of either altering or retaining the current rules. The result, Welch Suggs noted, was to turn that meeting "into a circus." The commission adopted twenty-three resolutions, fifteen unanimously. But within a few days, Foudy and de Varona, who found themselves in the minority on several issues, decided to oppose the entire report. They issued a twenty-page minority report that condemned the commission's procedures and offered twenty-three recommendations on how to strengthen Title IX.[38] Secretary Paige's effort to build a consensus had failed badly.

Most of the commission's unanimous recommendations were too vague to have much direct influence on OCR's regulatory program. But several of them suggested that OCR should move away from a rigid interpretation of the Three-Part Test: (1) "The designation of one part of the three-part test as a 'safe harbor' should be abandoned"; (2) if OCR retains the "substantial proportionality" standard, it should "allow for a reasonable variation in the relative ratio of athletic participation of men and women"; and (3) OCR should explore "additional ways of demonstrating equity beyond the existing three-part test."[39] Several of the non-unanimous recommendations went even further in this direction. One suggested, "For the purposes of Prong One, OCR should count only scholarship and recruited athletes, not walk-ons." Another recommended substantially changing OCR's interpretation of Prong Three by allowing schools to demonstrate compliance by "conducting continuous interest surveys." The commission also recommended that, in the future, OCR's policy statements and interpretations be "developed through the normal federal rule-making process"—an obvious swipe at OCR's use of DCLs, "interpretations," and "clarifications."[40]

The commission's report was greeted by harsh criticism not just from women's groups and Democrats in Congress, but also from the NCAA. NCAA president Myles Brand stated unequivocally, "Title IX is not broken, and it does not need to be fixed."[41] Secretary Paige agreed to "move forward" on the commission's unanimous recommendations. But when OCR issued its "Further Clarification of Intercollegiate Athletics Policy Guidance" a few months later, it did virtually nothing to alter its previous interpretation of the Three-Part Test, which, according to that 2003 document, had "worked well."[42] The new DCL emphasized that "each of the three prongs of the test is an equally sufficient means of complying with Title IX," but it did not make any of them easier to meet.

The only new element in the 2003 "Further Clarification" was the declaration that cutting men's teams in order to increase women's teams "is a disfavored practice." Reducing athletic opportunities "is contrary to the spirit of Title IX." Consequently, "In negotiating compliance agreements, OCR's policy will be to seek remedies that do not involve the elimination of teams."[43] In other words, competition for college resources should be resolved either by increasing the amount spent on athletics or by reducing football expenditures. Since the latter was unlikely at most schools, OCR's newly announced policy in effect amounted to pushing schools to spend more on varsity sports.

Two years later, with the 2004 election behind it, the Bush administration announced a more substantial change. In yet another DCL, this one with the comically awkward title, "Additional Clarification of Intercollegiate Athletics Policy: Three-Part Test, Part Three," OCR endorsed the use of e-mail surveys "to measure students' interest in participating in sports."[44] It provided a "Model Survey" and "User's Guide" developed by the department's technical assistance office. If the survey shows "insufficient interest to support an additional varsity team for the underrepresented sex," the school will be presumed to be in compliance with Prong Three. This presumption "can only be overcome" by "direct and very persuasive evidence," such as "recent elimination of a viable team" or "a recent, broad-based petition from an existing club team for elevation to varsity status." When the survey shows insufficient interest, "OCR will not exercise its discretion to conduct a compliance review." This gave schools the guidance that they had been seeking for many years on how to comply with Prong Three.[45]

The NWLC, WSF, and other advocacy groups reacted with outrage, arguing not only that such surveys are unreliable but also that they measure the wrong thing—current interest among female students, not potential interest. The NCAA called upon OCR "to rescind the Additional Clarification" and urged its members "to decline use" of the department's new Model Survey. The use of this survey, the NCAA declared, "conflicts with a key purpose of Title IX—to encourage women's interest in sports and eliminate stereotypes that discourage this form of participating."[46] The NCAA encouraged its members to increase the number of women's teams by working aggressively to stimulate female students' interest in the several "emerging sports" it had identified. The NCAA prevailed: over the next five years, very few schools tried to rely on the Model Survey. In 2010 the Obama administration withdrew both the "Additional Clarification" and the "User's Guide."[47]

Four features of these events during the Bush administration stand out. First is the extent to which the Three-Part Test, originally a minor provision buried in OCR's 1979 "interpretation," structured the entire debate for years. Almost no one proposed abandoning this framework. The only question was how Prongs One and Three could be adjusted to make them somewhat more or less demanding.

Second is the success of women's sports advocates in defeating any efforts to weaken the policies established by the courts and OCR in the 1990s. In part this is because defending the policy status quo is always easier in American politics than instituting a new policy. But the NWLC, WSF, and other groups were also remarkably adept at building broad coalitions. In 2003 they convinced over one hundred organizations to sign a letter opposing any change in OCR policy. Among these organizations were not just those representing women, but labor unions, civil rights groups, churches, and civil organizations. In the House, 140 Democrats sent a letter to President Bush urging him to withdraw the 2005 DCL.[48] Policies that can be described as reducing pressure on schools to increase athletic opportunities for women are clearly unpopular.

Third, those who defended existing policies and attacked the Bush administration's proposals relied heavily on the courts' interpretation of Title IX, especially the First Circuit's emphasis on counteracting gender stereotypes. In their minority report Donna de Varona and Julie Foudy wrote, "As courts have repeatedly recognized, what interest surveys measure is the discrimination that has limited opportunities for girls and women to participate in sports—*not* the interest that exists when girls are given unfettered opportunities to play."[49] Jocelyn Samuels, vice president of the NWLC, quoted the language of *Cohen v. Brown* and other circuit court opinions to support her claim that "courts have consistently recognized" that "interest cannot be measured apart from opportunity."[50]

Finally, the debate over Title IX has been dominated by those whose overriding concern is sports, not education. This was clearly true for the commission, which was composed almost entirely of athletic administrators and former athletes. (Ironically, the only college president on the commission was Penn State's Graham Spanier, who was later sentenced to prison for protecting a child molester in order to avoid embarrassing his football team.) On one side stood groups dedicated to increasing the number of women varsity athletes. On the other stood groups representing endangered men's teams. Tipping the balance was the NCAA, whose main goal has always been to increase the number of intercollegiate sports events it sponsors. It is not surprising, then, that all these participants could agree with OCR's 2003 declaration that "elimination of teams is a disfavored practice" and its 2005 pledge "to seek remedies that do not involve elimination of athletic opportunities." They could find common ground on this one point: expansion of highly competitive intercollegiate sports is always good.

The Obama Expansion: Guidelines

Given the polarization of American politics in the twenty-first century and the importance Democrats have placed on women's issues, it is hardly surprising that the Obama administration's approach to Title IX diverged significantly from that of its predecessor. In 2010 OCR released a thirteen-page DCL that withdrew the Bush administration's 2005 "Additional Clarification" and explained in detail how it would apply Prong Three.[51] The new policy was unveiled by Secretary Duncan and Vice President Biden before a large crowd in a college basketball arena. Biden lavished praise both on the female athletes in his family and on Title IX: "Making Title IX as strong as possible is a no-brainer. What we're doing here today will better ensure equal opportunity in athletics and allow women to reach their potential."[52] Duncan and Biden also announced that OCR would intensify its review of athletic opportunities at the elementary and secondary levels by opening investigations of thirty-two public school districts.

The 2010 DCL not only rejected the Bush administration's survey policy, but went further than the Clinton administration in requiring schools to use "a broad range of indicators" to prove that they have "fully" accommodated the interests and abilities of their female students under Prong Three. The assessments used to demonstrate compliance with Prong Three must include:

- interviews with students, admitted students, coaches, administrators, and others regarding interest in a particular sport;

- participation rates in sports in high schools, amateur athletic associations, and community sports leagues that operate in areas from which the institution draws its students;

- tryouts or other direct observations of participation in the particular sport in which there is interest;

- complaints from the underrepresented sex with regard to a lack of athletic opportunities or request for the addition of new teams; and

- routine monitoring of participation of the underrepresented sex in club and intramural sports.

These assessments must "take into account the nationally increasing level of women's interests and abilities."[53]

The DCL placed the burden of proof on schools to provide extensive documentation of a negative—that the requisite interest and ability for an additional women's team did not currently exist and would not soon appear on campus. "For example," the DCL says in a footnote, "if OCR's investigation finds that a substantial number of high schools from the relevant region offer a particular sport that the institution does not offer for the underrepresented sex," it will "ask the institution to provide a basis for any assertion that its students and admitted students are not interested in playing that sport." Not content to leave this assessment to schools, OCR investigators "may also interview students, admitted students, coaches, and others regarding that sport."

Schools that eliminate women's teams face a particularly demanding burden of proof. Cutting a team creates "a presumption that the institution is *not* in compliance with Part Three." To overcome this presumption the school must "provide strong evidence that interest, ability or competition no longer exists." OCR will not "consider the failure by students to express interest during a survey . . . sufficient to justify the elimination of a current and viable intercollegiate team for the underrepresented sex." If the Bush survey policy was designed to assess *current* interest among a school's undergraduates, the Obama "multiple indicators" policy was designed to *promote and develop* interest both among current students and in the students the school can recruit, admit, and train in coming years. As OCR explained in a footnote, students "may be unaware of whether they will have a future interest in athletic participation."[54]

The Obama Expansion: Enforcement

Between 2010 and 2016 the Obama administration launched a number of investigations of college athletic programs. These investigations examined not only the array of women's teams offered by the colleges in question but also the athletic facilities available to male and female teams, the number and salaries of coaches, travel allowances, publicity, schedules for games and practices, the availability of tutors and trainers, housing and dining facilities, recruitment, and scholarships. As a result, investigations often took months to complete and culminated in multipage agreements that extend to matters such as drainage in practice fields and the number of "sports information personnel" assigned to male and female teams. OCR also initiated systematic reviews of the interscholastic athletic programs of large public school districts, including New York, Chicago, Houston, Indianapolis, Tampa, and Columbus. This was the first time the agency had devoted significant enforcement resources to athletics at the high school level. A quick look at a few of these "letters of finding" and compliance agreements will provide a sense of the extent of this phase of federal regulation.

OCR's investigation of Rutgers University's athletic program culminated in a fifty-page letter of findings in 2015. Rutgers is a Division I school with a large student body (about 30,000 undergraduates) and a small number of varsity athletes (about 700). OCR found that from 2011 through 2014, the proportion of female athletes at Rutgers was only 1 percent below the proportion of female undergraduates, with the annual deficit of female athletes (between 10 and 16) less than the average size of a female varsity team (23). It therefore determined that Rutgers was one of the rare schools to pass Prong One.

But Rutgers was not yet off the hook. In its lengthy letter to the president of the university, OCR identified deficiencies in four areas: locker rooms, publicity, office space, and travel.[55] These were "substantial enough in and of themselves to deny equal athletic opportunity" to female Rutgers students. As a result, the school agreed to upgrade the locker rooms for female varsity athletes, provide more office space for the coaches of women's teams, and pay for charter flights for the women's basketball team. OCR also found that Rutgers had failed to provide "equal athletic opportunities to students of both sexes with regard to publicity." As a result, Rutgers agreed both to hire additional "sports information personnel" to cover women's teams, and to review the activities of the publicity office to ensure that it provides equal media coverage to women.[56] The entire agreement focused exclusively on providing additional resources to the approximately 350 undergraduates on women's varsity teams.

Merrimack College in northern Massachusetts did not get off nearly so easily. A school with only 1,900 undergraduates, Merrimack offered an array of varsity sports that in 2011 provided athletic opportunities to 25 percent of its male students and 15 percent of female students. (In contrast, varsity teams at Rutgers provided slots for only about 2 percent of male and female undergraduates.) The 12.6 percent gap between female undergraduate enrollments and female varsity slots meant that Merrimack could not comply with Prong One. Despite the fact that the school had added new women's teams in recent years, OCR determined that this "program expansion" was not sufficient because the college had added men's teams during the same period and the percentage of female athletes had not increased. Nor could Merrimack meet Prong Three: not only was its survey of student interest inadequate, but it had not made sufficient efforts to recruit female athletes.

For a small private school, the agreement Merrimack reached with OCR was remarkably expensive. The seventeen-page settlement laid out in great detail the schedule for creating a Division I women's hockey team that would compete in Hockey East; a new women's swimming and diving team; a new women's water polo team; and substantial expansion of the recently added women's track and field team, golf team, and crew. At the end of the seventh year the women's hockey team would be receiving $813,000 annually for scholarships and $372,000 for coaches, travel, and other expenses. The other two new women's teams would get a combined $650,000 annually for scholarships and a bit less than $100,000 for other expenses.[57]

Altogether the cost of this expansion would amount to more than $2.5 million annually—a big expense for a school with less than 2,000 students. To make sure that the school complied with these mandates, the agreement also required the school to "establish a full-time senior women's administrator who will report directly to the Director of Athletics" and a "Title IX Committee" that will meet at least three times a year "to review Title IX compliance as well as additional issues the department faces in the areas of Title IX and Diversity." Merrimack College also promised to provide annual reports to OCR listing the rosters of all teams, the amount of scholarship money provided to each team and each individual, and the operating budget for each team.

Why would a school sign such an expensive agreement rather than challenge OCR's finding that it had not complied with the Three-Part Test? The answer probably lies in the experience of Merrimack's neighbor to the south, Quinnipiac College. Quinnipiac lost a Title IX suit brought by members of the disbanded women's volleyball team (see chapter 1). After three and a half years of litigation Quinnipiac reached an agreement with those athletes and the Connecticut chapter of the American Civil Liberties Union that cost more than $8 million. Like Brown a decade and a half earlier, Quinnipiac fought and lost—at considerable expense to its budget and its reputation.

Although Title IX athletic rules have always applied to interscholastic as well as intercollegiate sports, OCR's guidelines have been molded with colleges in mind. Until recently, high school sports has received little attention from the agency.[58] This, too, changed during the Obama administration. A number of factors contributed to the shift. Interscholastic sports involve more than ten times as many students as intercollegiate sports. Since high school is usually the place where girls' athletic "interests and abilities" are formed, more interscholastic athletes mean a wider pool from which colleges can recruit. In recent years public schools have offered fewer physical education classes as a result of budget pressures and the demands of No Child Left Behind. Meanwhile childhood obesity rates have risen. Although a few states are approaching parity for interscholastic sports, in many other states the gap between boys' and girls' participation rates remains large. This is particularly true in the South and in schools with high concentrations of minority children.[59]

In 2010 the NWLC filed complaints against twelve school districts, one in each of OCR's regional offices.[60] This complaint not only forced OCR to investigate several very large districts, but also spurred it to initiate additional compliance reviews. Most of the NWLC complaints resulted in settlement agreements.

In many respects, these agreements were similar to those negotiated with colleges. They mandate new girls' teams, improvements in fields and locker rooms, better scheduling and publicity, and the appointment of Title IX sports coordinators. Even schools that seemed to be doing relatively well were subject to extensive additional requirements. For example, the high schools in Portland, Maine, could boast of high participation rates by both boys and girls—over 50 percent for each—and a male–female gap of only 3.7 percent. But it was required to add girls' volleyball immediately and another girls' team the following year.[61] Hingham, Massachusetts, a wealthy suburb near Boston, offered every interscholastic sport sanctioned by the state: thirteen female, twelve male, and four coed sports. Its male–female participation gap was only 2.45 percent. The settlement agreement required Hingham to eliminate that gap either by increasing squad sizes or creating new girls' teams. Hingham also agreed to construct new playing fields and spend more on girls' teams to compensate for the greater support boys' teams received from private booster clubs.[62]

OCR has required public school districts to complete a variety of studies in order to satisfy Prong Three. For example, the resolution agreement between OCR and the Indianapolis school district required the district to conduct an OCR-approved survey of current high school and eighth-grade girls, asking them about their interest in every sport offered by the city's high schools as well as sports that could be added. Among the data that the school district must provide to OCR are the following:

- female rates of participation in club, intramural, and community teams over the past three years;

- the number of girls cut from high school teams over the past three years, the reasons they were cut, and coaches' assessment of whether they had the ability to form an additional team;

- a list of the girls' teams eliminated over the preceding ten years;

- a review of requests for new girls' teams over the past three years; and

- coaches' assessment of the level of play in club, intramural, community, and middle school teams in the region.

For sports currently offered the school must consider adding new levels of competition (e.g., junior varsity, sophomore, or freshmen teams) and expanding roster size. If there is student interest in a sport not offered by other schools in the area, the district should take steps to increase the number of potential competitors.[63] The purpose of these reports is not just to survey current interest, but to discover areas for expansion of girls' programs. This search can stop only when the school reaches the parity standard set out in Prong One.

As has been the case with college sports, much of the litigation on interscholastic athletics has focused on increasing the competitiveness and the visibility of women's sports. A federal district court in Michigan (later upheld by the Sixth Circuit) required the state high school athletic association to move girls' soccer championships from the fall to the spring in order to allow college recruiters to view the games before they send their requests to admission committees and make scholarship offers.[64] The Seventh Circuit required a high school in Indiana to schedule more girls' basketball games on Fridays and Saturdays, arguing that relegating girls' games to "non-primetime" results "in a loss of audience" and "foster[s] feeling of inferiority." This could depress girls' interest in basketball, even in basketball-crazy Indiana: "Girls might be less interested in joining the basketball team because of lack of school and community support, which results in the perception that the girls' team is inferior and less deserving than the boys'."[65]

The Seventh Circuit's corollary to the "build it and they will come" thesis is "schedule games on Fridays and Saturdays, and the audience will appear." According to the court, "Disparate scheduling creates a cyclical effect that stifles community support, prevents the development of a fan base, and discourages females from participating in a traditionally male dominated sport." Title IX requires schools to counteract these "stereotyped notions of women's interests and abilities" by increasing the audience for girls' varsity games.[66] It is unclear what the school or the court should do if Hoosier basketball fans continue to turn out in greater numbers at boys' games. If increasing athletic opportunity for female students requires counteracting stereotypes not just within schools but in entire communities, it probably becomes a task beyond the reach of federal judges and administrators.

Conclusion

Ever since the revival of Title IX regulation of athletics in the early 1990s, judges and administrators, members of Congress and advocacy groups, reporters and professors, coaches and athletes have engaged in a heated debate over the extent and causes of different levels of male and female interest in competitive sports. For many years, court decisions and OCR guidelines have been based on the conviction that all such differences are "socially constructed" and must be counteracted by federal regulation. From a regulatory point of view, this debate has been conducted within a remarkably narrow framework: the meaning of Prong Three of the Three-Part Test first announced as one subsection of OCR's 1979 "interpretation" of its 1975 Title IX regulations. As a consequence, federal regulation has focused almost exclusively on varsity-level sports, which at most large schools provide athletic opportunities to only a small percentage of students.

This peculiarly narrow focus was in large part the result of the equally peculiar way in which federal policy has evolved. Courts and agencies slowly expanded federal regulation without ever admitting they were doing anything new or justifying their intense focus on the most competitive level of athletics. Women's advocacy groups placed more importance on increasing the visibility of high-level women's sports than on increasing the number of girls and women engaged in a variety of athletic endeavors. The NCAA has been happy to sponsor and subsidize highly competitive women's sports as long as this does not threaten its own cash cows. Seldom did any of these policymakers or advocates ask whether this regulatory approach was good for the vast majority of students, both male and female. That is the topic of the next chapter.

EIGHT

Athletic Opportunity Costs

In large part, regulation is the process of turning good intentions, lofty ambitions, and abstract legislative mandates into measurable performance standards and routinizable compliance procedures. This can rarely be done with ease or precision. Regulation inevitably imposes costs on some people and sectors of the economy in order to confer benefits on others. Some of these costs can be calculated with precision—such as the capital cost of a scrubber installed to reduce power plant emissions or the annual cost of adding a women's hockey team at Merrimack College. Predicting costs well into the future is more difficult. Even harder is estimating what economists call "opportunity costs," benefits forgone by using resources in one way rather than another. An athletic scholarship given to a hockey player is one not given to a budding musician or the academically gifted child of an immigrant. For every athlete who gets an admission boost at a selective college, someone else is turned away. As Brown University president Vartan Gregorian emphasized, money spent on athletics is money not spent on faculty salaries or libraries. Regulation also inevitably creates perverse incentives and unintended consequences. People and institutions subject to regulation will look for ways to get around legal rules and to comply with them at the lowest cost. This requires regulators to anticipate compliance strategies and to adjust their rules to take into account the response of those regulated. In the early days of most regulatory programs, all eyes are on the expected benefits. As time goes by, indirect costs, unanticipated consequences, and perverse incentives become more apparent.

As health, safety, environmental, consumer, and other forms of "social" regulation expanded rapidly in the 1970s, the federal government developed a variety of mechanisms to improve its ability to estimate the costs and benefits of its regulatory efforts and to anticipate the likely consequences. These include enhanced rulemaking procedures; the so-called hard look review by appellate courts; review of all major rules by the Office of Management and Budget; and the creation of policy analysis units within the regulatory agencies themselves.[1] Those familiar with regulation by the Environmental Protection Agency, the Food and Drug Administration, or the Occupational Safety and Health Administration will no doubt be surprised to learn that since 1975 the Office for Civil Rights (OCR) has managed to evade all these forms of scrutiny. Nowhere in any of its documents on athletics (or any other topic, for that matter) does one find serious discussion of direct costs, opportunity costs, or incentives. Nor is there any indication that the agency has attempted to anticipate how schools might try to game the new system. One could attribute this to the "rights talk" that dominates the civil rights state. But it is above all the product of the process described in chapters 6 and 7, a process that allowed OCR and judges alike to ignore these pivotal questions for decades.

To get a handle on the long-term costs and consequences of federal regulation of athletics, one must therefore look beyond the meager policy analysis presented by regulators and advocacy groups. One useful source is economic analysis of college sports as a whole. Another is the work of feminist scholars critical of what they describe as the "male model" of American intercollegiate and interscholastic sports.

A third source is the two-volume study of college athletics conducted by former Princeton president William Bowen and his coauthors, *The Game of Life: College Sports and Educational Values* (with James L. Shulman) and *Reclaiming the Game* (with Sarah A. Levin).[2] Bowen, Shulman, and Levin had access to decades of data on over 90,000 students at a wide variety of colleges and universities, ranging from small Division III colleges to large public Division I-A sports powerhouses. In the end their evaluation is similar to that provided by former *Chronicle of Higher Education* reporter Welch Suggs in his fine book, *A Place on the Team: The Triumph and Tragedy of Title IX*. On the one hand, regulation of athletics under Title IX has been a "triumph" because it opened up so many athletic opportunities for women. On the other hand, it has been a "tragedy" because intercollegiate sports have long been characterized by rampant corruption, exploitation of young athletes, and diversion of scarce educational resources (including, perhaps most important, the attention of students). In recent decades, Suggs laments, "female athletes have been sucked into this mess."[3]

Unanticipated Consequences

Although she celebrates the fact that "Title IX has encouraged a transformational amount of social change," the feminist historian Susan Ware notes that "the history of Title IX has been fraught with unintended consequences."[4] Some of these have been the result of what Gerald Gurney, Donna Lopiano, and Andrew Zimbalist call "roster inflation shenanigans," reporting tricks that increase the number of female athletes on paper but not on the field. For example, some schools (such as Quinnipiac) require female cross-country runners also to run indoor and outdoor track so they can count these athletes two or three times. Others have found crew to be an easy way to increase the number of female athletes since they can enter many boats in regattas, including those with inexperienced rowers. Arizona State adopted this strategy when it constructed a two-mile artificial lake to provide a site for women's crew—despite the fact that in that desert state not a single high school had a rowing team.[5] Still others have counted male fencers who practice with the women's team as female athletes. A few have included on the roster of women's teams students who never went to practice or games, and had no idea they were on the list.[6]

Many schools now place a hard cap on men's teams' rosters, turning away "walk-ons" despite the fact that they impose no additional costs and are usually happy to serve as benchwarmers. In fact, at most colleges "walk-ons"—the epitome of the "scholar athlete"—have all but disappeared from men's teams. Meanwhile, slots on women's teams sometimes go unfilled. Women, it seems, are less willing than men to be mere benchwarmers. This might be because they tend to be more serious about their studies.

Mary Jo Kane, director of the University of Minnesota's Tucker Center for Research on Girls & Women in Sport, argues that "the most significant unintended consequence of Title IX is the dearth of women in leadership positions."[7] When Title IX was enacted, nine out of ten women's college teams had a female head coach. In contrast, by 2014 only 40 percent of head coaches for women's teams were women.[8] Apparently, when colleges decide they wanted to produce winning women's teams, they turn to male coaches. An unfortunate side effect of this has been the increased risk of sexual harassment. According to Linda Flanagan and Susan Greenberg, between 1999 and 2012, "36 coaches from the U.S. national swim team—including the former director—have resigned or been banned from the sport following allegations of sexual misconduct or inappropriate sexual behavior."[9] The extent of sexual abuse might be even more extreme in gymnastics.[10]

Pressure to expand women's intercollegiate sports has also had unexpected racial effects. As surprising as it may seem given the visibility of women's basketball, female African Americans are underrepresented in intercollegiate athletics compared to their proportion of the wider undergraduate population. Bowen and Levin report that in the schools they studied "no more than 5 percent of recruited female athletes are minorities."[11] Their participation is concentrated almost entirely in basketball and track. Of the nine "emerging sports" pushed by the National Collegiate Athletic Association (NCAA) to increase the number of women's teams (synchronized swimming, team handball, water polo, archery, badminton, bowling, ice hockey, squash, and equestrian sports), only one (bowling) attracts a significant number of African American women. The others tend to be offered only at affluent suburban schools or prep schools—thus earning them the nickname "white-girl sports." In the 1990s the Black Coaches Association argued that cuts to men's teams hurt African American males while increasing athletic opportunities and scholarships for white females.[12]

Community colleges and historically black colleges have a particularly difficult time complying with Title IX because female students far outnumber males, sometimes by a ratio of 2 to 1. For schools such as Grambling State University, football and the marching bands that perform at halftime are hallowed traditions that help attract male students. Football's large squads combined with low levels of student interest in "white-girl sports" make it virtually impossible for these schools to have twice as many female as male varsity athletes, as parity requires. Cutting men's sports is likely to reduce the schools' attractiveness to male students, creating a vicious cycle.[13] Many community colleges face the same problem because they serve a large number of older women with children who are not likely to have time for varsity athletics.[14]

Equity wears many faces. It can mean increasing women's opportunities to participate in highly competitive varsity sports. Or it can mean increasing employment opportunities for women coaches. Or helping more minority students attend college. Or reducing the risk of sexual harassment. In the real world, these laudable goals often conflict.

Counting Costs: Dollars

Who bears the cost of providing more athletic opportunities for women? Especially during the 1990s the "minor" men's sports such as wrestling, gymnastics, and diving argued that they were paying the price: for several years the number of men's teams in these sports shrank as the number of women's teams increased. Advocates for women's sports replied that these displaced male athletes should aim their wrath at rapidly escalating spending on football rather than Title IX. What both sides could agree on was that men's athletic opportunities should not be reduced in order to increase opportunities for women. As Eleanor Smeal, former president of the National Organization for Women, put it, "Dropping men's teams is a violation of the spirit and the letter of Title IX. The purpose of saying you're not going to discriminate is not to limit opportunities of the other class. We should not be talking about a zero-sum game."[15] OCR has repeatedly taken the same position, insisting that cutting men's teams is a "disfavored practice," and that complying with Title IX should "not involve the elimination of athletic opportunities."[16]

This position certainly constitutes good politics. Neither OCR nor women's groups want to become locked in battle with well-organized, well-connected defenders of men's sports. Far better to join forces and expand the athletic budget as a whole, letting the cost be dispersed more broadly—and thus arousing less opposition. The problem, of course, is that what sports enthusiasts call "athletic opportunities" entails what economists call "opportunity costs." Hiring a new coach means there is less money for a new assistant professor (or two or three or four). More equipment for crew, less for laboratories.

The costs of intercollegiate sports come in several forms. The most obvious is financial. Calculating the average expenses of intercollegiate athletic programs is difficult in part because colleges differ so greatly in the nature of their programs and in part because many schools are less than forthright in reporting their cost. But a number of key points can be made with some confidence.

First, intercollegiate sports are expensive. Despite the huge increase in TV revenues for football and men's basketball, only about twenty schools nationwide—all of them in the so-called Power Five athletic conferences—show a surplus on paper. According to Gurney, Lopiano, and Zimbalist, "When capital expense and indirect costs are included in the accounting analysis, the number of college athletic programs running a true surplus in any given year dips below ten."[17] Even in the NCAA's Division I Football Bowl Subdivision (FBS), the home of the most televised teams, the median operating loss is almost $15 million. The median operating loss for the Division I Football Championship Subdivision (FCS) is $11 million, with some schools' losses approaching $40 million. At Division II and III schools revenues are only a small percentage of expenditures. At D-II schools with football those expenses range from $1.3 million to $15.4 million, D-II without football, $520,000 to $20 million; D-III with football, $800,000 to $16 million, and D-III without football $500,000 to $10 million.[18] These expenses are growing, especially at schools seeking to be nationally competitive in football and men's basketball. A Knight Commission report estimated that by 2020 the top ten public universities would be spending over $250 million on athletics, up from $100 million in 2009.[19] According to that report, in 2005 FBS schools spent an average of $11,000 on undergraduates as a whole, but over $60,000 on each athlete. By 2008 they were spending a little over $13,000 on undergraduates but $84,500 on athletes—6.3 times as much.[20] Colleges in the Southeastern Conference spend almost $145,000 on each athlete, 10.8 times as much as on the average student. A 2015 study by the *Chronicle of Higher Education* and the *Huffington Post* found that the net amount D-I public colleges spent on athletic programs had increased by 16 percent over the preceding five years.[21]

Second, a substantial amount of the money spent on intercollegiate sports comes from mandatory student fees and subsidies from the school's operating budget, not from sports-generated revenues. The 2010 Knight Commission report found that at most schools sports revenues "fall short of meeting the needs of athletic programs," and therefore "almost all programs must rely on allocations from general university funds, fees imposed on the entire student body, and state appropriations to meet the funding gaps." In fact, they warn, "reliance on institutional resources to underwrite athletics programs is reaching the point at which some institutions must choose between funding sections of freshman English or funding the football team."[22] Gurney, Lopiano, and Zimbalist estimate that by 2010 student athletic fees exceeded $4 billion annually at NCAA schools.[23] Even the handful of schools that generate enough revenue to cover their operating expenses receive a hidden subsidy from their institution since they are not charged for capital expenditures or the cost of acquiring the land on which their stadiums sit—land that could be used for classrooms or dormitories.

Third, especially at the biggest-spending schools, most of this money goes to a small number of teams and athletes. Most egregious by far is the amount spent on football and men's basketball. At FBS schools these two sports consume 83 percent of the budget for men's sports. At FCS schools the figure is 63 percent. At Division I schools without football, the fifteen to twenty members of the men's basketball team receive 41 percent of the men's sports budget. Obviously those who complain about the expense of the "arms race" in these two sports have much to complain about.

At the schools with the largest athletic budgets, the number of female athletes is remarkably small. Division I schools have come the closest to reaching parity as calculated by OCR. The average gap between the proportion of female undergraduates (53 percent) and female athletes (46 percent) is only 7 percent—as compared to 17 percent for D-II schools and 14 percent for D-III schools.[24] That is in part because between 1988 and 2013, D-I schools eliminated 320 men's sports and added 758 women's sports.[25] But it is also because many large D-I schools lavish their athletic funds on such a tiny group: at the University of Texas at Austin, 368 men and 321 women out of an undergraduate population of 36,000; West Virginia University, 299 male athletes and 261 females out of 21,000 undergraduates; Kansas State, 291 male athletes, 297 female, 18,000 students; Iowa State, 274 male, 234 female, 27,000 total; Texas Tech, 335 male, 232 female, 25,500 total.[26]

Contrary to the rhetoric of OCR, the NCAA, and advocates for women's sports, expanding the number of varsity women's teams *is* a "zero-sum game." At the vast majority of colleges, money that does not come from a reduction in men's sports comes from increases in tuition and fees or in cuts to other university programs. Those costs can be disguised, but not eliminated.

Counting Costs: Admissions and Student Culture

At most large D-I schools, the primary cost of athletics is mainly financial—paying for scholarships, often outlandish coaches' salaries, extensive travel, and lavish stadium and training facilities. D-III schools, in contrast, do not spend nearly as much because they do not offer athletic scholarships, they play more games within their region, and they seldom aspire to national championships. They also provide athletic opportunities to a much wider swath of students. At Ivy League and New England Small College Athletic Conference (NESCAC) schools, as much as a quarter (and at a few schools nearly half) of undergraduates play varsity sports at one point in their career.[27] For these colleges the biggest question is not how much money is spent on sports, but how intercollegiate athletics influences the makeup of the student body and the culture of the school.

This is the focus of William Bowen and his coauthors. When they examined the academic qualifications and classroom performance of male athletes, their findings were depressing but not surprising. Male athletes, especially those in "major" sports, entered college with lower SAT scores and grade point averages than their peers. They managed to do even worse in their college classes than their high school records predicted. They were disproportionately likely to end up near the bottom of their class. Athletes tended to hang out with other athletes, have closer connections with their coaches than with their teachers, and flock to a small number of less-demanding majors. This often had the effect of solidifying an anti-intellectual "jock" culture. All these trends have gotten worse since the 1970s. Although schools differ in the magnitude of these trends, the trajectory is downward across the board.

For women athletes the picture is a bit more surprising and definitely more depressing. Among the women who attended college in the mid-1970s, before Title IX regulations took hold, female athletes differed little from their peers. Few of them had been recruited. Their SAT and high school grades were similar to those of nonathletes. They graduated at the same rate. For these women "there was no evidence of systematic academic underperformance in college."[28] By one measure they *outperformed* their peers: after graduating they earned more M.D.s, more law degrees, more Ph.D.s, more master's degrees—and more money. They were, Shulman and Bowen hypothesize, more energetic, competitive, and focused than nonathletes.[29]

Over the next several decades, the picture for women athletes changed dramatically. Recruiting went up, and the gap between the SAT scores and grade point averages of athletes and nonathletes grew. So did the extent of academic underperformance by female athletes. By 1999, women athletes recruited by coaches at selective, nonscholarship schools had a 53 percent better chance of being admitted than nonathletes with a similar academic record, "essentially twice the degree of advantage enjoyed by legacies and minority students." Students applying to Ivy League schools in the late 1990s with a combined SAT score between 1300 and 1400 had only a 15 percent chance of being admitted. For recruited male athletes that jumped to 60 percent. For recruited female athletes it reached 70 percent.[30] The SAT deficits for women recruited to play ice hockey and basketball were particularly large.[31] After the 1970s SAT scores for the non-athletes admitted to these schools rose significantly, but the scores for recruited athletes fell. "For the 1989 and 1999 cohorts," Shulman and Bowen conclude, "the pattern of admissions advantage for women is amazingly similar to the pattern for men."[32]

By the 1990s women athletes were graduating less frequently than their peers, and were performing worse in their courses than those with similar academic qualifications upon entering college. Fewer graduated with honors or were inducted into Phi Beta Kappa. In this respect, Shulman and Bowen note, "The women athletes appear to have caught up with their male counterparts—a dubious distinction!"[33]

Such underperformance was not simply the result of time pressures. Women who spend as much time on school newspapers, musical performance, and student government tend to do better than expected in their classes, not underperform. Recruited athletes who stop playing sports and thus have more time to devote to studies continue to underperform academically. Conversely, nonrecruited walk-ons who manage to make the team do *not* underperform.[34] Regardless of sex, recruited athletes simply have less interest in and commitment to academic work than do their peers. According to the authors, "Whatever combination of peer effects, 'jock culture,' and the different priorities and incentives [that] has led male athletes to underachieve academically has now been replicated within women's sports, where underperformance appears to be at least as widespread."[35] Ironically, because coaches at schools that do not offer athletic scholarships cannot use financial pressure to keep their recruits on the team, they tend to look for students with a laser-like focus on their chosen sport. These are typically teenagers who have devoted most of their young lives to developing their talent for soccer or football or basketball or hockey, which helps explain the pattern of academic underachievement.[36]

The group that bears the cost of the sizable benefits bequeathed to male and female recruited athletes is made up of those anonymous students who were not accepted at selective schools. As Bowen and Levin put it, "Each recruited athlete who attends one of these schools has taken a spot away from another student who was, in all likelihood, more academically qualified—and probably more committed to taking full advantage of the educational resources available at these schools."[37] The value of these slots has increased markedly in recent decades.

The growth of a self-segregating athletic subculture made up of both male and female students has also had consequences for the culture of the larger college community. Bowen and Levin quote one faculty member who expressed a sentiment shared by many others. His major concern was "the impact on the classroom of academically disinterested athletes." Faculty, he reported, "are upset by the athletes' lack of preparation for classes, their underachievement, and their tendency to sit in the back row and do nothing." A special committee established at Amherst College to examine the role of athletics in that highly selective school devoted a section of its report to the anti-intellectual culture associated with college sports, quoting a student leader who stated, "It is demoralizing to the academic student that there are some athletes, especially on a few teams, who don't care about academic work." A similar theme was expressed in a faculty report at Amherst's archrival, Williams College. There the faculty of the economics and history departments, the majors of many athletes, were disturbed by "evidence of anti-intellectualism, of clear disengagement and even out-right disdain, on the part of varsity athletes. . . . Such an attitude is especially troubling because it affects the entire chemistry of the class."[38]

It is possible (indeed, quite likely) that male athletes bear more responsibility for this degradation of academic culture than do their female counterparts. But it is also likely that these costs fall disproportionately on women students. Female students are excelling both in high school and in college. Given the de facto quotas most selective schools establish for male applicants—they do not want the proportion of men to drop below 45 percent—the competition for admission at selective schools is particularly fierce for females. Female students are also generally more serious about their course work in college, which means they will be most offended and most harmed by the anti-intellectualism of the sports subculture.

Costs for Female Athletes

One might conclude that the trends affecting both male and female college athletes impose a few indirect costs on some women, but substantial benefits for those who do get a chance to participate in intercollegiate sports. On the fortieth anniversary of the enactment of Title IX, the National Women's Law Center (NWLC) made a compelling case for the benefits of athletic participation by women. It pointed out that women who play sports not only are healthier, but "have higher levels of self-esteem, a lower incidence of depression, and a more positive body image compared to non-athletes." They are "less likely to smoke or use drugs and have lower rates of both sexual activity and pregnancy," and "more likely to graduate from high school, have higher grades, and score higher on standardized tests than do non-athletes." In the long run, the NWLC claims, a larger number of female athletes "leads to an increase in women's labor force participation down the road and greater female participation in previously male-dominated occupations, particularly high skill, high wage ones."[39] While this may be true for the millions of high school students who play a sport, is it also true for the much smaller number of female athletes who move up to intercollegiate sports or for high school students who aspire to do so?

As many observers have noted, in order to be spotted by a college coach it is usually necessary for a young woman to have specialized in one sport for many years. Multisport athletes have disappeared from college campuses, and are rapidly disappearing from high school sports programs as well. For those who see soccer or lacrosse or crew as the ticket into college and an athletic scholarship, other activities, including schoolwork, recede in importance.[40] This often means summer camps and playing for year-round travel teams (in addition to or instead of a high school team). Those who do not start early will have a hard time catching up. But those who do start early are susceptible to burnout.

In 2012 the *Atlantic* published an article with the provocative title, "How Title IX Hurt Female Athletes: The groundbreaking legislation, which was supposed to help women thrive in sports, has had several unintended, negative consequences."[41] It featured a Boston College sophomore, Sophia Gouraige, who fit the profile of a specialized, highly competitive female athlete. During her sophomore year she developed interests outside lacrosse, and came to dread practice. Finally, she quit. "When you go to college, it's all about how to win the national championship." "Why can't sports just be fun?" she asked. Diane Auer Jones, a former assistant secretary of education, has argued that OCR's guidelines in effect put the parochial interests of the coaches (whose "job or salary may be determined by the number and type of sports offered") ahead of the welfare of students, who are likely to have a broader array of interests. Moreover, "as girls move from high school to college, they decide to focus on individual athletic activities, such as yoga, circuit training, or jogging, instead of competitive team sports"— hardly irrational choices. But, of course, what Jones describes as "life-fitness or life-wellness" sports do not count in the current Title IX calculus.[42]

To make matters worse, female athletes face more health risks than do their male counterparts. According to Susan Ware, eating disorders are so widespread among female athletes "that the term 'female athlete triad' was coined to describe how eating disorders and compulsive exercise can lead to muscle depletion and bone loss, as well as amenorrhea (cessation of menstruation), making women athletes more prone to injury as well as stress-induced immune disorders."[43] Female athletes are also four to six times more likely than male athletes to tear their anterior cruciate ligament (ACL).[44]

Competing Models of Competition

The columnist Jane Eisner has argued that instead of "moderating the role of athletics in higher education, Title IX too often has stimulated colleges simply to impose a flawed male model on women's sports." "Sadly," she writes, "this

hubristic sports culture is now entangling more and more women. The promise of Title IX . . . has given us Chamique Holdsclaw and Brandi Chastain. It's
also given us an increasing number of female student athletes who are as academically weak and socially isolated as the men."[45] Bowen and Levin similarly
lament the fact that "Title IX was, in effect, superimposed on the pre-existing
'male model' of athletics." This, they claim, was not inevitable. Title IX "could
have served as a signal to colleges and universities (and to the NCAA) that it
was time to recalibrate the entire athletics enterprise so that it would be more
congruent with educational goals." This would have meant "reducing the emphasis on recruiting, spending less money on athletic scholarships (if not eliminating them altogether), and in other ways carefully considering the adoption
of other aspects of the model of athletics that was pioneered and developed by
the AIAW."[46]

This refers to the Association for Intercollegiate Athletics for Women
(AIAW), which, as noted in chapter 5, served as the women's counterpart to
the NCAA during the 1970s. The AIAW was run by women who adamantly
rejected the NCAA's model of competition. The NCAA makes its money and
earns its power and prestige by promoting and commercializing competition
at the highest level. This means primarily big-time football and men's basketball,
most notably March Madness. Athletic scholarships and intensive recruitment
of promising high school athletes are integral parts of the NCAA's profession-
alized sports world. The leadership of the AIAW, in contrast, was serious about
promoting *student* athletes in practice as well as in name. This meant, above
all, prohibiting athletic scholarships and extensive recruiting. As Mary Jo Festle explains in her history of the organization, for its leaders "equality" did not
mean "sameness." "Women should not have to adopt all of men's practices or
get subsumed into a male-run organization." For them the AIAW was "the
vehicle through which they pursued both equality and difference—fighting
for more teams and bigger budgets but in a less commercialized, less exploit-
ative, less expensive, and more student-centered brand of competition."[47] "Must
the Women's Rights movement demand for our young girls a share of the things
that are wrong in sports today as well as a share in the rights in order fully to
prove equality?" asked one of the founders of the AIAW.[48] Their answer was
"no," but in the years that followed federal regulators in effect said "yes."

Although Title IX was initially a boon to the AIAW, it soon turned into a
threat. As the number of women athletes and college teams increased, so did the
AIAW's membership, rising from 280 schools in 1972 to 659 in 1974.[49] Some of
its members argued that raising the profile of women's sports required athletic
scholarships and recruiting. The AIAW's ban on scholarships, these internal critics maintained, violated Title IX, which seemed to require the same scholarship
rules for both sexes. Moreover, many colleges decided it would be easier to comply with Title IX if men's and women's teams were placed in a unified athletic

department. This almost always meant that men ran the women's athletics programs, a violation of another AIAW tenet, namely, that women should control the development of women's sports.

Facing a Title IX lawsuit, the AIAW capitulated on the scholarship issue. This seemingly small change had a domino effect on women's intercollegiate sports. Athletic scholarships, Suggs notes, "shifted the emphasis from women already enrolled to those who could be recruited. Armed with scholarships, coaches needed to get out and find the best possible recipients." Colleges expected to get something for their money, and that meant winning teams. To compete with other schools, they "had to choose athletes on the basis of athletic abilities, not as a way of providing students with a healthy extracurricular activity."[50] According to one longtime woman athletic administrator, this meant a "180-degree turn" for women's programs:

> I'd been here all these years trying to develop a program for the young women who came to the university to get an education, and liked to compete in sports. . . . Now suddenly with the [Title IX] act, we are going out to find the student-athletes who we thought the university should have. . . . And as soon as we began to do that, the emphasis for women's sports changed.[51]

Meanwhile, the NCAA—which during the 1970s had done all it could either to kill Title IX or to gain an exception for football and men's basketball—decided, "If you can't beat them, acquire them." It waged an aggressive and successful effort to lure women's sports programs away from the AIAW. Its crucial advantage was money: it proposed a number of championships for women's sports to begin in 1981–82. In contrast to the AIAW, which required schools to pay their own way to tournaments, the NCAA used the cash it received from men's sports to establish and publicize new championships as well as to subsidize women's teams' travel to them. Enticed by the NCAA's money, visibility, prestige, and media connections, most of the AIAW's members jumped ship. After losing an antitrust case against the NCAA, the AIAW declared bankruptcy and disappeared. So did its model for women's sports.[52] According to Jeffrey Orleans, an OCR attorney who helped write Title IX regulations during the 1970s and later advised the Ivy League on how to comply with them, for Title IX the consequences of the shift from the AIAW to the NCAA "cannot be underestimated."[53]

Absorbing women's sports did nothing to moderate the NCAA's commitment to highly competitive, thoroughly commercialized college sports. In fact, the lucrative TV deals produced by the expansion of cable TV intensified these traits. Increasingly, colleges chased the big money flowing into football and men's basketball, expecting—almost always incorrectly—to turn a profit. At the same time, they increased spending on women's teams to avoid Title IX suits, OCR investigations, and bad publicity.

Now inside the tent, supporters of women's programs convinced the NCAA to create a Gender Equity Task Force in 1992. Since then the task force has issued regular reports on the balance between male and female varsity athletes in the various NCAA divisions and member schools. It endorsed the goal of increasing the number of female varsity athletes until they match the proportion of female undergraduates. It also recommended cutting the number of football scholarships to make more money available for women's athletic scholarships. On this crucial issue they lost, largely because the five "power" conferences objected.[54] As usual, the NCAA membership and leadership bowed before the enormous financial resources of these conferences. In short, the NCAA has become a reliable defender of Title IX and competitive women's sports—as long as this does not interfere with football and men's basketball.

Although Title IX's most prominent advocates often complain about the money devoted to football and men's basketball, they have welcomed the NCAA's help in promoting highly competitive women's intercollegiate sports. Their embrace of the "male model" of intercollegiate and interscholastic sports is evident in their opposition to "competitive cheer and tumbling" and flag football, which do not provide "opportunities to play at the college level and earn athletic scholarships." According to former Women's Sports Foundation (WSF) president Nancy Hogshead-Makar, girls receive educational benefit from a sport only if they take it seriously: "That's one of the things that makes sports such an important experience. You're always striving for that next rung."[55] For high school girls the "next rung" is a college scholarship and a position on a varsity team. For a college athlete, it is an Olympic team or professional sports of the sort promoted by the former athletes who dominate the WSF. This now-dominant view among Title IX advocates is the antithesis of the alternative put forth by the AIAW.

To support their claim that the AIAW model of athletic competition is not an anachronism, Bowen and Levin point to the achievement of the University Athletic Association (UAA), the athletic league created by such leading schools as the University of Chicago, Emory University, Washington University in St. Louis, New York University, MIT, and Carnegie Mellon. Like the old AIAW, the UAA prohibits athletic scholarships, discourages extensive recruiting, and sponsors round-robin tournaments rather than several rounds of championship games. It schedules these competitions so as to avoid conflicting with exams.[56] As a result, its members have managed to avoid almost all the problems documented by Bowen and his coauthors for both male and female students at so many other schools.

Conclusion

Ever since the revival of regulation in the early 1990s, the debate over what Title IX requires for athletics has focused on the abstract question of whether males and females might naturally differ in their interest in competitive sports or whether any differences we currently observe are entirely "socially constructed." Current policy is based on the latter assumption. It has been endorsed repeatedly by appellate judges—stretching from the First Circuit's 1996 opinion in *Brown* to the Seventh Circuit's 2012 decision on the scheduling of girls' basketball games in Indiana—and it underlies OCR's interpretation of the Three-Part Test.

The equally important questions of what constitutes a "genuine athletic opportunity" and the appropriate role for sports within educational institutions, in contrast, have received virtually no attention from judges or administrators. As a result, the most easily quantified measure—the number of male and female varsity athletes—has dominated the debate and determined regulatory priorities. Rather then ask whether schools offer a variety of athletic programs that "equally accommodated the interests and abilities of both sexes," federal regulators demand that schools increase the number of intercollegiate and interscholastic teams for females in order to counteract widespread stereotypes about their lack of interest in competitive sports. That means more athletic scholarships, more recruiting, and more admission boosts for female athletes, usually resulting in more demands for them to focus on their sports rather than their studies. While most criticism of these policies has been that they discriminate against athletes in the "minor" men's sports, this chapter has suggested that the most serious costs fall on female athletes and the educational enterprise as a whole.

How did federal regulation come to focus on such a narrow slice of athletics? Part of the blame must go to the alliance between the NCAA (whose central purpose is to commercialize college athletics at its most competitive level) and the organizations that became the principal advocates for women on Title IX (who combined a professional interest in competitive athletics with the belief that creating female sports figures is the best way to counteract harmful stereotypes). Add to this the organizational imbalance between those students interested in intramural ultimate Frisbee, rock climbing, or yoga on the one hand, and the coaches whose livelihood depends on the survival of a varsity team, the team members hoping to hold on to their athletic scholarships, and high school students (and parents) who see sports as their ticket to a selective college on the other. The latter file complaints and suits. The former do not.

The most disturbing part of the story, though, is the way in which the peculiar Title IX policymaking process narrowed the political debate and the focus of regulation. The only time OCR and its parent department followed the full rulemaking procedures spelled out in the Administrative Procedure Act and Title IX was the one time they presented varsity sports as just one part of the larger athletic and educational picture. Throughout the 1990s the litigation that drove regulation focused entirely on one subsection of OCR's "interpretation" of those regulations, ripping it out of its broader context. Egged on by women's organizations and delighted to find it had readily quantifiable measures of compliance endorsed by the judiciary, OCR doubled down on a literal interpretation of Prong Three. Together the NCAA and women's groups were able to repulse the policy revisions of the Bush administration, which tried to make it somewhat easier for schools to comply with the Three-Part Test without engaging the larger issue of the meaning of "genuine athletic opportunities." The leapfrogging performed by federal courts and OCR produced a policy that became stricter and stricter, yet narrower and narrower. It also created organizational interests dedicated to its perpetuation. The problem with federal policy on athletics under Title IX is not that some wrestlers have lost their teams. The real problem is that to avoid the appearance of a "zero-sum game," regulators have created strong incentives for schools to increase spending on highly competitive sports and to embrace the NCAA's "male model" of athletics. That deserves the sort of debate one rarely gets under Title IX's convoluted and truncated form of policymaking.

Part III

Sexual Harassment

NINE

Controversies

In April 2014, the White House released a task force report on a problem that, according to President Obama, "is more than just a crime against individuals. It threatens our families, it threatens our communities; ultimately, it threatens the entire country. It tears at the fabric of our communities. . . . We have the capacity to stop [it], support those who have survived it, and bring perpetrators to justice."[1] The threat in question was not the usual presidential fare of international terrorism, the war on drugs, or nuclear proliferation. It was sexual violence on college campuses. The report states unequivocally that "one in five women is sexually assaulted in college." If this controversial statistic is correct, then in the sixteen years since the Department of Education's Office for Civil Rights (OCR) had first issued rules on sexual harassment, nearly 10 million college students had been sexually assaulted.[2] To those who believe this claim is accurate, the Obama administration's initiative is a long-overdue response to a problem that colleges have swept under the rug. To those who question that figure, it is a prime example of regulatory overreach by the federal government.

The White House report unleashed a barrage of media attention. The first wave—exemplified by *TIME* magazine's cover story "RAPE: A Crisis in Higher Education"—described an "epidemic" of sexual violence on campus. The *Huffington Post* dedicated a special section to documenting the prevalence of sexual assault and the inadequacy of colleges' investigations. The *New York Times* provided several front-page stories, including one on a Columbia University student who carried a mattress to protest the university's failure to punish an alleged assailant.[3] The second wave—exemplified by *Newsweek*'s cover story, "The Other Side of the College Sexual Assault Crisis," K. C. Johnson and Stuart Taylor's book *The College Rape Frenzy: The Attack on Due Process at America's Universities*, Laura Kipnis's *Unwanted Advances: Sexual Paranoia Comes to Campus*, and Emily Yoffe's extensively researched articles in *Slate* and *The Atlantic*—emphasized the ambiguity of many cases that come before college disciplinary bodies and the danger of false accusations.[4] The controversy over *Rolling Stone*'s discredited story of a gang rape at the University of Virginia first raised alarms about the problem of sexual violence, and then underlined the hazard of replacing the traditional presumption of innocence with a presumption of guilt.

In the fall of 2014 California sparked another round of controversy by enacting legislation requiring all colleges and universities that receive financial assistance from the state to add "affirmative consent" rules to their student conduct codes. This means that students who fail to receive "affirmative, conscious, and voluntary agreement" from their partners for every escalation of sexual activity— ranging from a hug or kiss to intercourse—can be charged with sexual assault. The editorial board of the *Los Angeles Times* decried this "extraordinarily intrusive" government effort "to micromanage sex so closely as to tell young people what steps they must take in the privacy of their own dorm rooms." But their brethren at the *New York Times* endorsed it as a strategy "worth trying" since "sexual assault is rampant on campuses, and colleges have failed to respond adequately."[5] The web pundit Ezra Klein described the California affirmative consent requirement as a "terrible law," but a "necessary extreme solution to an extreme problem." Undoubtedly some men would be treated unfairly under the new law, Klein conceded, but "men need to feel a cold spike of fear when they begin a sexual encounter."[6] By 2016 about 1,500 colleges had established "affirmative consent" rules.[7] Public fascination with the "affirmative consent" requirement is not hard to explain: people love to talk about sex, and "affirmative consent" is the rare policy innovation that can be practiced in the privacy of one's own bedroom.

Enter the Regulators

Many White House reports generate a brief flurry of media stories only to disappear without leaving a policy footprint. Not so with this one, largely because the task force built on the work of a variety of offices already committed to addressing the problem. The federal Centers for Disease Control and Prevention (CDC) published reports on "evidence-based prevention strategies that work." The Department of Justice's Office on Violence Against Women launched a "multi-year initiative on campus sexual assault," which would evaluate prevention programs used by colleges. Several other offices joined the effort, including the Department of Justice's National Center for Campus Public Safety, its Office of Sexual Offender Sentencing, Monitoring, Apprehending, Registering, and Tracking, and the Department of Education's National Center on Safe and Supportive Learning Environments. The Bureau of Justice Statistics developed the "campus climate surveys" that colleges would be expected to administer on a regular basis.

The keystone of this extensive government initiative was a series of guidelines issued by the Office for Civil Rights under Title IX.[8] On the same day the task force issued its report, OCR released a forty-six-page document, "Questions and Answers on Title IX and Sexual Assault," to explain in great detail what all educational institutions receiving federal money must do to eliminate sexual harassment. Those who fail to comply with its Title IX requirements, OCR insisted, would face termination of all federal funds. According to the assistant secretary for civil rights, Catherine Lhamon, this was not an empty threat: "It's one I've made four times in the 10 months I've been in office. So it's one that's very much in use."[9]

Lhamon never actually pulled the trigger on the funding cutoff, but she did initiate a large number of extensive and well-publicized investigations of major universities. With the release of "Questions and Answers" came the announcement that OCR would investigate 55 colleges, including Harvard, Dartmouth, Princeton, Brown, Swarthmore, the University of Virginia, and the University of California at Berkeley. Over the next three years that number increased more than sevenfold: by the summer of 2017 the agency had launched 396 investigations, but resolved only 62.[10] In the past OCR had refused to publicize or even acknowledge investigations until they had been completed. The new policy of releasing the list of those under investigation, the office explained in 2014, advances the Obama administration's goal of "putting an end to sexual violence—particularly on college campuses."[11] On average these investigations took a year and a half to complete, with several dragging on for five or six years.

These investigations put enormous pressure on schools to reach legally binding settlements with OCR. Schools not yet under an OCR-generated cloud had strong incentives to come into compliance with the agency's guidelines to avoid embarrassing and expensive investigations. As a result, schools across the country revised their disciplinary procedures and instituted new training programs for students, faculty, and administrators. For example, shortly after the release of the White House report, Tufts University signed a sixteen-page agreement that incorporated all OCR's requirements plus a few more.[12] As we saw in chapter 1, Harvard created a new procedure for sexual harassment complaints, giving its fledgling Office for Sexual and Gender-Based Dispute Resolution full authority to investigate all charges of sexual harassment and to make determinations of guilt. Under pressure from OCR, Princeton agreed to lower the burden of proof on complainants in sexual harassment cases.[13] Despite criticism from some of its law professors, the University of Pennsylvania also changed its procedures for handling such complaints.[14] New York's governor, Andrew Cuomo, announced that all sixty-four campuses within the State University of New York would not only adopt the grievance procedures required by the federal government, but also codify "affirmative consent" rules for sexual relations among students. The University of Michigan's new rules included in the definition of sexual violence "discounting the partner's feelings regarding sex; criticizing the partner sexually," and even "withholding sex and affection."[15] As these examples indicate, federal regulation had a snowball effect, not only forcing schools to change their practices but empowering those inside these institutions to go beyond what the federal government had explicitly required.

Countersuits filed by male students convicted of misconduct under the new federal mandates quickly multiplied, raising significant questions about the fairness of colleges' investigations. Between 2012 and 2016, federal and state courts issued fifty-one decisions in such cases. Over half found deficiencies in the schools' disciplinary process. In others judges found the accused students' cases strong enough to allow discovery to proceed.[16] According to a 2017 report issued by the National Center for Higher Education Risk Management, the leading consulting group offering legal advice to colleges on the topic, "Never before have colleges been losing more cases than they are winning, but that is the trend now. The courts are not expanding due process yet, but are insisting that colleges provide the full measure of college-based due process that has been required over almost 60 years of litigation by students."[17] A federal district court judge in Massachusetts described the process used by Brandeis University in a sexual harassment case as "closer to Salem, 1692, than Boston, 2015."[18] Another judge wrote that "due process has been completely obliterated" by the actions of the University of California, Davis.[19]

In the summer of 2017, Secretary of Education Betsy DeVos met with both sexual assault survivors and those who claimed to have been wrongly accused of misconduct, and promised to revisit her department's sexual harassment policies. Thirty-four Democratic senators told her they were "extraordinarily disappointed and alarmed by recent actions you and your staff have taken that have diminished . . . enforcement of federal civil rights laws."[20] Time has done little to settle these turbulent political waters.

Institutional Leapfrogging—With a Twist

OCR's 2014 guidance document did not come out of the blue. It was based on a lengthy Dear Colleague Letter (DCL) that OCR distributed to public school districts and institutions of higher learning in 2011. That, too, had been announced at a well-publicized event, this one featuring Vice President Joseph Biden and Secretary Arne Duncan. Although the White House task force described the 2011 DCL as "groundbreaking," OCR was considerably more modest: it maintained that it did not need to employ standard rulemaking procedures because its letter "does not add requirements to applicable law," but only provides schools with "information and examples" that explain how to comply "with their legal obligations."[21] Some of those "legal obligations" had been announced in "significant guidance documents" issued by OCR in 1997 and on the last day of the Clinton administration in January 2001. Those previous statements, too, were presented as mere clarifications of "longstanding nationwide practices" and "well established legal principles" developed throughout the 1980s and 1990s with the help of the federal courts and the Equal Employment Opportunity Commission (EEOC).[22] For a quarter century OCR has ratcheted up its regulatory demands, avoiding rulemaking procedures by claiming merely to clarify preexisting conditions on federal grants.

This pattern should sound familiar: it was in many regards the same process that produced Title IX guidelines on athletics. Despite the similarity, there are at least four major differences between the development of Title IX rules on athletics and those on sexual harassment. First, Title IX athletic rules are sui generis, that is, they were devised in response to the peculiarities of intercollegiate and interscholastic sports. Title IX rules on sexual harassment, in contrast, were imported from federal regulation of employment discrimination under Title VII. As we will see in chapter 10, the differences between students and employees and the contrasting structure of Title IX and Title VII complicated the transfer of regulation from one context to another.

Second, the Supreme Court was absent from the athletics controversy, but central to legal disputes over sexual harassment. Between 1986 and 1999 the Court issued five sexual harassment opinions under Title VII and three under Title IX. This led to a parting of the ways between OCR and the federal courts. Having decided that the Court's interpretation of Title IX was too conservative, OCR staked out a much more aggressive stance on schools' responsibility "to take effective action to prevent, eliminate, and remedy sexual harassment." This meant that OCR could not count on federal courts to enforce its guidelines through private suits, as had been the case with athletics.

Third, OCR's response to this enforcement problem was to use high-visibility and costly investigations to induce schools to comply with its extensive mandates. Each complaint filed by a private citizen was converted into a comprehensive review of the policies and practices of the entire educational institution. For educational institutions the investigative process has become the punishment.

Fourth, OCR's sexual harassment rules and enforcement practices have become even more contentious than its athletic rules. OCR policies on athletics periodically generate opposition from football coaches and wrestlers, groups whose self-interest is immediately apparent. Disputes over athletics are usually resolved in quiet negotiations between OCR and schools. The public accusations hurled against schools on sexual harassment, in contrast, have bred resentment among some (but hardly all) school officials. Even more important, criticism of OCR policies often comes from left-of-center groups and individuals. This included civil libertarians, legal associations, and professors.

The remainder of this chapter provides the background for the lengthy story of the evolution of Title IX practices on sexual harassment contained in chapters 10 and 11. It focuses on four main issues. The first three have been debated frequently and with great passion since 2014: due process, free speech, and the frequency of sexual assault on campus.

The fourth issue has received less attention, but is more fundamental: Why is sexual *harassment* a form of sexual *discrimination*? In other words, how does Title IX give the Department of Education authority to deal with an issue that is ordinarily considered a matter of state law? Today very few people deny that the federal government has authority to address forms of sexual harassment serious enough to limit students' opportunity to receive an education. But disagreement over the basis and extent of that authority lies at the heart of current controversies. Yale law professor Reva Siegel has noted that the courts' explanation of why sexual harassment constitutes a form of sex discrimination remains "terribly thin."[23] Even those who agree that harassment should be covered by these laws "disagree about the reasons why this is so." These differences are politically important because "disagreements about the normative basis of the prohibition on sexual harassment in turn produce disputes about the range and type of practices the prohibition constrains."[24]

The final section of this chapter examines the two leading explanations of why sexual harassment constitutes a form of sexual discrimination and the regulatory models associated with each. One approach views sexual harassment as a problem produced by a few "bad apples" (usually, but not always, male) who must be punished or removed from the school or workplace. Here the emphasis is on creating incentives for schools and employers to identify these "bad apples" and prevent them from engaging in misconduct again. Both courts and agencies have looked to tort law to create these incentives. This has been the predominant model for dealing with sexual harassment under Title VII. It was also the model followed by OCR until 2000. That, in large part, is the plot line of chapter 10.

The alternative viewpoint sees sexual harassment on the job and in schools as one part of a much broader pattern of subordination of women. According to its most famous proponent, feminist law professor Catharine MacKinnon, sexual harassment is just one of many features of society that "perpetuates the interlocked structure by which women have been kept sexually in thrall to men and at the bottom of the labor market."[25] By focusing so narrowly on individual perpetrators and individual victims, advocates of this "sociocultural" perspective charge, the tort-based approach prevents us from understanding the extent of the problem and making the fundamental changes needed to address it adequately.

As a result of its break with the Supreme Court in 2000, OCR explicitly moved away from the tort approach, and after 2011 implicitly adopted this "sociocultural" understanding of the problem. This can be seen in two main features of what the assistant secretary for civil rights has called the agency's "new paradigm": the assertion that a "rape culture" on campus has produced an "epidemic" of sexual assault; and the assumption that schools have been so complicit in this form of subordination of women that they must be forced to construct Title IX offices powerful and autonomous enough to counteract those traditional forces. That, in a nutshell, is the story told in chapter 11.

The Due Process Critique

When the White House released its 2014 report, it seemed that sexual assault was a classic example of what political scientists call a "valence" issue: no politician wants to defend campus rapists; those who call for more aggressive federal action can combine support for women's issues with a tough-on-crime stance. But substantial criticism of OCR's guidelines soon appeared.

The harshest and most specific criticism has come from civil libertarians and lawyers who blame OCR for pressuring colleges to adopt procedures that fail to provide accused students with an adequate opportunity to defend themselves. As noted in chapter 1, law professors at Harvard, the University of Pennsylvania, and other leading law schools have charged that their schools' policies were "overwhelmingly stacked against the accused."[26] A task force of the American College of Trial Lawyers produced a 2017 "White Paper on Campus Sexual Assault Investigations" warning that "in a well-intentioned effort to address the significant problem of campus sexual assault, OCR has established investigative and disciplinary procedures that, in application, are in many cases fundamentally unfair to students accused of sexual misconduct."[27] A few months later an American Bar Association task force was particularly critical of the single-investigator approach pushed by OCR. "Having an investigator also serve as decision-maker," it warned, "carries inherent structural fairness risks."[28] Four prominent women law professors at Harvard charged that OCR pressures schools to institute rules and procedures "so unfair as to be truly shocking." This sends the "dreadful message" that "fairness is somehow incompatible with treating sexual misconduct seriously."[29] The writings of Laura Kipnis and K. C. Johnson and Stuart Taylor offer multiple examples of badly flawed, one-sided investigations.[30] A number of judges have found that the disciplinary procedures established by schools under pressure from OCR violate constitutionally based due process rights (in public institutions) and contractual obligations (in private schools).[31]

OCR's most hotly contested procedural demand is that all schools use the lenient "preponderance of the evidence" standard in disciplinary matters rather than the somewhat more demanding "clear and convincing" standard previously used by some colleges. This means that if the story told by the accuser is just slightly more believable than that told by the accused, the disciplinary authority must find the accused student guilty of sexual misconduct. This burden of proof contrasts sharply with the "beyond a reasonable doubt" standard used in criminal proceedings on sexual assault. OCR's defenders argue that the "preponderance of the evidence" standard is regularly used in civil cases, and is appropriate for matters that at most culminate in expulsion from school rather than criminal penalties. Critics counter that a student should not be branded a rapist or a perpetrator of sexual assault if there is only a 50.1 percent chance he is guilty of the alleged misconduct.

OCR's rules also require the accuser and the accused student to have identical rights of appeal. That is, if the accused is able to appeal a guilty finding to a higher authority, then the accuser can also appeal a not guilty finding before that authority. If an appellate body has the authority to reduce the penalty at the request of the accused, it must also have the authority to increase the penalty at the request of the accuser. This means that a student found not guilty by a fact-finding body could later be found guilty on review. In a criminal proceeding this would most likely constitute unconstitutional double jeopardy. Allowing the appellate authority to increase the penalty makes it dangerous for the accused student to challenge the initial decision. OCR's guidelines also require schools to take steps to protect the accuser while the case is pending, even if that means imposing unilateral restrictions on the accused student. Like affirmative consent rules, this can subtly transform the traditional presumption of innocence into a presumption of guilt.

Perhaps most important, OCR has encouraged schools to do away with hearings entirely, and instead to use a "single investigator model" in which "trained investigators" not only gather evidence but also "render a finding, present a recommendation, or even work out an acceptance-of-responsibility agreement with the offender."[32] Eager to appease OCR, many schools have instituted this model. In most instances the investigator is hired by and accountable to the school's Title IX Coordinator, whose main job is to ensure compliance with OCR mandates. Judge F. Dennis Saylor has warned that "The dangers of combining in a single individual the power to investigate, prosecute and convict, with little effective power of review, are obvious. No matter how well-intentioned, such a person may have preconceptions and biases, may make mistakes, and may reach premature conclusions."[33] Law professors Elizabeth Bartholet, Nancy Gernter, Janet Halley, and Jeannie Suk offer a related critique: "Many schools improperly house the functions of investigation and adjudication in dedicated Title IX offices," which have "strong incentives to ensure that the school stays in OCR's good graces to safeguard the school's federal funding." Moreover, "Title IX officers have reason to fear for their jobs if they hold a student not responsible."[34]

Behind the disputes over particular procedures lies the question of whether it is appropriate for schools to handle sexual assault cases at all. Some argue that matters of such seriousness should be left to the police and criminal courts. Colleges, they insist, are incapable of investigating these charges thoroughly. Not only are they likely unfairly to brand some students as rapists, but their limited power to punish leaves those guilty of criminal behavior free to transfer to other schools. OCR and its defenders reply that the criminal justice process makes it too difficult to convict perpetrators, and deters women from filing charges. Because schools do not impose criminal penalties they can make the process less onerous for those filing complaints.

Do Federal Harassment Rules Threaten Freedom of Speech?

According to OCR's guidelines, sexual assault is but one form of sexual harassment prohibited by Title IX. "Sexual harassment" includes "verbal, nonverbal, graphic, or physical conduct of a sexual nature." The guidelines prohibit "unwelcome" sexual advances "whether or not they involved physical touching." This includes "making sexual comments, jokes, or gestures; writing graffiti or displaying or distributing sexually explicit drawings, pictures, or written material; calling students sexually charged names; spreading sexual rumors; rating students on sexual activity or performance; or circulating, showing, or creating e-mails or Web sites of a sexual nature."[35] The guidelines also prohibit "sexual stereotyping," which includes "persistent disparagement of a person based on a perceived lack of stereotypical masculinity or femininity." To violate Title IX harassment "does not have to include intent to harm, be directed at a specific target, or involve repeated incidents."[36]

Many schools have extended their definition of "sexual harassment" to prohibit even more forms of speech. Harvard's code prohibits "sexually suggestive comments, jokes, innuendoes, or gestures" and even "commenting about . . . an individual's body."[37] Since an "innuendo" is an "allusive or oblique remark or hint," this covers a lot of ground. Marshall University defines harassment as any expression that causes "mental harm, injury, fear, stigma, disgrace, degradation, or embarrassment"; Colorado State University at Pueblo as the "infliction of psychological and/or emotional harm upon any member of the University community through any means."[38] Several schools have expelled students for messages sent on social media, including tasteless jokes aimed at no one in particular.[39]

In 2003 OCR responded to concerns about the free speech implications of its sexual harassment guidelines by circulating a DCL emphasizing that "No OCR regulation should be interpreted to impinge upon rights protected under the First Amendment to the U.S. Constitution or to require recipients to enact or enforce codes that punish the exercise of such rights."[40] When OCR expanded its definition of harassment in 2011, Andrew Kloster at the Foundation for Individual Rights in Education (FIRE) warned: "Prohibiting all 'unwelcome verbal conduct of a sexual nature' means that a professor discussing sexual politics could be guilty of sexual harassment; a student asking another student out on a date could be sexual harassment; a student production of Hamlet ('Frailty, thy name is woman!') could be prohibited as well."[41]

The potential reach of OCR's rules became evident in 2015, when Northwestern University professor Laura Kipnis was subject to a Title IX investigation for writing an article in the *Chronicle of Higher Education* titled "Sexual Paranoia Strikes Academe." That same year Louisiana State University (LSU) School of Education professor Teresa Buchanan was stripped of tenure after being found guilty by school administrators of using "salty language" in her classes. LSU's president used the sexual harassment process to sidestep ordinary procedures for termination of a tenured professor. The American Association of University Professors (AAUP) censured LSU for this abuse of power. Buchanan has sued, challenging the federal guidelines LSU had relied upon. Citing these and other examples, former president of the American Civil Liberties Union (ACLU) Nadine Strossen devoted her 2015 Salant Lecture at Harvard to warning of the dangers to freedom of speech posed by OCR's sexual harassment policies.[42]

Elizabeth Bartholet and her Harvard colleagues point out that since the definitions of harassment endorsed by OCR and most schools "include mere speech about sexual matters," they "allow students who find class discussion about sexuality offensive to accuse instructors of sexual harassment."[43] In 2016 the AAUP issued a highly critical report on OCR's Title IX policies, claiming that "faculty in disciplines related to gender and sexuality" are particularly "vulnerable to the chilling effect of potential hostile environment charges and are disproportionally affected in their teaching and research due to universities' adoption of overly broad definitions."[44] The report called on OCR to "distinguish between allegations of sexual harassment based on conduct and allegations based on speech" in order "to adequately protect academic freedom." So intertwined are regulation of speech and regulation of conduct in OCR's guidelines that this would require a thorough rewriting of the rules—and of the codes of conduct colleges have composed to comply with them.

How Prevalent Is Sexual Assault on Campus?

Both the Obama White House and OCR argued that the federal government must take forceful action against sexual misconduct because traditional practices have failed to stem an epidemic of sexual violence on campus. The criminal justice system and schools' ordinary disciplinary procedures, they maintain, discourage victims from coming forward, make it too hard to prove misconduct, allow sexual predators to remain on campus, and send male students the message that colleges will turn a blind eye to even the most serious sexual misconduct. Consequently, the question of the frequency of sexual assault on campus lies at the heart of the debate over OCR's mandates.

The White House task force's claim that 20 percent of college women are sexually assaulted during their years on campus has become a staple of the argument for the federal government's aggressive role.[45] Some advocacy groups have gone farther, maintaining that one in every four students is the victim of sexual violence while in college.[46] Although violent crime, including rape, has declined sharply in the United States since the early 1990s, it is common to hear that in recent decades sexual assault has increased on college campuses, making them the most dangerous places in the country for young women. For example, Senator Kirsten Gillibrand, a leading defender of OCR's policies, has repeatedly decried "the fact that women are at greater risk of sexual assault as soon as they step onto a college campus."[47]

These claims have been subject to sustained criticism. The frequently repeated 20 percent figure comes from an online survey of female college students at two public universities. It suffers from two deficiencies common to almost all such studies: a small, probably skewed sample; and an ambiguous definition of "assault." Since the study was limited to two schools in the Midwest, its lead author has conceded, "We don't think one in five is a nationally representative statistic."[48] The survey's low response rate (30 percent) raised the possibility that those who had been subject to sexual assault were more likely to respond than those who had not. Moreover, its definition of sexual assault included not just rape and attempted rape, but "unwanted touching" and sexual encounters while intoxicated. "By lumping uninvited advances and alcohol/drug-influenced encounters together with forcible rape," criminologists James Alan Fox and Richard Moran note, "the problem can appear more severe than it really is, creating alarm when cool heads are required."[49] In their review of the academic literature on violence against college women, Callie Marie Rennison of the University of Colorado and Lynn Addington of American University emphasize that researchers' failure to adopt clear and consistent definitions of sexual violence and assault has made it hard to quantify the extent of the problem, to map trends over time, or to compare college with noncollege women.[50]

In late 2014 the Department of Justice's Bureau of Justice Statistics issued a special report on "Rape and Sexual Assault Victimization among College-Age Females, 1995–2013."[51] The bureau's survey had a much higher response rate than the studies discussed above, and it provided respondents with clearer definitions of various forms of assault. Four of its findings stand out:

1. According to the Bureau, the annual rate of rape and sexual assault among college students is just over half of 1 percent—6.1 per 1,000 students. If

we assume that most students spend four years on campus, this means that female students face an assault rate of 2.44 percent, about one-tenth of the figure cited by the task force.

2. Since 1997 the rate of rape and sexual assault among female college students has not escalated, but in fact has been cut in half.

3. Females between eighteen and twenty-four who do *not* attend college are 1.2 times *more* likely to be the victims of sexual assault than those who attend college. Professor Rennison has noted that although "people have been bombarded with the notion that universities and colleges are hotbeds of sexual violence," the available evidence indicates that "young women who don't go to college are more likely to be raped." In fact, the rate of sexual victimization of women without a high school education is "more than 400 percent greater than those with a bachelor's degree or more."[52]

4. College students are less likely to report assaults to the police than are nonstudents, despite the fact that they were also more likely to believe the police will help them. The major reasons they gave for not reporting were that this was a "personal matter" (26 percent), it was "not important enough" (12 percent), the victim "did not want to get the offender in trouble with the law" (10 percent), and "fear of reprisal" (20 percent).

To get a better handle on the extent of the problem, twenty-seven universities worked with the Association of American Universities (AAU) to develop a model "Campus Climate Survey on Sexual Assault and Sexual Misconduct." The questions on this survey were more precise than the previous "climate checks" used by colleges, particularly in describing the various forms of assault and misconduct. The finding emphasized by most newspapers was that 23 percent of the responding female undergraduates reported "sexual contact involving physical force or incapacitation since enrolling in college." This figure includes "unwanted touching or kissing" as well as "penetration by force or incapacitation."[53] For the latter, by far the most serious form of sexual misconduct, 10.8 percent of the responding female undergraduates reported having been victimized. Although this is about half of the frequently repeated one-in-five statistic, it remains a disturbingly large percentage.

Like the Bureau of Justice Statistics, the AAU found that only a quarter of those who have experienced "physically forced penetration" have reported this to college authorities or the police. Reporting was even less common for "sexual touching or kissing involving physical force (7%) or incapacitation (5%)." According to the AAU report, "When asked why the incident was not reported, the dominant reason was it was not considered serious enough. . . . Even for penetration involving physical force, over half (58.6%) of students gave this reason."[54]

Given the seriousness of these offenses, the intense publicity given to the issue, and colleges' efforts to protect and provide services to those filing complaints, it is hard to know what to make of the small number of complaints filed by students. It might mean that despite recent changes the process remains difficult and stigmatizing for students making accusations. It might mean that the social pressure for remaining silent remains intense. It might mean that victims fear that the punishment imposed would be too harsh. It might be that the perpetrator has somehow intimidated the victim. Probably all these factors are in play.

As the authors of the AAU report admit, a major problem with their survey was the low response rate at most schools: the median was only 17.4 percent for undergraduates and 19.3 percent overall. Since those who do not respond to such surveys tend "to be less likely to report victimization," the survey's estimates "may be biased upward (i.e. somewhat too high)." Moreover, the AAU found "a wide range of variation" across the twenty-seven schools it studied, but could not "find a clear explanation for why there is such wide variation." For this reason they cautioned against invoking the common 1-in-5 figure.[55]

Another oddity of the AAU results is that in practice far fewer students actually report sexual assault to school officials than claim to have done so in the survey. The AAU found that 2.2 percent of female undergraduates claim to have reported "penetration without consent" to their college. Projected nationwide, that would constitute about 44,000 reports per year—ten times the number of college sexual assault reports of any type in 2013.[56] According to a *Boston Globe* story that compiled statistics collected by the Department of Education, the number of reports filed by students in thirty-one New England colleges was 0.99 per 1,000 students, or 0.1 percent in 2014—one-twentieth of the number of students who claim on the survey to have filed a report.[57] The AAU study did not investigate why so many students find "penetration by force or incapacitation" not "serious enough to report," and why the number of reports actually filed is so much smaller than the number claimed in surveys. These are but two of the questions that remind us how much we have yet to learn about the extent of the problem or the effectiveness of proposed solutions.

Disputed Foundations

When women first brought sexual harassment complaints to court under Titles VII and IX in the mid-1970s, judges were reluctant to equate sexual harassment with sexual discrimination. Some judges found such "personal" matters to be outside the control and the responsibility of employers. Others argued that improper behavior might violate state law, but does not constitute sexual discrimination. Authorizing judges to scrutinize these issues, many predicted, would open the proverbial "floodgates of litigation." One federal judge warned that "if the plaintiff's view were to prevail, no superior could, prudently, attempt to open a social dialogue with any subordinate of either sex. An invitation to dinner could become an invitation to a federal lawsuit if a once-harmonious relationship turned sour at some later time."[58]

As we will see in chapter 10, the tide began to change in the late 1970s. The rationale on which most judges fastened was that when a heterosexual male harasses a woman, it is "because" of her "sex." A heterosexual male would not similarly harass another male. This means that Title VII or Title IX also applies when a straight woman harasses a man, when a gay male harasses another male, or when a lesbian harasses another woman. But, as several judges reluctantly concluded, a bisexual man does not violate Title VII or Title IX if he harasses both men and women. Since he does not discriminate on the basis of sex—his harassment would be literally indiscriminate—such an equal-opportunity harasser violates no federal law. This led the syndicated humor columnist Art Buchwald to advise lecherous bosses to bring a male employee along on their trysts with employees of the opposite sex.[59]

Buchwald was not the only one to find this anomalous. In their dissent in *Vinson v. Taylor*, the first sexual harassment suit to reach the Supreme Court, three judges on the D.C. Circuit, Robert Bork, Antonin Scalia, and Kenneth Starr, observed that much of the "doctrinal difficulty in this area" resulted from "the awkwardness of classifying sexual advances as 'discrimination.'" While harassment is "reprehensible," Title VII (like Title IX) "was passed to outlaw discriminatory behavior and not simply behavior of which we strongly disapprove."[60]

The "artificiality" of the courts' interpretation of these laws, Judge Bork argued for the dissenters, is apparent in the distinctions they made among categories of perpetrators. On the one hand, "if a man makes unwanted sexual overtures to a woman, a woman to a man, a man to another man, or a woman to another woman" they have engaged in illegal discrimination. On the other hand, "this court has twice stated that Title VII does *not* prohibit sexual harassment by a 'bisexual superior because the insistence upon sexual favors would apply to male and female employees alike.'" According to this interpretation, "only the differentiating libido runs afoul of Title VII, and bisexual harassment, however blatant and however offensive and disturbing, is legally permissible." This "bizarre result," Bork maintained, indicates that Congress had not intended to address this issue when it passed Title VII: "Had Congress been aiming at sexual harassment, it seems unlikely that a woman would be protected from unwelcome heterosexual or lesbian advances but left unprotected when a bisexual attacks."[61]

The awkwardness of the "discriminating harasser" became even more apparent in 1998 when the Supreme Court decided *Oncale v. Sundowner Offshore Services*.[62] The author of the opinion for a unanimous court was Justice Scalia, who as a circuit court judge had joined Bork's dissent. *Oncale* involved the verbal and physical abuse of a man working on an offshore oil rig. The Court made no effort to establish whether Oncale's tormenters were gay or straight, whether they had been animated by animus, amour, or some strange amalgam of the two, or whether Oncale himself was gay or straight—matters that the courts' previously announced "bisexual harasser exception" had seemed to make crucial. Scalia's brief opinion stressed that Title VII protects men as well as women, and that it prohibits discriminatory behavior by some men against other men. Since dissecting motives in such cases is difficult, it is enough to show that some sort of sexual conduct or language was involved.

Justice Scalia acknowledged that this rather open-ended understanding of the type of sexual harassment prohibited by nondiscrimination statutes had the potential to "transform Title VII into a general civility code for the American workplace." To mitigate this danger he insisted that "the statute does not reach genuine but innocuous differences in the way men and women routinely interact with members of the same and of the opposite sex," but "forbids only behavior so *objectively offensive* as to alter the 'conditions' of the victim's employment." To violate Title VII, conduct must be *"severe and pervasive* enough to create an *objectively* hostile or adversarial environment."[63] These are the same limitations that featured prominently in Justice O'Connor's interpretation of Title IX in 1998 and 1999—only to be ignored by OCR soon thereafter.

Readers perplexed about why Oncale's tormenters were guilty of sex *discrimination* are not alone. Feminist law professor Katherine Franke notes that in *Oncale* the Supreme Court "was forced to articulate its conception of the wrong of sexual harassment with more specificity than it had in the past." "Unfortunately," she concluded, "rather than forging a principled path out of the thicket of previously muddled sexual harassment jurisprudence, the Supreme Court compounded the errors perpetuated by lower courts."[64]

When Congress passed Title VII and Title IX, it was primarily concerned with the exclusion of women from jobs and educational programs, but possibly with the exclusion of men as well. Sexual harassment law focuses on a different meaning of the key word, "sex." To appreciate the two meanings of the word, it is useful to call to mind the old joke about the employer filling out a government questionnaire. To the query "Number of employees broken down by sex?" he replies, "A few have succumbed to drink, but I can't recall any who have been broken down by sex." Court decisions culminating in *Oncale* established that Titles VII and IX cover not just behavior that discriminates against males or females, but *any* form of misconduct involving *sexual activity or words*.

Legal and academic efforts to establish a firmer foundation for sexual harassment law tend to fall into one of the two camps briefly outlined above. The approach most commonly endorsed by judges is based on a tort model of individual misbehavior and individual harm. Margaret Crouch points out that according to what she calls the "liberal" approach, "sexual harassment is not intrinsically connected to gender." Of course, due to "gender disparities in our society, men will tend to be the harassers and women the harassed." But "advocates of this perspective tend to attribute sexual harassment to misbehaving individuals, rather than to any group-based cause."[65]

Legal scholar Judith Resnik has emphasized the many ways in which the courts' invocation of tort law enshrines this individualistic understanding of the problem. Most legal claims are brought by "individual complainants and occasionally small groups of individuals" who "seek redress, first through an administrative apparatus inside a workplace or school, then in an agency, and finally in court." These plaintiffs and their lawyers usually seek monetary damages rather than broader injunctive relief "because settlements that lead to structural change do not ensure payments of fees to attorneys as surely as do settlements and judgments resulting in monetary payments and because obtaining wide-reaching relief is labor intensive."[66] Writing in 2004, Resnik found that "administrative responses generally mimic the tort paradigm rather than invent new regulatory modes." That remains true of the EEOC and Title VII, but is no longer accurate for OCR and Title IX.

As Crouch and Resnik suggest, this understanding of sexual harassment assumes that sexual harassment is the work of a few "bad apples"—usually, but not always males—who need to be identified, punished, and most likely removed from the workplace or school. This can best be done by giving victims opportunities and incentives to complain, and by giving schools and employers strong incentives to create grievance procedures and to take action when faced with credible evidence of harassment. Tort remedies are designed to create both sets of incentives. The greater the liability placed on employers and schools, the stronger their incentives to identify, discipline, and eliminate "bad apples."

A central irony of sexual harassment law is that Catharine MacKinnon, usually considered the intellectual godmother of these legal doctrines, has from the beginning attacked the tort-based, individualistic understanding of sexual harassment adopted by most judges. It is a fundamental mistake, MacKinnon argued, to view sexual harassment as wayward behavior by a few individuals:

> Rather, it is a group-defined injury which occurs to many different individuals regardless of unique qualities or circumstances, in ways that connect with other deprivations of the same individuals, among all of whom a single characteristic—female sex—is shared. Such an injury is *in essence* a group injury. The context which makes the impact of gender cumulative—in fact, the context that makes it injurious—is lost when sexual harassment is approached as an individual injury, however wide the net of damages is cast.[67]

Sexual harassment must be viewed as part of a much larger pattern of subordination, just one of many features of society that "perpetuates the interlocked structure by which women have been kept sexually in thrall to men and at the bottom of the labor market." The proper understanding of sexual harassment requires us to see that "Women historically have been required to exchange sexual services for material survival, in one form or another. Prostitution and marriage as well as sexual harassment in different ways institutionalize this arrangement."[68] In short, the problem is sexual inequality; the victims are women, and the perpetrators men.

MacKinnon insisted that legal doctrines that ignore these crucial facts produce only incoherent, ineffective liability rules and remedies. "Tort theory," she argued, "fails to capture the broadly social sexuality/employment nexus that comprises the injury of sexual harassment." Because it treats "the incidents as if they were outrages particular to an individual woman rather than integral to her social status as a woman worker, the personal approach on the legal level fails to analyze the relevant dimensions of the problem."[69] The tort law approach attempts only to shave off the tip of the patriarchal iceberg: "Tort law considers *individual* and *compensable* something which is *fundamentally social* and should be *eliminated*."[70] Rather than focus on the crass, immoral, or unethical behavior of a few individual supervisors, fellow employees, teachers, or students, her "inequality" approach "sees women's situation as a structural problem of enforced inferiority that needs to be radically altered."[71] Sexual harassment on the job and in schools is not a random, occasional event, but rather an omnipresent threat that maintains the economic and physical subordination of women.

Many others feminist writers and activists have adopted this "sociocultural" or "dominance" understanding of the problem. Although they recognize that courts and agencies have taken a few steps to reduce sexual harassment, they are critical of judges—and especially Supreme Court justices—who fail to provide "a systematic account of the social order sustained by 'discrimination.'"[72] According to Katherine Franke, for example, "Completely ignored in the Supreme Court's sexual harassment jurisprudence are notions of structural inequality and the relationships between gender-based power and sex."[73]

The feminist critique of the individual malfeasor model is usually couched in highly abstract terms. But three specific claims lie at the heart of this alternative approach. First, sexual harassment in its many forms is the inevitable result of a culture that condones and encourages it. This is reflected in the rhetoric now common on college campuses: the "epidemic" of sexual assault is a direct result of our "rape culture." For example, a January 2014 report by the White House Council on Women and Girls, "Rape and Sexual Assault: A Renewed Call to Action," offered this statement: "Sexual assault is pervasive because our culture still allows it to persist. According to the experts, violence prevention can't just focus on the perpetrators and the survivors. It has to involve everyone."[74] When we listen to "the experts" we will realize that we are *all* responsible for the "tide of violence" sweeping over us. That is why wholesale cultural change is in order.

Second, the institutions that tort law calls upon to stop sexual harassment—above all employers and schools—are complicit in the abuse of women. They have turned a blind eye to the problem not only because they want to guard their reputation, but also because they are determined to protect powerful internal interests. For schools this includes money-making athletic programs, fraternities with influential alumni, and old-boy networks that generate financial contributions. Consequently, one simply cannot trust established institutions to confront or eliminate the problem. Nor will a small change in incentives of the sort achieved by tort law be nearly enough to change deeply embedded institutional assumptions and practices. The 2015 documentary *The Hunting Ground* seems to reflect this dark understanding of the problem on college campuses.[75]

Third, the sexual harassment problem is not a product of the complexities of human nature or intimate relationships. Rather, it is a consequence of contemporary culture and power relationships. The individual malfeasor approach assumes that while the problem can be reduced, like other forms of criminal and unethical behavior it cannot be eliminated. Although the inequality/subordination approach views the problem as much more severe and deeply rooted in social practices than does the tort/individual malfeasor approach, its adherents repeatedly argue that sexual harassment can indeed be *eliminated* and federal regulators should not relax their supervision of educational institutions until it is.

This understanding of the nature of sexual harassment became particularly evident in the strange events at the University of Iowa in the winter of 2015. The university's president, Sally Mason, responded to student protests by discussing with the student newspaper her own distressing experience with sexual assault as an undergraduate. In passing she said that ending sexual assault altogether is "probably not a realistic goal just given human nature and that's unfortunate." Student activists immediately attacked her for assuming that sexual violence has some foundation in human nature. The university's board of trustees demanded an explanation.[76] It is unlikely that the mayor or police chief of Iowa City would have faced a similar reaction for suggesting that the rate of murder, assault, and other felonies in that city cannot be reduced to zero. Outside college campuses most people still believe that unfortunate features of human nature place some limits on what public policy can accomplish.

MacKinnon's views on sexual harassment have left their mark on the new advocacy groups that have played such a major role in shaping the current debate. In a *New York Times Magazine* article, Emily Bazelon found that "Nationally the leaders of the survivor movement include law students for whom MacKinnon is an intellectual touchstone." According to Know Your IX cofounder and National Women's Law Center fellow Alexandra Brodsky, MacKinnon "resonates with us for recognizing that sexual violence holds back individuals and classes of marginalized people from flourishing."[77] Know Your IX's statement of "values" contains these declarations on the pervasiveness of sexual violence and its connection to institutional power:

> We recognize that sexual and dating violence are manifestations of systemic gender oppression, which cannot be separated from all other forms of oppression, including but not limited to imperialism, racism, classism, homophobia, transphobia, and ableism. The experiences of survivors are shaped by their individual identities and these connected systems of oppression. We also recognize that institutions play a central role in enabling these systems of violence and oppression.

> We recognize that surveillance, incarceration, imperialism, and ideologies of normalcy are tools of state dominance, and we recall the (continuing) histories of the state's co-optation of progressive movements' practices and goals. We aim to resist and reject the violence of the state in and through our work.[78]

As we will see, some of the university Title IX compliance offices established through negotiations with OCR have endorsed a similarly dark view of the world (see chapter 11).

Those who adopt the inequality/subordination position insist that four decades of sexual harassment law have done little to reduce the frequency of harassment. They imply that the "epidemic" of sexual violence on campus began in the 1990s, just as OCR and the federal courts were beginning to address the problem. Despite her praise for the judges who made sexual harassment actionable under Title VII, MacKinnon maintains that "men sexually harass women as often as they did before sexual harassment became illegal."[79] "While courts have developed a comprehensive set of legal rules governing workplace harassment," Joanna Grossman asserts, "the incidence of harassment has not changed."[80] In 2016 Vice President Biden wrote a letter to the nation's college and university presidents claiming that although "domestic violence rates have dropped by 72%" since enactment of the 1994 Violence against Women Act, nothing has changed on campus: "Twenty-two years ago, approximately 1 in every 5 women in college experienced rape or sexual assault. Today that number is the same."[81]

In *The Women's Movement against Sexual Harassment*, Carrie Baker notes that "early feminist activists" not only understood sexual harassment to be "symptomatic of a deeply flawed patriarchal, capitalist, racist system," but also "hoped to use the issue to inspire collective action to fight the root causes of injustice and transform society."[82] Once sexual harassment cases were funneled into the courts and the EEOC, though, "individualized solutions to sexual harassment" predominated, undermining "collective efforts that might have led to deeper social transformation." The challenge for those who view sexual harassment as an element of the broader problem of sexual subordination is to use the political momentum generated by egregious cases of sexual harassment to create a systematic attack on gender inequality, rather than fall into the trap of looking for ways to compensate individual victims and punish individual miscreants.

Although it is unlikely that anyone quite understood it at the time, OCR's abandonment of the standard tort liability approach in 2000 laid the foundation for a switch from the individual malfeasor to the inequality/subordination understanding of the problem. The agency's focus shifted from how schools handle individual cases of misconduct to comprehensive efforts to prevent all forms of sexual harassment. OCR insisted that schools accept responsibility for remedying the effects of harassment regardless of its source and regardless of schools' efforts to punish perpetrators. It required all schools—not just those where harassment had been demonstrated to be widespread—to provide regular training for all students, faculty, and administrators. In short, the emphasis shifted from individual cases to systematic efforts to change institutional structure and organizational culture.

Conclusion

Stepping up federal efforts to reduce sexual violence on campus and in public schools might seem like a "no-brainer"—to use Vice President Biden's favorite term for describing Title IX regulations. No one wants to defend perpetrators of sexual assault. But soon after OCR announced new guidelines in 2011 and 2014, it became clear that even those with big brains in academia, think tanks, and the media had serious criticisms of how these rules affect due process, free speech, and the power of federal administrators. It also became clear that we know less about the extent and causes of the problem or the effectiveness of various prevention strategies than OCR, the Department of Justice, and the White House had claimed.

The next two chapters examine how these controversial rules were developed by federal courts and agencies. This is a long story, not just because policy evolved slowly, with judges and administrators repeatedly denying that they were doing anything new, but also because it involved two statutes, one on employment (Title VII) and the other on education (Title IX). Policymakers applied rules initially developed for adults working in highly structured employment settings to children playing in schoolyards and teenagers doing who knows what in college dorms. OCR's sexual harassment guidelines and investigations have been unusually visible and contentious. Yet for better or worse, they illustrate the usual operation of the American civil rights state.

TEN

A Tale of Two Titles

During Title IX's first two decades, neither the courts nor the Office for Civil Rights (OCR) had much to say about sexual harassment. In the early 1990s, though, a combination of events substantially increased the number of Title IX sexual harassment suits in court and pushed the issue toward the top of OCR's agenda. To address this new issue, both judges and administrators looked to the regulations and case law previously developed under Title VII of the Civil Rights Act. When OCR issued its first set of comprehensive guidelines on the topic in 1997, it not only adopted the main structure of Title VII rules, but also relied on Title VII cases to provide judicial support for this expansion of its regulatory program.

As useful as it was for getting a regulatory initiative underway, this heavy reliance on Title VII precedent overlooked two key differences between the laws. Most obviously Title VII governs the workplace, where most employees are adults. Title IX, in contrast, covers schools, where most students are minors and the rest are less than fully mature. The workplace also tends to be more structured than school life, especially for college students (as college graduates quickly learn to their dismay). Few employers need be worry about what happens during recess and bus rides or in dormitories and fraternity houses. Employees who drink on the job can be fired, unlike college students who can engage in repeated binge drinking and remain in good standing. As a result, the transfer of Title VII rules to the educational context has not gone uncontested. For example, in 1999 Justice Anthony Kennedy argued that "analogies to Title VII" are "inapposite" because "the norms of the adult workplace that have defined hostile environment sexual harassment . . . are not easily translated to peer relationships in schools, where teenage romantic relationships and dating are a part of everyday life."[1]

Just as important are the differences between the regulatory schemes created by Titles VII and IX. Title VII imposes monetary penalties on employers who engage in discrimination: back pay and injunctive relief before 1991, plus compensatory and punitive damages thereafter. Only courts—and not the Equal Employment Opportunity Commission (EEOC)—can impose these penalties on employers. The central role of the courts is indicated by the fact that nearly 15,000 Title VII cases are filed every year.[2] Title IX, in contrast, imposes conditions on recipients of federal grants. After the Supreme Court recognized "implied" private rights of action under Title IX and authorized judges to award monetary damages to victims of sex discrimination, a two-tiered enforcement process developed: one administrative and backed by the threat of termination of federal funds; the other judicial and backed by the threat of injunctions and monetary damages.

Initially everyone expected these two enforcement mechanisms to be guided by the same substantive mandates. But in 2000–01 the Clinton OCR claimed that it could use its administrative enforcement tools to impose requirements going far beyond those mandated by courts in private suits. Precipitating this shift was a duo of Supreme Court decisions that limited schools' liability for sexual harassment perpetrated by teachers (*Gebser v. Lago Vista Independent School District*) and peers (*Davis v. Monroe County School District*).[3] These decisions were roundly condemned by women's groups and in the law reviews. During the Bush administration these critics held out little hope for administrative enforcement of tougher standards. They pinned their hopes on congressional efforts to override the Supreme Court's *Gebser* and *Davis* decisions. But that legislation never got out of committee. As a result, for a full decade OCR's 2001 midnight guidelines appeared to be nothing more than a cri de coeur from an administration rushing out the door.

This chapter traces the development of sexual harassment rules in the employment context under Title VII, and then turns to the equally complicated story of how this framework was applied to educational institutions between 1992 and 2001. It lays the groundwork for chapter 12, which explains how the Obama OCR extended the logic of the 2001 guidelines and developed an enforcement strategy that did not rely on the courts.

Title VII: Finding Common Ground through Common Law

When the word "sex" was added to Title VII on the floor of the House in 1964, no one gave any thought to the problem of sexual harassment. In fact, the term had yet to be invented. As Carrie Baker notes, it was not until 1975 that "a group of feminist activists in Ithaca, New York coined the term 'sexual harassment' to name something they had all experienced but rarely discussed—unwanted sexual demands, comments, looks, or sexual touching in the workplace."[4] As women entered the workforce in greater numbers and took jobs traditionally held by men, the long-simmering problem became a political and legal issue. Some feminist activists focused on consciousness-raising and political organizing; others on changing management practices; and still others on developing legal arguments on behalf of aggrieved female employees.[5] Lin Farley, the leader of the Ithaca group and author of *Sexual Shakedown: The Sexual Harassment of Women on the Job*, became an adviser to Eleanor Holmes Norton, who chaired the EEOC when it issued its first sexual harassment guidelines in 1980. While working on her influential 1979 book *Sexual Harassment of Working Women*, the feminist legal scholar Catharine MacKinnon helped organize a Title IX suit against Yale.[6] The National Organization for Women's Legal Defense and Education Fund launched an effort both to publicize the issue and provide legal support to women filing suit under Title VII.[7]

Early Court Decisions

As noted in the previous chapter, early rounds of litigation did not go well. Judges were reluctant to equate harassment with discrimination or to attribute to Congress an intent to supervise "personal" relationships in the workplace. Between 1976 and 1981 the tide slowly changed due to the combined efforts of the EEOC and federal judges in the District of Columbia (for the Title VII chronology, see table 10-1).

In a 1976 case, *Williams v. Saxbe*, Judge Charles Richey concluded that the conduct of a supervisor who allegedly fired a female subordinate because she would not submit to his demands for sexual favors "created an artificial barrier to employment which was placed before one gender and not the other."[8] The following year the D.C. Circuit became the first appellate court to find that Title VII covers what was quickly becoming known as "quid pro quo" sexual harassment. In *Barnes v. Costle*, Judge Spottswood Robinson explained that the plaintiff "became the target of her superior's sexual desires because she was a woman, and was asked to bow to his demands as the price for holding her job. . . . No male employee was susceptible to such an approach by appellant's supervisor."[9] According to the court, this should be viewed not as a "personal escapade" by the plaintiff's

Table 10-1   Title VII Sexual Harassment Chronology

1970s	Women's groups and feminist lawyers develop arguments characterizing sexual harassment as a form of sex discrimination actionable under Title VII
1976	After losing most sexual harassment cases, plaintiffs finally get a win in *Williams v. Saxbe* (D. D.C. 1976)
1977	The D.C. Circuit becomes the first federal appeals court to recognize sexual harassment as a form of sex discrimination under Title VII (*Barnes v. Costle*)
1980	Shortly after President Carter loses the November election, the EEOC promulgates rules establishing sexual harassment as a form of sex discrimination
1981	D.C. Circuit holds that Title VII covers "hostile environment" harassment, relying in part on Catharine MacKinnon's arguments (*Bundy v. Jackson*)
	Reagan administration tries, unsuccessfully, to rescind EEOC rules
1983	EEOC votes to retain its sexual harassment rules, citing "widespread public and judicial support"
	The number of sexual harassment cases in federal court reaches 52
1986	In *Meritor v. Vinson* the Supreme Court rules that sexual harassment constitutes sex discrimination under Title VII, but declines to endorse the EEOC's rules on liability
1991	Hill–Thomas hearings shine a media spotlight on sexual harassment, making it a major political issue and increasing the number of Title VII suits
	Congress passes Civil Rights Act of 1991, substantially increasing damages in Title VII cases; the number of Title VII cases filed increases sharply soon thereafter
1993	Supreme Court issues its decision in *Harris v. Forklift*; EEOC issues new guidelines reflecting its ruling
1998	Supreme Court decides *Oncale, Burlington Industries v. Ellerth*, and *Faragher v. Boca Raton*
1999	EEOC publishes new guidelines incorporating the three Court decisions

supervisor, but as an action by the supervisor's employer, the Environmental Protection Agency (EPA), which should be held liable for the actions of its agents.[10]

Barnes v. Costle resolved one issue—whether "quid pro quo" harassment constitutes sex discrimination—but it raised an issue that took decades to resolve: Exactly *when* is an employer responsible for sexual harassment by one or more of its employees? Two members of the D.C. Circuit panel implied that an employer is always "strictly liable" for the tangible employment decisions of its supervisors—that is, held responsible regardless of how much they knew about it or tried to prevent it. The third, George MacKinnon (father of Catharine) preferred the more lenient "negligence" ("knew or should have known") standard.[11]

In 1981 another panel of the D.C. Circuit took a step beyond *Barnes v. Costle*, holding that so-called "hostile environment" harassment—in which no tangible employment action has been taken against the plaintiff—also violates Title VII. Writing for the court in *Bundy v. Jackson*, Judge J. Skelly Wright agreed with the plaintiff that "the sexually stereotyped insults and demeaning propositions to which she was indisputably subjected and which caused her anxiety and debilitation" had "illegally poisoned" her "psychological and emotional work environment."[12] Gender-based stereotypes and insults, Judge Wright insisted, are just as serious as the raced-based insults and stereotypes federal judges had previously determined could create a discriminatory "hostile environment." "How then," he asked, "can sexual harassment, which injects the most demeaning sexual stereotypes into the general work environment and which always represents an intentional assault on an individual's innermost privacy, not be illegal?" Citing Catharine MacKinnon's recently published *Sexual Harassment of Working Women*, Judge Wright argued that sexual harassment on the job should be understood both as pervasive and as linked to women's unequal status: "So long as women remain inferiors in the employment hierarchy, they may have little recourse against harassment beyond the legal recourse [the plaintiff] seeks in this case."[13] Years later MacKinnon praised judges on the D.C. Circuit for using "the common law process to build a sex equality doctrine that, instead of reflecting the interests of the dominant . . . advanced the interests of the less powerful."[14]

This was hardly the D.C. Circuit's first effort to transform the law on behalf of "the less powerful." During the 1970s that court was the most liberal in the country. It took the lead in pushing for more stringent environmental and consumer protection regulation, and was the primary architect of the "new administrative law" that sought to increase the power of public interest groups and reduce the influence of business interests.[15] Judge Wright was the author of one of the most ambitious desegregation plans in the country.[16] The court's rulings in the protracted *Adams v. Richardson* litigation pushed OCR to enforce civil rights laws more aggressively (see chapter 4). Not only was the list of the D.C. Circuit's legal innovations in those years long, but its reputation for going its own way led to confrontations with the Supreme Court.[17] It is therefore not surprising that the first sexual harassment case heard by the Supreme Court came from the D.C. Circuit, and on the key question of liability the justices refused to endorse that court's position.

The EEOC's Midnight Guidelines

Judge Wright bolstered his opinion in *Bundy v. Jackson* by claiming that judges "owe considerable deference" to the guidelines the EEOC had issued two months before.[18] Over the next decade federal judges cited these guidelines as often as the opinions of the D.C. Circuit. The combination of the two created a bandwagon onto which almost all judges jumped.

As early as 1975 the EEOC had taken the position that "quid pro quo" harassment constitutes sex discrimination under Title VII.[19] Two years later it investigated a complaint lodged by a woman forced to dress provocatively in order to keep her job as a "lobby hostess." The commission concluded that an employer violates Title VII when it "injects sexual stereotypes into the work environment."[20] Far more important were the rules it announced in November 1980, a few days after Ronald Reagan defeated President Carter (see table 10-2).[21] These rules were largely the work of EEOC chair Eleanor Holmes Norton, an energetic and outspoken Carter appointee. While they were brief, only seven paragraphs, they provided the framework for almost all subsequent discussion of sexual harassment.

The EEOC guidelines offered what became the standard definition of sexual harassment: "Unwelcome sexual advances, requests for sexual favors, and other verbal or physical conduct of a sexual nature." Adopting Catharine MacKinnon's terminology, the EEOC then distinguished between (a) "quid pro quo" harassment—where submission "is made either implicitly or explicitly" a condition of employment or "used as the basis for employment decisions"—and (b) "hostile environment" harassment—where the conduct in question "has the purpose or effect of unreasonably interfering with an individual's work performance, or creating an intimidating, hostile, or offensive working environment."[22]

The 1980 guidelines made a second distinction, one that became controversial almost immediately. Employers would be held liable for sexual harassment by *co-workers* only if the employer "knew or should have known" about the offending behavior and failed to take "immediate and appropriate corrective action." But employers would be held "strictly liable" for the behavior of *supervisors*, regardless of whether it took the form of quid pro quo or hostile environment harassment. This meant employers would be held responsible for *all* misbehavior by a supervisor, regardless of what they knew, what measures they had taken to stop sexual harassment, or whether the person subject to abuse had filed a complaint. Although the guidelines advised employers to "take all necessary steps to

Table 10-2   Key Elements of 1980 EEOC Guidelines

1. "Unwelcome sexual advances, requests for sexual favors, and other verbal or physical conduct of a sexual nature constitutes sexual harassment" when submission "is made either implicitly or explicitly" a condition of employment or "used as the basis for employment decisions." ["quid pro quo" harassment]

2. Such conduct also violates Title VII when it "has the purpose or effect of unreasonably interfering with an individual's work performance, or creating an intimidating, hostile, or offensive working environment." ["hostile environment" harassment]

3. Employers are strictly liable for harassment of either sort by supervisors "regardless of whether the specific acts complained of were authorized or even forbidden by the employer and regardless of whether the employer knew or should have known of their occurrence."

4. For "conduct between fellow employees" or between customers and employees, the employer is liable when the employer or any of its supervisors "knows or should have known of the conduct, unless it can be shown that it took immediate and appropriate corrective action."

5. Since "prevention is the best tool for elimination of sexual harassment," employers "should take all steps necessary to prevent sexual harassment from occurring, such as affirmatively raising the subject, expressing strong disapproval, developing appropriate sanctions, informing employees of their right to raise and how to raise the issue . . . and developing methods to sensitize all concerned."

prevent sexual harassment from occurring," such preventative measures would never insulate employers from liability for supervisors' misconduct.

The fact that these rules were issued so soon after President Carter's unexpected electoral defeat infuriated the incoming Reagan administration and some members of the newly Republican Senate. The Task Force on Regulatory Relief chaired by Vice President George H. W. Bush targeted them for special scrutiny. Meanwhile Senator Orrin Hatch, the incoming chair of the Senate Committee on Labor and Human Resources, held hearings on the subject and proposed legislation narrowing the EEOC's jurisdiction over sexual harassment. When Clarence Thomas became chair of the EEOC, he devoted few resources to enforcing the 1980 guidelines.

In the end, though, the EEOC's guidelines survived. Democrats in the House held hearings to demonstrate popular support for the rules. Women's groups mobilized their supporters. In 1983 the full commission voted to retain them, "citing widespread public and judicial support."[23] But that hardly turned

Reagan administration officials into converts. When the sexual harassment issue first went to the Supreme Court in 1986, both Solicitor General Charles Fried and Chairman Thomas urged the Court *not* to follow the EEOC's guidelines on the liability issue. As we will see, the Court chose to punt on the contentious liability question.

The EEOC was not the only federal agency to attack sexual harassment in the workplace. Responding to pressure from a House subcommittee, the Office of Personnel Management issued a policy statement similar to the EEOC's to guide the employment practices of federal agencies. The Department of Labor's Office of Federal Contract Compliance Programs applied the same rules to companies receiving federal contracts.[24] The issue was clearly striking a chord with many women and public officials.

Many Cases, Little Clarity

One sign of the growing acceptance of the argument that sexual harassment constitutes a form of sex discrimination came in 1982, when a panel of the Eleventh Circuit held for the plaintiff in a hostile environment case. *Henson v. City of Dundee* laid out an elaborate five-part test that was adopted by many other courts as they confronted a growing number of sexual harassment suits.[25] The Eleventh Circuit, though, refused to endorse the EEOC's strict liability standard for supervisors' misconduct. Instead it found that an employer could be held responsible for the creation of a hostile environment by a supervisor only if the employer "knew or should have known" of the misconduct in question. This dispute over liability rules roiled the federal courts for a decade and a half. Judges were all over the map on this question until the Supreme Court finally resolved it in 1998—more than two decades after federal courts had declared sexual harassment a form of sex discrimination (see table 10-3).

That was but one of the many issues on which federal judges disagreed in the 1980s and 1990s. How serious or pervasive must harassment become to create an actionable hostile environment? When is it reasonable to say that an employer "should have known" about harassment by supervisors or co-workers? How does one determine whether conduct is "welcome"? What evidence should be admissible in the common he-said–she-said controversy? Does the display of pornography by itself create a hostile environment?

In 1986 the Supreme Court made its first attempt to address these questions. Chief Justice William Rehnquist's terse opinion for a unanimous Court in *Meritor Savings Bank v. Vinson* held that both quid pro quo and hostile environment harassment constitute forms of sex discrimination prohibited by Title VII.[26] But Rehnquist made little effort either to explain *why* this is so or what liability standards should apply. He insisted that the court below had "erred in concluding that employers are always automatically liable for sexual harassment by their

Table 10-3   Major Supreme Court Decisions on Sexual Harassment

1986   *Meritor Savings Bank v. Vinson*
      Confirmed that sexual harassment constitutes a form of Title VII sex
         discrimination
      Unanimous, Rehnquist for the Court

1992   ***Franklin v. Gwinnett County Public Schools***
      Authorized monetary damages in Title IX sex harassment cases brought by
         private parties
      Unanimous, White for the Court
      Scalia, Rehnquist, and Thomas concur in judgment only (concurring
         opinion by Scalia)

1993   *Harris v. Forklift Systems, Inc.*
      Explained the extent of harm needed to sustain "hostile environment" claims
      Unanimous, O'Connor for the Court
      Ginsburg and Scalia each write concurring opinions

1998   *Oncale v. Sundowner Offshore Services*
      Ruled that same-sex sexual harassment is actionable under Title VII
      Unanimous, Scalia for the Court

1998   *Burlington Industries v. Ellerth*
      Established Title VII liability standard for sexual harassment by supervisors
      7-2, majority opinion by Kennedy
      Concurring opinion by Ginsburg
      Dissenting opinion by Thomas for himself and Scalia

1998   *Faragher v. City of Boca Raton*
      Established Title VII liability standard for sexual harassment by supervisors
      7-2, majority opinion by Souter
      Dissenting opinion by Thomas for himself and Scalia

1998   ***Gebser v. Lago Vista Independent School District***
      Established Title IX liability standard for sexual harassment by teachers
      5-4, majority opinion by O'Connor
      Dissenting opinions by Stevens and Ginsburg for themselves, Souter,
         and Breyer

1999   ***Davis v. Monroe County Board of Education***
      Established Title IX liability standard for peer sexual harassment
      5-4, majority opinion by O'Connor
      Dissenting opinion by Kennedy for himself, Rehnquist, Scalia, and Thomas

Note: Title VII cases in italics; Title IX cases in bold and italics.

supervisors." Title VII "surely evinces an intent to place some limits on the acts of employees for which employers under Title VII are to be held responsible." But Rehnquist refused to endorse the more lenient negligence standard recommended by the solicitor general, and "decline[d] the parties' invitation to issue a definitive rule on employer liability."[27] The chief justice offered only the enigmatic guidance that "Congress wanted courts to look to agency principles for guidance in this area," while warning that "such common law principles may not be transferable in all particulars to Title VII."[28] What these limits might be, the Court refused to say. Rehnquist was equally inscrutable on the status of EEOC's guidelines: "While not controlling upon the courts by reason of authority," they "do constitute a body of experience and informed judgment to which courts and litigants may properly resort for guidance." By saying so little, employment law scholar David Oppenheimer observed, "the *Meritor* Court gave us a decade of confusion."[29]

A similar reluctance to establish clear rules was evident seven years later when the Court handed down *Harris v. Forklift Systems* in 1993.[30] Justice Sandra Day O'Connor's opinion for a unanimous Court addressed the question of when co-workers' insults and "unwanted sexual innuendos" became severe enough to constitute a hostile environment. She tried to discover "a middle path between making actionable any conduct that is merely offensive and requiring the conduct to cause a tangible psychological injury." On the one hand, the "mere utterance of an epithet which engenders offensive feelings in an employee" or conduct that is "not severe or pervasive enough to create an objectively hostile or abusive work environment—an environment that a reasonable person would find hostile or abusive" does not violate Title VII.[31] On the other hand, "Title VII comes into play before the harassing conduct leads to a nervous breakdown."[32] This meant that a court could determine whether a work environment in question is "hostile" "only by looking at all the circumstances," including the frequency and severity of the conduct, "whether it is physically threatening or humiliating," and whether it "unreasonably interferes with an employee's work performance." In typically O'Connoresque fashion, Justice O'Connor concluded that "no single factor is required." In a masterpiece of understatement, she conceded, "This is not, and by its nature cannot be, a mathematically precise test."[33]

In *Harris v. Forklift Systems* the Supreme Court could have helped out lower court judges by either relying upon or disagreeing with two 1990 EEOC guidance documents spelling out what constitutes a hostile environment. But it did neither, seeing no need "to answer today all the potential questions" raised by the case. In a concurrence, Justice Antonin Scalia complained, "As a practical matter, today's holding lets virtually unguided juries decide whether sex-related conduct engaged in (or permitted by) an employer is egregious enough to warrant an award of damages." But he conceded that he knew "of no test more faithful to the inherently vague statutory language than the one the Court today adopts."[34]

The EEOC Strives for Uniformity and Clarity

The difficulties created by the Supreme Court's reluctance to provide guidance to lower courts became more severe as sexual harassment complaints and court suits surged in the 1990s. In 1990 the EEOC received 5,557 sexual harassment complaints. By 1995 that figure had nearly tripled to 15,549.[35] Damage awards quadrupled. Two factors contributed to this growth. First was the Clarence Thomas–Anita Hill controversy in the fall of 1991. Never before had sexual harassment in the workplace received such sustained media and public attention. Second, Congress included in the Civil Rights Act of 1991 provisions allowing judges to award compensatory and punitive damages in all Title VII cases. This made Title VII litigation much more attractive for lawyers working on a contingency fee basis.[36]

One consequence of the joint court–agency responsibility for enforcing civil rights laws is that agencies—here both the EEOC and OCR—must find a way to cope with disagreements among federal courts that can fester for years without resolution by the Supreme Court. Most federal agencies are committed to applying the law in a nationally uniform manner rather than interpreting the law differently in each circuit.[37] They have stronger mechanisms for ensuring national uniformity than do the federal courts, which must rely on a Supreme Court that accepts fewer than eighty cases per year. As a result, agencies frequently try to interpret court decisions so as to discover (or exaggerate or invent) their common ground. They also try to identify the general direction that courts are taking and to explain why they believe some court decisions are incorrect. In effect, agencies are forced to play the role of junior varsity Supreme Court, struggling to identify an elusive coherence in conflicting lower court decisions. If the EEOC's 1980 midnight regulations were a bold act of administrative entrepreneurship, its later guidance was largely an effort to establish uniform standards for processing thousands of complaints.

The guidelines it issued in 1990, 1994, and 1999 were largely commentaries on court decisions and on complaints the EEOC itself had investigated. The 1990 guidelines addressed several issues "in light of the developing law" after *Meritor v. Vinson.* The commission devoted its second set of guidelines to "analyz[ing] the Supreme Court's decision in *Harris* and its effects on Commission investigations." The third explained and built upon the liability rules established by the two 1998 Supreme Court cases discussed below, *Burlington Industries v. Ellerth* and *Faragher v. City of Boca Raton.*[38] In marked contrast to

OCR, the EEOC made no attempt to strike out on its own. Recognizing its limited enforcement authority, it modified its rules on liability to conform to Supreme Court decisions.

The Supreme Court's Liability Framework

Until 1998 the EEOC continued to hold employers strictly liable for supervisors' conduct that creates a hostile environment. Some circuit courts agreed, others did not. The federal judiciary's disarray became particularly apparent in 1997, when the full Seventh Circuit could not find majority support for *any* liability standard. Not only did the court produce eight lengthy opinions, but three of them were written by particularly eminent jurists, Richard Posner, Frank Easterbrook, and Diane Wood. This case finally forced the Supreme Court to recognize that the lower courts had failed "to derive manageable standards to govern employer liability for hostile environment harassment perpetrated by supervisory employees."[39]

In his opinion for the majority in *Burlington Industries v. Ellerth*, Justice Kennedy tried to stake out a middle position between the strict liability and negligence standards.[40] Justice David Souter did the same in a companion case, *Faragher v. City of Boca Raton*.[41] The two dissenters in these cases, Justices Thomas and Scalia, described the Court's liability rules as "a product of willful policy-making pure and simple," a "whole-cloth creation that draws no support from the legal principles" it cited, and "Delphic pronouncements" that "leave the dirty work to the lower courts."[42] Kennedy and Souter made little effort to hide or deny their innovation, claiming that "Congress has left it to the courts to determine controlling agency law principles in a new and difficult area of federal law."[43]

The liability scheme created by the Supreme Court in 1998 had three parts. First, when sexual harassment takes the form of "tangible employment action" (such as a raise, promotion, change in work requirements, or termination taken by a supervisor), the employer will be held strictly liable for the supervisor's conduct. Second, when sexual harassment takes the form of creation of a hostile environment by a fellow employee, the employer will be held liable only if he "knew or should have known" about the conduct of the co-workers. Third, when sexual harassment takes the form of a hostile environment created by a supervisor who does not take "tangible employment action" against the complainant, the employer will be held strictly liable *unless* he can demonstrate (a) that he "exercised reasonable care to prevent and correct promptly any sexually harassing behavior," and (b) that the complaining employee "unreasonably failed to take advantage of any preventative or corrective opportunities provided by the employer or to avoid harm otherwise." The burden is on the employer to demonstrate both (a) and (b). In 1999 the EEOC incorporated these liability rules into its guidelines, and they have provided the basic framework for Title VII cases ever since.

The Supreme Court's justification for this compromise was long on discussion of "agency" principles and the 1957 Restatement (Second) of Agency, but short on explanation of why this constitutes sound public policy. One of the few judges to weigh the costs and benefits of alternative liability rules was Richard Posner, whose position in the Seventh Circuit case was quite similar to that eventually adopted by the Supreme Court. Posner's opinion offers the clearest rationale for the liability rules that have governed Title VII sexual harassment regulation since 1998. His opinion also helps explain many of the issues that later emerged under Title IX.

The main purpose of sexual harassment law, Judge Posner argued, is deterrence. Compensation is secondary since the harm suffered by the victim is not primarily pecuniary. From this perspective, it does little good to hold employers responsible for employees' actions of which employers have no knowledge and over which they have no control. This would impose costs on employers, employees, and customers—many of whom are women—without providing any additional deterrence. At the same time, Title VII should not create incentives for employers to stick their heads in the sand or make sure that no complaints reach their desks. The goal must be to ensure that employers have a clear policy prohibiting all forms of sexual harassment; that they establish and publicize grievance procedures that allow victims to complain; that they quickly and fairly investigate the complaints; and that they take action adequate to stop the harassment and address its effects. The "knew or should have known" standard accomplishes this for hostile environment harassment by co-workers. On this almost everyone seemed to agree.

In contrast, strict liability is appropriate for "tangible employment actions" taken by supervisors because they are far easier for the employer to monitor than are informal relationships among peers. A strict liability standard creates strong incentives for employers to "monitor the exercise of this delegated authority very carefully, knowing that it will be liable if the authority is abused." Such monitoring "should be relatively easy to do," since in "well-managed companies" such decisions are already "subject to rules, and to review by higher-ups." Indeed, "it is usually a mistake for a firm, quite without regard to any potential legal liability, to give a supervisor unilateral authority to alter a subordinate's terms or conditions of employment significantly."[44]

Sexual harassment by supervisors that does not culminate in a tangible employment action, Posner reasoned, is the most difficult part of the problem. On the one hand, because supervisors can exert informal pressure on subordinates, employees may be less inclined to file complaints against the supervisors. This consideration supports a higher level of employer liability for hostile environment harassment by a supervisor than by a peer. On the other hand, holding employers responsible for behavior that is completely hidden from them has serious disadvantages. Unlike most torts, sexual harassment is usually observed only by the victim and the perpetrator. An employer will almost always know "whether one of his employees sustains a physical injury on the job," but "he is much less likely to know that one of his employees is being sexually harassed."[45] Posner's analysis thus provides a basis for imposing a somewhat higher liability standard for hostile environment conduct perpetrated by supervisors, but not one that rises to the level of strict liability. In effect that is what the Supreme Court did by placing the burden on employers to demonstrate that they had taken "reasonable care to prevent and correct promptly any sexually harassing behavior," and that the plaintiff had "unreasonably" failed to take advantage of grievance procedures.

In an observation that anticipated some of the most difficult issues later confronted by universities, Posner noted that employers cannot succeed in "stamping out this sort of harassment without going to extreme expense and greatly curtailing the privacy of its employees, as by putting them under continuous video surveillance." "Large companies have thousands of supervisory employees. Are they all to be put under video surveillance? Subjected to periodic lie-detector tests? Trailed on business trips by company spies? Even the EEOC does not go so far." Moreover, "Romantic encounters, including romantic encounters between supervisors and supervised, are a fact of the workplace. Title VII does not purport to forbid them, and would be quixotic if it did." Some of these relationships "are abusive from the start, and some start well and turn ugly and engender charges of sexual harassment that sometimes have and sometimes lack merit." The features that distinguish a "fully consensual" relationship from a "coercive" one "will often be invisible to the supervisor's superiors." To the claim that imposing strict liability will force employers to transform the organizational culture, Posner replied that this is "easy to say," but "hard to do."[46]

The Durable Compromise

The *Ellerth–Faragher* rules incorporated many of the measures advocated by women's groups and the EEOC in 1980, but at the same time provided business with a framework it could readily accept. The Supreme Court's framework has won praise from many quarters. Charles Epp has convincingly argued that the potent combination of Title VII rules and the zeal of personnel administration professionals for changing organizational practices have proved to be "key mechanisms for reducing harassment."[47] According to David Oppenheimer, a law professor who wrote an amicus brief on behalf of the plaintiff in *Burlington Industries v. Ellerth*, the Supreme Court's liability decisions "promise that rare thing in employment discrimination law—a rule that encourages employers to take meaningful steps to prevent discrimination while increasing the possibility that victimized employees will be able to recover damages for their injuries."[48] Labor law experts Michael Harper and Joan Flynn describe these twin cases as both "an extraordinary example of the Supreme Court exercising its authority to engage in lawmaking in the manner of a traditional common law court" and a rare instance in which "the Court not only brought much-needed clarity to the law, but also produced a coherent and logically defensible rule with which both plaintiffs and employees could readily live."[49] The *New York Times*'s Linda Greenhouse agreed, noting that "Few Supreme Court decisions in recent memory have been received as enthusiastically across the spectrum of interested parties . . . praised by women's rights leaders, the Chamber of Commerce, and federal trial judges alike for providing the first clear set of rules in this rapidly evolving area of employment law."[50] Greater clarity contributed to a decline in litigation. The number of Title VII sexual harassment suits had risen steadily between 1991 and 1998. Over the next decade the number declined by 25 percent.[51]

Given the extent of legal change since 1976, it is striking to hear feminist legal scholars declare how little progress has been made in reducing workplace harassment. In 2004 Catharine MacKinnon gloomily concluded, "So far as is known, men sexually harass women as often as they did before sexual harassment became illegal."[52] Hofstra Law professor Joanne Grossman sounds a similar refrain, calling the Supreme Court's 1998 decisions "the final triumph of form over substance in sexual harassment law."[53] When attention shifted from employment to schools, women's groups and feminist legal scholars urged OCR and the courts to impose liability standards more demanding than the *Ellerth–Faragher* framework. But the Supreme Court moved in just the opposite direction, holding that Title IX demands less of schools than Title VII demands of employers. This eventually led OCR to abandon the tort model altogether and to construct an alternative regulatory strategy.

Sexual Harassment Regulation Goes to School

For a quarter century after enactment of Title IX, OCR paid little attention to the sexual harassment issue. In 1981 it circulated an internal memo stating that sexual harassment constitutes a form of sex discrimination. It periodically distributed a pamphlet titled "Sexual Harassment: It's Not Academic," describing conduct by school "employees and agents" (but not peers) that might violate Title IX.[54] OCR neither devoted resources to enforcement nor provided schools with substantial guidance. The courts, too, remained silent. Most of the plaintiffs in the Title IX suit that Catharine MacKinnon and others brought against Yale in the late 1970s were dismissed, and the court found that those who remained had not suffered harassment that violated Title IX.[55]

In the first half of the 1990s three sets of factors converged to move sexual harassment to the top of OCR's agenda (see table 10-4). The first was publicity. On the heels of the 1991 Hill–Thomas hearings, *Seventeen* magazine published

Table 10-4   Title IX Sexual Harassment Chronology

1980	Second Circuit dismisses *Alexander v. Yale*, the first sexual harassment case brought under Title IX
1991	Hill–Thomas hearings and *Seventeen* magazine articles put media spotlight on sexual harassment both in the workplace and in schools
1992	In *Franklin v. Gwinnett County Schools*, Supreme Court authorizes monetary damage awards against school districts that turn a blind eye to sexual misconduct by teachers
1993	First reported federal lower court decision finding a school district liable for peer-on-peer sexual harassment; over the next five years twenty-four federal district court decisions and six circuit court decisions are handed down on peer harassment
1996	OCR releases "proposed policy guidance" on sexual harassment under Title IX
1997	OCR publishes in *Federal Register* the final version of "Sexual Harassment Guidance: Harassment of Students by School Employees, Other Students, or Third Parties"
1998	Supreme Court holds school districts liable for harassment of a student by a teacher only if school officials have "actual notice" of the misconduct and are "deliberately indifferent" to it (*Gebser*)
1999	Supreme Court holds school districts liable only for student-on-student harassment "serious enough to have the *systemic* effect of denying the victim equal access" to education (*Davis*)
2000	OCR proposes "revised guidance" explaining why it will *not* revise its 1997 guidelines in response to *Gebser* and *Davis*
2001	On the day before President Clinton left office, OCR releases "Revised Sexual Harassment Guidance," asserting its authority to enforce Title IX rules more stringent than those endorsed by the Supreme Court in *Davis* and *Gebser*
2010	OCR distributes "Dear Colleague Letter" on bullying that includes new rules on racial, sexual, and "gender-based" harassment
2011	OCR issues Dear Colleague Letter on steps to reduce sexual violence
2013	OCR and the Department of Justice sign consent agreement with the University of Montana that will serve as a "blueprint" for agreements with other universities
2014	White House releases "Not Alone" report on sexual violence; OCR simultaneously releases forty-six-page guidance document, "Questions and Answers on Title IX and Sexual Violence"
	OCR announces investigation of scores of universities for Title IX violations

an article on sexual harassment in elementary and secondary schools, and it encouraged readers to report on their experiences. Over 4,000 students did so. A subsequent article in the magazine reported that 90 percent of the respondents had been subject to some form of sexual harassment, nearly 40 percent on a daily basis. In 1993 the American Association of University Women published a study entitled *Hostile Hallways* claiming that the vast majority of high school girls had been subject to sexual harassment of some form.[56] Although hardly systematic studies, these finding were widely reported in the press.

The second factor was congressional action. In 1990 Congress passed the Clery Act, which requires colleges to report the frequency of campus crimes, including sexual assault, to the Department of Education. In 1994 it enacted the Violence Against Women Act (VAWA), which, among many other things, provided funding to reduce sexual assault on campus. VAWA's chief sponsor was Senator Joseph Biden (D-Del.), who as vice president became a driving force behind the expansion of Title IX regulation.

The Supreme Court Opens the Door

The third development was the Supreme Court's 1992 ruling in *Franklin v. Gwinnett County Public Schools*. A unanimous Court held that a student who had been subjected to serious and repeated sexual misconduct by a teacher could sue the school district for monetary damages under Title IX. The outcome was surprising because time and again the Rehnquist Court had restricted the use of private suits to force state and local governments to comply with federal mandates.[57] As chapter 3 explained, in 1979 a narrow majority on the Court had made an exception for Title IX, arguing in effect that federal courts had already entertained too many Title IX suits to put the genie back into the bottle.[58] Instead of confining that exception, the Court's *Franklin* decision expanded plaintiffs' incentives to file private rights of action under Title IX. The Court ruled that when the judiciary finds an "implied" private right of action, it must infer that Congress intended to create an effective judicial remedy. As Justice Scalia pointed out in his concurrence, this means "that the most questionable of private rights will also be the most expansively remediable."[59]

Franklin v. Gwinnett is probably an instance in which the facts of the case before the Court influenced the development of legal doctrine. If the allegations were true and the issue of who was telling the truth remains in doubt years later—this was a case of severe abuse of authority by a high school teacher against a fifteen-year-old student.[60] Unlike many Title IX cases, this controversy did not seem to require the application of educational expertise. It was just the sort of tort suit that judges are accustomed to handling. Since the facts of this case seemed to indicate that state courts had not dealt adequately with serious abuse of school authority, why shouldn't the federal courts step in?

Especially after the Court's 1986 decision in *Meritor, Franklin* did not seem like a big leap. If sexual harassment of an employee by a supervisor constitutes sex discrimination, Justice White wrote, "the same rule should apply when a teacher sexually harasses and abuses a student."[61] A number of women's groups and civil rights groups filed amicus briefs on behalf of the plaintiff, but not a single educational group offered support for the local school district.[62] This may have assured the Court that it was not imposing a heavy burden on schools. All the questions that had bedeviled courts for years under Title VII—what constitutes harassment, when employers are responsible for the behavior of supervisors and other employees, what steps employers must take to reduce harassment—remained unanswered. The Supreme Court simply announced that monetary damages were available, and left everything else to the lower courts.

Most of the cases subsequently arriving in federal court involved peer harassment, not the sort of misconduct by teachers found in *Franklin*. They required the lower courts to determine when public schools should be held responsible for the "hostile environment" created by other elementary and secondary school students. The first reported decision on school liability for student-on-student harassment appeared in 1993.[63] By 1998 there were twenty-four published federal district court decisions on the subject, as well as rulings by six circuit courts.[64] Once again, federal courts were all over the map on the liability standard to apply. Some ruled that schools were liable if they "knew or should have known" about behavior that created the hostile environment. Others held that schools would be held responsible only if they had "actual knowledge" of the behavior and failed to take corrective action. The Fifth Circuit argued that a school violates Title IX only "if it treated sexual harassment of boys more seriously than sexual harassment of girls."[65]

In 1997 a federal district court judge in New Hampshire noted with distress that "whether and to what extent school districts can be found liable under Title IX for peer sexual harassment" was "an issue undecided" by the Supreme Court. Neither the Court nor the law's legislative history offered much guidance for "interpreting the scope of Title IX." He urged Congress "to carry out its legislative responsibilities and to address these issues squarely so that policy will be made where it should be made—in Congress—and not by default in the courts."[66] Congress remained silent.

The resulting legal uncertainty—especially when combined with the threat of significant punitive damages—alarmed school officials. To make matters worse, as the legal sociologist Jodi Short has documented, articles in professional journals such as *Education Week* "provided an exaggerated assessment of the state of the law on peer harassment at the time," seriously overstating both the frequency of litigation and the size of monetary awards while "ignoring or downplaying the controversy in the courts."[67] Realizing that it would take years for the Supreme Court to address all the issues raised in the lower courts, school officials pressed OCR to explain what Title IX requires of them.

Working VII to IX

In 1997 OCR announced its first set of sexual harassment guidelines, rules that were far more detailed than any previously issued under either Title VII or Title IX. These guidelines took an ambiguous form. On the one hand, for the first time in nearly twenty years, OCR employed some elements of notice-and-comment rulemaking. It issued proposed guidelines in October 1996, and published a final version six months later. In the interim it made a few adjustments in response to suggestions by school officials. On the other hand, OCR refused to call the process "rulemaking," claiming only to offer "policy guidance." The public was not asked to comment on the wisdom of its mandate, but only "on whether the Guidance is *clear and complete*."[68] As usual, OCR insisted that it was doing nothing new: "The standards in the Guidance reflect OCR's longstanding nationwide practice and reflect well established legal principles developed under Title VII of the Civil Rights Act."[69] Nor did it make submitting comments easy. It held no public hearings, required interested parties to obtain a copy of the proposal from the Department of Education, and insisted that they respond within a month. Not surprisingly, it received only eighty comments, a number far less than the thousands received for most major rules.[70] OCR did not submit its guidelines to review by the Office of Management and Budget or comply with Title IX's requirement that rules be signed by the president.

Procedure aside, the most striking feature of the 1997 guidelines (as well as those issued in 2001) was their laser-like focus on legal precedent. They read like a heavily footnoted appellate decision, devoid of any discussion of the frequency of sexual harassment, the consequences of various forms of harassment, or alternative methods for attacking the problem. Since Title IX cases were inconsistent and relatively few in number, OCR relied most heavily on Title VII case law. Where federal courts disagreed, agency lawyers did not hesitate to weigh in on the "correct" legal answer. Where its rules were more demanding than judicial rulings, OCR advised schools that "following the Guidance may be the safest way for schools in these States to ensure compliance with the requirements of Title IX." Nervous school officials could easily interpret this as a veiled threat: even where the circuit courts have limited your liability for monetary damages, we can still investigate you and generate bad publicity.

Nevertheless, OCR clearly saw itself as establishing rules that would be enforced by federal judges rather than through the congenitally ineffective funding cutoff. Since courts "generally benefit from and defer to the expertise of an agency" with "authority to interpret and enforce" a statute, a "beneficial result of the Guidelines will be to provide courts with ready access to the standards used" by OCR.[71] It promised to work with the Department of Justice in litigation before the federal courts "to shape the evolution of Title IX law in a manner consistent with the Guidance." No doubt the Supreme Court's decision in *Franklin* increased OCR's confidence that the Court would follow its lead.

The 1997 guidelines hewed closely to the Title VII rules developed by the EEOC and the courts over the preceding twenty years. Their definition of harassment was nearly identical to that of the EEOC, emphasizing the distinction between "welcomed" or "unwelcomed" conduct. Like the EEOC it distinguished between "quid pro quo" and "hostile environment" harassment, and between harassment by teachers and by students. Although OCR did not explicitly establish strict liability for "hostile environment" harassment by teachers, its interpretation of "agency principles" was so broad that it would be unlikely for a school district *not* to be found responsible for any form of harassment by a school employee.[72]

OCR justified these rules by linking them to the underlying purpose of Title IX, equal educational opportunity. The wording it used to describe prohibited conduct (and speech) is worth quoting since it is significantly broader than the version eventually endorsed by the Supreme Court (see table 10-5 for a comparison). According to OCR's 1997 and 2001 guidance, "conduct of a sexual nature" creates a "hostile environment" and consequently violates Title IX if it is "sufficiently severe, persistent, or pervasive to limit a student's ability to participate in or benefit from the educational program or to create a hostile or abusive educational environment." Conduct that is "sufficiently severe, but not persistent or pervasive," it maintained, "can result in hostile environment sexual harassment." To determine "whether conduct is sufficiently severe, persistent, or pervasive, the conduct should be considered from both a subjective and objective perspective."[73] The agency further broadened the class of prohibited conduct by stipulating that a "hostile environment may exist even though there is no tangible injury to the student" at whom it is directed, and "can occur even if the harassment is not targeted specifically at the individual complainant." Nor must harassment be directed at members of the opposite sex to violate Title IX.

The most important divergence between Title VII rules and OCR's Title IX guidelines was the level of detail the latter included on grievance procedures, training, and remedies. To some extent this reflects the contrasting structures and contexts of Titles VII and IX. Courts and the EEOC established *liability* rules under Title VII. Especially since workplace grievance procedures are often governed by union contracts, the EEOC and the courts were content to judge the adequacy of these procedures on a case-by-case basis. In the employment context remedies are relatively straightforward: firing or reassigning the miscreant; reinstating or promoting the victim; paying back wages to those wrongfully dismissed; and emphasizing to others that sexual harassment will not be permitted in the workplace. The emphasis is not on what employers *must* do, but on what they *can* do to avoid liability. Regulators offer "safe harbors" rather than impose specific mandates.

OCR, in contrast, is expected to explain to educational institutions what they *must* do to qualify for federal funds. It was not shy about doing so in the 1997 guidelines, and it became more directive in each subsequent iteration. For example, schools violate Title IX if their grievance procedures fail to incorporate every element specified by OCR—"regardless of whether harassment occurred." Schools must designate a Title IX coordinator, and ensure that everyone in that office has "adequate training as to what constitutes sexual harassment." Schools must take "corrective action" to "address the effects on those who have been subject to harassment." This can include providing new housing, issuing no-contact orders, course and grade changes, tutoring, professional counseling, and tuition adjustments. In some cases schools will be expected "to provide training for the larger school community." Since public schools cannot expel all harassers, they must be prepared to offer counseling to those who remain in school. In short, schools must not only end the specific form of harassment that led to an individual complaint but also "take steps reasonably calculated to end *any* harassment, *eliminate* a hostile environment if it has been created, and *prevent* harassment from occurring again"—a task that is extraordinarily difficult if not Sisyphean in large institutions.

In 1996–97 OCR recognized that sexual harassment rules can infringe upon due process and free speech rights. It urged schools to institute procedures "that ensure the Title IX rights of the complainant, while at the same time according due process rights to the parties involved."[74] In a separate "First Amendment" section of the final version of the guidelines, OCR explained that "Title IX is intended to protect students from sex discrimination, not to regulate the content of speech. OCR recognizes that the offensiveness of a particular expression as perceived by some students, standing alone, is not a legally sufficient basis to establish a sexually hostile environment under Title IX. . . . [A] school must formulate, interpret, and apply its rules so as to protect academic freedom and free speech rights."[75] To be sure, the agency was not particularly clear on how schools can reconcile these potentially conflicting rights. But at least it recognized the problem in 1996–97—something that cannot be said for OCR a decade and a half later.

The Supreme Court Takes a Contrary Position

In June 1998, the Supreme Court issued not only the two major Title VII decisions described above, but the first of two decisions on schools' liability for sexual harassment under Title IX, *Gebser v. Lago Vista Independent School District*. A year later the other shoe dropped in *Davis v. Monroe County School Board*. In both instances the Court split along predictable liberal–conservative lines. Justice O'Connor wrote both opinions, siding with the Court's conservative bloc in

Gebser and with its liberals in *Davis*. *Gebser* involved serious—indeed most likely criminal—misconduct by a public school teacher against a middle school girl. *Davis* involved repeated and unquestionably offensive behavior by an elementary school boy aimed at an elementary school girl. Together they established the liability standards that federal courts would apply in Title IX cases brought by private parties for monetary damages. In both *Gebser* and *Davis* the Court emphatically rejected the liability standards it had recently developed under Title VII and those announced by OCR in 1997.

Justice O'Connor's majority opinion in *Gebser* concluded that a school district would not be held liable for teacher-on-student sexual harassment "unless an official of the school district who at a minimum has authority to institute corrective measures on the district's behalf has *actual notice of, and is deliberately indifferent to*, the teacher's misconduct."[76] The Clinton administration's solicitor general had argued for the stronger strict liability standard applied to employers under Title VII, and had urged the Court to defer to OCR. But the majority would not impute such a liability standard to a statutory provision that (unlike Title VII) failed to make any explicit provision for individual damage suits. Title IX, Justice O'Connor argued, explicitly gives school districts the opportunity to correct deficiencies before facing administrative enforcement action. "It would be unsound," she concluded, to allow courts to use "a judicially *implied* system of enforcement" to penalize schools for deficiencies of which they had no notice.[77] Title IX was designed "to avoid diverting education funding from beneficial uses where a recipient was unaware of discrimination . . . and is willing to institute prompt corrective measures." The strict liability standard favored by OCR and the solicitor general "is at odds with that basic objective." Title IX does not aim "centrally to compensate victims," but to prevent discrimination by those who receive federal funds.[78]

In his dissent, Justice Stevens argued that the majority opinion not only conflicted with the logic of the *Franklin* decision, but failed to acknowledge OCR's expertise. Most important, the Court's "exceedingly high standard" had made it nearly impossible for "plaintiffs who have been victims of intentional discrimination" to recover damages. "As a matter of policy," Stevens charged, "the Court ranks protection of the school district's purse above the protection of immature high school students."[79]

A year later the Court addressed peer harassment under Title IX. Justice O'Connor tried to stake out a middle path between the conservatives—who argued that school districts should never be held responsible for peer harassment—and the "knew or should have known" standard favored by OCR and the Court's liberal wing. Her opinion in *Davis* applied to peer harassment the lenient "actual notice/deliberate indifference" standard first enunciated in *Gebser*. To this O'Connor added a further limitation: "Such an action will lie only for harassment that is so severe, pervasive, and objectively offensive that it effectively bars the victim's access to an educational opportunity or benefit."[80] She repeatedly emphasized the limited scope of judicial review of schools' practices. The "deliberate indifference" standard "narrowly circumscribe[s] the set of parties whose known acts of sexual harassment can trigger some duty to respond," and it "cabins the range of misconduct that the statute proscribes."[81] The lower courts "should refrain from second-guessing the disciplinary decisions made by school administrators." To avoid liability schools "must merely respond to known peer harassment in a manner that is not clearly unreasonable."[82] She warned that judges "must bear in mind that schools are unlike the adult workplace and that children may regularly interact in a manner that would be unacceptable among adults." Although "students often engage in insults, banter, teasing, shoving, pushing, and gender-specific conduct that is upsetting to the students subjected to it," damages are not available unless it is "serious enough to have the systematic effect of denying the victim equal access to an educational program or activity."[83]

In addition to this series of limitations on Title IX damage suits, Justice O'Connor added two more constraints that conflicted with OCR's later guidelines for colleges. First, she suggested that colleges be granted even more leeway than elementary and secondary schools: "A university might not, for example, be expected to exercise the same degree of control over its students that a grade school would enjoy . . . and it would be entirely reasonable for a school to refrain from a form of disciplinary action that would expose it to constitutional or statutory claims."[84] This section of her opinion seems to anticipate the due process and free speech claims later brought by students and faculty convicted of misconduct by college disciplinary boards.

Second, O'Connor directly challenged OCR's definition of "hostile environment" harassment. "Although, in theory, a single instance of sufficiently severe one-on-one peer harassment" could have the effect of denying students equal access to educational programs, "we think it unlikely that Congress would have thought such behavior sufficient to rise to this level in light of the inevitability of student misconduct and the amount of litigation that would be invited by entertaining claims of official indifference to a single instance of one-on-one peer harassment."[85] Limiting suits for damages "to cases having a systemic effect on educational programs or activities," Justice O'Connor argued, would "reconcile the general principle that Title IX prohibits official indifference to known peer sexual harassment with the practical realities of responding to student behavior, realities that Congress could not have meant to be ignored."[86] The contrast between the Court's interpretation of Title IX and that of OCR was stark (see table 10 5).

In a dissenting opinion for himself, Rehnquist, Thomas, and Scalia, Justice Kennedy warned that while "the majority's opinion purports to be narrow," the "limiting principles it proposes are illusory." According to Kennedy, "The fence the Court has built is made of little sticks, and it cannot contain the avalanche of liability now set in motion." "The only certainty flowing from the majority's decision," he claimed, "is that scarce resources will be diverted from educating our children."[87]

The ambiguities of the Court's interpretation of Title IX would allow judges, juries, and administrators to expand federal regulation, "transforming Title IX into a Federal Student Civility Code" and "justify[ing] a corps of federal administrators in writing regulations on student harassment."[88] School districts will be so "desperate to avoid Title IX peer harassment suits" that they "will adopt whatever federal code of student conduct and discipline the Department of Education sees fit to impose on them." Kennedy also predicted that extending Title IX to cover peer harassment would create special problems for universities "which do not exercise custodial and tutelary power over their adult students," and that efforts to discipline college students for verbal harassment would raise serious First Amendment issues. In the end, Kennedy argued, the majority "clears the way for the federal government to claim center stage in America's classrooms."

OCR Goes Its Own Way

Justice Kennedy's prediction that federal regulation would expand was correct. But he did not foresee *how* that would happen, namely, through OCR's refusal to accept the Court's narrow reading of Title IX. *Gebser* and *Davis* received scathing reviews from women's groups and in the law reviews. One law review article, for example, suggested that the *Gebser* decision had caused "the metastasization of the sexual harassment epidemic in educational institutions."[89] Another asked, "Why has the Supreme Court allowed schools to put their heads in the sand?"[90] Yet another concluded that the two decisions "signal that the protection against discrimination that Title IX originally seemed to offer is an empty promise."[91] Adding to their anger was the Rehnquist Court's 2000 decision in *United States v. Morrison*, which struck down as unconstitutional the provision in the Violence Against Women Act that allowed victims of sexual assault to bring civil suits against their attackers in federal court.[92]

In the waning days of the Clinton administration OCR responded to *Gebser* and *Davis* by reaffirming its 1997 guidelines and even expanding federal regulation a bit here and there. Once again, OCR employed a truncated form of rulemaking. On November 2, 2000, less than a week before the presidential election, it published a proposed "Revision of Sexual Harassment Guidelines" in the *Federal Register*. On January 19, 2001, the day before the inauguration of George W. Bush, it published a short notice announcing that the department had settled on a final set of guidelines that would soon be made available to the public. Apparently, OCR was in such a rush to beat the presidential clock that it could not get its thirty-seven pages of guidelines into the *Federal Register* on time.[93]

The central argument of OCR's guidelines was that the liability standards announced by the Court in *Gebser* and *Davis* apply only to private suits for money damages, not to administrative enforcement of Title IX. According to OCR, "the *Gebser* Court recognized and contrasted lawsuits for money damages with the incremental nature of administrative enforcement of Title IX." OCR's "enforcement actions, therefore, do not raise the Court's concern." In fact, OCR contended that the Supreme Court's recent decisions had "confirmed several fundamental principles articulated by the Department in the 1997 guidance." Consequently, "our proposed revised guidance does not change the standards that we use."[94]

OCR's determination to circumvent *Gebser* and *Davis* was apparent in its explanation of how serious sexual harassment must be to constitute a violation of Title IX and when schools should be held responsible for harassment by employees and peers. OCR conceded that "the terms used by the Court in *Davis* are in some ways different from the words used to define hostile environment harassment in the 1997 guidance," but it unconvincingly insisted that "the definitions are not inconsistent." The divergence between the positions of OCR and the Supreme Court are laid out in table 10-5.

OCR's 2001 rules broke the link between its administrative guidelines and the liability standards that had evolved under Titles VII and IX. In bland legalistic language that belied the major step it was taking, the agency explained, "Because the focus of the guidance is on a school's administrative responsibilities under the nondiscrimination requirements of the Title IX statute and regulations, rather than its liability to private litigants, the proposed revised guidance no longer describes a school's compliance in terms of 'liability' or 'Title VII agency law.' " Instead of explaining what schools can do to escape liability, "the proposed revised guidance explains the regulatory basis for a school's Title IX responsibility to take effective action to prevent, eliminate, and remedy sexual harassment occurring in its program."[95] OCR lawyers justified this switch with many pages of intricate legal argument, abundantly footnoted.

This was deft work, but it ignored one fundamental point: for nearly thirty years OCR had relied on judicial enforcement of Title IX because it could not terminate federal funding for any but the most egregiously discriminatory actions. When OCR's rules became more demanding than those recognized by the courts, how could it enforce its dictates? Why would school districts subject to adverse administrative action not challenge OCR in court, claiming that its interpretation of Title IX not only conflicted with *Gebser* and *Davis*, but had flouted the rulemaking procedures established in Title IX and the APA?

The 2001 Guidelines in Limbo

The Bush administration made little effort either to revise or to enforce the Clinton administration's midnight guidelines. Todd Jones, the incoming head of OCR's enforcement division, maintained that since the Clinton OCR had not followed standard rulemaking procedures, the 2001 guidelines "were not more official than a brochure" and had no legal force. For this he earned the scorn of several women's groups.[96] In 2003 the Bush OCR issued a statement emphasizing that the

Table 10-5 OCR v. the Supreme Court

When is a school responsible for sexual harassment by an employee?

OCR, 2001: A school is responsible for quid pro quo and hostile environment harassment by an employee whenever that harassment occurs "in the context of the employee's provision of aid, benefit, or services to a student." In other words, the school is always responsible, except in those rare circumstances where the harassment is unconnected to the employee's role and authority within the school.

The Supreme Court, in *Gebser*, 1998: A school district will *not* be held liable for teacher-on-student sexual harassment "unless an official of the school district who at a minimum has authority to institute corrective measures on the district's behalf has *actual notice of, and is deliberately indifferent to, the teacher's misconduct.*"

When is a school responsible for peer sexual harassment?

OCR, 2001: A school is responsible for responding to peer harassment whenever a "responsible employee" either *"knew or in the exercise of reasonable care should have known" about it.*

The Supreme Court, in *Davis*, 1999: A school district will *not* be held liable for the creation of a hostile environment by other students "unless an official of the school district who at a minimum has authority to institute corrective measures on the district's behalf has *actual notice of, and is deliberately indifferent to"* such peer harassment.

When does conduct by a school employee or student create a "hostile environment"?

OCR, 2001: The conduct must be "sufficiently severe, persistent, *or* pervasive to *limit* a student's ability to participate in or benefit from the educational program." The conduct should be "considered from *both a subjective and objective perspective.*"

The Supreme Court, in *Davis*, 1999: "Such action will lie only for harassment that is so severe, pervasive, *and objectively* offensive that it *effectively bars* the victim's access to an educational opportunity or benefit." It must be "serious enough to have the *systematic effect* of denying the victim equal access to an educational activity or program."

Can a single instance of harassment create a "hostile environment"?

OCR, 2001: "The more severe the conduct, the less the need to show a repetitive series of incidents; this is particularly true if the harassment is physical. . . . Indeed *a single or isolated incident of sexual harassment may, if sufficiently severe, create a hostile environment.*"

Table 10-5   (*continued*)

The Supreme Court, in *Davis*, 1999: "Although, *in theory*, a single instance of sufficiently severe one-on-one peer harassment" could have the effect of denying students equal access to educational programs, "we think it unlikely that Congress would have thought such behavior sufficient to rise to this level in light of the inevitability of student misconduct and the amount of litigation that would be invited by entertaining claims of official indifference to a *single instance* of one-on-one peer harassment."

How much control should the federal government exercise over school officials?

OCR, 2001: Its thirty-seven pages of guidelines explained in detail how schools should handle various categories of harassment.

The Supreme Court, in *Davis*, 1999: Judges "should refrain from second-guessing the disciplinary decisions made by school administrators."

---

guidelines should not be interpreted to limit First Amendment rights.[97] Yet in 2006 Assistant Secretary Stephanie Monroe recirculated the 2001 guidance, promising to "conduct compliance reviews of sexual harassment in schools."[98]

Why did the Bush administration so meekly accept the 2001 shift? The answer seems to be that those guidelines had little significance unless backed by an aggressive enforcement effort that at that time appeared to exceed the agency's capacity. OCR never undertook the compliance reviews promised by Assistant Secretary Monroe. Instead it investigated only the small number of complaints it received. For example, OCR's annual report for fiscal years 2001 and 2002 listed only two sexual harassment complaints, one of which involved the hazing of a boy who had become a cheerleader. Both cases were resolved through negotiations with the public school.[99] Similarly, OCR's report for the fiscal years 2007 and 2008 mentioned only three sexual harassment complaints, one on inappropriate conduct during pledging for a literary society (resolved when the school issued a warning and required the perpetrators to undergo training), one on retaliation, and one on reporting procedures. Of the sixty-five compliance reviews that OCR conducted in those two years, none involved sexual harassment.[100] If schools chose to follow the advice that OCR had offered in 2001, fine—that might reduce the rate of sexual harassment. If not, there was little the agency could do. Why invite political controversy by revoking rules that were virtually unenforceable?

In 2008 Fatima Goss Graves, at the time senior counsel at the National Women's Law Center and later its president, wrote an essay arguing that the federal government could restore "effective protections" against sexual harassment only by "moving beyond the *Gebser* and *Davis* standards." Those two decisions, she explained, "raised the bar, in perverse and unacceptable ways, for bringing private lawsuits for damages under Title IX," imposing a "crippling burden" on students who experience harassment at the hands of teachers and peers. The decisions also "eliminated incentives for school districts to take steps to address and prevent" such harassment.[101] But she did not, as one might have expected, call for vigorous enforcement of the 2001 guidelines. In fact, she barely mentioned them. "The Supreme Court majority in *Gebser*," she argued, "placed any additional relief for students under federal law *squarely on the shoulders of Congress*." By enacting the Civil Rights Act of 2008 sponsored by Senator Edward Kennedy and Congressman John Lewis, "Congress can and should remove the unfair burdens imposed by the Court and reinstate its commitment to protecting students from sex discrimination."[102] That legislation sought to overturn a number of Rehnquist Court decisions on civil rights. One section was devoted to reversing "*Gebser* and its progeny," which had created incentives for schools "to insulate themselves from knowledge of harassment."[103] In addition, Graves argued, advocates should try to convince state legislators and state judges to ease the burden placed on plaintiffs in sexual harassment suits filed in state court.

The Civil Rights Act of 2008 did not get out of committee in either house of Congress even after Democrats seized control of the House, the Senate, and the presidency. When Republicans retook the House in the 2010 election, hope for legislative change evaporated. Those unhappy with the *Gebser/Davis* standard had only two choices: to turn their attention back to the administrative process or to give up on the federal government.

Conclusion

When OCR and the courts first began to address in a serious way sexual harassment in school, they adopted the tort-based approach developed with glacial speed by the courts and the EEOC under Title VII. The Title VII liability scheme announced by the Supreme Court in 1998 seemed to satisfy all interested parties, except feminist legal scholars who considered it an ineffective product of an overly individualistic understanding of the sexual harassment problem. Within a year, though, the Supreme Court established liability rules for schools under Title IX considerably weaker than those it had established for employers under Title VII. In the waning days of the Clinton administration OCR refused to accept this understanding of schools' responsibility under Title IX. It claimed authority to impose stricter requirements, but could offer no credible enforcement strategy. Critics of the Court's lenient liability standards looked to Congress for help, but came away empty-handed. During the eight years of the Bush administration and first two years of the Obama administration, OCR's activity was limited to investigating the few individual complaints it received. How this suddenly changed is the topic of the next chapter.

ELEVEN

Changing Culture, Building Institutions

For nearly a decade the sexual harassment guidelines issued by the Office for Civil Rights (OCR) in 2001 remained in limbo, neither revised nor repudiated, generating few complaints, investigations, or news stories. Immersed in other education issues, the Obama administration said nothing on the topic for over a year. But in early 2010 Secretary of Education Arne Duncan traveled to Selma, Alabama, to announce the administration's intention to "reinvigorate civil rights enforcement."[1] A few months later OCR issued a Dear Colleague Letter (DCL) on school bullying, a term that encompassed harassment based on race, sex, gender identification, or disability. On the day the president announced his reelection bid in 2011, Secretary Duncan and Vice President Joseph Biden unveiled OCR's nineteen-page DCL on sexual assault at a well-attended event at the University of New Hampshire.[2] In 2013 OCR and the Department of Justice (DOJ) negotiated a thirty-one-page settlement with the University of Montana, and announced that it would "serve as a blueprint for colleges and universities throughout the country to protect students from sexual harassment and assault."[3] When the White House Task Force to Protect Students from Sexual Assault issued its 2014 report, OCR simultaneously distributed a forty-six-page "Questions and Answers" on how to comply with Title IX guidelines, and it initiated its extensive investigation of hundreds of colleges.[4]

New Politics, New Paradigm

The most obvious difference between the development of sexual harassment policy in the 1990s and in the post-2010 period is the public visibility of the issue and the support OCR's efforts received from the White House and Democrats in Congress. When OCR announced its sexual harassment guidelines in 1997 and 2001, it did so with little fanfare. It was responding primarily to court decisions and to schools' requests for advice on how to comply with federal mandates. Its 2010, 2011, and 2014 guidance documents, in contrast, received the full blessing of the Obama administration, with Vice President Biden often playing a leading role.

OCR's efforts also had vocal advocates in Congress, most notably Senators Kirsten Gillibrand (D-N.Y.) and Claire McCaskill (D-Mo.). They sponsored legislation to embed OCR's guidelines in statute and to strengthen its enforcement authority. The proposed Campus Accountability and Safety Act (CASA) would go beyond OCR's guidelines in spelling out the steps colleges must take to prevent sexual violence, punish perpetrators, and protect victims. It would also allow OCR to impose fines of up to 1 percent of a school's operating budget for each violation of the act—a more credible sanction than the current Title IX funding cutoff. Among CASA's thirty-seven Senate cosponsors were several Republicans. This issue not only had strong appeal for the Democratic Party's base, but also placed Republicans in the awkward position of having to choose between their general opposition to expansion of federal regulation and their desire to reach out to women voters and avoid being branded "rape apologists." These political dynamics were evident in 2013, when Congress amended the Violence Against Women Act to require schools to increase reporting of sexual violence and to document their prevention efforts.

Another novel feature of the post-2010 political landscape was the emergence of new groups organized by women who describe themselves as sexual violence survivors. Organizations such as SurvJustice, Know Your IX, End Rape on Campus, and Students Active for Ending Rape were founded by women who had lodged complaints of sexual assault and found the response of college administrators and federal regulators inadequate. Some of these groups retained a local focus, counseling students on how to recognize, report, and cope with the aftermath of sexual assault. Others, most notably SurvJustice and Know Your IX, have become active at the national level. Social media helped victims of sexual assault find one other, and use of social media has become a key element of their organizational strategy. What these new groups share is the conviction that sexual violence on campus has reached epidemic proportions, largely because schools have failed to acknowledge the "rape culture" that prevails within their institutions. Many leaders of these groups have been influenced by the "sociocultural/dominance" model of sexual harassment put forth by Catharine MacKinnon and other feminist scholars (see chapter 9).

Traditional media helped these groups bring their concerns to a wider audience. In 2009 the Center for Public Integrity (CPI), an organization of investigative journalists funded by several major foundations, "fielded a team of reporters and researchers to lift the curtain on how colleges and universities respond to reports of sexual assault." Partnering with National Public Radio (NPR), the center produced a hundred-page report and a six-part radio series charging that "lax enforcement of Title IX campus sexual assault cases" left "students at risk." One of its stories focused on the experience of Laura Dunn, the founder of SurvJustice, who claimed that both the University of Wisconsin and the federal OCR had mishandled her charge of rape against a fellow student. The CPI/NPR series helped make Dunn a major participant in the debate: she was later named to the president's task force and was one of the "stakeholders" in the negotiated rulemaking mandated by the 2013 amendments to the Violence Against Women Act. The CPI/NPR series first attacked the Obama administration for inaction, then praised its aggressive post-2010 policies. It gave credence to the claims that campuses are experiencing an epidemic of sexual violence and that college administrators have tried to sweep this under the rug. The series won several prestigious journalism awards, and most likely influenced OCR as it wrote its 2011 DCL.[5]

In a 2010 interview with a reporter for the Center for Public Integrity, Assistant Secretary for Civil Rights Russlynn Ali indicated the extent to which OCR came to embrace the perspective of these new activists. She claimed that recent Title IX settlements with colleges reflected "a new paradigm" for addressing sexual assault on campus: "Taken as a whole, these settlements will change the culture on the college campuses, and that is hugely important if we are to cure the epidemic of sexual violence on our college campuses across the country."[6] In retrospect, we can see that OCR's 2000–01 break with the Supreme Court opened the door to this "new paradigm" by jettisoning the individualistic tort-based approach that for years had provided the foundation for federal regulation under both Title VII and Title IX.

What the alternative approach would look like in practice and how it would be enforced remained unclear until 2011–14. The following pages focus on five key features of OCR's new policy: (1) the expanded definitions of "sexual harassment" and "hostile environment"; (2) procedures for investigating complaints; (3) remedies for identified victims and the entire student body; (4) schools' responsibility for taking preventative measures; and (5) OCR's strategy for enforcing its extensive new demands.

What Constitutes "Sexual Harassment" and a "Hostile Environment"?

Despite the attention paid to sexual assault in the press, OCR's guidelines are based on a much broader understanding of sexual harassment. They define sexual harassment as "unwelcome conduct of a sexual nature." This includes not only "touching of a sexual nature" but "verbal conduct" such as "making sexual comments, jokes, or gestures," "spreading sexual rumors," "rating students on sexual activity or performance," and "creating e-mails or Web sites of a sexual nature."[7] The extent to which speech or conduct is "welcome" or "unwelcome"—which means whether it will be considered a punishable offense or an appreciated mating overture—will depend on the response of the target, which might not be knowable until after the remark has been uttered or the action taken.

The forms of "verbal conduct"—usually known as speech—covered by OCR's rules include those aimed at a broad audience. To violate Title IX harassment need not "be directed at a specific target," "involve repeated incidents," or be motivated by "intent to harm." Some schools (for example, Colorado College) have suspended students for posting on social media offensive jokes not directed at anyone in particular. Northwestern University investigated a professor for an article she wrote for the *Chronicle of Higher Education*. Administrators at Louisiana State University used these sexual harassment rules as the basis for stripping an education professor of tenure for using "salty language" in her classes.

Nor must speech be related to sexual activity to violate Title IX. OCR's guidelines also prohibit "gender-based harassment," which includes "verbal hostility based on sex or sex-stereotyping." A school thus violates Title IX whenever "students are harassed either for exhibiting what is perceived as stereotypical characteristics for sex, or for failing to conform to stereotypical notions of masculinity or femininity."[8] OCR's rule on combating "sex-stereotyping" formed the basis for its controversial guidelines on treatment of transgender students (see chapter 12). In its 2010 guidelines on bullying, OCR explained that one part of a school's "comprehensive response" to the problem should be "educating the entire school community on civil rights and the expectation of tolerance, especially as they apply to sexual stereotypes."[9] This suggests that schools should take steps to prevent students from criticizing their peers' behavior or appearance—a monumental task that could involve extensive monitoring and censoring of speech.

OCR's post-2010 guidelines thus go far beyond the Supreme Court's interpretation of schools' responsibility for monitoring and punishing misconduct by students (see table 10-5). The implications of OCR's expansive definition of sexual harassment became apparent in 2013, when OCR and DOJ negotiated the agreement with the University of Montana that they described as a "blueprint" for future accords.

The university had originally defined sexual harassment as conduct "sufficiently severe or pervasive as to . . . unreasonably interfere with a person's work or educational performance," language that tracks the Supreme Court's opinion in *Davis v. Monroe County Board of Education.* OCR objected to this formulation, and forced the school to revise it policies. Sexual harassment, the agency told the University of Montana, must be defined as "*any* unwelcome conduct of a sexual nature." That is because the university's narrower definition "leaves unclear when students should report unwelcome conduct of a sexual nature and risks having students wait to report to the University until such conduct becomes severe or pervasive or both." The university should "encourage students to report sexual harassment early, before such conduct becomes severe or pervasive, so that it can take steps to prevent the harassment from creating a hostile environment."[10]

OCR also objected to the university's rule that limited the definition of sexual harassment to conduct that is "objectively offensive"—another phrase the school had borrowed from the Supreme Court. This is improper, the agency explained, because "the United States considers a variety of factors, from both a subjective and objective perspective, to determine if a hostile environment has been created."[11] The "environment" in question is not that of the school as a whole, but that of individual students; what constitutes a "hostile environment" will depend in part on how those students interpret the interaction.[12]

Why such strong objections to language the school had lifted directly from the leading Supreme Court decision on the topic? OCR's position is based on two propositions. The first is that Title IX requires schools not just to prevent the formation of a macro-level, systemic "hostile environment" serious enough to deprive a number of students of educational opportunity, but to eliminate any micro-level "hostile environment" that, from a "subjective" point of view, could limit an *individual* student's ability to profit from her education. The second proposition is that in order to do this, schools must, in effect, nip misconduct in the bud, taking action against improper behavior before it becomes "severe or pervasive" enough to infringe on the education of some students. For example, jokes that some people find offensive might not by themselves create a "hostile environment," but they could constitute "sexual conduct" that from a "subjective perspective" contributes to such an "environment." For that reason the joker can be subject to disciplinary action.

OCR's recent guidelines also insist that school officials are responsible for harassment of students perpetrated by people not affiliated with their institution and for harassment that takes place off campus. This applies not just to peer harassment in off-campus educational programs and extracurricular activities (such as field trips or football games), but also to harassment "that initially occurred off school grounds, outside a school's education program or activity," such as off-campus bars or concerts. Schools must process complaints "regardless of where the conduct occurred" because "students often experience the *continuing effects* of off-campus sexual harassment in the educational setting." For that reason schools must "consider the effects of off-campus conduct when evaluating whether there is a hostile environment on campus."[13] Of course, if the perpetrator is not a student or an employee of the school, the school may not be able to take action against him. But the school "must still take steps to provide appropriate remedies for the complainant, and, where appropriate, the broader school population."[14] In other words, even if a school has no control over those who created the "hostile environment," it still bears responsibility for minimizing its long-term effects.

OCR's 2011 and 2014 guidances focus on the most serious form of harassment, sexual violence, that is, "physical sexual acts perpetrated against a person's will or when a person is incapable of giving consent due to the victim's use of drugs or alcohol."[15] This includes rape and sexual assault as defined by most criminal statutes, but also conduct that is not covered by the criminal law of some states.[16] Although OCR has made it clear that consent is the key for distinguishing between ordinary sex and sexual violence, it has not attempted to explain how schools should determine consent. When the Department of Education engaged in the negotiated rulemaking required by amendments to the Clery Act, it first proposed defining consent as "the affirmative, unambiguous, and voluntary agreement to engage in a specific sexual activity during a sexual encounter." It eventually dropped that definition without substituting an alternative. As Harvard law professors Jacob Gersen and Jeannie Suk have pointed out, "The federal bureaucracy's agnosticism on what is nonconsent—the very concept on which the definition of sex offense relies—combined with the need to have some definition, has led schools to overshoot, and to define consent to render most sexual interactions nonconsensual."[17] Examples of such "overshooting" abound. At Elon University, "Only a comprehensible, unambiguous, positive and enthusiastic communication of consent for each sexual act qualifies as consent."[18] Georgia Southern University tells its students, "Consent is a voluntary, sober, imaginative, enthusiastic, creative, wanted, informed, mutual, honest, and verbal agreement."[19] According to a training video for incoming students at Brown, "Consent is knowing that my partner wants me just as much as I want them."[20] As Gersen and Suk emphasize, as the definition of consent grows more demanding, the difference between sexual violence and ordinary sex becomes harder and harder for students as well as adjudicators to discern.[21]

OCR's definition of sexual harassment thus covers an enormous range of activities, from name-calling by kindergarten students to tasteless junior high jokes to rape in off-campus bars. On the one hand, OCR has prudently urged schools to take into account the context and the age of the students involved. For example, it may be appropriate for a football coach to slap a player on the butt as he runs off the field, but certainly not for a professor to do the same as a student exits his classroom. A kindergarten teacher can get away with hugging students at the end of the day, but a high school teacher cannot. (Whether a kindergartner who keeps trying to kiss a fellow student creates a hostile environment is a closer legal question.[22]) OCR's insistence that harassment need not be "systemic" to violate Title IX makes this ambiguity particularly treacherous for schools. Since it is hard for schools to know in advance what will trigger an OCR investigation, they have a very strong incentive to define harassment broadly to show how serious they are about addressing the problem.

Procedures for Soliciting, Investigating, and Resolving Complaints

No section of OCR's 2011 guidelines has been more controversial than the requirements for schools' adjudicatory procedures. Both in its general policy statements and in the resolution agreements negotiated with particular schools, OCR has prescribed in great detail timelines, investigative practices, evidentiary rules, hearing and appeals procedures, and confidentiality protocols. OCR's practices contrast sharply with the Supreme Court's claim that Title IX requires schools "merely [to] respond to known peer harassment in a manner that is not clearly unreasonable," and its caution that "courts should refrain from second guessing the disciplinary decisions made by school administrators."[23] In fact, the agency's 2014 guidance devotes twenty-nine single-spaced pages to such second-guessing. This guidance is based on a profound distrust of schools' willingness to confront the sexual abuse problem without strict federal rules.

Some of these procedural requirements are unexceptionable. For example, schools must regularly disseminate to all students and staff information on what constitutes sexual harassment and how to report it. A second set of demands seems reasonable in theory, but is likely to prove difficult to carry out in practice. For example, schools must investigate *all* complaints, regardless of how serious or credible they may seem to school officials, and they are expected to complete these investigations promptly, usually within sixty days. School investigators can wait for the police to complete their initial gathering of information in an assault case (usually three to ten days), but schools cannot delay their own proceedings pending completion of that investigation. OCR has criticized many schools for failing to resolve cases promptly, and has required them to establish strict time limits for completion of disciplinary proceedings.[24] This puts schools under pressure to hire outside investigators (who, according to the *Chronicle of Higher Education*, "typically charge $5,000 to $20,000 per case"[25]) and to expand the office of the Title IX coordinator.

A third set of procedural requirements ignited the current debate over due process described in chapter 9. These include OCR's demand that schools use the "preponderance of the evidence" standard in disciplinary proceedings, limits on cross-examination and use of lawyers, and procedures for appeals. Although OCR allows schools to hold hearings to resolve sexual harassment complaints, it has emphasized that "Title IX does not necessarily require a hearing." The White House task force report praised colleges for adopting the "single investigator" model,[26] and in negotiations with individual schools OCR has strongly encouraged them to do so. Lawyers who work with schools estimate that about one-third of colleges now empower a "single investigator" not just to collect evidence, but to determine guilt or innocence.[27]

For example, as a result of OCR's investigation of Harvard, its Faculty of Arts and Sciences dispensed with hearings in sexual harassment cases. An investigator selected by the Title IX office interviews witnesses individually, makes summaries of these interviews available to the parties, and then issues a ruling on whether the accused student violated the school's "Sexual and Gender-Based Harassment Policy." Either party can appeal this determination, but only to the Title IX coordinator and only on the grounds of procedural error or pertinent new information. The administrative board that determines the proper punishment "must accept as final and non-reviewable the [investigative] report's finding of fact and its conclusions as to whether a violation of the Policy has occurred."[28]

Critics argue that these procedures turn the "single investigator" into a de facto investigator, judge, and jury. To make matters worse, they are usually employed or hired by the school's Title IX office, which is expected to demonstrate to OCR that it is cracking down on sexual harassment. Harvard law professor Janet Halley has charged that the entire process is "structurally biased" since the Title IX officer's *very job depends on showing a high rate of enforcement.*[29] A 2017 report issued by the American Bar Association (ABA) Task Force on College Due Process Rights and Victim Protections discouraged use of the single investigator model because it "carries inherent structural fairness risks especially as it relates to cases in which suspension or expulsion is a possibility."[30]

A fourth set of procedures mandated by OCR is designed to reduce the burden on those lodging complaints and to make investigators and adjudicators more sympathetic to the plight of complainants. For example, OCR insists that school officials engaged in the evaluation of complaints should recognize "that use of alcohol and drugs never make the victim at fault for sexual violence." Not only should "questioning about the complainant's sexual history with anyone other than the alleged perpetrator" never be permitted, but schools "should recognize that the mere fact of a current or previous consensual dating or sexual relationship between the two parties does not itself imply consent or preclude a finding of sexual violence." Schools should also remove from their sexual harassment policy statements any language that appears to discourage anonymous complaints.[31]

Fifth, schools must provide investigators and members of disciplinary committees with extensive training on sexual harassment and violence. OCR's settlements with individual schools often spell out in great detail what this training must include. The Tufts University agreement, for example, states that its Title IX coordinator and all investigators, adjudicators, and "liaisons" must understand Equal Employment Opportunity Commission and OCR guidance, other federal laws, university policies, confidentiality rules, and "victim behavior, dynamics of power, [and] implicit bias."[32] To help school officials, OCR, the White House task force, and other federal agencies have showered them with numerous documents laying out "best practices" for all phases of the process. The task force alone has produced "sample reporting and confidentiality protocols"; "promising policy language" on "definitions of various forms of sexual misconduct"; "training programs for campus officials involved in investigating and adjudicating sexual assault cases"; and sample "Memorandums of Understanding" for establishing divisions of labor with police and rape crisis centers. Schools under investigation realize that they ignore such officially recognized "best practices" at their peril.

Finally, OCR requires all students at a university to be covered by the same procedures. This means not just no special rules for athletes, but also identical rules for undergraduates and students at professional schools, part-time students who live off campus and full-time students living in college dorms, seventeen-year-old kids and forty-year-old adults. The rationale for this requirement has never been made clear. It is likely, though, that it reflects OCR's larger effort to take sexual harassment cases out of schools' ordinary disciplinary committees and to create separate sexual harassment tribunals under the control of the Title IX coordinator. As we will see, strengthening the Title IX office in each school is a key part of OCR's enforcement strategy.

Remedial Measures

OCR has emphasized that taking disciplinary action against harassers is not enough to cure the problem. It mandates three additional forms of remedial action: (a) interim measures to protect the complainant while the matter is being decided; (b) long-term services, protections, and ameliorating arrangements for identified victims; and (c) remedies "for the broader student population," which can include "changes in the school's overall services and policies."

Even before the school's investigation has been completed and a finding announced, the school must "take steps to protect the complainant." This may include allowing the complainant "to change academic or living situations" in order to "avoid contact with the alleged perpetrator." In most situations it will also mean prohibiting the alleged perpetrator "from having any contact with the complainant." In separating the two students, "a school must minimize the burden on the complainant." In other words, if anyone must change classes, dormitories, or activities it must be the accused—an obvious deviation from the ordinary assumption of innocent until proven guilty. Moreover, the school must protect the complainant against "retaliatory harassment," including "name-calling and taunting." How the school can accomplish this—and how it can distinguish "retaliation" from reasonable criticism of the actions of the claimant—is left unclear. There is no mention of protecting the accused student from "name-calling and taunting," another indication that the presumption of innocence has been abandoned.

Once it has been established that a student or employee has been the victim of sexual misconduct, schools are expected to offer a number of additional services. These include "comprehensive, holistic victim services, including medical, counseling, and academic support services, such as tutoring" at no cost to the victim; "arranging for the complainant to re-take a course or withdraw from a class without penalty"; and "providing an escort to ensure that the complainant can move safely between classes and activities." These steps "also can be used as interim measures before the school's investigation is complete."

It takes OCR two full single-spaced pages to list remedies "for the broader student population" that should be considered by the school. These include "but are not limited to":

- "offering counseling, health, mental health and comprehensive victim services to all students affected by sexual harassment or sexual violence" wherever it occurred;

- "designating an individual from the school's counseling center to be 'on call' to assist victims of sexual harassment or violence whenever needed";

- adding discussion of sexual harassment policies to student orientations;

- creating a committee of students and school officials to identify strategies for combating sexual harassment;

- "conducting periodic assessments of student activities to ensure that the practices and behavior of students do not violate the school's policy against sexual harassment and violence";

- and "investigating whether school employees with knowledge of allegations of sexual harassment or violence failed to carry out their duties."

Since it is rare for any but the smallest college to be completely free of all forms of sexual harassment, almost every school in the country is expected to take these steps.

One might wonder why a school that has diligently solicited and investigated complaints, punished perpetrators, and assisted identified victims should be expected to institute so many additional remedial measures. Why should it be held responsible for the consequences of behavior it has swiftly and severely punished? The answer, it would seem, is that the measures listed by OCR are not so much remedies for specific acts of sexual harassment as measures that *all* schools are expected to adopt to address the *general* problem of sexual misconduct. Since most colleges fear being charged with violating Title IX and being subjected to a public investigation by OCR, it is likely that most of these "remedies" will be adopted to pre-empt such charges and investigations.

Prevention: Training Staff and Remaking School Culture

The central theme underlying OCR's guidelines, one repeated in several White House reports, is that reducing sexual assault requires deep cultural change. Getting students to understand that "sexual assault is simply unacceptable" will require a "sea change" in attitudes.[33] Consequently, effective prevention programs must be "sustained (not brief, one-shot educational programs), comprehensive, and address the root individual, relational and societal causes of sexual assault."

To this end schools must provide training to faculty, adjudicators, investigators, law enforcement personnel, general counsels, resident assistants, medical and counseling staff, and, of course, students. Indeed, no word is repeated more frequently in OCR guidance documents than "training." The types of mandatory training are too numerous to list here, but they include:

- training for all employees on their responsibility to report sexual harassment that they witness or hear about, on how to recognize the "warning signs" of sexual harassment, and on how to encourage students to file grievances without breaching confidentiality;

- training for law enforcement personnel on how to investigate sexual harassment cases;

- training for those who will sit on disciplinary boards on how to evaluate sexual harassment claims;

- training for students who serve as advisers in residence halls;

- and special training for student athletes and their coaches, and for fraternities and sororities.

Schools must also "have methods for verifying that the training was effective." The best way to do this, OCR has insisted, is to conduct the annual "climate checks" described below. The Title IX coordinator is responsible for all these forms of training, with help from the many "best practices" documents provided by federal agencies.

All the settlements OCR has reached with individual schools contain lengthy provisions on training. Usually one section is devoted to training the Title IX coordinator's staff and those involved in investigating and adjudicating individual complaints. Another will cover training for "administrators, professors, instructors, resident assistants, coaches, university police . . . and other staff who interact with students on a regular basis."[34] Several more sections will focus on training for students. The Ohio State agreement, for example, includes one lengthy paragraph on freshmen orientation programs, a second on "orientation sessions for returning students," a third on the Student Wellness Center, and a fourth on "additional training needs for specific groups, including but not limited to, fraternities, sororities, band, cheerleaders, and athletes."[35]

Given the prominence of "training" in OCR's guidance documents, the lack of detail on what this means is striking. The compliance agreements OCR has reached with particular institutions are only slightly more specific. This means that the background of those chosen as trainers and the materials they use are crucial. Another important feature of these agreements is the requirement that OCR "review and approve" all training materials before they are deployed by the school. Especially given the tight schedule established by the agreements, OCR investigators wield great control over what faculty, staff, and students are told about what constitutes sexual harassment and how it can best be prevented. Few schools will be willing to contest OCR's determination of what constitutes "best practices," acceptable training material, or suitable training consultants.

Janet Halley, who had a chance to examine Harvard's training material, claimed that it "is 100% aimed to convince" those sitting on adjudicatory boards "to believe complainants, precisely when they seem unreliable and incoherent."[36] Emily Yoffe's 2017 *Atlantic* article, "The Bad Science Behind Campus Response to Sexual Assault," explains how a number of unsubstantiated and most likely exaggerated claims about the effects of trauma on assault survivors have become a standard part of many schools' training material.[37] Evaluating the quality of these training materials is possible only when schools make them available to the public. Unfortunately, as K. C. Johnson and Stuart Taylor discovered, "At the overwhelming majority of universities, training materials for people who mete out discipline for alleged sexual assault have been kept secret."[38]

The 2013 amendments to the Violence Against Women Act require schools to report their sexual violence prevention programs to the federal government. In 2014 the Department of Education announced extensive rules requiring "primary prevention and awareness programs for all incoming students and new employees." These must include "programming, initiatives, and strategies informed by research or assessed for value, effectiveness, or outcomes" designed "to stop dating violence, domestic violence, sexual assault, and stalking before they occur" by promoting "positive and healthy behaviors that foster healthy, mutually respectful relationships and sexuality, encourage safe bystander intervention, and seek to change behavior and social norms in healthy and safe directions."[39] In undertaking this daunting task, these prevention programs must "consider environmental risk and protective factors as they occur in the individual, relationship, institutional, community, and societal levels."[40]

This language tracks the public health framework developed by the federal Centers for Disease Control and Prevention (CDC) to address the problem of sexual violence. According to the CDC, "individual risk factors" include alcohol and drug use, empathic deficits, general aggressiveness, early sexual initiation, coercive sexual fantasies, preferences for impersonal sex and sexual risk-taking, exposure to sexually explicit media, adherence to traditional gender role norms, and hypermasculinity. "Relationship factors" include a history of childhood abuse; poor parent–child relationships, particularly with fathers; and association with sexually aggressive, hypermasculine, and delinquent peers. "Community factors" include poverty, lack of employment opportunities, lack of institutional support from policy and the judicial system, and general tolerance of sexual violence within the community. "Societal factors" include "social norms that support male superiority and sexual entitlement," "social norms that maintain women's inferiority and sexual submissiveness," "weak laws and policies related to sexual violence and gender equality," and high levels of crime and violence.[41]

There are not many acceptable steps that colleges can take to reduce the majority of these "risk factors." The most effective would be simply to stop admitting applicants who are most likely to have been exposed to these pernicious influences—which would probably have the perverse effect of reducing the number of poor and minority students admitted. Schools could also try to screen students on the basis of their sexual preferences and habits or their opinions on proper gender rules. Or they could ban the fraternities and competitive sports that breed "hypermasculinity." For obvious reasons the vast majority of schools will be reluctant to do any of these.

The training that most schools now offer students in order to comply with federal mandates involves extensive discussion of what constitutes a "healthy, mutually respectful" sexual relationship and appropriate "bystander intervention." Brown, for example, tells its students that since "communication, respect, and honesty are fundamental to great sex and relationships," consent is "not just getting a yes or no answer, but about understanding what a partner is feeling." Yale tells its students: "Hold out for enthusiasm. In general, it's easy to tell if someone is enthusiastic about an encounter or not." The University of Georgia provides this advice to students: "If you are not accustomed to communicating with your partner about sex and sexual activity the first few times may feel awkward. But, practice makes perfect. Be creative and spontaneous. Don't give up." (Of course, according to OCR's guidelines overtures that are repeatedly rejected constitute sexual harassment.) Clark University's training material states, "We want you to have great sex if you choose to have sex—safe, mutually enjoyable, consensual sex."

American University explains that in healthy relationships partners "are open and communicate needs and desires," are "free to be themselves," respect each other's privacy, and enjoy "independence within the relationship."[42]

In their important and alarming article on the expansion of federal regulation of sexual behavior, Gersen and Suk note that the "college sex bureaucrats" who run these federally mandated programs "are not simply training students on the rules of rape, sexual assault, and sexual harassment." Rather,

> They are instructing on, advising on, counseling on, defining, monitoring, investigating, and adjudicating questions of sexual desire. . . . Sexual violence education and prevention programming is rapidly morphing into sex instruction reminiscent of guidance provided by sex therapists like Dr. Ruth. This jibes well with the public health framework that has so strongly influenced the federal regulatory orientation to sexual violence. Since the sex bureaucracy's role is regulating health and safety, explanations of consent easily lead to instruction about what is "healthy" or "positive" in sex and relationships.[43]

In short, for OCR, "changing the culture" means not just condemning violence, but teaching new expectations about sex and gender roles that govern even the most intimate personal relationships.

In 2014 OCR added the requirement that schools establish "methods for verifying that the training was effective." The main tool for judging effectiveness is the "climate check," questionnaires sent to students to evaluate the frequency of sexual assault and their familiarity with university policies and procedures. The 2014 task force report asked all schools "voluntarily to conduct the survey next year," provided them "with a new toolkit for developing and conducting a climate survey," and promised to "explore legislative or administrative options to require colleges and universities to conduct an evidence-based survey in 2016."[44] The Campus Accountability and Safety Act introduced by eight senators shortly thereafter included a provision requiring every school to administer such a survey every year and directing the Department of Education to establish rules for the design of these surveys.

Although that legislation has yet to pass, OCR has included mandatory annual climate checks in each of its settlements. The agency not only demands that schools preclear these surveys with the agency, but in some cases has specified how the questionnaires will be developed. For example, its 2014 resolution agreement with Tufts requires the university to "submit for OCR review and approval a description of and underlying documentation of its tools for conducting a climate check" that will allow it to "assess the effectiveness of steps taken by the University toward providing a campus free of sexual misconduct." The agreement also requires the university to "formulate a working group of students and staff to help gather and provide feedback on how the climate checks are conducted, and how to respond to its results." Any revision of the climate check must also be submitted to OCR "for review and prior approval."[45] Tufts must conduct OCR-approved climate checks annually until federal monitoring ends. When that will be remains unclear, but the agreement implies that Tufts must first demonstrate that it is a "campus free from sexual misconduct." Unless Tufts has an unusually virtuous student body, that is not likely ever to occur.

Enforcement I: Well-Publicized, Systemic Investigations

If OCR's post-2000 break with the Supreme Court provided an unexpected opportunity to move federal regulation beyond the once dominant individualistic, tort-based framework, it also posed a major enforcement problem. Despite OCR's fierce rhetoric, everyone knows that the funding cutoff will never be used in these circumstances. Since the agency could no longer count on private lawsuits to put teeth into its enforcement program, how could it induce thousands of schools to comply with its extensive and detailed demands? Would this be another instance in which OCR issued extensive guidelines and then did little to enforce them?

The answer to the latter question clearly is no. OCR has induced many schools to sign legally binding compliance agreements, and many more have complied with its guidelines to avoid becoming the target of complaints filed with the agency. OCR developed a sophisticated, two-part enforcement strategy. Part 1 involved turning each individual sexual assault complaint against a school into a well-publicized and costly investigation of the practices of the entire institution. Part 2 used the pressure created by these investigations to build within schools compliance units more responsive to OCR than to anyone else.

Two novel elements of OCR's investigations were designed to put pressure on schools to sign legally binding agreements with the agency. The first was publicity. Previously investigations had remained under wraps until they were concluded. In 2014 OCR announced that it would publicly identify schools subject to sexual assault investigations from the outset to advance the Obama administration's goal of "putting an end to sexual violence—particularly on college campuses."[46] By first going after some of the nation's best known universities—schools that jealously guarded their reputations—OCR sought both to win some quick victories and to show that any educational institution could find itself on the agency's list of shame.

The second key feature of these investigations was their scope: any complaint lodged by an individual about a particular incidence of alleged misconduct would trigger a systematic investigation of the practices of the institution as a whole. In a 2015 interview with the Associated Press, Assistant Secretary Catherine Lhamon explained that OCR now viewed each complaint as "an opportunity for a broader assessment of a school's overall compliance." Rather than focusing on the facts presented by an individual complainant, "it's better to look at a school's policies, and other case files, to see if what happened to that student is an aberration." She explained, "We are more systemic in the way we evaluate because I think that's the way to get at civil rights compliance more effectively."[47] In another interview, Lhamon conceded that this means it can take years to complete such investigations: "A review is onerous. I don't love how much time it takes for my staff, and I don't love how much time it takes for schools. But I do love ensuring safety for all students on campus."[48]

By the summer of 2017, OCR had opened 410 investigations, but resolved only 65, leaving 345 ongoing. The average duration of completed investigations grew from about one year in 2010–12 to a year and a half in 2013, and nearly five years in 2014. By 2015 the average length was 940 days, nearly three years. An October 2015 article in the *Chronicle of Higher Education* reported: "The latest settlements show that federal inquiries into how colleges handle sexual assault are growing longer, tougher, and more demanding."[49] Assistant Secretary Lhamon told Congress that these investigations were so resource-intensive for the agency that it needed a substantial increase in its staff and appropriation. In 2016 Congress provided only a modest increase. A year later OCR faced the prospect of a substantial cut in its budget.

These investigations proved even more costly for the targeted schools. The direct, financial costs of replying to all the agency's demands for information can be substantial. More important are the reputation costs, especially when groups on campus use the investigations to charge the school with turning a blind eye on assault. OCR has certainly attracted the attention of top school officials. According to a *Chronicle of Higher Education* report, "Longtime leaders can't recall another issue that so consumed colleges. . . . Just about every campus has a task force. Some presidents say they've spent half their time on the issue— and serious money, limiting their ability to add another mental-health counselor, for example, or hold down a tuition increase. Chancellors can rattle off the percentage of students and faculty members who have completed new training programs."[50] Few investigations result in a finding of no violation—even if the only specific infractions involve deficient record-keeping. According to Peter Lake of Stetson University, one of the country's leading experts on Title IX compliance, "They come into your closet and say, 'Everything is in order, but we just went into your dresser and your socks aren't matching.'"[51] In the first of her three 2017 *Atlantic* articles, Emily Yoffe was more blunt: "Several former OCR investigators and one current investigator told me the perceived message from Washington was that once an investigation into a school was opened, the investigators in the field offices were not meant to be objective fact finders. Their job was to find schools in violation of Title IX."[52] Since the ultimate objective of the investigations is not to discover the extent of wrongdoing, but to induce schools to sign an agreement that incorporates OCR's demands, few issues escape the agency's attention.

Even though schools are eager to demonstrate that they are serious about addressing sexual misconduct, OCR's investigatory strategy has often created an adversarial relationship between its staff and school officials. Student affairs administrators at some schools under investigation told a *Chronicle of Higher Education* reporter that they were "buckling under the pressure of trying to meet the government's approval with their prevention and adjudication efforts." To avoid antagonizing government regulators, these school administrators "would not allow their names to be used in sharing their frustration with the process."[53] One student affairs officer wrote an anonymous essay in *Inside Higher Ed* arguing that his so-called colleagues in OCR "do not know my work." They "do not know what I face every day in responding to a student culture of alcohol infused hook-ups, where regrettable sex is a daily occurrence." In particular, "I do not appreciate having my hands tied by the presumption of guilt the Dear Colleague Letter portrays." He doubted that the practices of his or any other school "could hold up to the intense scrutiny of the team of lawyers OCR will send after us should a complaint arise." As a result, "My fear—yes it's fear—of seeing my institution's name in *Inside Higher Ed* or the *Chronicle of Higher Education* as the subject of an investigation, or, even worse, having the 'letter of agreement' OCR makes public displayed for all to read—makes me toe the line in a way I sometimes have trouble justifying to myself."[54]

Some school officials have been understandably angered by the fact that OCR requires schools to sign legally binding agreements before they see the "letter of finding" issued by OCR that explains whether and how the school has violated the law. When Tufts University discovered that OCR had charged it with violating Title IX, its president temporarily withdrew his approval of the lengthy agreement it had negotiated with OCR. Faced with the prospect of continuing scrutiny and controversy, he soon relented. According to *Inside Higher Ed*, when Assistant Secretary Lhamon spoke at a conference of the National Association of College and University Attorneys, she "was roundly booed." When Trump appointees spoke to them about their proposed changes in enforcement practices, in contrast, "the reaction seemed largely favorable."[55] This might have been the first time a group associated with higher education showed more support for the Trump administration than the Obama administration.

OCR's approach to investigations has also received criticism from those speaking for assault survivors. According to a lawyer for the Boston-based Victim Rights Law Center, OCR's determination to "look at everything from soup to nuts" was "a great thing" overall, but "it's terrible for victims" who have filed complaints. The enforcement strategy of the Obama OCR, she claimed, "utterly fails to provide remedies to individual victims." She described OCR's response to individual complainants as, "Thanks for the complaint, we'll see you in four years while we do a compliance review."[56] In a 2016 *Yale Law Journal* article, Alyssa Peterson and Olivia Ortiz wrote that "while OCR has dramatically improved its effort to reform structural Title IX compliance . . . it has done relatively little to promote complainants' immediate access to education." As a result, "most survivors must wait years—sometimes even until after they graduate or withdraw from the institution—to get redress."[57]

In the summer of 2017 the acting assistant secretary of education for civil rights, Candice Jackson, sent a memo to the agency's regional directors stating, "Effective immediately, there is no mandate that any one type of complaint is automatically treated differently than any other type of complaint with respect to the scope of the investigations." In particular, "OCR will no longer follow the existing investigative rule of obtaining three years of past complaint data" for sexual assault complaints. It will "only apply a 'systemic' or 'class-action' approach where the individual complaint allegations themselves raise system or class wide issues or the investigative team determines a systemic approach is warranted through conversations with the complainant." OCR's primary goal is "to swiftly address compliance issues raised by individual complaint allegations." These instructions "are designed to empower our investigative staff to clear case backlogs and resolve complaints within a reasonable time-frame, thus providing effective resolution and justice to complainants and recipients."[58]

Almost immediately the memo was leaked to the press, provoking outrage among those who saw this as "another sign of retreat on civil rights" by the Trump administration.[59] These critics included thirty-four Democratic senators who described Jackson's memo as "scaling back and narrowing the way OCR will approach civil rights enforcement."[60] The newly installed chair of the U.S. Commission on Civil Rights, Catherine Lhamon, described the departure from the enforcement strategy she had instituted while head of OCR as "stunning," "dangerous," and inconsistent with the agency's legal mandate.[61] She announced that the commission would hold two years of hearings to monitor the Trump administration's enforcement of civil rights laws. These critics failed to mention that OCR's post-2014 use of investigations had been a novel effort to enforce guidelines that went far beyond those enforceable in court, one that had left schools and individual complainants in suspended animation for years.

Enforcement II: Building Powerful Compliance Offices

Given the fact that OCR does not have enough staff to investigate the schools now on its list, how can it hope to monitor compliance with the detailed plans it negotiates? The answer is that OCR fastened upon the strategy of building well-staffed compliance offices within universities, increasing their internal autonomy, and cementing professional ties between these Title IX offices and federal administrators. OCR has required Title IX coordinators to exercise control over a growing cadre of investigators, trainers, and service providers. The more responsibilities placed on schools—from providing educational programming to carrying out "climate checks" to evaluating the effectiveness of prevention programs to organizing student groups to reporting regularly to OCR—the larger and more influential Title IX offices become. The result, as Gersen and Suk put it, is "the burgeoning of specified mini-bureaucracies within nongovernmental institutions to administer these procedural obligations, including investigation, discipline, and prevention."[62] These compliance offices will remain in place even if OCR alters its sexual harassment policy.

A number of recent studies of affirmative action and sexual harassment have shown that "human resources" professionals within corporations, schools, and local governments have been a major factor behind the institutionalization of these practices.[63] Harvard sociologist Frank Dobbin writes, "In the United States, once harassment was defined as employment discrimination, it gained a natural constituency among corporate personnel experts handling Title VII."[64] These personnel administrators offered two solutions, grievance procedures and training—both designed and run, of course, by those same personnel administrators.

In his study of local government compliance with Title VII rules, Charles Epp found that "to win executive backing, personnel experts often exaggerated federal support for training just as they had exaggerated support for grievance procedures." Although "the personnel administration profession initially received feminists' complaints of sexual harassment coolly," before long "the profession accepted many of the feminists' policy recommendations and endorsed policies that reached significantly beyond the Supreme Court's narrow suggestions." The "growth of employees rights in the 1970s and 1980s," Epp writes, "offered personnel administration a virtual lifeline, a new rationale for its existence and role."[65]

OCR's post-2011 guidelines require schools to grant a variety of powers to their Title IX coordinators. Coordinators are responsible not just for reviewing all Title IX complaints, but for "identifying and addressing any patterns or systematic problems that arise during the review of such [sexual harassment] complaints."[66] To do so they must have access to the entire record of complaints, adjudicatory determinations and punishments, including law enforcement records. Title IX coordinators also bear responsibility for conducting all the training exercises described above, as well as the "climate checks" that have been all but mandated by OCR. The guidelines strongly imply that the coordinator should hire and supervise all Title IX complaint investigators.

In April 2015, OCR issued yet another DCL, this one devoted exclusively to the structure of Title IX offices. Title IX coordinators, Assistant Secretary Lhamon told school leaders, "must have the full support of your institution." She highly recommended that each institution employ a "full-time Title IX coordinator" in order to "minimize the risk of conflict of interest and . . . ensure sufficient time is available to perform all the role's responsibilities." The coordinator "should be independent to avoid any potential conflict of interest" and "should report directly" to the school's "senior leadership."[67]

To underscore the institutional autonomy of the Title IX office, the 2015 DCL offered this novel claim: "Title IX's broad anti-retaliation provision protects Title IX coordinators from discrimination, intimidation, threats, and coercion for the purpose of interfering with the performance of their job responsibility." More specifically, a recipient of federal funding "must not interfere with the Title IX coordinator's participation in complaint investigations and monitoring of the recipient's efforts to comply with and carry out its responsibility under Title IX."[68] This suggests that no one within a school can modify, overrule, or even question the decisions and policies of the Title IX coordinator. Nor, apparently, can the Title IX coordinator be fired as the result of a disagreement with the school's leadership. At the very least, this DCL sends the clear message that any school that second-guesses its Title IX coordinator risks being investigated by OCR.

The same 2015 DCL recommends that to provide the requisite "regular training to the Title IX coordinator," schools take advantage of "technical assistance" provided by OCR's regional offices and training programs offered by the Department of Education's "Equity Assistance Centers." The federal government has deluged Title IX coordinators with suggestions on what constitutes "best practices" for almost all their tasks. To strengthen their ties with like-minded professionals outside their school, OCR encourages Title IX coordinators "to seek mentorship from a more experienced Title IX coordinator and to collaborate with other Title IX coordinators in the region."

In *Bureaucracy: What Government Agencies Do and Why They Do It*, James Q. Wilson notes that in a bureaucracy, "Professionals are those employees who receive some significant portion of their incentives from organized groups of fellow practitioners located outside the agency." As a result, "the way such a person defines his or her task may reflect more the standards of the external reference group than the preferences of the internal management."[69] The flip side of insulating the Title IX office from internal control is strengthening the signals that come from outside the university. The measures described in the preceding paragraphs indicate that OCR intends to ensure that the "reference group" for the "professionals" hired by Title IX coordinators are those the federal government has recently called into being and instructed.

In its agreements with particular schools, OCR has asserted even more control over schools' Title IX offices and placed them under continuing surveillance. For example, the Tufts resolution letter specifies fifteen tasks the office of the Title IX coordinator must perform, the Ohio State agreement twelve. The Tufts letter lists thirteen items that office must report to OCR on every student complaint it investigates. Tufts also promised to "provide access to its files during OCR's monitoring" to confirm the accuracy of these reports. It must submit all training material to OCR for its approval. It cannot alter the pamphlets it distributes to students without an OK from OCR. The agreement stipulates that "OCR may visit the University, interview staff and students, and request additional reports" to determine whether the university has complied with the agreement and all Title IX rules. Most strikingly, Tufts may not make any changes in its grievance procedures or "climate check" without prior approval by OCR.[70]

The *Chronicle of Higher Education* reports that since OCR started its sexual harassment investigations in 2013, schools have been "scrambling to find people with experience responding to sexual-violence complaints and the ability to interpret federal regulations. Among new hires are former lawyers with the Office for Civil Rights and longtime equal-opportunity advocates."[71] For example, as part of its agreement with OCR, Harvard hired a new Title IX coordinator and a new chief investigator. Both were former OCR lawyers. Peter Lake estimates that from 2011 to 2015 colleges spent more than $100 million to comply with Title IX sexual harassment guidelines, much of it in the form of salaries to those employed by the Title IX coordinator. As a result of the government's focus on prevention, Lake claims, "Title IX coordinators are now starting to become almost like an academic department, teaching people about culture change."[72]

One way to attract top candidates, a headhunter told the *Chronicle of Higher Education*, is to show that the university is thinking about the job "not only in the narrow compliance sense, but in the spirit of Title IX." According to Kaaren Williamsen, then the Title IX coordinator at Swarthmore (and previously director of the Gender and Sexuality Center at Carleton College), "These new jobs are really not just about compliance anymore," but are about "campus climate."[73] Since 2013, Swarthmore, a college with only 1,500 students, has appointed four new Title IX deputy coordinators and a Title IX fellow plus a "violence prevention educator and advocate" in its health center and a new sexual misconduct investigator in the college police department. It has also added staff positions in a new Office of Student Engagement, and created a Student Title IX Advisory Team, "a group of 10 dedicated Swarthmore students who will advise on policy, procedures, events, and initiatives."[74] By 2016 Harvard had more than fifty full-time and part-time Title IX coordinators, and Yale had thirty. At the University of California, Berkeley, Title IX spending rose by over $2 million between 2013 and 2016.[75] The University of North Carolina (UNC) now has seven full-time Title IX compliance officers. The UNC Title IX coordinator, a former OCR lawyer, has complained that his well-staffed office is not getting enough sexual harassment complaints.[76] This is a good example of how expansion of government regulation increases the number and influence of academic administrators—an institutional shift of great significance in higher education.

As the Tufts example shows, the settlement agreements that OCR negotiates with schools often require Title IX offices to organize and work with student groups that share their sense of mission. George Washington University agreed to "establish a committee of students, with representation from various student groups, including women's groups, student athletes, and others, to assist students understand their rights under Title IX . . . and recommend strategies to prevent sex discrimination and harassment."[77] The University of Mississippi agreed to set up a similar student task force that included "women's groups, female/male student athletes, Sorority/Fraternity leaders and other student leaders."[78] This ensures that schools' Title IX offices have an engaged constituency within the student body.

In 2016 OCR reprimanded the University of New Mexico (UNM) for its failure to "adequately engage student groups to ensure that it is meeting the needs of a diverse campus community." Since religion, race and ethnicity, sexual orientation, disability, and gender identity "can affect how students address and respond to sexual harassment," the university's prevention efforts "should take account of and include students from diverse backgrounds." According to OCR, "LGBTQ students report that the University's messaging around sexual harassment, including sexual assault, uses a heterosexist frame" and that the school "does not have a counselor trained or competent to help LGBTQ individuals at the faculty/staff counseling center." Consequently, the agency expected UNM's Title IX office to work more closely not only with groups representing LGBTQ students, but also "campus community groups" representing African American, American Indian, and Latino students.[79]

Mission Creep

Given these features of universities' Title IX offices, it is not surprising that they often develop a very strong sense of mission. For example, during a panel discussion at the University of Virginia, Amanda Childress, coordinator of Dartmouth's Sexual Assault Awareness Program, asked, "Why could we not expel a student based on an allegation?" She claimed that since only a tiny fraction of accusations are unfounded and the vast majority of assaults go unreported, "It seems to me that we value fair and equitable process more than we value the safety of our students. And higher education is not a right. Safety is a right. Higher education is a privilege."[80] In other words, expulsion first, a hearing only later, if at all.

The aspirations of some of these newly empowered administrators was expressed by Laura Bennett, the president of the Association for Student Conduct Administration, a group sure to benefit from OCR's mandates. Bennett was one of the people asked by the *Chronicle of Higher Education* to explain when we will know we have made progress combating sexual violence on campus. She responded that the following "would demonstrate institutional and systemic progress to me":

> First, there is adequate staffing for prevention and response, ample funding, and ongoing training. . . . Title IX coordinators, student-conduct administrators, and campus law enforcement are empowered by presidents and attorneys to make relevant policy decisions.

> Second, faculty discuss consent and healthy and unhealthy relationships in every course. . . . Students confront misogynistic and homophobic behaviors and statements . . . [and] the student party culture changes as a result of healthier concepts of masculinity and multiple positive identities for all genders and orientations.[81]

Bennett's statement captures the link between bureaucratic expansion and the demand for sweeping cultural change that has informed OCR's regulatory initiative.

Perhaps the most ambitious presentation of the aspirations of the new Title IX bureaucracies comes from the Harvard Office of Sexual Assault Prevention and Response (OSAPR). Four features of this office's explanation of its mission stand out. The first is how closely its understanding of sexual harassment mirrors the systemic paradigm first put forth by Catharine MacKinnon and other feminist legal scholars:

> Rape culture is ubiquitous—it manifests in the print, music, and film media we consume, the language we use to talk about sex and relationships, and the laws that govern our public and private spaces. Rape culture promotes sexual objectification and coercion . . . and dismissal of feminine-presenting or gender non-conforming individuals as not "fully human." . . . Understanding how to give and get consent in our interactions is essential to creating long-term, sustainable culture change. . . . A person's ability to say "yes" or "no" is influenced by the interplay of power, identity, and privilege between those involved. . . . Every day we are bombarded with messages that teach us to believe coercion is consent. This is how rape culture is created and perpetuated through deeply-embedded social norms, normalizing the belief that violence is not only sexy, but unavoidable.[82]

Second, combating "rape culture" requires changing the way we speak, not just the way we act. This means creating "social spaces free from harassing language and harmful behavior." Students need to "understand how attitudes and behavior are connected," and should be taught to "feel comfortable and empowered to confront harmful language, attitudes, and behavior at any time"—including when "someone makes a sexually suggestive comment about someone else's body on the street." To cleanse ourselves of oppressive beliefs, "We all need to look inward" and ask ourselves, "What implicit biases do we hold that contribute to oppressive structures and systems?"

Third, students need to be reeducated on how to create "healthy" personal relationships. One component of Harvard's OSAPR is called "Consent Advocates and Relationship Educators" (CARE). "Through strategic educational advocacy, outreach, and programming, CARE work to create a culture free from the threat or experience of sexual violence for all people." To accomplish this they "plan culturally-competent health communication campaigns" and "conduct peer-to-peer training surrounding consent, healthy relationships, and gender equity." To prepare for their role as "relationship educators," students "undergo 40 hours of training . . . that focuses on intersectionality, primary prevention through a public health model, and meaningful student engagement."

Finally, the campaign against sexual violence is but one part of a much broader fight against "oppressive structures" and for "social justice." According to its brief mission statement, the office "seeks to eliminate harm, violence, and oppression through the intersectional promotion of gender equality and social justice." Sexual violence is inseparable from gender inequality: "The less equity that exists between genders in a culture (men having more power than women and trans* people), the more likely rape, sexual assault, and harassment are likely to occur." Consequently, "addressing gender inequality requires reflection, action, and vision that is rooted in an anti-oppression, social justice framework." This in turn requires a "consistent and unwavering" commitment to the "anti-oppression" cause and an understanding of its "connection to sexual violence." In their biographies, the director and associate director stress their "history of community advocacy and social justice" and commitment to "inspiring social change through intersectional activism and strengthening community capacity to sustain cultural reform by confronting oppression in all forms."

The extent to which serious efforts to provide professional help to those who have experienced sexual assault have been combined with ideological attacks on "masculinity" in the name of "social justice" is evident in Princeton's 2017 description of a new position for an "Interpersonal Violence Clinician and Men's Engagement Manager." The person who fills this job, offered by the University Health Services' Sexual Harassment/Assault Advising Resources and Education office (SHARE), will "develop and implement men's programming initiatives geared toward enhancing awareness and challenging gender stereotypes, increasing the community's understanding of interpersonal violence dynamics." One-third of this person's time will be devoted to providing traditional counseling services. The rest will involve "promoting an environment for healthy male social development by challenging belief systems and social constructs that contribute to violence and offering alternative options." This may include "compulsory accountability programs for students *accused* of sexual misconduct under Title IX." (Apparently an accusation will be sufficient to trigger such mandatory training.) In addition to the advanced degrees, clinical experience, and certifications required for counseling, applicants must "possess knowledge about the challenges and privileges of male identity formation and the relationship with violence." They must demonstrate "expertise in . . . social justice issues," and the ability "to balance strong commitment to social justice with a capacity to navigate complex organizational systems."[83] In other words, addressing the problem of sexual assault requires us to go beyond dealing with individual cases to challenge "belief systems" about "gender stereotypes," to expose the "privileges of male identity formation and the relationship with violence," and to work toward "social justice." Princeton has yet to find a suitable candidate. Apparently finding an able clinician who also has "expertise in social justice" (requiring a Ph.D. in political philosophy perhaps?) is not easy.

Such language used to be the preserve of a few students on the ideological fringe and of professors in identity studies programs. Now it is embedded in the mission statements of university administrators empowered by federal regulators. The combination of OCR's broad interpretation of Title IX combined with its sophisticated enforcement strategy—both of which were informed by the "sociocultural" model of sexual harassment described in chapter 9—have left their mark on campuses throughout the country.

Conclusion

When OCR announced its new sexual harassment guidelines on the last day of the Clinton administration, it rejected both the limits the Supreme Court had placed on the responsibility of schools and the tort-based approach to regulation that had slowly evolved under Titles VII and IX. Among the matters left unclear were these: (1) Would this new approach survive the Bush administration? (2) How could the agency enforce its guidelines when they go beyond judicial interpretations of the statute? and (3) What would replace the individualistic, "bad apple" understanding of sexual harassment that undergirded the tort model?

The answer to the first question was "Yes," largely because without an alternative enforcement mechanism the 2001 guidelines did not amount to much. They remained in place, but essentially unenforced. The answer to the second question was the two-prong enforcement strategy described in this chapter. First use extensive, well-publicized investigations to force schools to the bargaining table, and then convince them to sign detailed compliance agreements monitored by newly empowered internal compliance offices.

Although the answer to the third question is harder to pin down, OCR's 2011 and 2014 guidelines and the agreements it reached with many schools reflect many elements of the "sociocultural" model described in chapter 9. Most important, sexual assault and other forms of harassment were seen not as the work of a few misguided souls, but as the product of a deeply embedded culture that threatens the safety of women. If "rape culture" is the problem, only changing the culture will solve it. That means extensive training on sexual mores and the meaning of masculinity and femininity. Moreover, existing institutions are so complicit in this "rape culture" that they cannot be trusted to address it adequately. Fiddling with incentives, the basic approach of tort law, will not suffice. New institutions must be created within schools to take over the job. Their job is not simply to reduce the incidence of assault and other forms of misconduct, but to *eliminate* them and address the effects of misconduct that takes place beyond the campus.

As we saw in chapter 9, this expansive reading of Title IX and the authority of OCR sparked opposition both inside and outside the university, largely on due process and free speech grounds. The Trump administration first modified OCR's policy of turning every sexual assault complaint into a full-blown, institution-wide compliance review, and then withdrew OCR's 2011 and 2014 guidelines. Meanwhile, hundreds of investigations continue, agreements already negotiated remain in place, and Title IX offices within universities retain their power. Many colleges followed the pattern set by Duke, whose dean told a reporter, "Right now we are staying where we are. . . . What we have in place now actually is a fair balance so we aren't going to go anywhere until we see what happens with rulemaking."[84] Once instituted, government policies are hard to reverse. Much more than inertia lies behind the policies first established by the Obama administration. They were based on understandings of the purposes of civil rights legislation and the authority of federal regulators that have many proponents in all three branches of government, in advocacy groups, and in academia. That is the topic of the following chapter.

Part IV

Expansion and Retrenchment

TWELVE

The Logic of Expansion

For most of its history Title IX regulation proceeded with glacial speed and little publicity. A long series of federal rules, interpretations, clarifications, negotiated agreements, and court decisions slowly extended the reach of federal mandates. Such incremental expansion paused under Republican administrations, and resumed when Democrats captured the White House. Only those intensely interested in Title IX policy could keep up with the evolution of this convoluted, opaque regulatory regime.

By 2016 this pattern had changed: the aggressiveness of the Obama administration put Title IX and the Office for Civil Rights (OCR) in the national spotlight, and the unexpected election of Donald Trump made regulatory retrenchment a real possibility. The apotheosis of the Obama administration's expansion of civil rights regulation was the Dear Colleague Letter (DCL) on the rights of transgender students issued by OCR and the Department of Justice (DOJ) in May 2016.[1] That letter required schools to grant access to bathrooms, locker rooms, showers, and overnight accommodations on the basis of students' gender identity (that is, their "internal sense of gender") rather than on the basis of their biological sex. The DCL insisted that respecting the identity of transgender students must take priority over responding to other students' concerns about privacy and safety. Schools' "desire to accommodate others' discomfort cannot justify a policy" that denies transgender students the right to choose the

225

sex-segregated facilities they will use, the sports teams on which they will play, and their preferred names and pronouns.[2]

The 2016 DCL was one part of an administration-wide effort to extend coverage of Title VII and Title IX to transgender employees and students. This became front-page news in 2016 when the Department of Justice filed suit against the state of North Carolina, which had recently enacted legislation requiring that access to public restrooms be determined solely by the sex listed on an individual's birth certificate. North Carolina responded by challenging the legality of the federal guidelines. Faced with boycotts by the National Basketball Association, the National Collegiate Athletic Association (NCAA), and an array of entertainers and corporations, North Carolina eventually modified its infamous "bathroom bill." But the controversy continued in the federal courts: one district court judge found that federal administrators had exceeded their authority in issuing the DCL and enjoined its enforcement. The Fourth Circuit, in contrast, deferred to federal administrators' interpretation of Title IX and issued an injunction enforcing it. Several other states subsequently considered legislation similar to North Carolina, but nowhere were these laws enacted.

The Obama administration's aggressive use of Title IX served as a convenient foil for the Republicans' attacks on political correctness and excessive federal regulation. Twenty-five Republican senators wrote to the secretary of education objecting to the department's repeated use of Dear Colleague Letters. Devoting a separate section to Title IX, the 2016 Republican platform declared that the Obama administration's "distortion of Title IX to micromanage the way colleges and universities deal with allegations of abuse contravenes our country's legal traditions and must be halted."[3]

In the fall of 2016 the Supreme Court—which in forty-four years had never heard a single Title IX case on athletics—agreed to review the Fourth Circuit's opinion in *G. G. v. Gloucester County School Board* to resolve the conflict in the lower courts. Soon after the Trump administration took office, though, the new leadership at DOJ withdrew the 2016 DCL. The Supreme Court then sent the *G. G.* case back to the circuit court for reconsideration in light of the new circumstances.

Whether this marked the end of the transgender rights experiment or merely a temporary setback will be determined by the federal courts. A few months after the Trump administration withdrew the DCL, the Seventh Circuit found that Title IX requires schools to follow the policies laid out by the Obama OCR. It is likely that before long the Supreme Court will address (and perhaps even resolve) this matter.

Although the Obama administration's transgender policy was in place only briefly, its history highlights two assumptions that undergird Title IX rules on both athletics and sexual harassment: first, that Title IX should be read as a "dynamic" statute whose meaning changes and expands over time; and second, that the law's principal purpose is to eliminate all forms of "sex stereotyping." After reviewing the actions of OCR and the courts on transgender rights, this chapter examines how these two assumptions have guided all aspects of Title IX regulation.

Transgender Rights

For nearly forty years—from 1972 through 2010—neither OCR nor federal courts interpreted Title IX to address discrimination on the basis of "gender identity." Indeed, almost no one had given any thought to the difference between "sex"— that is, the anatomical differences between male and female—and "gender identity"—that is, "an individual's internal sense of gender,"[4] or considered the possibility that the two might diverge. In the 1980s and 1990s the courts heard a handful of Title VII employment discrimination cases brought by transgender plaintiffs, but judges invariably held that federal law bans only discrimination based on sex, not gender identity.[5]

That began to change around 2000. Increasingly federal courts held that firing or refusing to hire an individual because that person's gender identity diverges from his or her biological sex constitutes a form of "sexual stereotyping" prohibited by Title VII.[6] These courts relied almost entirely on dicta in a plurality opinion announced by the Supreme Court in 1989, *Price Waterhouse v. Hopkins.* Although that case dealt primarily with the burden of proof in so-called mixed motive employment discrimination disputes, four members of the Court agreed that failure to promote a woman for not acting in a sufficiently "lady-like" fashion constitutes sex discrimination. An employer violates Title VII, they maintained, if that employer's decisions were "the product of sex stereotyping" or were "likely influenced by sex stereotyping."[7] According to Justice William Brennan's opinion, "Congress intended to strike at the entire spectrum of disparate treatment of men and women resulting from sex stereotypes."[8] Although the case involved neither sexual orientation nor gender identity, the wording of the plurality opinion suggests that gender nonconforming employees cannot be subject to adverse employment action simply because they refuse to conform to "sex stereotypes"—such as men wearing dresses or insisting upon being referred to as "she."[9]

If the evolution of transgender rights in the judiciary was slow and halting, between 2014 and 2016 the executive branch moved with remarkable speed and unity (see table 12-1). In 2014 President Obama issued an executive order prohibiting federal contractors from discriminating on the basis of sexual orientation or gender identity.[10] A few months later, Attorney General Eric Holder announced that the position of the Justice Department on the transgender issue had "evolved over time." While previously the department had maintained that

Table 12-1   Transgender Chronology

1975	The Department of Health, Education, and Welfare's Title IX regulations authorize schools to provide "separate toilet, locker room, and shower facilities on the basis of sex" as long as they are of comparable quality
1980s	Most federal courts find that Title VII does *not* cover gender identity or sexual orientation
1989	Plurality decision in *Price Waterhouse v. Hopkins* holds that employers violate Title VII if their decisions are "the product of sex stereotyping"
2000s	Relying on language in *Price Waterhouse*, most federal courts find that Title VII prohibits employment discrimination based on gender identification and sexual orientation
2007	Rep. Barney Frank introduces the Employment Non-Discrimination Act, which would amend Title VII to cover discrimination based on sexual orientation or gender identity
2010	Dear Colleague Letter on bullying covers bullying based on gender identity; OCR begins to investigate complaints about schools' treatment of transgender students
2012	Equal Employment Opportunity Commission rules that Title VII covers employment discrimination against transgender applicants (*Macy v. Holder*)
2013	OCR's agreement with Acadia Unified School District allows transgender students to use bathrooms matching their gender identity
2014	President Obama issues executive order prohibiting discrimination on the basis of gender identity by federal contractors
	In two sets of "Questions and Answers" OCR states that Title IX covers some forms of discrimination based on transgender status
	Attorney General Holder changes the position of the Department of Justice (DOJ), declaring that Title VII prohibits employment discrimination based on gender identity
2015	Ferg-Cadima letter states that OCR policy with regard to sex-segregated facilities is that schools must "treat transgender students consistent with their gender identity"
2016	Fourth Circuit defers to OCR's transgender policy in *G. G. v. Gloucester County School Board*
	OCR and DOJ issue their transgender DCL

Table 12-1 (*continued*)

	DOJ sues North Carolina over its bathroom bill; North Carolina countersues, challenging the legality of the DCL
	Supreme Court grants certiorari in *G. G. v. Gloucester County School Board*
	Federal district court in Texas rules that the DCL violates Title IX and issues nationwide injunction stopping its enforcement
2017	DOJ withdraws DCL; Supreme Court sends *G. G.* back to the Fourth Circuit
	Seventh Circuit finds that both Title VII and Title IX cover discrimination based on gender identity, and require schools to allow students to choose sex-segregated facilities that match their gender identity

Title VII does *not* cover discrimination against transgender individuals, it now realized that Title VII prohibits "discrimination based on a perceived failure to conform to socially constructed characteristics of males and females."[11] In another forum Holder described "the fight for equality for our lesbian, gay, bisexual, and transgender—or LGBT—citizens" as "the defining civil rights challenge of our time."[12] Shortly thereafter, the Office of Federal Contract Compliance Programs in the Department of Labor issued guidelines explaining that "discrimination based upon gender identity, gender expression, and sex stereotyping" now constitutes a "form of prohibited sex discrimination."[13]

The immediate catalyst for the Obama administration's effort appears to have been Congress's failure to enact either the Employment Non-Discrimination Act (ENDA) or the Student Non-Discrimination Act, legislation that would have explicitly amended Titles VII and IX to cover discrimination on the basis of sexual orientation and gender identity. Both these bills had the support of a large number of congressional Democrats, but could not win approval in the Republican-controlled House. LGBT groups had for some time urged President Obama to make more aggressive use of administrative tools, most importantly an executive order on discrimination by government contractors. According to a 2012 *New York Times* article, "President Obama disappointed and vexed gay supporters" by his initial refusal to do so.[14] The president preferred to go the legislative route—at least until it became evident that such a strategy would fail. At that point the president expanded his We Can't Wait agenda to include the demands of a key constituency in the Democrats' coalition.[15]

From the Workplace to the Classroom . . . and Beyond

While President Obama waited for Congress to act, OCR began to include protections for transgender students in its Title IX guidelines. As usual, it did so in a series of small steps with little explanation. OCR first mentioned the issue in its 2010 DCL on bullying, which included this head-scratching statement: "Although Title IX does not prohibit discrimination based solely on sexual orientation, Title IX does protect all students, including lesbian, gay, bisexual, and transgender (LGBT) students, from sexual discrimination." According to the DCL, Title IX gives OCR authority to attack all forms of bullying that are the result of "hostility based on sex or sex-stereotyping. . . . Thus it can be sex discrimination if students are harassed either for exhibiting what is perceived as stereotypical characteristics for their sex, or for failing to conform to stereotypical notions of masculinity and femininity."[16] At first OCR only told schools to take steps to prevent harassment based on students' "LGBT status." But as the agency investigated specific complaints about bullying of transgender students, it extended its demands to cover a much different issue, namely, access to sex-segregated facilities. Over the next four years it signed six resolution agreements with schools requiring them to take action against bullying and to base access to sex-segregated facilities on students' gender identity, not their biological sex.[17]

As was the case with sexual harassment, OCR applied to Title IX legal doctrines originally developed under Title VII, never acknowledging the differences between the two contexts. One obvious difference is age. Most students are much younger than most employees. They are more likely to be experimenting with new identities. Even those who are sure that their gender identity does not match their physical attributes are usually too young to undergo hormone treatment or surgery. Their transitions pose especially difficult challenges for the school personnel who must deal with these complex psychological and interpersonal issues.

A second key difference is that although some employers claim the right to deny employment to transgender applicants, no one has claimed that schools should be able to *exclude* transgender students. That would violate state law and invite an Equal Protection challenge without serving any legitimate public purpose. Rather, the central issue in the education setting is how to classify transgender students in those few arenas where schools can legally segregate by sex. This significantly narrows the question of what constitutes discrimination.

What Does "Sex" Mean?

To understand the access-to-bathrooms issue, it is important to recall that Title IX provides several exceptions to the general rule that educational institutions receiving federal funding cannot discriminate on the basis of sex. Title IX does not prohibit single-sex private undergraduate schools, or single-sex religious or military schools. It does not prohibit schools from sponsoring father–son or mother–daughter events, providing separate housing for male and female students, or maintaining single-sex athletic teams. A noncontroversial section of the Department of Health, Education, and Welfare's 1975 regulations stated, "A recipient may provide separate toilet, locker room, and shower facilities on the basis of sex, but such facilities provided for students of one sex shall be comparable to such facilities provided for students of the opposite sex."[18] In areas where personal privacy is especially important, separate-but-equal has long been the general rule.

There are three possible answers to the question of how schools can allocate access to these sex-segregated facilities. The first—in effect the one that has governed school life until very recently—is that school officials have discretion to use *either* biological sex or gender identity. Not surprisingly, schools usually resolve these issues on an ad hoc basis, taking into account the requests of transgender students (many of whom prefer single-occupancy facilities), their physical attributes, the stage of their gender transition, and the reactions of other students.

The second position is that taken by OCR and DOJ in 2016: the student's gender identity is the *sole* criterion schools can use. The difficulty with this position is that it requires us to read the word "sex" in Title IX and its regulations to mean *only* "gender identity" and *not* "biological sex." This not only runs counter to the common understanding of the term, but it ignores the fact that the term "gender identity" was coined precisely to *differentiate* transgender individuals' subjective understanding of themselves from their anatomical or chromosomal sex. The third position is the one initially taken by the state of North Carolina in response to OCR's mandate: schools *must* base such decisions on the biological sex listed on the student's birth certificate.

OCR's Policy Statements

Given the novelty of the transgender access issue, the tenuous legal foundation for OCR's position, and the intense political opposition it was likely to provoke, one might have expected the agency to offer a full-throated explanation of its legal and policy arguments. It never did so. In two "Question and Answer" documents released in 2014, it merely asserted that "Title IX's sex discrimination prohibition extends to claims of discrimination based on gender identity," and that schools "must treat transgender students consistent with their gender identity in all aspects of the planning, implementation, enrollment, operation, and evaluation of single-sex classes."[19]

When OCR did finally issue a general policy statement, it employed a strange form: a letter from the acting deputy assistant secretary for policy responding to an e-mail inquiry from a transgender advocate.[20] According to this January 2015 letter, "When a school elects to separate or treat students differently on the basis of sex" in situations authorized by the department's Title IX regulations, it "must treat transgender students consistent with their gender identity." But OCR also "encourages schools to offer the use of gender-neutral, individual-user facilities to any student who does not want to use shared sex-segregated facilities." This letter was never made public and contains no justification for its mandate. Yet the Fourth Circuit soon recognized it as the authoritative interpretation of Title IX regulations to which courts should defer.[21]

In its initial ruling in *G. G. v. Gloucester County School Board*, the Fourth Circuit did not argue that Title IX *must* be read in this way, but only that the text of the law and the 1975 regulations is sufficiently ambiguous to *permit* OCR's interpretation. Judicial review of an agency's interpretation of its own regulations, the court held, must be "highly deferential." The panel split 2-1, with Judge Paul Niemeyer arguing in dissent that the word "sex" in Title IX and its regulations cannot plausibly be read to mean "gender identity" as OCR claimed. The majority, he charged, "misconstrues the clear language of Title IX and its regulation" to arrive at "an unworkable and illogical result."[22]

In April 2016, one month after the Fourth Circuit announced its *G.G.* decision, OCR and DOJ issued their eight-page transgender DCL. In a classic example of institutional leapfrogging, the two agencies claimed that their policy statement "is consistent with the courts' and other agencies' interpretation of Federal laws prohibiting sex discrimination." They could offer only one such court interpretation of Title IX, namely, the Fourth Circuit decision deferring to the interpretation OCR had offered in the January 2015 letter. All the other court rulings involved a different issue, employment discrimination under Title VII.[23]

If the 2016 DCL was short on legal or policy justification, it was long on mandates. Because schools cannot "treat a transgender student differently from the way it treats other students of the same gender identity," they must do the following:

- use a transgender student's preferred pronoun and name both in the classroom and in official records, even if this differs from the student's legal name;

- keep strictly confidential any information that might reveal the fact that the student has undergone gender transition;

- allow transgender students access to restrooms, locker rooms, housing, single-sex classes, and single-sex public schools "consistent with their gender identity";

- not "rely on overly broad generalizations or stereotypes about the differences between transgender students and other students of the same sex" when deciding who is eligible to play on all-male or all-female sports teams.

Schools must abide by these rules "even in circumstances in which other students, parents, or community members raise objections or concerns." The students whose objections must be disregarded include those required to share shower, dormitory rooms, or other overnight accommodations with a transgender student.

OCR had little opportunity to apply its new policy. In early August the Supreme Court took the unusual step of staying the Fourth Circuit's order until it either denied certiorari in the *G. G.* case or upheld its decision.[24] In October it granted certiorari, thus keeping the stay in place. A few weeks later, a federal district court judge in Texas issued a nationwide injunction prohibiting OCR from enforcing its transgender DCL. Ruling in a case brought by a number of states and local school districts, Judge Reed O'Connor found (1) that the agency had violated the Administrative Procedure Act by not using notice-and-comment rulemaking to establish its policy; and (2) that OCR's policy was incompatible with the clear meaning of Title IX and the 1975 regulations.[25]

What's Done by DCL Can Be Undone by DCL . . . Or Maybe Not

Judge O'Connor lifted his injunction only after the Trump administration withdrew the 2016 DCL a month after the president's inauguration.[26] According to press reports, the new secretary of education, Betsy DeVos, defended the 2016 DCL, but lost a White House debate with Attorney General Jeff Sessions.[27] The withdrawal letter stated that the Obama administration's 2015 and 2016 policy statements were deficient both because they did not "undergo any formal public process" and because they failed to "explain how the position is consistent with the express language of Title IX." The Trump administration's letter emphasized, though, that "withdrawal of these guidance documents does not leave students without protection from discrimination, bullying, or harassment." A few months later OCR headquarters sent instruction to its field offices explaining that complaints regarding any form of harassment, retaliation, or "different treatment based on sex stereotyping" must be investigated "with great care and individualized attention."[28]

During the second round of litigation in the Fourth Circuit, two former secretaries of education, Arne Duncan and John B. King Jr., joined with Catherine Lhamon and other Obama subcabinet officials to submit an amicus brief on behalf of the transgender plaintiff, Gavin Grimm. They urged the court to follow "the practice and history of the Departments of Education and Justice" by "interpreting Title IX's prohibition against sex discrimination to include protections against gender identity discrimination."[29] OCR's policy, they maintained, was "based on a thorough review and analysis of the law and facts, a substantial record of jurisprudence and agency decision making, and scientific studies."[30] What the Obama administration had done in many tiny steps, they insisted, could not be undone by the Trump administration in one DCL. This implied that the more obscure the basis of a policy determination, the more deference it deserves from the courts.

Once the Trump administration switched the government's position on the transgender issue, the big question became how the federal courts would interpret Title IX. As noted above, the two courts that had previously confronted the issue came to opposite conclusions. The Fourth Circuit found that the word "sex" in Title IX was sufficiently ambiguous to give OCR authority to insist that the word be equated with "gender identity." The federal district court judge in Texas, in contrast, held that the term is *not* ambiguous: "the plain meaning of the term sex" as it was used in HEW's 1975 regulations "meant the biological and anatomical differences between male and female students as determined at their birth."[31] Consequently, that court ruled, OCR's recent policies were invalid. The withdrawal of the 2016 DCL changed the burden of proof in subsequent legal disputes. Previously the issue had been whether Title IX and the 1975 regulations were *sufficiently ambiguous* to justify the Obama administration's actions. But after the Supreme Court sent the *G. G.* case back to the Fourth Circuit, the question became whether the language of the statute and the 1975 regulations was *sufficiently specific* to require that the Obama administration's policies remain in place.

Representing Gavin Grimm in the Virginia case, the American Civil Liberties Union (ACLU) assembled an impressive list of amicus briefs in the second round of litigation. One was filed by the Obama administration officials mentioned above. The National Association for the Advancement of Colored People argued that prohibiting a transgender boy from using the boys' locker room was the equivalent of segregating buses and schools on the basis of race. The National Education Association argued that reversing the Obama administration's policy would not only harm transgender students, but would "sow confusion and discord in public schools" by leaving teachers uncertain about how to handle these issues. A number of associations representing health professions argued that medical science provides a firm basis for the previous OCR/DOJ policy.[32]

After initially arguing that courts should defer to the agencies' interpretation of ambiguous terms, the ACLU now did an about-face, asking the appeals court to interpret the law "de novo and without deference."[33] Lawyers for the school board, in contrast, used Title IX's legislative and regulatory history to show that when legislators and regulators used the term "sex," they meant anatomy, not "gender identity." Their brief concluded: "Instead of joining *G. G.* in rewriting Title IX, this Court should simply adopt the intuitive interpretation that the Board is permitted by Title IX to separate the sexes in restrooms and locker rooms based on the physiological distinctions between males and females, as school districts around the nation have been doing in reliance on Title IX for the past five decades."[34]

Although most media attention focused on the *G. G.* case, it was the Seventh Circuit that first addressed the issue in its new political context. In April 2017, the full Seventh Circuit ruled that Title VII covers employment discrimination based on sexual orientation.[35] A month later a three-judge panel of that court held in *Whitaker by Whitaker v. Kenosha Unified School District* that both Title IX and the Equal Protection clause require schools to respect students' gender identification when assigning them to sex-segregated facilities.[36]

Nowhere in its long *Whitaker* opinion did the unanimous panel discuss the meaning of the word "sex." Instead, it focused entirely on "sex stereotyping." In enacting Titles VII and IX, the circuit court claimed, Congress "intended to strike at the entire spectrum of disparate treatment of men and women resulting from sex stereotypes."[37] "By definition," it noted, "a transgender individual does not conform to the sex-based stereotypes of the sex that he or she was assigned at birth."[38] A school "policy that requires an individual to use a bathroom that does not conform with his or her gender identity punishes that individual for his or her gender non-conformance, which in turn violates Title IX."[39]

To this the *Whitaker* panel added an Equal Protection argument. Whenever a state uses a sex-based classification, "the burden rests with the state to demonstrate that its proffered justification is exceedingly persuasive." Here the harm done to the transgender student is severe, and the harm done to other students is "based upon sheer conjecture and abstraction."[40] Therefore, the school's policy violates the Constitution.

The fact that the Seventh Circuit panel relied in part on such a novel constitutional argument increased the likelihood that the Supreme Court would review the issue. On the one hand, it seems unlikely that Chief Justice Roberts and Justices Thomas, Alito, Gorsuch, and Kennedy (the author of the spirited dissent in *Davis v. Monroe County School Board*) will adopt such a broad reading of Title IX. On the other hand, Justice Kennedy has regularly deserted the conservative bloc in constitutional cases involving sexual orientation. However the Supreme Court resolves the case, its decision is likely to affect the trajectory of all forms of Title IX regulation for years to come.

From Exclusion to Stereotyping

One could offer a rather simple political explanation for these developments. The LGBT community and its advocacy organizations have become an important constituency of the Democratic Party. Especially after the Supreme Court's same-sex marriage decision, transgender rights rose to the top of their agenda. When Congress refused to amend Titles VII and IX to cover sexual orientation and gender identity, the Obama administration did so through bureaucratic means.

The rigidity of the federal government's command—schools must *always* defer to the gender identity of students, regardless of other students' concerns about safety and privacy—led to an equally rigid response from states like North Carolina—transgender individuals can *only* use the sex-segregated facilities that correspond to the sex listed on their birth certificate. The unnecessary harshness of North Carolina's legislation provoked understandable outrage among many people who had hardly ever thought about the issue before. Once this issue was drawn into the vortex of the culture wars, the usual political alliances (and animosities) quickly formed and hardened. In this political environment, Title IX served as a statutory Swiss Army knife: new, specialized tools could be grafted onto the original structure in order to deal with an emerging issue.

What this political explanation misses is the extent to which OCR's 2016 DCL on transgender rights was in an important respect—as the agency maintained—an extension of an understanding of Title IX that stretched back to the early 1990s. Guided by this understanding, Title IX has been transformed from a law designed to prevent schools from establishing educational practices that exclude or disadvantage female students to a far more sweeping effort to eliminate all forms of "sex stereotyping." This meant not just preventing educational institutions from making decisions on the basis of stereotypes, but training students, faculty, and staff to change the way they think about sex differences, about "femininity and masculinity," about what constitutes appropriate sexual conduct, and about whether sexual differences have any basis in nature rather than convention. This reeducation effort extends to women—who must learn to reject the roles and limitations placed on them by the dominant culture—and to the general public outside educational institutions—who must be provided with new female role models and jolted out of conventional ways of thinking about sex differences.

During the 1970s, neither members of Congress nor federal administrators paid much attention to the issue of gender stereotypes. They focused primarily on practices that prevented female students from gaining entrance to particular schools, departments, programs, or courses as well as on the discriminatory hiring practices that had made it nearly impossible for women to hold teaching positions in many university departments. To the extent stereotypes were mentioned at all during the brief congressional debate, it was to decry the fact that educational institutions had justified exclusionary policies by relying on inaccurate and outmoded views of women's interests and abilities.[41]

When some women's groups urged the Department of Health, Education, and Welfare (HEW) to include in its 1975 regulations a provision requiring the federal government to review textbooks to eliminate gender stereotypes, Caspar Weinberger, then the secretary of HEW, declared that he would never approve such a rule.[42] Although "sexual stereotyping in textbooks and curricular materials is a serious matter," such a review would "place the Department in a position of limiting free expression in violation of the First Amendment." Especially since "there is no evidence in the legislative history that the proscriptions in title IX against sex discrimination should be interpreted in this way," the department would not open this can of worms.[43]

As schools eliminated overt barriers facing female students, the attention of regulators and judges shifted to more subtle consequences of conventional understandings of male and female roles, drawing them deeper and deeper into realms previously considered private. Attention first shifted from the policies and practices of educational institutions to the behavior of students, then from the conduct of those students to their speech and their beliefs, and finally to the beliefs and mores of the public at large.

The shift first became apparent in intercollegiate athletics. As judges and administrators struggled with the tricky question of how to ensure "equal athletic opportunity," they maintained that "Title IX was enacted in order to remedy discrimination that results from stereotyped notions of women's interests and abilities." Evidence purporting to show that female students are less interested in varsity athletics than their male counterparts, the First Circuit wrote in the leading case, "provides only a measure of the very discrimination that is and has been the basis for women's lack of opportunity to participate in sports."[44] Title IX was designed to change these social norms, however well-established they may be: "Had Congress intended to entrench, rather than change, the status quo . . . it need not have gone to all the trouble of enacting Title IX."[45] Similarly Ninth Circuit judge Cynthia Holcomb Hall insisted that "women's attitudes toward sports are socially constructed and have been limited by discrimination and gender stereotypes." Congress expected Title IX to be used to combat those stereotypes, "thereby changing the social environment in which girls and women develop, or do not develop, interest in sports."[46] The motto "Build it and they will come" is based on the assumption that all differences between males and females are "socially constructed," that gender equality requires new construction (both literally and figuratively), and that the practices of schools can weaken destructive stereotypes in society at large.

This focus on changing public attitudes was even more evident several years later when the Seventh Circuit held that when Indiana high schools relegate girls' basketball games to "non-primetime" slots, the result is a small audience and "the perception that the girls' team is inferior and less deserving than the boys'." This "disparate scheduling creates a cyclical effect that stifles community support, prevents the development of a fan base, and discourages females from participating in a traditionally male dominated sport." Title IX requires schools to counteract these "stereotyped notions of women's interests and abilities" by increasing the audience for girls' varsity games.[47] In a similar vein OCR has required college athletic departments to increase publicity and media coverage for women's teams: schedule it, publicize it, and fans will come.[48]

The assumption that schools have an obligation to change the way prospective students and the public at large think about women and sports helps explain why so much attention has been lavished on intercollegiate sports (which at most schools provide athletic opportunities to only a tiny fraction of the student body), why OCR's recent agreements have required women's teams to receive more publicity, and why "competitive cheer" has become such a contentious issue.[49] The more visible the sport, the more important it becomes for changing public perceptions. Thus the unlikely alliance between feminists, who are usually suspicious of testosterone-driven competitiveness, and proponents of the most visible and commercialized form of college athletics.

Although sexual harassment did not become a significant Title IX issue until the early 1990s, it is easy to understand how sexual harassment can substantially limit the educational opportunities available to women. If female students face constant disparagement, or if working with a particular professor exposes them to the threat of assault, retaliation, or indignity, then their opportunities are hardly equal to those of their male counterparts. The central regulatory problem is that addressing harassment by staff members and peers raises difficult monitoring and enforcement issues. Since harassment is not an official policy that can quickly be changed by those at the top, schools must devise procedures for policing hundreds, thousands, even tens of thousands of people and changing their habits. It took the courts and the EEOC over two decades to devise a tort mechanism for holding employers responsible for harassment by superiors and fellow workers. Finding ways to address harassment by fellow students is even more difficult since they are far more numerous and engage in informal behavior that remains unobserved by institutional monitors. Being immature, elementary and secondary school students engage in all sorts of objectionable behavior during recess, free time, and bus rides. College students spend countless hours in dorm rooms and fraternity houses unsupervised by parents or anyone *in loco parentis*.

The Supreme Court's response to this enforcement dilemma was to expect schools to stop harassment by teachers and administrators as soon as they learn of it, and to address peer harassment that becomes serious and systematic enough to deprive students of educational opportunity. Under this reading of Title IX the federal government's role remained limited. It was to step in only when schools conspicuously failed in their responsibility to protect students from abuse by teachers or staff or when schools overlooked systematic misbehavior by students. The justices did not expect Title IX to eliminate all sexual harassment, and warned that stricter measures would both place unrealistic demands on schools and require too much intrusion into the lives of students. They did not intend to transform Title IX into a "general civility code" for American schools.[50]

OCR rejected this narrowly circumscribed role. Under the "new paradigm" it unveiled in 2011–14, once a school has evidence that one or more students face a "hostile environment," Title IX requires it to "take immediate action to *eliminate* the hostile environment, *prevent its recurrence*, and *address its effects*." At the same time, OCR so lowered the threshold for what constitutes a "hostile environment" that virtually no school can escape these responsibilities. No longer is the goal to punish a few "bad apples": if schools are experiencing an "epidemic" of assault, expelling a few miscreants will hardly suffice to solve the problem. Rather, schools must change the way students think about sexuality. As Assistant Secretary Russlynn Ali explained when she announced several agreements with colleges in 2010, "Taken as a whole, these settlements will change the culture on the college campuses, and that is hugely important if we are to cure the epidemic of sexual violence on our college campuses across the country."[51]

One of the most important but least noted features of what Ali described as OCR's "new paradigm" is the extent of training schools must provide to students, faculty, and staff. This training is not aimed primarily at convincing them that rape and other forms of sexual assault are serious crimes that should be reported to the police. Rather, it is aimed at changing their understanding of what *constitutes* sexual assault and what rises to the level of harassment. The "affirmative consent" rules adopted on many campuses are designed to restructure sexual relations among students. As Jacob Gersen and Jeannie Suk show, the training and codes instituted by colleges under intense pressure from OCR are designed to redraw the line between "normal" and prohibited sex by jettisoning pernicious and outmoded assumptions and stereotypes.[52] Since "welcomeness" is the criterion that separates acceptable sexual behavior from serious misconduct, schools must provide instruction not only on sexual etiquette but also on how to read oblique signals from other adolescents and young adults.

Behind these extensive federal rules—enshrined not only in OCR's guidance documents but also in the detailed agreements negotiated with individual schools—is the assumption that mistreatment of women is so ingrained in our culture that convincing students that "sexual assault is unacceptable" will require a "sea change" in attitudes. A report issued by the White House Council on Women and Girls—which worked closely with OCR on this issue—explains: "Sexual assault is pervasive because our culture still allows it to persist." Consequently, "violence prevention can't just focus on the perpetrators and the survivors. It has to involve everyone." As a result, the prevention programs mandated by Title IX must be "sustained (not brief, one shot-education programs), comprehensive, and address the root individual, relational, and societal causes of sexual assault."[53] In 2014 the Department of Education embraced this understanding of the problem when it announced new rules for "primary prevention and awareness programs for all incoming students and new employees." The purpose of these federally mandated programs is to prevent sexual violence "through the promotion of positive and healthy behaviors that foster healthy, mutually respectful relationships and sexuality, encourage safe bystander intervention, and seek to change behavior and social norms in healthy and safe directions."[54] In other words, the federal government requires schools to change how their students think about intimate sexual relations. Establishing sexual norms became the newest form of health and safety regulation.

In this context, the logic behind OCR's 2016 DCL on transgender students becomes easier to understand. To be sure, the link to educational opportunity here is attenuated at best: the central issue is access to bathrooms and locker rooms, not classrooms; the number of students affected is tiny, and none of them have been denied access to anything even vaguely curricular in nature. Nor does this involve the question at the heart of the debate over athletics, that is, whether sex-segregated facilities are in fact equal in quality. The only controversial issue is how one decides who has access to which sex-segregated facilities.

One could imagine the federal government using Title IX to emphasize that transgender students cannot be denied access to any educational programs, urging schools to treat these students sympathetically and humanely, and asking them to provide a reasonable balance between respect for the wishes of transgender students and the privacy concerns of other students. That is what most schools were already doing. Why, then, did it insist that the wishes of transgender students on these sensitive questions must always prevail and the concerns of other students must be given zero weight?

The answer is that Title IX regulation is no longer primarily concerned with traditional education in the classroom, but rather with the education of both students and the general public on all matters sexual. Sexual stereotyping—which can include virtually all conventional thinking about sex and gender—must be identified, condemned, and corrected. Outmoded stereotypes about "masculinity and femininity"—based as they are on a mistaken bimodal, biological understanding of gender—should be replaced by an understanding that recognizes both the fluidity and the socially constructed nature of gender. Shortly after she left OCR, Assistant Secretary Catherine Lhamon told an interviewer, "The bathroom question never was just about a bathroom. It is about who that child is at school and how that child will be perceived and seen."[55] Any stigma that currently attaches to transgender status must be eliminated, which means changing how transgender students are "perceived and seen" by other students and school officials.

In 2010 OCR issued its first significant statement on "gender-based harassment." It emphasized that responding to individual instances of harassment is not enough. Among the elements that must be part of the schools' "more comprehensive response" is "educating the entire school community on civil rights and expectations of tolerance, specifically as they apply to gender stereotypes."[56] If one hopes to eliminate "hostility based on sex or sex-stereotyping," one must teach "tolerance" as it applies to gender stereotypes, which in effect means teaching students to reject those stereotypes.

Eliminating the stigma that might attach to students' failure to act according to gender stereotypes is a far cry from Title IX's original purpose of removing institutional barriers to education by women and girls. It is also a huge job for a small agency with weak enforcement authority. But, as we have seen, OCR has many allies, and their alliance is fortified by the conviction that in the long run the "arc of history" bends in the direction of deconstructing conventional understandings of male and female.

Statutory Revision through "Dynamic" Interpretation

The project of civil rights has always demanded creativity. It requires being bold. Often that means going against the grain of current-day popular thinking. Or it requires going to the more expansive reading of the law to ensure we are actually ensuring equal protection for everyone. [This means using power] to bend the arc of history itself—not merely by serving your clients, but by harnessing the law as a force for positive change.

—Vanita Gupta, coauthor of the 2016 transgender DCL

I would prefer to see us acknowledge openly that today we, who are judges rather than members of Congress, are imposing on a half-century-old statute a meaning of "sex discrimination" that the Congress that enacted it would not have accepted. This is something courts do fairly frequently to avoid statutory obsolescence and concomitantly to avoid placing the entire burden of updating old statutes on the legislative branch. We should not leave the impression that we are merely the obedient servants of the 88th Congress (1963–1965), carrying out their wishes. We are not. We are taking advantage of what the last half century has taught.

—Seventh Circuit Judge Richard Posner, 2017

Title IX is a dynamic statute . . . [that] envisions continued progress toward the goal of equal opportunity.

—Ninth Circuit Judge Cynthia Holcomb Hall, 1999

This shift in focus from exclusion to stereotyping was made possible by the more specific changes in Title IX described in the previous chapters. Most important are the following:

1. The sole enforcement power granted by the 1972 law was the authority to terminate federal funds to educational institutions that discriminate on the basis of sex. Not once in the following forty-five years did federal

administrators use the funding cutoff. Instead, Title IX has been enforced through an "implied" (that is, not explicitly mentioned in the statute) private right of action and the threat of embarrassing and expensive investigations by OCR.

2. In granting funding agencies authority to issue regulations under Title IX, the law not only subjected them to the standard rulemaking procedures, but required the signature of the president. Since 1975 OCR has seldom followed these procedures, and recently has resorted entirely to regulation by unilateral DCLs. Procedural checks on agency rulemaking have evaporated.

3. Title IX explicitly prohibits federal regulators from granting "preferential treatment" to members of one sex "on account of an imbalance which may exist with respect to the total number or percentage of that sex participating in or receiving the benefits of any federal supported program." The judicial and administrative insistence that schools move toward "parity" in athletics does exactly that.

4. The original law limited federal enforcement action to "the particular program, or part thereof" in which noncompliance has been found. This meant that OCR could not threaten to terminate funding to university programs (such as intercollegiate athletics) that do not themselves receive federal money. Today, in contrast, Title IX regulations apply to all parts of a school that receives federal funding in any form.

Of these changes, only the last was the result of congressional action. In fact the 1988 Grove City Bill that expanded Title IX's definition of "program or activity" was the *only* significant legislative change in the law in its forty-five-year history. Both the Voting Rights Act and the Civil Rights Act, in contrast, have been amended several times over the past several decades. All the other changes listed above came through administrative and judicial interpretation of the original statute.

To be sure, every statute contains gaps and ambiguities that administrators and judges must fill and resolve. When the central mandate of a statute is as vague as that of Title IX—terminate funding to educational institutions that discriminate on the basis of sex—the discretion delegated to administrators and judges is enormous. How agencies interpret ambiguous statutes changes over time in response to the new issues, new demands, new complaints, and new implementation problems that inevitably arise. Each presidential administration tries to put its own spin on policy. That's life in the administrative state.

As the number and scope of regulatory statutes ballooned in the late 1960s and 1970s, Congress, the president, and the courts all scrambled to channel and constrain such agency discretion. Congress wrote increasingly detailed statutes, with more specific standards, multiple deadlines, complex procedures, and liberal judicial review provisions. Presidents expanded the Office of Management and Budget's (OMB) review of administrative rules. Federal judges developed a more elaborate rulemaking process designed to ensure that administrators consult a wide array of interests, gather data on both the costs and benefits of regulation, consider alternative approaches for addressing the problem, and explain their policy in a way that is accessible to attentive publics and reviewing judges. Those judges would then take a "hard look" at the administrative record to see that the agency had interpreted the statute correctly and applied it reasonably. As Richard Stewart explained, these time-consuming and resource-intensive proceedings were designed to assure "fair representation for all affected interests in the exercise of the legislative power delegated to agencies."[57]

One of the most remarkable features of Title IX regulation is the extent to which OCR has managed to sidestep almost all these constraints. It almost never uses notice-and-comment rulemaking or subjects its policy statements to OMB, presidential, or interagency review. The combination of "guidelines" announced in Dear Colleague Letters and investigations culminating in resolution agreements makes judicial review of OCR policies extremely difficult and rare. Meanwhile Congress has done nothing to clarify the meaning of Title IX. It has seldom even conducted oversight hearings—except occasionally to complain about a particular policy that has upset some members' constituents.

As the quotations at the beginning of this section indicate, judges and administrators have bestowed upon themselves the authority to "update"—read amend—Title IX through the opaque forms of institutional leapfrogging described in the preceding chapters. Title IX provides a graphic example of the type of "dynamic statutory interpretation" best described and promoted by Yale law professor William Eskridge. Judges, he argues, should allow a statute's meaning to evolve not just "beyond original expectations," but even "against" those original expectations.[58]

The archetype of this form of interpretation is Justice Brennan's opinion in the famous affirmative action case *Weber v. Steelworkers*. Brian Weber had argued that Title VII outlawed precisely the type of affirmative action plan instituted by Kaiser Aluminum under intense pressure from the federal government. Title VII not only makes it illegal for an employer to "refuse to hire . . . or otherwise discriminate against any individual . . . because of such individual's race," but also included a separate section with the heading "Preferential treatment not to be granted on account of existing number or percentage imbalance." Justice Brennan conceded that Weber's "literal interpretation" of Title VII was "not without force." Justice William Rehnquist's dissent was more blunt: "Were Congress to act today specifically to prohibit the type of racial discrimination suffered by Weber, it would be hard pressed to draft language better tailored to the task."[59]

Nonetheless, citing a then-obscure nineteenth-century Supreme Court decision, Justice Brennan maintained: "A thing may be within the letter of the statute and yet not within the statute, because not within its spirit, nor within the intention of its maker."[60] What is most important in statutory interpretation, Brennan argued, is not what the text of the statute says, but what judges decide was Congress's fundamental purpose in enacting it. He claimed that Congress's overriding goal in 1964 was not preventing employers from using racial preferences, but "the integration of blacks into the mainstream of American society." Even the Court's defenders concede that here and in many other Title VII cases, judges played fast and loose with statutory language. Paul Frymer, for example, writes, "Courts significantly rewrote aspects of the law" and "in the process, got rid of very carefully placed loopholes that unions and other civil rights opponents had demanded in order to pass the act, turning it from one that emphasized color-blindness to one that underscored affirmative action."[61] As the *Weber* case shows, what constitutes "updating" rather than "distorting," "progress" rather than "backsliding" can be a matter of intense political controversy.

Two factors greased the skids for applying such "dynamic" interpretation to Title IX. The first is the close connection between Title IX and the Equal Protection clause of the Fourteenth Amendment. Title IX resides in a "quasi-constitutional" twilight zone: in part simply a policy choice made by legislators and in part a legislative effort to enforce constitutional norms; at once both a condition placed on receipt of federal spending and an individual right that can be vindicated through litigation in federal court. As the Supreme Court expanded its reading of Equal Protection to invalidate not only laws containing explicit sex classifications, but policies allegedly based on "animus" against sexual minorities, these constitutional arguments migrated to interpretation of Title IX, which also covers private schools not subject to the Fourteenth Amendment. One of the best examples of this is the Seventh Circuit's 2017 transgender ruling, which appended a rather tendentious interpretation of Title IX to a novel and more forceful constitutional argument. "Dynamic" statutory interpretation is a younger, less familiar sibling of "living constitution" jurisprudence. By smuggling novel constitutional claims into statutory rulings, judges can claim to follow rather than confront popularly elected legislators.

The second factor is the institutional leapfrogging we have repeatedly encountered in this book. Such incrementalism disguises innovation. The clearest description of the link between "dynamic" interpretation and this institutional pattern appeared in the dissenting opinion of Justice John Paul Stevens in *Alexander v. Sandoval* (see chapter 3). There Stevens described in glowing terms the "integrated remedial scheme" that courts and agencies had developed under Titles VI and IX for "attacking the often-intractable problem of racial and ethnic discrimination." This "inspired model," Stevens argued, allowed courts and agencies to go beyond merely forbidding intentional discrimination to attacking "more subtle forms of discrimination." This model "empowers the relevant agencies to evaluate social circumstances to determine whether there is a need for stronger measures," and "builds into the law flexibility, an ability to make nuanced assessments of complex social realities, and an admirable willingness to credit the possibility of progress."[62] Justice Scalia's textualism, he implied, frustrates this incremental progress by tying federal policy to the wording of statutes enacted decades ago, before we understood the causes of inequality as well as we do now.

Title IX and the Idea of Progress

Describing the Warren Court, Alexander Bickel wrote, "What informed the enterprise was the idea of progress." Belief in "man-made progress was the new faith, and the supremacy of judges as its carriers and executors was not denied."[63] If he were alive today, Bickel would probably add administrators to the list of these "carriers and executors." "Dynamic" interpretation requires both judges and administrators to acquire the capacity to distinguish "progress" from "obsolescence" and thus to trace "the arc of history."

This understanding of the meaning of civil rights laws and the responsibilities of government officials was eloquently expressed in an extraordinary statement issued by the two Fourth Circuit judges who had previously upheld the 2016 DCL in the Gavin Grimm case. When Grimm graduated from high school in 2017, the circuit court agreed to the school board's unopposed motion to vacate the injunction that had applied to his case. Judges Andre Davis and Henry Floyd took the unusual step of appending a memo describing the plaintiff as one of the "modern-day human rights leaders who strive to ensure that, one day, equality will prevail, and that the core dignity of every one of our brothers and sisters is respected by lawmakers and others who wield power over their lives." Like Fred Korematsu, Linda Brown, Jim Obergefell, and other civil rights heroes, Gavin Grimm "explained why it is humiliating to be segregated from the general population. He knew, intuitively, what the law has in recent decades acknowledged: the perpetuation of stereotypes is one of many forms of invidious discrimination." "G. G.'s case is about much more than bathrooms," they explained. "It's about government validation of the existence and experiences of transgender people, as well as the simple recognition of their humanity. His case is part of a larger movement that is redefining and broadening the scope of civil and human rights so that they extend to a vulnerable group that has traditionally been unrecognized, unrepresented, and unprotected." His case shines a light on "the inequities that arise when the government organizes society by outdated constructs like biological sex and gender." Gavin Grimm's "struggle for justice" may have been "delayed and rebuffed," but as Reverend Martin Luther King Jr. reminded us, "'the arc of the moral universe is long, but it bends toward justice.'" "Fortunately," the judges wrote, "the law eventually catches up to the lived facts of people."[64]

In this statement Judges Davis and Floyd make it clear that they were not simply deferring to OCR's expertise in the original case, nor were they concerned principally with the text of Title IX or Supreme Court precedent. Rather they were determined to oppose "the perpetuation of stereotypes" and to counteract "the inequities that arise when the government organizes society by outdated constructs like biological sex and gender." Rather than look back at what Congress meant when it enacted a law, judges should ensure that "the law eventually catches up to the lived facts of people." In this way they can quicken the pace at which "the arc" of history "bends toward justice."

The closer one looks at the public policy issues that have arisen under Title IX, though, the harder it becomes to make determinations about the direction of progress with confidence. Does providing "equal educational opportunity" really require us to spend more money on highly competitive sports rather than on libraries, scholarships, or teachers' salaries? Does it require colleges to recruit more athletes at the expense of talented mathematicians or cellists? Is it necessary to weaken due process protections, to threaten free speech, and to lavish money and responsibilities on Title IX compliance offices in order to reduce sexual assault and harassment? Must schools ignore some students' concerns about personal privacy in order to reduce embarrassment and discomfort to others? Above all, does it require that these hard choices be made by a few administrators and judges at the federal level rather than by local officials and school personnel who are likely to be more familiar with "lived facts" on the ground? It is easier to speculate about the direction of progress when one only focuses on problems rather than working on the details of solutions. The "arc of history," apparently, does not stoop to recognize hard policy choices.

THIRTEEN

The Politics of Retrenchment

The Trump administration's withdrawal of the 2016 Dear Colleague Letter (DCL) on transgender students was the first time an incoming administration had directly repudiated a Title IX policy initiative of its predecessor. Not that previous Republican administrations hadn't tried. The Reagan administration entered office critical of federal guidelines on athletics and sexual harassment, but succeeded only in delaying their enforcement. The Bush administration's efforts to make it somewhat easier for college athletic programs to comply with Title IX ended in failure, largely because the National Collegiate Athletic Association (NCAA) objected so strongly to them. Until 2017 the evolution of Title IX regulation could best be described as a ratchet: it expands under Democrats, pauses under Republicans, and grows again under the next Democratic administration.

Will this time be different? There are two reasons for thinking it might. First, the Obama administration was unusually aggressive on Title IX, and it consequently generated more opposition than ever before. Second, Donald Trump came to Washington promising to "drain the swamp." While Republicans have routinely promised to reduce federal regulation, this administration seemed more determined to shake up the governmental status quo than any of its predecessors.

The manner in which current Title IX policies came into being would seem to make reversal relatively simple. They are not the product of legislation, which in the United States is difficult to enact and even harder to repeal (as Republicans learned with the Affordable Care Act). Nor did the Obama administration use notice-and-comment rulemaking to establish its Title IX guidelines. The Supreme Court has held that rules promulgated under the Administrative Procedure Act's time-consuming rulemaking procedures can be revoked only by using those same procedures.[1] Reversing a unilateral DCL, in contrast, just takes another unilateral DCL. That is what happened on the transgender issue in early 2017. A few months later the Office for Civil Rights (OCR) issued an internal enforcement memo explaining that individual sexual assault complaints would no longer trigger full-blown investigations of entire institutions.[2] Administrative enforcement strategies, like DCLs, can be altered by a few strokes on a laptop keyboard. In September 2017 Secretary of Education Betsy DeVos withdrew her department's 2011 and 2014 sexual assault guidelines. She also announced that in the future OCR would use notice-and-comment rulemaking for all major policy initiatives: "The era of 'rule by letter,' is over."[3]

The Title IX regulatory regime described in this book, though, rests on more than a few easily reversible DCLs. It is quite possible that other courts will join the Seventh Circuit in finding that Title IX and the Equal Protection clause enshrine the transgender policies first announced in the 2016 DCL. Many schools have responded to withdrawal of the 2011 and 2014 guidelines by stating that they have no intention of revising the sexual harassment policies developed under them. As the title of a postelection article in the *Chronicle of Higher Education* put it, "Trump Administration May Back Away from Title IX, but Campuses Won't."[4] Some states are considering legislation requiring schools to follow the outlines of OCR's 2011 and 2014 guidelines on sexual harassment.[5] Any attempt to alter federal rules on athletics will run into stiff opposition from the NCAA and women's organizations. They would stand a good chance of prevailing in the litigation that would inevitably follow. In short, once put it place, most government policies develop constituencies that vigorously defend them.

This book goes to press during the first year of the Trump administration. As James Q. Wilson frequently noted, political scientists have enough trouble predicting the past; they should be hesitant to claim they can predict the future. This is particularly true when dealing with an administration led by a man as mercurial as Donald Trump. Instead of engaging in what would be little more than rank speculation, this chapter begins by explaining why retrenchment is generally so difficult, and then explores the sources of support and opposition to the policies described in the preceding chapters. This provides an opportunity to review the broader politics of Title IX.

Obstacles to Retrenchment

The growing academic literature on retrenchment—that is, efforts to roll back previously established government programs and policies—emphasizes how the politics of retrenchment differs from the politics of expansion.[6] Most of this work has focused on legislatures and administrative agencies. A few recent studies have examined retrenchment within the judiciary.[7] What can we say about the politics of retrenchment in a policy realm characterized by extensive interaction between courts and agencies?

In a nutshell, we know that retrenchment is difficult for three reasons: institutional, psychological, and organizational. First, in the United States new policies are hard to establish because of the many veto points created by our constitutional system and traditions. This is particularly true for legislation, which ordinarily must go through several committees, survive a Senate filibuster, gain the approval of both houses of Congress, and be signed by the president. Rescinding previous enactments requires an identical trip through "the obstacle course on Capitol Hill." Since administrative regulations are easier to promulgate, they are easier to withdraw. But administrators have several mechanisms for locking in their preferred policies. One is to use notice-and-comment rulemaking, which can be reversed only by going through another lengthy round of rulemaking. Another is to negotiate legally binding consent agreements with regulated parties. These remain in force until both parties agree to revise them—and in some circumstances receive the blessing of a reviewing court. This has become a popular and controversial method for binding a subsequent administration.[8]

Court rulings, too, can be reversed, either through subsequent judicial action or (in the case of statutory rulings) legislation. As the Grove City Bill shows, the latter route can take years to accomplish. In recent years presidents have devoted a great deal of attention to nominating judges who will revise or overturn precedents that their party finds objectionable. Once granted life tenure, though, judges do not always vote as the president who selected them expected. A president may be able to change the balance of power on the Supreme Court with one or two appointments. It is more difficult to change the lower courts, which, as we have seen, decide the vast majority of federal cases, including those issued under Title IX. Even more important, judges' respect for precedent means that judicial change ordinarily comes very slowly.

A second key factor is the psychological phenomenon known as "loss aversion" or "negativity bias." Virtually all of us work longer and harder to avoid losses than to achieve gains, even when the magnitude of these losses and gains is the same. This asymmetry seems to be baked into the human psyche. The current distribution of costs and benefits provides a powerful anchor for the way we see the world and judge what is fair. In his seminal book, *Thinking, Fast and Slow*, Daniel Kahneman describes loss aversion as "a powerful conservative force that favors minimal changes from the status quo in the lives of both institutions and individuals" and "the gravitational force that holds our life together near the reference point."[9] In politics, Paul Pierson explains, "The well-documented imbalance between the way that voters react to losses and gains further enhances the political position of retrenchment opponents" because "individuals will take more chances—seeking conflict and accepting the possibility of even greater losses—to prevent any worsening of their current position."[10] Loss aversion is even stronger when issues are framed in terms of rights: to deprive someone of his rights seems even more threatening than depriving him of a concrete, particularized benefit. That is why the claim that an administration is trying to "roll back civil rights" has such rhetorical bite.

Third, new policies create organized constituencies and bureaucracies that vociferously defend their own survival. For example, the expansion of athletic opportunities for women has produced thousands of teams, coaches, and high school athletes hoping to be recruited by colleges. The NCAA is now heavily invested in sponsoring women's championships. Women's professional leagues and Olympic teams expect colleges to develop their best players. Years of federal regulation have created compliance offices within schools and a cottage industry of consultants, lawyers, investigators, and trainers offering (for a fee) to help them meet OCR's demands. Such compliance "experts" oppose retrenchment not only because they want to save their jobs, but also because they are deeply committed to the causes that define their professions.

An equally significant source of organizations' support for the regulatory status quo, of course, is the regulatory agency itself. Only a handful of positions in OCR will have changed hands when the Trump administration finally gets around to making its subcabinet appointments. The other 550 people working at OCR will continue investigating complaints under existing guidelines and negotiating the details of compliance agreements until ordered to do otherwise. Few are likely to give their enthusiastic support to major changes in agency policy. It takes considerable management skill to change the standard operating procedures and sense of mission of these "street level bureaucrats."[11]

These factors do not operate uniformly across the three policies examined in this book. Support for them varies according to (1) their institutional foundations, (2) the clout of their allies within regulated institutions and among interest groups, and (3) public perceptions of their merits. For that reason we should expect their trajectories to differ in significant ways. Current athletic policies are most secure, recent policies on transgender least secure, and sexual harassment policies in the middle.

Institutional Foundations

Since 1995 no complaint about American politics has been repeated more frequently than this hardy perennial: the combination of partisan polarization and divided government has produced nearly endless gridlock; as a result, the federal government just cannot get anything done.[12] One hardly finds such stasis when looking at regulation under Title IX. In fact, just the opposite. Regulation has grown most rapidly during two periods of divided government and intense partisan conflict: 1994–2000 and 2010–16. As table 13-1 shows, major policy changes and enforcement campaigns almost always began *after* Democratic administrations effectively lost their majorities in Congress. For them Title IX has become a policy instrument best deployed once the president's legislative program has stalled.

A principal theme of this book has been the peculiar form of court–agency interaction I call "leapfrogging." The policy archaeology of the preceding chapters describes how courts and agencies have each extended regulation in a large number of small steps, with each claiming to defer to the other. Court decisions on athletics relied on guidelines issued by the Clinton and Obama administrations, which were based on previous circuit court decisions that looked to OCR's 1979 interpretation of the Department of Health, Education, and Welfare's 1975 regulations. OCR's post-2011 sexual harassment rules were extensions of the guidelines issued by OCR in 1997 and 2001, which claimed to follow judicial interpretations of Title VII, which were based in large part on regulations of the Equal Employment Opportunity Commission (EEOC), which in turn built on previous Title VII court decisions. OCR's 2016 DCL on transgender rights relied in large part on judicial interpretations of Title IX and VII despite the fact that the sole pre-2016 Title IX court decision rested on judicial deference to an OCR letter that had in turn relied on previous Title VII opinions on a quite different matter (see table 13-2). Such complexity produces what William Safire called the MEGO (My Eyes Glaze Over) response, providing political camouflage to these policy innovations.[13]

This form of incrementalism differs significantly from the form celebrated by political scientists such as Charles Lindblom and Aaron Wildavsky in the 1950s and 1960s.[14] They argued that by taking small steps policymakers learn from experience; each step provides feedback about what is working and how the policy affects a variety of parties. The form of incrementalism described in this book, though, is designed to accumulate *authority*, not evidence or experience. All OCR's recent DCLs and guidelines have in effect proclaimed, "We have legal authority to do this *without* gathering evidence or seeking public input."

Some might view this as an example of the autonomy of the "administrative state," an ambiguous term that has become popular since the election of Donald

Table 13-1   Divided Government and Regulatory Expansion

Athletics	
1975 regulations	Divided government, unusually weak president
1979 interpretation	President Carter had effectively lost his majority in Congress
1995–98	Clinton administration issued new guidelines after Republicans took control of Congress
2010–16	Obama administration reinstated previous rules and negotiated multiple compliance agreements primarily after Republicans gained control of House[a]
Sexual Harassment	
1980–81	Equal Employment Opportunity Commission issued "midnight" regulations shortly after Democrats lost the White House and Senate
1996–97	Clinton administration issued new guidance after Democrats lost control of House and Senate
2001	OCR issued new guidelines after Democrats lost the presidential election
2011–16	OCR issued new guidelines and mounted extensive investigations after Republicans gained a House majority
Transgender	
2015–16	Administration-wide effort to extend civil rights protections to LGBT students and employees began after it became clear that Republican House would not pass legislation on the topic

[a] One exception: the DCL on athletics was issued before the 2010 election, but after the administration had passed its major education program, Race to the Top.

Trump. To the extent this means that policymaking takes place outside the legislative branch and in a form that seems highly technical, that is certainly the case. But if it implies that Title IX policy is the product of a "runaway bureaucracy" or a "deep state" impervious to external control, it is demonstrably false for two reasons.

First, since the creation of the Department of Education in 1980, OCR has rarely been out of step with the department secretary, the White House staff, or the Department of Justice. This was particularly evident during the Obama administration. Many of OCR's policies were announced or publicly supported

Table 13-2   Cross-Institutional Leapfrogging

Athletics
    Health, Education, and Welfare's 1975 regulations →
    OCR's 1979 interpretation →
    Supreme Court opinion on remedies (*Franklin*) →
    Circuit court opinions (especially *Cohen v. Brown*) →
    OCR's 1996 "clarification" →
    OCR's 1998 DCL on scholarships →
    Defeat of Bush administration's "additional clarification" →
    Obama administration's 2010 "clarification" and negotiated agreements

Sexual Harassment
    Long series of Equal Employment Opportunity Commission and court
        rulings under Title VII →
    Supreme Court decision in *Franklin v. Gwinnett* →
    Lower court decisions on peer harassment →
    Guidance issued by OCR in 1996–97 →
    Supreme Court decisions in *Gebser* and *Davis* →
    OCR's revised guidance in 2000–01 →
    OCR's DCLs in 2010 and 2011, and its 2014 "Questions and Answers" →
    OCR's new enforcement/investigation strategy, 2014–16

Transgender
    Supreme Court's dicta on "sex-stereotyping" in *Price Waterhouse v.*
        Hopkins →
    Lower court interpretations of Title VII →
    OCR's 2010 DCL on bullying →
    OCR settlement agreements with individual schools and 2015 letter →
    Fourth Circuit decision in *G. G.* deferring to OCR's expertise →
    OCR's 2016 DCL →
    Withdrawal of DCL in 2017 →
    Seventh Circuit ruling in *Whitaker v. Kenosha Unified School District*, 2017

not just by Secretaries Arne Duncan and John King, but also by Vice President Joseph Biden, the attorney general, and the president himself. Republican administrations have had a bit more trouble restraining lower-level officials dedicated to the policies of the previous administration. But that is in large part because they have declined to change written policies, preferring instead to weaken them through relaxed enforcement. The Reagan administration developed relatively successful administrative strategies for reducing the autonomy of lower-level officials in the regional offices, and subsequent Republican administrations have followed suit.

Second, courts have played as large a part in this story as administrative agencies. Students of the administrative process often claim that American federal agencies are relatively weak because judicial review is so ubiquitous in the United States. But under Title IX, courts have most often enabled and empowered agencies rather than enervated them. The major reason Republican presidents have had such trouble revising Title IX rules is that they are so embedded in court precedent.

This raises the question of why the conservative majorities on the Rehnquist and Roberts Courts have not left more of a mark on Title IX. To the contrary: a number of Supreme Court decisions, especially *Cannon* and *Franklin* on private rights of action, *Meritor* and *Oncale* on sexual harassment, and *Price Waterhouse* on gender stereotyping—contributed significantly to the expansion of Title IX regulation. Two decisions that seemed to limit the reach of Title IX, *Gebser* and *Davis*, have been all but ignored by OCR. Ironically, these decisions were the catalyst for OCR's aggressive post-2014 sexual assault investigation strategy. The Court's 1984 decision in *Grove City*, in contrast, shut down enforcement of OCR's athletic rules for several years. But within four years Congress had re-written the law to overturn it.

Part of the explanation lies in the fact that the Supreme Court has generally *not* been conservative on gender-related issues. In *United States v. Virginia* (1996) and *Sessions v. Morales-Santana* (2017), the Court applied "intermediate scrutiny" to invalidate overly broad gender classifications in state and federal laws.[15] In *Romers v. Evans* (1996), *Lawrence v. Texas* (2003), *United States v. Windsor* (2013), and *Obergefell v. Hodges* (2015), the Court struck down state and federal laws it found to be based on unconstitutional animus against homosexuals.[16] In most of these cases the Court's two swing voters, Justices Anthony Kennedy and Sandra Day O'Connor, deserted the Court's conservative bloc.

More puzzling is why the Court's conservatives have not prevailed on procedural issues. Steven Burbank and Sean Farhang have shown that on seemingly technical issues regarding who can get into federal court and the sort of remedies available, the Supreme Court's conservatives have succeeded in limiting the role of federal courts. They provide this summary of their exhaustive review of court decisions: "Incrementally at first but more boldly in recent years, over the past four decades, the Supreme Court has transformed federal law from friendly to unfriendly, if not hostile toward enforcement of rights through private lawsuits. Although the Court's anti-enforcement work has ranged broadly across fields of federal regulatory policy, it has especially focused on civil rights."[17] For some reason, though, Title IX seems to be an exception to this general rule. The Supreme Court not only recognized private rights of action in 1979, but made them more attractive to plaintiffs and their attorneys by authorizing monetary damages in 1992. The Court's 2001 decision in *Alexander v. Sandoval* exemplified the trend Burbank and Farhang describe. But a few years later in *Jackson v. Birmingham*, the Court backed away from the implication of that ruling as it applied to Title IX (see chapter 3). So far, at least, the Supreme Court has left only a faint imprint on Title IX jurisprudence. The most important judicial action has taken place in the lower courts, most of which have been enthusiastic participants in the institutional leapfrogging described above.

Interests: Schools, Advocacy Groups, and the Compliance Industry

A cynical student of regulation looking at Title IX in the early 1970s might well have dismissed it as merely a symbolic measure. Women are such a large, diverse group that they are hard to organize. At that time only a few national organizations claimed to speak for women. In contrast, many well-organized groups represent educational interests: the National School Boards Association, the Council of Chief State School Officers, the National Association of Elementary School Principals, the Council of the Great City Schools, the American Council on Education, the American Association of University Professors, the Association of American Universities, the National Education Association, the American Federation of Teachers—to name but a few. Just as important, local school board members and school superintendents often have the ear of members of Congress. So do the leaders of state universities and the presidents of elected officials' alma maters. To make matters worse, the federal Office of Education (soon to become the Department of Education) had many reasons to cultivate good relations with school officials. Threatening to terminate federal funding undermines such institutional comity. Title IX seemed destined to fall prey to regulatory "capture," that is, domination by regulated interests, in this instance, educational institutions.

That obviously did not happen. Why not? Why did advocacy groups prove stronger and educational interests weaker than expected? The organizations that pushed for stronger Title IX regulation were hardly household names or major campaign contributors. Most of them did not even exist when Title IX was first proposed. On athletics the most important were the National Women's Law Center (NWLC, founded in 1972) and the Women's Sports Foundation (formed in 1974). In the 1990s the NWLC, the American Association of University Women, and the National Organization for Women called attention to the sexual harassment/sexual assault problem. Two decades later a different type of group led the charge on this issue. Know Your IX, SurvJustice, and End Rape on Campus were organized by younger women who used social media to attract attention to their cause. Yet another set of organizations pushed OCR and the White House to extend protections to gay and transgender students. This included GLSEN (the Gay, Lesbian, and Straight Education Network), the Human Rights

Campaign, the National Center for Transgender Equality, and the American Civil Liberties Union. If these groups seemed to be punching above their political weight, they were not alone. Jeffrey Berry's extensive research on public interest groups demonstrates not only that the number of liberal advocacy groups grew rapidly during the 1960s and 1970s, but also that they succeeded in forming alliances with members of Congress and federal administrators. As he wrote in his 1999 book, *The New Liberalism*, "Although the liberal citizen groups are only a small proportion of the thousands and thousands of lobbies in Washington, the analysis in this book shows that they have been remarkably successful in influencing public policy."[18]

At least three factors contributed to the success of these advocacy groups on Title IX issues. First was their ability to attract media attention. This was particularly apparent with the sexual harassment and transgender issues. Second, these organizations proved adept at forming broad coalitions with advocacy groups that focus on different issues. During the 1970s groups representing African Americans, Latinos, people with disabilities, and women frequently found themselves sparring over scarce resources and priorities at OCR. But over the years such competition faded. Far more apparent was their ability to unite in causes such as enacting the Grove City Bill and the 1991 Civil Rights Act. One example of this was a 2003 letter signed by over one hundred organizations opposing changes in OCR's Title IX policies on athletics (see chapter 7). Another was the array of groups filing amicus briefs in the *G. G.* transgender case (see chapter 12).

Third, in the five decades since enactment of Title IX, these advocacy organizations have become important elements of the Democratic coalition. In 1972 the two parties did not differ significantly on women's issues or civil rights. As odd as it might seem today, back then Republicans were somewhat more pro-choice than Democrats. A higher percentage of Republican members of Congress voted for the 1964 Civil Rights Act than Democratic members. No longer. For example, voting on the 1991 Civil Rights Act split largely along party lines, with Democrats supporting and Republicans opposing legislation that expanded remedies and lowered the burden of proof in discrimination cases. In 2013 the Employment Non-Discrimination Act (ENDA), which would have amended Title VII to outlaw discrimination on the basis of sexual orientation and gender identity, passed the Senate with overwhelming Democratic support, but died in the House when Republican leaders refused to bring it to the floor. In 2017 Democratic senators and Democratic state attorneys general denounced the Trump administration's effort to change how OCR investigates sexual harassment complaints. Democrats have shown strong support for measures important to their coalition partners.

Organizations representing schools and school officials have never replicated the intensity of these advocacy groups on Title IX issues. Although they frequently complain about excessive federal regulation in general, they have been reluctant to suggest that they place anything but the highest priority on providing equal educational opportunity to women and girls. Bernice Sandler, who worked closely with Congresswoman Edith Green on Title IX, tells this revealing story about organizing hearings in 1971–72:

> The American Council on Education is the main player in the world of higher education. Just about every college president is a member. The Council monitors all legislation that would have an impact on colleges and universities. The lobbyist for the American Council on Education was contacted about the hearings, and he declined to testify, stating, "There is no sex discrimination in higher education," and "even if there was, it wasn't a problem." . . . [Most of higher education] knew nothing about the bill in the House of Representatives. Those few who did know about the bill did not believe it would have any meaningful impact.[19]

Organized opposition to Title IX regulation has been sporadic and halfhearted. The National School Boards Association (NSBA) objected strenuously to OCR's 2010 DCL on bullying, but it attracted few allies and lost. The next year it said little about OCR's sexual harassment guidelines, which affected universities more than elementary and secondary schools. Both the American Council on Education and the American Association of University Professors have criticized those regulations—and have been ignored by OCR. Brown University's president Vartan Gregorian—the rare educational leader who showed passion for protecting the autonomy of the university—was able to convince sixty universities and several higher education associations to join his appeal to the Supreme Court. But signing an amicus brief is relatively cheap talk. None of these schools or associations put up anything approaching the fight Gregorian did. Lawyers for the Gloucester County School Board presented a forceful brief to the Fourth Circuit in the second round of the *G. G.* litigation. Although a number of conservative advocacy groups signed an amicus brief on behalf of the local school board, few educational organizations joined them.

The major exceptions, of course, were the NCAA and coaches of intercollegiate male teams. In an effort to protect their jobs (and in some instances their empires) they were vocal and persistent. Although they succeeded in delaying enforcement of OCR's guidelines for many years, they routinely lost in court and in Congress. Eventually the NCAA decided, "If you can't beat 'em, join 'em." It established a standing committee on gender equity, collected detailed information on men's and women's varsity teams sponsored by its members, and promoted a number of "emerging sports" for women. Since the NCAA's raison d'être and major source of revenue is the sponsorship of national championships, this reinforced the emphasis on highly competitive women's sports. One thing the NCAA would not do is challenge the major athletic conferences by taking steps to reduce expenditures on men's football and basketball.

Regulators do not just respond to pressure from established interests. They create new ones. This is particularly clear with athletics. We now have thousands of intercollegiate women's teams with their own coaches, trainers, fans, scholarship athletes, and high school students hoping to become scholarship recipients. Similarly, OCR's sexual harassment regulation created an extensive network of private consultants, lawyers, and student advocacy groups that provide schools' internal Title IX offices with services, advice, and political support. The vice president of the American Association of University Women warned the Trump administration "to think carefully before making wholesale changes because lots of universities have invested time and resources to come up to speed."[20] A college official told the *Chronicle of Higher Education* that schools had "worked so hard to raise awareness on this issue in the last few years that students are really attuned, and they won't allow institutions to walk away from this commitment." A lawyer who represents accused students presented a more jaundiced view: "It's like a perpetual-motion machine."[21]

For reasons explained above, groups are most likely to organize politically and to attract a sympathetic audience when they face losses. This was apparent in the 1990s when both OCR and the courts made it extremely difficult for colleges to eliminate women's teams, regardless of how diligent these schools had previously been in expanding opportunities for female athletes. This, of course, also led to loud complaints from men's teams facing elimination for budgetary reasons. Everyone seemed to agree that it would be best to avoid any cuts to athletic programs—and avoid any discussion of opportunity costs. As they say in the tax policy world, "Don't tax me; don't tax thee; tax the man behind the tree."

Public Perceptions

Most members of the public strongly support Title IX. They just know precious little about it. They believe that female students (especially their daughters) should have the same opportunities as their male counterparts, but have given little thought to what this should mean in practice. Almost no one has heard of the Three-Part Test or can explain the rationale behind the parity standard. Despite all the controversy over sexual harassment and the treatment of transgender students, even well-informed voters continue to associate Title IX almost entirely with athletics. Most people want schools to reduce sexual violence and other forms of sexual harassment, but few can explain why sexual harassment constitutes sex discrimination or what OCR now requires of all educational institutions. Even the reader who has slogged through this entire book will probably have difficulty reproducing those arguments. In short, public support for Title IX is wide but shallow.

This means that politicians must be concerned not only with pleasing groups that pay a great deal of attention to these issues, but with anticipating what Douglas Arnold has called the "mobilization of previously inattentive publics."[22] In other words, they must worry about how advocacy groups, political parties, and challengers in future elections will use their voting record to whip up opposition. If I criticize OCR's guidelines on sexual misconduct, will I be branded a "rape apologist"? If I agree that transgender students should be allowed to use facilities that match their gender identity, will I be accused of endangering other students? If I question the Three-Part Test, will I be charged with undermining policies that opened athletic opportunities to millions of girls and women? But if I endorse those policies, will I be charged with establishing gender quotas? Given these perils, it is not surprising that Congress seldom weighs in on these matters.

We usually think of interest groups and parties as the primary framers of these complicated issues. Certainly advocacy organizations such as the National Women's Law Center, the Women's Sports Foundation, and Know Your IX have had great success in defining Title IX issues. Increasingly, though, voters view all these matters through the prism of partisanship: many Democrats believe Republicans are waging a "war on women"; many Republicans believe Democrats are building an "administrative state" that threatens their liberty. The preceding chapters show how courts and agencies have also played a role in framing Title IX issues, and how regulators have taken advantage of the way these issues have been framed by others.

Half a century ago, Lloyd Free and Hadley Cantril offered a proposition about American politics that is just as helpful today as it was in 1967.[23] Americans, they claimed, are "ideologically conservative" but "operationally liberal." By that they meant that most American voters favor a wide array of government programs to promote full employment, increase economic security, improve public health, reduce crime, protect the environment, improve education, reduce discrimination, and promote equality of opportunity. But they are also distrustful of government in general, and centralized, bureaucratic government in particular. They want more government benefits, services, and protections, but less government regulation, taxation, and interference. Democrats, of course, emphasize the former, and Republicans the latter. Since 1968 neither has succeeded in becoming the dominant party in the United States, largely because neither can adequately address both of these powerful elements of our political culture.

This political schizophrenia is evident in policymaking under Title IX. Today we quickly jump from the finding that a serious problem exists—whether it is bullying on the playground or sexual misconduct in college dorms or painful gender transitions—to the conclusion that the federal government must do something about it. A few decades ago the idea that the federal government would establish national rules on bathroom use, sexual harassment training, or roster rules for collegiate teams would have seemed bizarre. Now we quickly accept the argument that most problems demand not just a governmental response, but a nationally uniform one. In 1979 James Q. Wilson described this expansion of the agenda as a consequence of "the lowering of the legitimacy barrier."[24] If he were writing today, he would probably change that to the *collapse* of the legitimacy barrier.

At the very time social regulation was expanding in leaps and bounds, public trust in the federal government was plummeting. In the mid-1960s three-quarters of the American public told pollsters they "trusted the government in Washington just about always or most of the time." By 2015 less than one-fifth gave that response.[25] A 2015 Gallup poll found that half the public thinks that "the federal government poses an immediate threat to the rights and freedoms of ordinary Americans."[26]

Only recently have we begun to appreciate the extent of fear and resentment this has generated among some Americans, especially those who live outside the Northeast and the Pacific Coast. High levels of anger at and distrust of government have produced a large pool of voters receptive to appeals by demagogues who give voice to their conviction that distant Beltway elites are not just looking down at them, but threatening their way of life. For them, what is a better example of federal overreach and bicoastal nuttiness than the mandate that people with male anatomy be allowed to use women's locker rooms? Title IX provides each party with issues they can use to attack and discredit the other.

When Title IX was enacted in 1972, it seemed unlikely that it would be pulled into the vortex of partisan polarization or what we now call the "culture wars." It was sponsored by Democrats, but passed with large bipartisan majorities and signed by President Nixon. Throughout the 1970s OCR's athletics policy drew as much heat from Democrats as from Republicans. Opening educational programs to women and girls encountered so little opposition that it was hard to see how the issue would create a sharp ideological or partisan divide.

That schism appeared and then widened as Title IX's emphasis changed from ending exclusionary institutional practices to correcting public stereotypes. This not only raised divisive cultural issues—such as what we should teach our children about masculinity and femininity—but required the federal government to delve deeper and deeper into areas previously considered private. As the national government took on more complex and difficult tasks, it had to assert more authority with less legislative authorization. New Title IX policies have contributed to our new, more inflamed politics.

A Modest Proposal for Depolarizing the Policy Debate

Distrust of the Trump administration on Title IX issues runs high—and justifiably so. This is, after all, an administration headed by a man who has bragged about committing sexual assault and routinely makes startlingly demeaning comments about women. He has launched personal attacks on federal judges and sought to undermine confidence in the judiciary as a whole. His secretary of education came into office without an adequate command of the legal responsibilities of her office. It took the administration nearly a year to nominate an assistant secretary for civil rights. Just as profound distrust of the administration led several circuit courts to enjoin enforcement of its hastily conceived travel ban, the new leadership at OCR is likely to run into stiff resistance in court unless it can provide a thorough and convincing explanation for its actions.

To put the matter more bluntly, OCR's new leaders will have a chance to improve Title IX regulations only if they are willing to be everything our current president is *not*. Rather than act precipitously and unilaterally, they should demonstrate their commitment to the rule of law and public participation by following the Administrative Procedure Act's notice-and-comment rulemaking procedures. In doing so, they should collect reliable information on such matters as the prevalence of sexual assault on campus and the effectiveness of proposed remedies. They should invite debate rather than shove disagreements under the rug, as the civil rights office has so often done in the past. This means they must explain how and why they are modifying existing policy, not claim disingenuously to be doing nothing new. They should show respect for Supreme Court interpretations of civil rights law, rather than devise clever end runs around them. They should demonstrate renewed fidelity to due process, freedom of speech, local self-government, and academic freedom—fundamental elements of liberal, constitutional democracy. In doing so, they will gain grudging appreciation from those of us who find so many of the actions taken by the Trump administration in its first year deeply disturbing.

The obvious place to start is with OCR's sexual harassment guidelines. The transgender issue is now in the hands of the courts. As flawed as they are, Title IX athletic rules have powerful allies and in recent years have elicited few complaints from organized constituencies. (Rising television revenues lift all crew shells.) Current sexual harassment regulation, in contrast, has accumulated an array of critics, many of them on the left. Moreover, OCR can convincingly argue that by moderating its policies on the topic it is bringing them into line with the Supreme Court's interpretation of Title IX.

To its credit, the Department of Education has taken the first step in this direction, promising to initiate notice-and-comment rulemaking to revise its sexual harassment guidelines. So far that debate has focused on procedures for resolving sexual misconduct accusations: the preponderance-of-the-evidence requirement, limitations on cross-examination, access to legal advice, the division of labor between schools' disciplinary panels and the criminal justice system, and the "single investigator" model that OCR has encouraged schools to adopt. These have all been subject to sustained and serious criticism from legal and academic organizations across the political spectrum.

Reassessment of the sexual harassment guidelines should not stop there. OCR's current definition of sexual harassment sweeps in far too much speech that should be protected, especially on college campuses. Current rules demand expensive and extensive training whose effectiveness has yet to be demonstrated, and that provides student affairs offices and their allies in student advocacy groups far too many opportunities to engage in ideologically charged indoctrination. Current guidelines also demand that schools take responsibility for counteracting the effects of off-campus misconduct by nonstudents—misconduct over which they have no control. To achieve this ambitious "culture change," schools are required to develop large internal Title IX bureaucracies insulated from supervision by all but the most senior school officials. All this needs to be reexamined in a forum that invites public debate and explicitly considers the costs and benefits of alternative regulatory strategies, anticipation of possible unintended consequences and perverse incentives, and recognition of the limited legal authority granted by Title IX. Other regulatory agencies routinely go through such a demanding process. There is no reason why OCR should be exempt. Invocation of the words "civil rights" should not be a talisman that protects regulatory action from rigorous analysis and criticism.

Title IX rules on athletics could benefit from a similar top-to-bottom review. But here allies would be rare, and the analytical task even more difficult. In this context OCR would be forced to address questions it has avoided for decades. Here are just a few: What is the relationship between athletic participation and *educational* opportunity? What athletic opportunities other than intercollegiate and interscholastic sports enhance educational opportunity? To what extent do highly competitive sports do just the opposite, draining resources from and corrupting classroom instruction? Do current Title IX guidelines disadvantage the large number of female students not interested in highly competitive sports?

Over the past forty years neither OCR nor the courts have given any serious consideration to how Title IX regulation has contributed to the pathologies of commercialized college sports. Never before has college sports so needed a thorough reexamination. Title IX rules should be a part of that. It will probably take a serious financial crisis to force such a rethinking. Given the rising financial cost of college, the growing deficits of almost all athletic programs, the demands of college athletes for adequate compensation, and the drumbeat of misconduct by coaches and tutors, such a crisis might soon be upon us.

Given the political risks of open, participatory rulemaking, the Trump administration might fall back on the strategy used by previous Republican administrations: keeping existing guidelines in place but easing up on enforcement. Soon after Trump's election the *Washington Post* warned that the president might "starve civil rights enforcement funding, slowing hundreds of open investigations and narrowing their scope."[27] This approach has a variety of serious disadvantages. It leaves schools unsure about what is expected of them. Being risk averse, many schools—especially those still under investigation—will respond by following the older guidelines despite their many flaws. Those who previously reached agreements with OCR will have no idea which parts might be renegotiable. Private enforcement suits will proliferate, with lower courts offering a wide variety of interpretations of Title IX. Once again, policymaking will move underground.

The most important thing administrators, judges, and legislators can do in coming years is to bring Title IX regulation back to its original focus on *educational* opportunity. We know that many people in this country are being left behind economically and socially because they lack the skills rewarded in the global economy. We also know that our educational system has not responded adequately to this challenge. In truth, the federal government has very little control over education in this country. It does not provide much money, and it does not control curriculum or personnel. It does, though, have the ability to focus public debate. Increasingly, Title IX regulation has steered attention away from the skills, knowledge, and analytical tools students acquire in the classroom to what students learn about gender roles and about "masculinity and femininity" in the hallways, dorm rooms, sports arenas, and bathrooms of our schools. The resulting controversies have added to the divisions within our already polarized nation. Is that the best way for the federal government to use its limited power and dwindling moral authority? This book has argued that over the past several decades Title IX regulation has been subtly but fundamentally transformed without any serious discussion of the new goals it has taken on. That debate is long overdue. We might learn that real progress involves going back to basics.

Notes

Chapter One

1. Hanna Rosin, *The End of Men and the Rise of Women* (New York: Riverhead Books, 2012), p. 149; Thomas DiPrete and Claudia Buchmann, *The Rise of Women: The Growing Gender Gap in Education and What It Means for American Schools* (New York: Russell Sage Foundation, 2013), pp. 1–3, 39.

2. DiPrete and Buchmann, *The Rise of Women*, pp. 36–42, 79–80, 106–09; Rosin, *The End of Men*, pp. 152–53; Christina Hoff Sommers, *The War against Boys: How Misguided Policies Are Harming Our Young Men* (New York: Simon and Schuster, 2013), pp. 11–17.

3. DiPrete and Buchmann, *The Rise of Women*, p. 1.

4. Gerald Gurney, Donna A. Lopiano, and Andrew Zimbalist, *Unwinding Madness: What Went Wrong with College Sports and How to Fix It* (Brookings, 2017), pp. 145–46.

5. *Cohen* v. *Brown University*, 991 F.2d 888, 898 (1st Cir. 1993).

6. Quoted in Kenneth S. Lowande and Sidney M. Milkis, "'We Can't Wait': Barack Obama, Partisan Polarization, and the Administrative Presidency," *The Forum* 12, no. 1 (2014), p. 3.

7. Republican Platform, 2016, p. 35 (www.gop.com/the-2016-republican-party -platform).

8. Quote in John D. Skrentny, *The Minority Rights Revolution* (Harvard University Press, 2002), p. 241 (Abzug), p. 240 (Bayh).

9. *Reed* v. *Reed*, 404 U.S. 71 (1971).

10. *Frontiero* v. *Richardson*, 411 U.S. 677 (1973).

11. DiPrete and Buchmann, *The Rise of Women*, p. 1.

12. Rosin, *The End of Men*, p. 149.

13. By chance I was in the Yale admissions office for an interview the day in the fall of 1968 when Yale announced it would accept women. My interviewer explained that the office was in a frenzy because so many alumni wanted their daughters to receive interviews.

14. *Biediger* v. *Quinnipiac University*, 728 F. Supp. 2d 62 (D. Conn. 2010).

15. The consent decree is available at http://counsel.cua.edu/res/docs/Consent.pdf. The discussion of this case is based on that document plus the district court's "Ruling on Defendant's Motion to Lift Injunction" (https://scholar.google.com/scholar_case ?case=9181417747683813087&q=biediger+v.+quinnipiac,++ruling+on+request+to+l ift+injunction&hl=en&as_sdt=6,30&as_vis=1). Other features of the litigation are explained in Kiersten McKoy, "Biediger v. Quinnipiac," 58 *New York Law Review* 457 (2013/14).

16. *PGA Tour* v. *Martin*, 532 U.S. 661, 700 (2001) (Scalia dissenting).

17. Gregg Easterbrook, "No 'Cheers' for Latest Title IX Decision," July 27, 2010 (www.espn.go.com/espn/print?id=5413428).

18. Nancy Hogshead-Makar, "Title IX Remains Viable and Necessary," August 9, 2010 (www.espn.go.com/espn/print?id=5443367).

19. Elizabeth Bartholet and others, "Rethink Harvard's Sexual Harassment Policy," *Boston Globe*, October 15, 2014.

20. David Rudovsky and others, "Open Letter from Members of the Penn Law School Faculty," February 18, 2015 (http://media.philly.com/documents/OpenLetter .pdf).

21. Theodore R. Delwiche and Andrew M. Duehren, "New Law School Sexual Harassment Procedures Break from University Framework," *Harvard Crimson*, January 3, 2015 (www.thecrimson.com/article/2015/1/3/pending-procedures-law-school -title-ix); Andrew M. Duehren, "After Federal Feedback, Law School Implements New Title IX Standards," *Harvard Crimson*, August 7, 2015 (www.thecrimson.com /article/2015/8/6/law-school-implement-titleix/).

22. Elizabeth Bartholet and others, "19 Harvard Law Professors Defend Law Student Brandon Winston, Denouncing His Portrayal in 'The Hunting Ground,'" *Harvard Law Record*, November 11, 2015 (http://hlrecord.org/2015/11/19-harvard-law -professors-defend-law-student-brandon-winston-denouncing-his-portrayal-in-the -hunting-ground/).

23. Kamilah Willingham, "Why Harvard Should #JustSaySorry for How It Handled My Sexual Assault" (https://theestablishment.co/why-harvard-should-justsaysorry-for -how-it-handled-my-sexual-assault-c4ba18f72b5b). Emily Yoffe examines the troubling racial implications of some campus efforts to crack down on sexual assault in "The Question of Race in Campus Sexual-Assault Cases," *The Atlantic*, September 11, 2017.

24. David Cantor and others, "Report of the AAU Campus Climate Survey on Sexual Assault and Sexual Misconduct, Harvard University," September 21, 2015, pp. 13–17 (https://sexualassaulttaskforce.harvard.edu/files/taskforce/files/final_report _harvard_9.21.15.pdf).

25. Some of these, perhaps as many as half, were closed with a finding of no violation. Andrew M. Duehren, "After 34 Cases, Central Sexual Harassment Office Aims to Increase Staff," *Harvard Crimson*, February 25, 2016 (www.thecrimson.com/article /2016/2/24/odr-hears-34-cases/).

26. The number of reports filed by students in thirty-one New England colleges was 0.99 per 1,000 students, or 0.1 percent in 2014. See "Campus Sex Assault Reports Climbing," *Boston Globe*, October 6, 2014. For example, at Yale only thirteen of the school's 2,700 female undergraduates filed complaints with the school's sexual assault office in 2014–15. Emily Yoffe, "The Problem with Campus Sexual Assault Survey," *Slate*, September 24, 2015 (www.slate.com/articles/double_x/doublex/2015/09/aau _campus_sexual_assault_survey_why_such_surveys_don_t_paint_an_accurate.html).

27. Letter of December 3, 2015, Adele Rapport (OCR) to Daniel Cates (https://adc .d211.org/wp-content/uploads/2015/12/Letter-from-OCR-on-December-3-2015.pdf).

28. Associated Press, "No Decision Yet in Illinois Transgender Bathroom Case," August 15, 2015; Kate Thayer and Robert McCoppin, "Transgender Controversy Dominates High School Board Election," *Chicago Tribune*, April 3, 2017; "Attempt to Overturn Palatine School Transgender Policy Fails," *Chicago News*, April 5, 2017.

29. Catherine Lhamon (OCR) and Vanita Gupta (DOJ), Dear Colleague Letter on Transgender Students, May 13, 2016 (www2.ed.gov/about/offices/list/ocr/letters /colleague-201605-title-ix-transgender.pdf).

30. "Attorney General Loretta E. Lynch Delivers Remarks at Press Conference Announcing Complaint against the State of North Carolina to Stop Discriminating against Transgender Individuals," May 9, 2016 (www.justice.gov/opa/speech/attorney -general-loretta-e-lynch-delivers-remarks-press-conference-announcing-complaint).

31. Quoted in David A. Graham, "North Carolina's Suit to Keep Federal Funding after HB2," *The Atlantic*, May 9, 2016.

32. *Texas* v. *United States*, 201 F. Supp. 3d 810 (N.D. Tex. 2016).

33. *G. G.* v. *Gloucester County School Board*, 822 F.3d 709 (4th Cir. 2016).

34. Sandra Battle (OCR) and T. E. Wheeler II (DOJ), Dear Colleague Letter, February 22, 2017 (www2.ed.gov/about/offices/list/ocr/letters/colleague-201702-title -ix.pdf).

35. *Whitaker by Whitaker* v. *Kenosha Unified School District Board of Education*, 858 F.3d 1034 (7th Cir. 2017).

36. EEOC Compliance Manual, Section 13-V, A (www1.eeoc.gov/policy/docs /national-origin.html#VA).

37. *Code of Federal Regulations* 24, sec. 5.300—Subpart C.

38. Sean Farhang, *The Litigation State: Public Regulation and Private Lawsuits in the U.S.* (Princeton University Press, 2010), p. 3 and chs. 4–5.

39. The Court's decision in *Bakke* v. *Regents of the University of California*, 438 U.S. 265 (1978) provides a good example of this. Five of the justices based their opinions on the Fourteenth Amendment. The four dissenters relied entirely on Title VI of the Civil Rights Act.

40. I develop the latter point more fully in R. Shep Melnick, "Courts and Agencies in the American Civil Rights State," in Jeffrey Jenkins and Sidney Milkis, eds., *The Politics of Major Policy Reform in Postwar America* (Cambridge University Press, 2014); and "Adversarial Legalism, Civil Rights, and the Exceptional American State," in Thomas Burke and Jeb Barnes, eds., *Varieties of Legal Order: The Politics of Adversarial and Bureaucratic Legalism* (New York: Routledge, 2017). On the federalism rulings of the Rehnquist and Roberts Courts and their implication for enforcement of federal statutes, see Melnick, "Deregulating the States: The Political Jurisprudence of the Rehnquist Court," in Tom Ginsburg and Robert Kagan, eds., *Institutions and Public Law: Comparative Approaches* (New York: Peter Lang, 2005).

41. I first encountered this metaphor in St. John Barrett, "The New Role of the Courts in Developing Public Welfare Law," 1970 *Duke Law Journal* 1, 23 (1970). Gordon Silverstein also uses it in *Law's Allure: How Law Shapes, Constrains, Saves, and Kills Politics* (Cambridge University Press, 2009).

42. These events are discussed at much greater length in chapter 12.

43. Those decisions are *Cannon* v. *University of Chicago*, 441 U.S. 677 (1979); *North Haven Board of Education* v. *Bell*, 456 U.S. 512 (1982); *Grove City College* v. *Bell*, 465 U.S. 555 (1984); *Franklin* v. *Gwinnett County Public Schools*, 503 U.S. 60 (1992); *Gebser* v. *Lago Vista Independent School District*, 524 U.S. 274 (1998); *Davis* v. *Monroe County Board of Education*, 526 U.S. 629 (1999); *Jackson* v. *Birmingham Board of Education*, 544 U.S. 167 (2005); and *Fitzgerald* v. *Barnstable School Committee*, 555 U.S. 246 (2009). All these cases, except for *North Haven* and *Fitzgerald*, will be discussed at length in this book. The former involved employment discrimination, which has largely been handled by the EEOC under Title VII rather than by OCR under Title IX. The latter revolved around a complex §1983 issue, and has had little effect on Title IX regulation so far.

44. James Q. Wilson, *Bureaucracy: What Government Agencies Do and Why They Do It* (New York: Basic Books, 1989), p. 168.

45. Quoted in R. Shep Melnick, *Between the Lines: Interpreting Welfare Rights* (Brookings, 1994), p. 148.

46. Personal interview, May 7, 2015, Austin, Texas.

47. Charles Epp, *Making Rights Real: Activists, Bureaucrats, and the Creation of the Legalistic State* (University of Chicago Press, 2009).

48. Mary Ann Glendon, *Rights Talk: The Impoverishment of Political Discourse* (New York: Free Press, 1993).

49. Quoted in Welch Suggs, "Title IX at 30," *Chronicle of Higher Education*, June 21, 2002.

50. "Foreword: Constitutional Adjudication and the Promotion of Human Rights," 80 *Harvard Law Review* 91, 91 (1966).

51. *Cohen* v. *Brown*, 101 F.3d 155, 179 (1st Cir. 1996).

52. I develop this argument at greater length in "Gridlock and the Madisonian Constitution," in Benjamin Wittes and Pietro Nivola, eds., *What Would Madison Do? The Father of the Constitution Meets Modern American Politics* (Brookings, 2015).

53. "Secretary DeVos Prepared Remarks on Title IX Enforcement," September 7, 2017 (www.ed.gov/news/speeches/secretary-devos-prepared-remarks-title-ix-enforcement).

54. In an interview for the website "The 74" conducted shortly after she left OCR, Catherine Lhamon demonstrated both her conviction that she was on the side of the angels and her lack of self-doubt: "What motivates me in the work is love of civil rights, love of people, and deep care for satisfying the promises that Congress has made to all of us. . . . I don't know how we could have done the work better, differently, or more than we did. We were working at breakneck speed trying to achieve as much justice as was possible with the time that we had. And looking back, with the benefit now of six months' time to reflect, I continue to not be able to think of another way to have done more good than we did" (www.the74million.org/article/74-interview-catherine-lhamon -takes-on-trump-with-probe-into-cutbacks-on-student-civilrights?).

55. Vartan Gregorian, quoted in Marvin Lazerson and Ursula Wegener, "Missed Opportunities: Lessons from the Title IX Case at Brown," *Change* 28 (July–August 1996), p. 50.

Chapter Two

1. Abigail Saguy, *What Is Sexual Harassment? From Capitol Hill to the Sorbonne* (University of California Press, 2003).

2. Kathrin S. Zippel, *The Politics of Sexual Harassment: A Comparative Study of the United States, the European Union, and Germany* (Cambridge University Press, 2006), p. 42.

3. Saguy, *What Is Sexual Harassment?*, p. 10.

4. Zippel, *The Politics of Sexual Harassment*, p. 42.

5. Robert Lieberman, "Weak State, Strong Policy: Paradoxes of Race Policy in the United States, Great Britain, and France," *Studies in American Political Development* 16 (Fall 2002), p. 139. See also Robert Lieberman, *Shaping Race Policy: The United States in Comparative Perspective* (Princeton University Press, 2005). For other works that support Lieberman's conclusions, see Steven Teles, "Positive Action or Affirmative Action? The Persistence of Britain's Antidiscrimination Regime," and Erik Bleich, "The French Model: Color-Blind Integration," both in John Skrentny, ed., *The Color Lines: Affirmative Action, Immigration, and Civil Rights Options for America* (University of Chicago Press, 2001).

6. Erik Bleich, *Race Politics in Britain and France: Ideas and Policymaking since the 1960s* (Cambridge University Press, 2003), ch. 4.

7. Nicholas Pedriana and Robin Stryker, "The Strength of a Weak Agency: Enforcement of Title VII of the 1964 Civil Rights Act and the Expansion of State Capacity, 1965–71," *American Journal of Sociology* 110 (2004), pp. 709–60; Frank Dobbin and John R. Sutton, "The Strength of a Weak State: The Rights Revolution and the Rise

of Human Resources Management Divisions," *American Journal of Sociology* 104 (1998), pp. 441–76; Frank Dobbin, *Inventing Equal Opportunity* (Princeton University Press, 2009). The first chapter of Dobbin's book is titled, "Regulating Discrimination: The Paradox of a Weak State."

8. Stephen C. Halpern provides a vivid illustration of this pattern in *On the Limits of the Law: The Ironic Legacy of Title VI of the Civil Rights Act* (Johns Hopkins University Press, 1995). For perceptive analyses of the role courts have played in building the American "state," see John Skrentny, "Law and the American State," *Annual Review of Sociology* 32 (2006), pp. 213–44, and Paul Frymer, "Law and American Political Development," *Law and Social Inquiry* 33 (2003), pp. 779–803.

9. Gary Orfield, *The Reconstruction of Southern Education: The Schools and the 1964 Civil Rights Act* (New York: Wiley-Interscience, 1969).

10. *South Carolina* v. *Katzenbach*, 383 U.S. 301, 309, 334–35 (1966).

11. In 2013 a divided Supreme Court struck down one part of the Voting Rights Act, its criteria for determining which states and counties are subject to the preclearance provision. Like Chief Justice Warren, Chief Justice Roberts argued that in 1965 Congress had "employed extraordinary measures to address an extraordinary problem." Nearly half a century later, he claimed, the "exceptional conditions" that justified this "extraordinary departure form the traditional course of relations between the States and the Federal Government" no longer existed. The Supreme Court's controversial decision in *Shelby County* v. *Holder*, 570 U.S. 2 (2013) stands out as the *only* instance in which the Supreme Court limited the authority of Congress to extend to other times, places, and forms of discrimination the powers it had acquired in the 1960s to attack the racial caste system in the South.

12. Malcolm M. Feeley and Edward L. Rubin, *Judicial Policy Making and the Modern State: How the Courts Reformed America's Prisons* (Cambridge University Press, 1999), pp. 39–40.

13. Hugh Davis Graham, *The Civil Rights Era: Origins and Development of National Policy* (Oxford University Press, 1990), ch. 9; Jack Greenberg, *Crusaders in the Courts: Legal Battles of the Civil Rights Movement*, Anniversary ed. (Northport, N.Y.: Twelve Tables Press, 2004), ch. 30.

14. The formal name of the law is the Civil Rights Restoration Act of 1988. Because its main purpose was to overturn the Supreme Court's interpretation of Title IX in *Grove City College* v. *Bell*, 465 U.S. 555 (1984), it is widely known as the Grove City Bill (see chapter 3). That term will be used throughout the book.

15. Hugh Davis Graham, "After 1964: The Paradox of American Civil Rights Regulation," in Morton Keller and R. Shep Melnick, eds., *Taking Stock: American Government in the Twentieth Century* (Cambridge University Press, 1999), pp. 197–99.

16. Peter Schuck provides a useful discussion of these issues in *One Nation Undecided: Clear Thinking about Five Hard Issues That Divide Us* (Princeton University Press, 2017), pp. 56–60 and 276–77.

17. Richard Kluger, *Simple Justice* (New York: Vintage, 1975); Joshua Dunn, *Complex Justice: The Case of Missouri v. Jenkins* (University of North Carolina Press, 2008).

18. See Schuck, *One Nation Undecided*, pp. 287–89.

19. Richard Neustadt, *Presidential Power: The Politics of Leadership from FDR to Carter* (New York: Macmillan, 1980), p. 26.

20. Sean Farhang, *The Litigation State: Public Regulation and Private Lawsuits in the U.S.* (Princeton University Press, 2010); George Rutherglen, *Employment Discrimination Law: Visions of Equality in Theory and Doctrine*, 2nd ed. (New York: Foundation Press, 2007); Pedriana and Stryker, "The Strength of a Weak Agency"; Dobbin and Sutton, "The Strength of a Weak State"; Dobbin, *Inventing Equal Opportunity*.

21. Jeb Barnes and Thomas F. Burke, *How Policy Shapes Politics: Rights, Courts, Litigation, and the Struggle over Injury Compensation* (Oxford University Press, 2015).

22. Robert Katzmann, *Institutional Disability: The Saga of Transportation Policy for the Disabled* (Brookings, 1986).

23. Halpern, *On the Limits of the Law*; Gary Orfield, *Reconstruction of Southern Education* and *Must We Bus? Segregated Schools and National Policy* (Brookings, 1978); R. Shep Melnick, "Taking Remedies Seriously: Can Courts Control Public Schools?" in Joshua M. Dunn and Martin R. West, eds., *From Schoolhouse to Courthouse: The Judiciary's Role in American Education* (Brookings, 2009).

24. Gareth Davies, *See Government Grow: Education Politics from Johnson to Reagan* (University of Kansas Press, 2007), ch. 6; John D. Skrentny, *The Minority Rights Revolution* (Harvard University Press, 2002), ch. 7; and Rachel Moran, "The Politics of Discretion: Federal Intervention in Bilingual Education," 76 *California Law Review* 1249 (1988).

25. See, for example, Christopher Howard, *The Welfare State Nobody Knows: Debunking Myths about U.S. Social Policy* (Princeton University Press, 2007); and Walter A. Rosenbaum, *Environmental Politics and Policy*, 10th ed. (Washington: CQ Press, 2016).

26. U.S. Commission on Civil Rights, *Federal Title VI Enforcement to Ensure Nondiscrimination in Federally Assisted Programs: A Report of the U.S. Commission on Civil Rights* (June 1996), pp. 618–30.

27. Hanes Walton Jr., *When the Marching Stopped: The Politics of Civil Rights Regulatory Agencies* (State University of New York Press, 1988), pp. 30–31. Walton's careful efforts to estimate the number of staff members dedicated to civil rights compliance in 1984 (the only such estimate I have found) arrived at a total of 12,074 (p. 45). Because the staff of the EEOC and OCR has declined since then, it is likely that the current figure is lower.

28. Farhang, *Litigation State*, chs. 4–5.

29. Graham, "After 1964," p. 202.

30. United States Courts Statistics and Reports, Caseload Statistics Data Tables, Table C-2 (www.uscourts.gov/sites/default/files/data_tables/jb_c2_0930.2016.pdf), pp. 1–2.

31. Donald Horowitz, *The Courts and Social Policy* (Brookings, 1976), p. 13.

32. See R. Shep Melnick, *Between The Lines: Interpreting Welfare Rights* (Brookings, 1994), pp. 36–38. Chief Justice Warren Burger's opinion in *Griggs* v. *Duke Power*,

401 U.S. 424 (1971), perhaps the most important of the Court's many interpretations of Title VII, exemplifies this approach.

33. Sean Farhang and Stephen Burbank, *Rights and Retrenchment: The Counterrevolution against Federal Litigation* (Cambridge University Press, 2017).

34. Those decisions are *Cannon* v. *University of Chicago*, 441 U.S. 677 (1979); *North Haven Board of Education* v. *Bell*, 456 U.S. 512 (1982); *Grove City College* v. *Bell*, 465 U.S. 555 (1984); *Franklin* v. *Gwinnett County Public Schools*, 503 U.S. 60 (1992); *Gebser* v. *Lago Vista Independent School District*, 524 U.S. 274 (1998); *Davis* v. *Monroe County Board of Education*, 526 U.S. 629 (1999); *Jackson* v. *Birmingham Board of Education*, 544 U.S. 167 (2005); and *Fitzgerald* v. *Barnstable School Committee*, 555 U.S. 246 (2009).

35. Robert Kagan, *Adversarial Legalism: The American Way of Law* (Harvard University Press, 2001).

36. Suzanne Mettler, *The Submerged State: How Invisible Government Policies Undermine American Democracy* (University of Chicago Press, 2011).

Chapter Three

1. Susan Ware, *Title IX: A Brief History with Documents* (Long Grove, Ill.: Waveland Press, 2007), pp. 1, 3. One indication of how common this "simple statute" meme has become is an ESPN.com video celebrating the law's forty-fifth anniversary. It begins, "It's 45 Years Old and Only 37 Words Long" (www.espn.com/video/clip?id=19696040).

2. Quoted in John Skrentny, *The Minority Rights Revolution* (Harvard University Press, 2002), p. 247.

3. Andrew Fishel and Janice Pottker, *National Politics and Sex Discrimination in Education* (Lexington, Mass.: Lexington Books, 1977), ch. 5; and Skrentny, *The Minority Rights Revolution*, ch. 8.

4. Skrentny, *The Minority Rights Revolution*, p. 232.

5. *INS* v. *Chahda*, 462 U.S. 919 (1983). This did not deter Congress from enacting additional legislative vetoes. See Louis Fisher, "The Legislative Veto: Invalidated, It Survives," 56 *Law and Contemporary Problems* 273 (1993).

6. For useful discussions of congressional influence over administrative agencies, see Herbert Kaufman, *The Administrative Behavior of Federal Bureau Chiefs* (Brookings, 1981); and Christopher H. Foreman, *Signals from the Hill: Congressional Oversight and the Challenge of Social Regulation* (Yale University Press, 1989).

7. In 2006 the Department of Education promulgated Title IX regulations creating a limited exception to the 1975 regulation's prohibition on single-sex primary and secondary schools. This is one of those rare cases in which the exception does in fact prove the rule. The administration was forced to go through the full panoply of procedures because it wanted to change existing requirements. The process took two years. The department received and responded to 5,860 comments. It revised its original proposal in several ways, and offered a detailed explanation for the final rule. 71 *Federal Register* 62530–62543 (October 25, 2006). This shows how time-consuming and

resource-intensive notice-and-comment rulemaking can be. The more controversial the issue, the longer and more costly the process.

8. When OCR employed a similar tactic for its Title VI bilingual education guidelines in the late 1970s, a federal district court ordered it to comply with the APA. Betsy Levin, "An Analysis of the Federal Attempt to Regulate Bilingual Education: Protecting Civil Rights or Controlling Curriculum?" 12 *Journal of Law and Education* 29 (1983). That rulemaking process generated so much opposition to OCR's proposal that it never issued a final rule on bilingual education—and did everything it could to avoid the standard rulemaking process in the future.

9. Letter to Senators Harkin and Alexander, June 25, 2014 (www.acenet.edu /news-room/Documents/Letter-Senate-HELP-Sexual-Assault-Hearing.pdf).

10. Brief for the United States, quoted in *Texas* v. *United States*, 201 F. Supp. 3d 810, 817 (N.D. Tex. 2016).

11. Jake New, "Senators Challenge Legality of U.S. Guidance on Campus Sexual Assault," *Inside Higher Ed*, January 7, 2016.

12. *Sexual Assault on Campus, Working to Ensure Student Safety: Hearings before the Senate Health, Education, Labor, and Pensions Committee*, 114th Cong., June 26, 2014. The exchange between Senator Alexander and Assistant Secretary Lhamon can be viewed at minutes 49:00 to 56:00 of the hearing (www.help.senate.gov/hearings /sexual-assault-on-campus-working-to-ensure-student-safety).

13. Letter, Senator James Lankford to Acting Secretary John B. King Jr., January 7, 2016, pp. 2–3 (www.lankford.senate.gov/imo/media/doc/Sen. Lankford letter to Dept. of Education 1.7.16.pdf).

14. Letter, Assistant Secretary Catherine E. Lhamon to Senator James Lankford, February 17, 2016, p. 3 (www.chronicle.com/items/biz/pdf/DEPT.%20of%20 EDUCATION%20RESPONSE%20TO%20LANKFORD%20LETTER%202 -17-16.pdf).

15. Letter, Senator James Lankford to Acting Secretary John B. King Jr., March 4, 2016, pp. 1, 4 (www.lankford.senate.gov/imo/media/doc/3.4.16 Lankford letter to Dept. of Education.pdf).

16. Letter, NWLC and others to Secretary John King, July 13, 2016 (nwlc.org/wp -content/uploads/2016/07/2016.7.13-Title-IX Support-Sign-On-Letter.final.pdf).

17. Letter, Senator James Lankford to Secretary John King, May 17, 2016 (www .lankford.senate.gov/imo/media/doc/Senator Lankford letter to Secretary King on OCR transgender guidance 5.17.16.pdf).

18. "Secretary DeVos Prepared Remarks on Title IX Enforcement," September 7, 2017 (www.ed.gov/news/speeches/secretary-devos-prepared-remarks-title-ix-enforcement).

19. OCR is far from the only agency to circumvent APA procedures. For a review of the larger problem and an explanation of the federal courts' inability to grapple adequately with it, see Hale Melnick, "Guidance Documents and Rules: Increasing Executive Accountability in the Regulatory World," 44 *Boston College Environmental Affairs Law Review* 357 (2017).

20. Quoted in Hugh Davis Graham, "The Storm over Grove City College: Civil Rights Regulation, Higher Education, and the Reagan Administration," *History of Education Quarterly* 38 (Winter 1998), pp. 417–18.

21. *Grove City College* v. *Bell*, 465 U.S. 555, 573 (1984).

22. Ibid. at 582 (Brennan dissenting).

23. These developments are described in Graham, "Storm over Grove City College."

24. Beryl Radin, *Implementation, Change, and the Federal Bureaucracy: School Desegregation Policy in H.E.W., 1964–1968* (New York: Teachers College Press, 1977), p. 14.

25. Joseph A. Califano Jr., *Governing America: An Insider's Report from the White House and the Cabinet* (New York: Simon and Schuster, 1981), pp. 252–53.

26. U.S. Commission on Civil Rights, *Federal Title VI Enforcement to Ensure Non-discrimination in Federally Assisted Programs: A Report of the U.S. Commission on Civil Rights* (Washington, June 1996), p. 40.

27. Radin provides a good summary of the deficiencies of the funding cutoff in *Implementation, Change, and the Federal Bureaucracy*, pp. 125–26.

28. *Brown* v. *Califano*, 455 F. Supp. 837, 842 (D.D.C. 1978).

29. *U.S.* v. *Jefferson County Board of Education*, 372 F.2d 836, 852, 856 (5th Cir. 1966).

30. *U.S.* v. *Jefferson County* at 847–48.

31. *U.S.* v. *Jefferson County Board of Education*, 380 F.2d 385, 413 (5th Cir. en banc 1967) (Bell dissenting).

32. *Lau* v. *Nichols*, 414 U.S. 563 (1974).

33. I explain this change in greater detail in Melnick, "Taking Remedies Seriously: Can Courts Control Public Schools?" in Joshua M. Dunn and Martin R. West, eds., *From Schoolhouse to Courthouse: The Judiciary's Role in American Education* (Brookings, 2009), pp. 36–40.

34. Leading examples include *J. I. Case* v. *Borak*, 377 U.S. 426 (1964) and *King* v. *Smith*, 392 U.S. 309 (1968).

35. See, for example, *National Railroad Passengers Corp.* v. *National Association of Railroad Passengers*, 414 U.S. 453 (1974); *Securities Investor Protection Corp.* v. *Barbour*, 421 U.S. 412 (1975); *Pennhurst State School and Hospital* v. *Halderman*, 451 U.S. 1 (1981); *Middlesex Co. Sewage Authority* v. *National Seaclammers Association*, 453 U.S. 1 (1981); and *Atascadero State Hospital* v. *Scanlon*, 473 U.S. 234 (1985).

36. *Cannon* v. *University of Chicago*, 441 U.S. 677 (1979).

37. Ibid. at 705–06.

38. Ibid. at 726 (White dissenting).

39. Ibid. at 747 (Powell dissenting).

40. I describe these later cases in Melnick, "Deregulating the States: The Political Jurisprudence of the Rehnquist Court," in Tom Ginsburg and Robert Kagan, eds., *Institutions and Public Law: Comparative Approaches* (New York: Peter Lang, 2005), pp. 82–87.

41. *Franklin* v. *Gwinnett*, 503 U.S. 60, 77 (1992) (Scalia concurring). A more extended discussion of this case can be found in chapter 10.

42. In 2009 a unanimous Court held that Title IX does not preclude §1983 peer sexual harassment suits that allege unconstitutional sex discrimination. *Fitzgerald* v. *Barnstable School Committee*, 555 U.S. 246 (2009). This is another deviation from the Rehnquist and Roberts Courts' general tendency to restrict access to the federal courts. So far, the ruling has had little effect on sexual harassment litigation.

43. The only discussion of the status of the OCR memo came in one brief paragraph in Justice Stewart's concurring opinion.

44. *Alexander* v. *Sandoval*, 532 U.S. 275, 287 (2001).

45. *Sandoval* at 306–07.

46. *Jackson* v. *Birmingham Board of Education*, 544 U.S. 167, 173–74 (2005).

47. Ibid. at 180. Lynda Dodd has noted that many retaliation cases decided by the Rehnquist and Roberts Courts do not fit the more general pattern of restricting judicial remedies. *The Rights Revolution Revisited* (Cambridge University Press, 2017), ch. 9.

48. *Jackson* at 195.

49. Ibid. at 178.

Chapter Four

1. Office for Civil Rights, *Securing Equal Educational Opportunity: Report to the President and Secretary of Education, 2016*, p. 6 (www2.ed.gov/about/reports/annual/ocr/report-to-president-and-secretary-of-education-2016.pdf).

2. Ibid., p. 4.

3. *Adams* v. *Richardson*, 351 F. Supp. 636 (D.D.C., 1973), upheld in *Adams* v. *Richardson*, 480 F.2d 1159 (D.C. Cir. 1973). The long story of this extensive litigation, which produced several more court decisions, is recounted in Stephen Halpern, *On the Limits of the Law: The Ironic Legacy of Title VI of the Civil Rights Act* (Johns Hopkins University Press, 1995); and Jeremy Rabkin, *Judicial Compulsions: How Public Law Distorts Public Policy* (New York: Basic Books, 1989), ch. 5.

4. For a summary of these guidance documents, see the Obama administration's report on OCR's accomplishments, *Achieving Simple Justice: Highlights of Activities, Office for Civil Rights, 2009–2016*, pp. 4, 6, 7, 9, 10, 13 (www2.ed.gov/about/reports/annual/ocr/achieving-simple-justice.pdf). The documents are available at OCR's online "reading room" (www2.ed.gov/about/offices/list/ocr/frontpage/faq/readingroom).

5. Andy Thomason, "Why Isn't Baylor Under Title IX Investigation? A Records Request Yields Laughably Little," *Chronicle of Higher Education*, August 3, 2016.

6. Catherine Y. Kim, "Presidential Control across Policymaking Forms," UNC Legal Studies Research Paper no. 2571068, December 9, 2015, pp. 31–33 (https://ssrn.com/abstract=2571068).

7. Rabkin, *Judicial Compulsions*; Gary Orfield, *The Reconstruction of Southern Education* (New York: Wiley-Interscience, 1969); Gary Orfield, *Must We Bus? Segregated*

Schools and National Policy (Brookings, 1978); Halpern, *On the Limits of the Law*; Beryl Radin, *Implementation, Change and the Federal Bureaucracy: School Desegregation Policy in H.E.W., 1964–1968* (New York: Teachers College Press, 1978); Rosemary Salomone, "Judicial Oversight of Agency Enforcement: The Adams and WEAL Litigation," in Barbara Flicker, ed., *Justice and School Systems: The Role of the Courts in Education Litigation* (Temple University Press, 1990); Michael Rebell and Arthur Block, *Equality and Education: Federal Civil Rights Enforcement in the New York City School System* (Princeton University Press, 1985).

8. *Civil Rights Enforcement by the Department of Education: Hearings Before the Subcommittee on Human Resources and Intergovernmental Relations, House Committee on Government Operations*, 100th Cong., 1st sess., April 23, 1987; Majority Staff of the Committee on Education and Labor, *Report on the Investigation of the Civil Rights Enforcement Activities of the Office for Civil Rights, U.S. Department of Education*, 100th Cong., 2nd sess. 1988; U.S. Commission on Civil Rights, *Federal Title VI Enforcement to Ensure Nondiscrimination in Federally Assisted Programs* (June 1996) (https://babel.hathitrust.org/cgi/pt?id=pst.000026196725;view=1up;seq=3).

9. OCR/DOJ letter explaining the agreement with University of Montana, May 9, 2013, p. 1 (www2.ed.gov/documents/press-releases/montana-missoula-letter.pdf).

10. "Secretary DeVos Prepared Remarks on Title IX Enforcement," September 7, 2017 (www.ed.gov/news/speeches/secretary-devos-prepared-remarks-title-ix-enforcement).

11. These personal interviews were conducted as background; interviewees are not quoted directly without their permission.

12. The office was initially located within HEW's Office of Education. After the "Chicago fiasco" described in the text, it was transferred to the Office of the Secretary of HEW.

13. Panetta and Peter Gall provide a detailed description of his confrontation with the Nixon administration in *Bring Us Together: The Nixon Team and the Civil Rights Retreat* (Philadelphia: Lippincott, 1971).

14. Joseph Califano Jr., *Governing America: An Insider's Report from the White House and the Cabinet* (New York: Simon and Schuster, 1981), pp. 215, 217–19.

15. Republican Platform, 2016, p. 35 (www.gop.com/the-2016-repubican-party-platform/).

16. Office for Civil Rights, *1995 Annual Report to Congress,* p. 1 (www2.ed.gov/about/offices/list/ocr/AnnRpt95/edlite-ocr95rp1.html).

17. U.S. Department of Education, "Crossing the Next Bridge: Secretary Arne Duncan's Remarks on the 45th Anniversary of 'Bloody Sunday' at the Edmund Pettus Bridge, Selma, Alabama," March 8, 2010 (www.ed.gov/news/speeches/crossing-next-bridge-secretary-arne-duncan's-remarks-45th-anniversary-bloody-sunday-edmund-pettus-bridge-selma-alabama).

18. *Report on the Investigation of the Civil Rights Enforcement Activities*, p. 20.

19. The following analysis is informed by James Q. Wilson's discussion of bureaucratic tasks in *Bureaucracy: What Government Agencies Do and Why They Do It* (New

York: Basic Books, 1989), especially chs. 3–4. I use Michael Lipsky's felicitous term "street-level bureaucrat" instead of Wilson's favored term, "operators." See Lipsky, *Street-Level Bureaucracy* (New York: Russell Sage Foundation, 1980).

20. Quoted in Orfield, *Must We Bus?*, p. 352.

21. Ibid., pp. 309, 281, 298.

22. Quoted in Gareth Davies, *See Government Grow: Education Politics from Johnson to Reagan* (University Press of Kansas, 2007), pp. 112–13.

23. Quoted in Orfield, *Reconstruction of Southern Education*, p. 76.

24. Rebell and Block, *Equality and Education*, p. 153. For their general evaluation, see pp. 201–02.

25. Betsy Levin provides a concise description of these events in "An Analysis of the Federal Attempt to Regulate Bilingual Education: Protecting Civil Rights or Controlling Curriculum?" 12 *Journal of Law and Education* 29 (1983).

26. For a detailed description of this complex litigation, see Halpern, *On the Limits of the Law*, pp. 95–152, 202–35.

27. *Women's Equity Action League* v. *Cavazos*, 906 F.2d 741, 744–45 (D.C. Cir. 1990).

28. Quoted in Halpern, *On the Limits of the Law*, p. 221.

29. *Adams* v. *Weinberger*, 391 F. Supp. 269, 273 (D.D.C. 1975).

30. 40 *Federal Register* 24148–49 (June 4, 1975).

31. These statements come from Tatel's affidavit in the *Adams* litigation, as quoted in Halpern, *On the Limits of the Law*, pp. 140–41. Gary Orfield agreed, concluding that by 1977, "The office was under so many court-imposed deadlines for so many contradictory enforcement tasks that virtually no staff was available for any fresh policy initiative." Orfield, *Must We Bus?*, p. 317.

32. Halpern, *On the Limits of the Law*, p. 144.

33. Department of Education, OCR, *Fiscal Year 2018 Budget Request*, p. Z-13 (www2.ed.gov/about/overview/budget/budget18/justifications/z-ocr.pdf).

34. *Report on the Investigation of the Civil Rights Enforcement Activities*, p. 11.

35. Halpern, *On the Limits of the Law*, p. 151.

36. Rabkin, *Judicial Compulsions*, p. 168.

37. Ibid., p. 170.

38. Califano, *Governing America*, p. 226.

39. Department of Education Office for Civil Rights, *Annual Report to Congress: Fiscal Year 1993*, p. 10 (https://ia600202.us.archive.org/15/items/ERIC_ED422667/ERIC_ED422667.pdf).

40. OCR, *Protecting Civil Rights, Advancing Equity: Report to the President and Secretary of Education, FY 2013–14* (April 2015), p. 28.

41. OCR, *Achieving Simple Justice*, p. 10.

42. The source for the former figure is OCR, *Securing Equal Educational Opportunity*, p. 24; for the latter, testimony by Assistant Secretary Lhamon, reported in the *Washington Post*, March 18, 2015 (www.washingtonpost.com/news/local/wp/2015/03/18/civil-rights-complaints-to-u-s-department-of-education-reach-a-record-high/?utm_term=.0fede3cf3850).

43. *Report on the Investigation of the Civil Rights Enforcement Activities*, p. 26.

44. Ibid., p. 5.

45. *Investigation of Civil Rights Enforcement by the Department of Education: Hearings Before the Subcommittee on Intergovernmental and Human Relations of the House Committee on Government Operations*, 99th Cong., 1st sess., July 18 and September 11, 1985 (testimony of Assistant Secretary Harry Singleton), p. 93.

46. *Report on the Investigation of the Civil Rights Enforcement Activities*, p. 103.

47. Kim, "Presidential Control," p. 28.

48. Ibid., pp. 37, 39.

49. Office for Civil Rights, *Protecting Civil Rights, Advancing Equity: Report to the President and Secretary of Education, FY 2013–14*, p. 4 (www2.ed.gov/about/reports /annual/ocr/report-to-president-and-secretary-of-education-2013-14.pdf).

50. *Securing Equal Educational Opportunity*, pp. 18, 24. The report does not mention any other compliance reviews.

51. Interview with Associated Press reporter Juliet Linderman, published in *U.S. News and World Report*, June 8, 2015 (www.usnews.com/news/us/articles/2015/06/08 /broader-probes-of-campus-sex-assaults-leave-victims-hanging).

52. These events are described in greater detail in chapter 13. The memo, which was leaked to ProPublica, can be found at www.documentcloud.org/documents/3863019 -doc00742420170609111824.html.

53. One major exception was the massive settlement between OCR and the New York City school system announced in the waning days of the Carter administration. Liberal icon Judge Jack Weinstein temporarily halted enforcement of the agreement on the grounds that such "drastic governmental action" that "affects the lives of hundreds of thousands of citizens" should not "result solely from secret, informal negotiations conducted exclusively by a handful of government officials. . . . No matter how benign and well intentioned, those government officials who can, in practical effect, turn on or off the source of hundreds of millions of dollars, must conduct themselves with scrupulous regard for procedural protections. Not only must the result be just, but, if the people are to retain their faith in their government, the means used to achieve the result must be fair." *Caulfield* v. *Board of Education*, 449 F. Supp. 1203, 1206–07 (E.D. N.Y. 1978). Judge Weinstein was later overruled by the Second Circuit.

54. For example, letter to George Washington University, August 3, 2011 (www2 .ed.gov/about/offices/list/ocr/docs/investigations/11112079-a.pdf); and letter to Harvard Law School, December 30, 2014 (https://www2.ed.gov/documents/press-releases /harvard-law-letter.pdf).

55. Letter from Comptroller General Elmer Staats to Senator Birch Bayh, March 30, 1977 (www.gao.gov/assets/120/117641.pdf), pp. 7–8.

56. Jeremy Rabkin, "Office for Civil Rights," in James Q. Wilson, ed., *The Politics of Regulation* (New York: Basic Books, 1980), p. 347.

57. *Report on the Investigation of the Civil Rights Enforcement Activities*, pp. 33–35.

58. It added, "OCR has not defined the phrase equal educational opportunity in any of its policies or guidance memoranda." U. S. Commission on Civil Rights, *Equal Educational Opportunity Project Series*, vol. 1 (December 1996), p. 196 (https://www .law.umaryland.edu/marshall/usccr/documents/cr12ed8az.pdf).

59. Report of the Commission on Civil Rights, *Equal Employment Opportunity and Nondiscrimination for Minority Students: Federal Enforcement of Title VI in Ability Grouping Practices* (September 1999), p. 121.

60. U.S. Commission on Civil Rights, *Ten-Year Check-Up: Have Federal Agencies Responded to Civil Rights Recommendations?* (September 2004), p. 20 (www.usccr.gov /pubs/10yr04/10yr04.pdf).

Chapter Five

1. Quoted in Susan Ware, *Title IX: A Brief History with Documents* (Long Grove, Ill.: Waveland Press, 2007), p. 3.

2. *Congressional Record* 117 (August 6, 1971), p. 30407.

3. U.S. House of Representatives, Committee on Education and Labor, *Sex Discrimination Regulations: Hearings Before the Subcommittee on Post-Secondary Education*, 94th Cong., 1st sess. 1975, p. 439.

4. Thomas A. Diprete and Claudia Buchmann, *The Rise of Women: The Growing Gender Gap in Education and What It Means for American Schools* (New York: Russell Sage Foundation Press, 2013), p. 109; and Jessica Gavora, *Tilting the Playing Field: Schools, Sports, Sex and Title IX* (San Francisco: Encounter Books, 2002), pp. 142–43. On the extent to which female students generally outpace their male counterparts in education, see Hanna Rosin, *The End of Men and the Rise of Women* (New York: Riverhead Press, 2012), and Diprete and Buchmann, *The Rise of Women*.

5. Quoted in William G. Bowen and Sarah A. Levin, *Reclaiming the Game: College Sports and Educational Values* (Princeton University Press, 2003), p. 246.

6. I have adopted the useful term "parity" from Earl C. Dudley Jr. and George Rutherglen, "Ironies, Inconsistencies, and Intercollegiate Athletics: Title IX, Title VII, and Statistical Evidence of Discrimination," 1 *Virginia Journal of Sport and the Law* 117 (1999). The term "relative interest" pervades the long debate over athletic rules discussed in subsequent chapters.

7. Quoted in Chanan Tigay, "Women and Sports: Do Schools Give Female Athletes Enough Opportunities?" *CQ Researcher* 21 (March 25, 2011), p. 271.

8. Gavora, *Tilting the Playing Field*, p. 60.

9. James L. Shulman and William G. Bowen, *The Game of Life: College Sports and Educational Values* (Princeton University Press, 2001), p. xxv.

10. Mark Snyder, "Michigan Is First Football Program with 3 Assistants Making $1 Million," *Detroit Free Press*, January 24, 2017.

11. Welch Suggs, "Title IX at 30," *Chronicle of Higher Education*, June 21, 2002.

12. Quoted in Ware, *Title IX*, p. 20.

13. Dudley and Rutherglen, "Ironies, Inconsistencies, and Intercollegiate Athletics," p. 183.

14. Department of Education, Equity in Athletics Data Analysis, Revenues (https://ope.ed.gov/athletics/Trend/public/#/answer/6/601/main?row=-1&column=-1).

15. This term was used repeatedly by the district and appellate courts in the Quinnipiac case: *Biediger* v. *Quinnipiac University*, 728 F. Supp. 2d 62, 64, 66, 94 (D. Conn. 2010); *Biediger* v. *Quinnipiac University*, 691 F.3d 85, 95, 99 (2nd Cir. 2010). The implication—that nonvarsity athletic participation "opportunities" are not "genuine"—cannot hold up under serious examination. But that implication is never examined in the regulatory debate. This issue will be explored in greater detail in chapter 8.

16. Remarks of Jocelyn F. Samuels (vice president for education and employment, National Women's Law Center) and Judith Sweet (former senior vice president of the NCAA for Championships and Educational Services), in *Title IX Athletics: Accommodating Interests and Abilities*, Briefing before the United States Commission on Civil Rights (2010), pp. 30, 28.

17. *Cohen* v. *Brown*, 101 F.3d 155, 179–80 (1st Cir. 1996).

18. See Gavora, *Tilting the Playing Field*, ch. 3; and a summary of the remarks of Jocelyn Samuels, in *Title IX Athletics: Accommodating Interests and Abilities*, pp. 11–13.

19. Statement of Abigail Thernstrom, in *Title IX Athletics: Accommodating Interests and Abilities*, p. 84.

20. Dear Colleague Letter, "Further Clarification of Intercollegiate Athletics Policy Guidance regarding Title IX Compliance," July 11, 2003, p. 2 (www2.ed.gov/about/offices/list/ocr/title9guidanceFinal.html).

21. The opportunity costs of creating more athletic opportunities will be explored in chapter 8.

22. For a dispiriting review of the extensive academic fraud linked to intercollegiate athletics, see also Gerald Gurney, Donna A. Lopiano, and Andrew Zimbalist, *Unwinding Madness: What Went Wrong with College Sports and How to Fix It* (Brookings, 2017), pp. 75–83, 147–61.

23. Ibid., chs. 1 and 7.

24. Ware, *Title IX*, p. 11.

25. The best descriptions of the AIAW are provided by Mary Jo Festle, *Playing Nice: Politics and Apologies in Women's Sports* (Columbia University Press, 1996); and Ying Wushanley, *Playing Nice and Losing: The Struggle for Control of Women's Intercollegiate Athletics, 1960–2000* (Syracuse University Press, 2004). See also Shulman and Bowen, *The Game of Life*, pp. 119–25; and Welch Suggs, *A Place on the Team: The Triumph and Tragedy of Title IX* (Princeton University Press, 2005), pp. 45–65.

26. For more on the AIAW, see chapter 8.

27. National Women's Law Center, *The Next Generation of Title IX: Athletics*, (June 2012), p. 4 (www.nwlc.org/wp-content/uploads/2015/08/nwlcathletics_titleixfactsheet.pdf); see Walter Villa, "A Touchdown for Girls' Sports?" (June 21, 2012)

(www.espn.com/high-school/girl/story/_/id/8080354/flag-football-growing-high
-school-sport-girls).

28. NCAA, *Student Athlete Participation, 1981–82—2015–16*, p. 7 (www.ncaa
publications.com/productdownloads/PR1516.pdf).

29. R. Vivian Acosta and Linda Jean Carpenter, "Women in International Sport: A
Longitudinal, National Study Thirty-Seven Year Update, 1977–2014," p. 5 (http://
acostacarpenter.org/AcostaCarpenter2012.pdf).

30. Suggs, *A Place on the Team*, pp. 95–96.

Chapter Six

1. "Nondiscrimination on the Basis of Sex in Education Programs and Activities
Receiving or Benefiting from Federal Financial Assistance," 40 *Federal Register* 24135
(June 4, 1975).

2. The best descriptions of the rulemaking process are Andrew Fishel and Janice
Pottker, "Sex Discrimination and the Administrative Rule-Making Process: The Development of the Title IX Regulations," in *National Politics and Sex Discrimination in
Education* (Lexington, Mass.: Lexington Books, 1977); and John Skrentny, *The Minority Rights Revolution* (Harvard University Press, 2002), ch. 8.

3. *Adams* v. *Richardson*, 351 F. Supp. 636 (D.D.C., 1973) and 356 F. Supp. 92
(D.D.C. 1973). The significance of this case is discussed in chapter 4.

4. Weinberger told the committee that HEW's regulations "do not require women
to play football with men," do "not require coeducational showers, locker rooms, and
toilet facilities," and do "not mean that the National College Athletic Association will
have to be dissolved and will have to fire all of its highly vocal staff." U.S. House of
Representatives, Committee on Education and Labor, *Sex Discrimination Regulations:
Hearings Before the Subcommittee on Post-Secondary Education*, 94th Cong., 1st sess.
(1975), p. 329.

5. Ibid., p. 441.

6. §86.41, 40 *Federal Register* 24142 (June 4, 1975).

7. Ibid., p. 24134.

8. Letter from Peter E. Holmes to Chief State School Officers, Title IX Obligations in Athletics, September 1975 (www2.ed.gov/about/offices/list/ocr/docs/holmes
.html). The significance of this letter is discussed in Welch Suggs, *A Place on the Team:
The Triumph and Tragedy of Title IX* (Princeton University Press, 2005), pp. 72–73.

9. 40 *Federal Register* 24143 (June 4, 1975).

10. Quoted in Susan Ware, *Title IX: A Brief History with Documents* (Long Grove,
Ill.: Waveland Press, 2007), p. 55.

11. J. Cameron, "Nader's Invaders Are Inside the Gates," *Fortune*, October 1977,
p. 252.

12. Joseph A. Califano Jr., *Governing America: An Insider's Report from the White
House and the Cabinet* (New York: Simon and Schuster, 1981), p. 225.

13. Ibid., p. 224.

14. "Title IX of the Education Amendments of 1972; a Proposed Policy Interpretation," 43 *Federal Register* 58070–76 (December 11, 1978).

15. Ibid., pp. 58072, 58074.

16. Califano, *Governing America*, p. 266.

17. Ibid., pp. 266–68, 224; Suggs, *A Place on the Team*, pp. 77–78.

18. Califano, *Governing America*, p. 225.

19. "Title IX of the Education Amendments of 1972; a Policy Interpretation; Title IX and Intercollegiate Athletics," 44 *Federal Register* 71413 (December 11, 1979).

20. Ibid., p. 71414.

21. Ibid., pp. 71517–18.

22. Norma Cantú, Dear Colleague Letter, "Clarification of Intercollegiate Athletics Policy Guidance: The Three-Part Test," January 16, 1996, p. 3 (www2.ed.gov /about/offices/list/ocr/docs/clarific.html).

23. *OCR Title IX Intercollegiate Athletics Investigator's Manual, 1980*, p. 122 (emphasis added), quoted in Brown University's petition for writ of certiorari, p. 5 (www .brown.edu/Administration/News_Bureau/1996-97/96-085p.html).

24. *OCR Title IX Intercollegiate Athletics Investigator's Manual, 1990*, prepared by Valerie Bonnette, pp. 23, 27 (http://files.eric.ed.gov/fulltext/ED400763.pdf).

25. For the clearest statement, see Earl C. Dudley Jr. and George Rutherglen, "Ironies, Inconsistencies, and Intercollegiate Athletics: Title IX, Title VII, and Statistical Evidence of Discrimination," 1 *Virginia Journal of Sport and the Law* 117 (1999).

26. Welch Suggs, "Title IX at 30," *Chronicle of Higher Education*, June 21, 2002; Jeffrey H. Orleans, "An End to the Odyssey: Equal Athletic Opportunities for Women," 3 *Duke Journal of Gender Law and Policy* 131, 137–38 (1996).

27. 47 *Federal Register* 1662 (January 13, 1982).

28. Quoted in Suggs, *A Place on the Team*, p. 88.

29. *University of Richmond* v. *Bell*, 543 F. Supp. 321 (E.D. Va. 1982).

30. *Grove City College* v. *Bell*, 465 U.S. 555 (1984). The Court's opinion is discussed in chapter 3.

31. Hugh Davis Graham, "The Storm over Grove City: Civil Rights Regulation, Higher Education, and the Reagan Administration," *History of Education Quarterly* 38 (Winter 1998), p. 418; Suggs, *A Place on the Team*, p. 89.

32. The only significant debate involved abortion, and it was resolved by a compromise offered by Senator Danforth. Graham, "Storm over Grove City," pp. 420–23.

33. Department of Education, Office for Civil Rights, *Annual Report to Congress: Fiscal Year 1991*, p. 17 (http://files.eric.ed.gov/fulltext/ED421804.pdf); U.S. Commission on Civil Rights, *Equal Educational Project Series*, vol. 1 (December 1996), p. 174.

34. Douglas Lederman, "U.S. Drafts Memo on Sex Equality in College Sports," *Chronicle of Higher Education*, February 5, 1992.

35. "CUNY's Brooklyn College to Drop Its Sports Program," *Chronicle of Higher Education*, June 17, 1992.

36. Quoted in Douglas Lederman, "Women's-Sports Advocates Take the Offensive," *Chronicle of Higher Education*, March 25, 1992.

37. Quoted in Lederman, "U.S. Drafts Memo on Sex Equality in College Sports."

38. Quoted in Lederman, "Women's-Sports Advocates Take the Offensive."

39. Suggs, *A Place on the Team*, p. 94.

40. Gavora, *Tilting the Playing Field*, p. 44.

41. *Franklin* v. *Gwinnett County Public Schools*, 503 U.S. 60 (1992).

42. Suggs, *A Place on the Team*, p. 106.

43. Ware, *Title IX*, p. 16.

44. Douglas Lederman, "Women's-Sports Advocates Take the Offensive"; Debra Blum, "Women Sue University to Reinstate 2 Teams," *Chronicle of Higher Education*, October 14, 1992; "U. of Mass. at Amherst Agrees to Reinstate 3 Women's Teams," *Chronicle of Higher Education*, October 28, 1992; Blum, "Judge Sees 'Stonewalling' at Colorado State," *Chronicle of Higher Education*, March 31, 1993; Blum, "Southeastern Conference Approves Equity Plan," *Chronicle of Higher Education*, June 16, 1993; "9 Women Sue Cornell U. for Sex Bias," *Chronicle of Higher Education*, July 21, 1993; Blum, "University of Texas Settles Sex-Bias Suit," *Chronicle of Higher Education*, July 28, 1993; Blum, "Sex Equity Takes Big Step in California," *Chronicle of Higher Education*, October 27, 1993.

45. Quoted in Debra Blum, "Education Department Criticized on Rights," *Chronicle of Higher Education*, March 3, 1993.

46. Quoted in Debra Blum, "Getting Tough on College Sports," *Chronicle of Higher Education*, September 15, 1993.

47. Blum, "Getting Tough on College Sports"; and Blum, "OCR Urged to Heed Results of 2 Recent Sex-Bias Suits," *Chronicle of Higher Education*, September 15, 1993.

48. U.S. General Accounting Office, "Gender Equity: Men's and Women's Participation in Higher Education," GAO-01-128, December 2000, p. 30; Suggs, *A Place on the Team*, p. 129.

49. *Hearing on Title IX of the Education Amendments of 1972 Before the Subcommittee on Postsecondary Education, Training, and Life-Long Learning of the House Committee on Economic and Educational Opportunities*, 104th Cong., 1st sess. (May 9, 1995), pp. 35–49.

50. Mike Zapler, "Protecting Men's Sports," *Chronicle of Higher Education*, January 6, 1995.

51. Douglas Lederman, "House Targets Enforcement of Sex-Bias Law in College Sports," *Chronicle of Higher Education*, August 4, 1995.

52. Ibid.

53. Quoted in Gavora, *Tilting the Playing Field*, p. 29.

Chapter Seven

1. After fourteen days of testimony, District Court judge Pettine found that Brown had violated Title IX and he issued a preliminary injunction, *Cohen* v. *Brown*, 809 F. Supp. 978 (D. R.I. 1992). The First Circuit upheld the district court in *Cohen* v. *Brown*, 991 F.2d 888 (1st Cir. 1993). After a thirty-day trial on the merits,

Judge Pettine again held that Brown had violated Title IX, *Cohen* v. *Brown*, 879 F. Supp. 185 (D. R.I. 1995), and ordered it to submit a plan for compliance. Brown again appealed to the First Circuit, and again lost. *Cohen* v. *Brown*, 101 F.3d 155 (1st Cir. 1996). It then asked the Supreme Court to hear the case, but its petition was denied, *Cohen* v. *Brown*, 520 U.S. 1186 (1996). For informative descriptions of this extended litigation, see Welch Suggs, *A Place on the Team: The Triumph and Tragedy of Title IX* (Princeton University Press, 2005), ch. 7, and Jessica Gavora, *Tilting the Playing Field: Schools, Sports, Sex and Title IX* (San Francisco: Encounter Books, 2002), ch. 3.

2. *Favia* v. *Indiana University in Pennsylvania*, 7 F.3d 332 (3d Cir. 1993); *Roberts* v. *Colorado State Board of Agriculture*, 998 F.2d 824 (10th Cir. 1993); *Kelley* v. *Board of Trustees*, 35 F.3d 265 (7th Cir. 1994); *Neal* v. *Board of Trustees*, 198 F.3d 763 (9th Cir. 1999); *Pederson* v. *Louisiana State University*, 213 F.3d 858 (5th Cir. 2000); *Horner* v. *Kentucky High School Athletic Association*, 206 F.3d 685 (6th Cir. 2000); *Chalenor* v. *University of North Dakota*, 291 F.3d 1042 (8th Cir. 2002).

3. Marvin Lazerson and Ursula Wagener, "Missed Opportunities: Lessons from the Title IX Case at Brown," *Change* 28 (July–August 1996), p. 47.

4. *Cohen* v. *Brown*, 991 F.2d 888, 892 (1st Cir. 1993).

5. Whether the players sought out Bryant or Bryant sought out the players is a matter of some dispute.

6. The first quotation comes from Gregorian's testimony in *Hearing on Title IX of the Education Amendments of 1972 Before the Subcommittee on Postsecondary Education, Training, and Life-Long Learning of the House Committee on Economic and Educational Opportunities*, 104th Cong., 1st sess. (May 9, 1995), p. 115. The second from Lazerson and Wagener, "Missed Opportunities," p. 50.

7. 44 *Federal Register* 71414 (December 11, 1979) (emphasis added).

8. Brown's lawyers placed special weight on the Supreme Court's decision in *Adarand Constructors* v. *Pena*, 515 U.S. 200 (1995), which had been decided in the years between the First Circuit's two rulings.

9. *Cohen* v. *Brown*, 991 F.2d at 900.

10. *Cohen* v. *Brown*, 101 F.3d at 155, 174, 179 (1st Cir. 1996).

11. Ibid. at 177.

12. Ibid. at 179–80.

13. *Cohen* v. *Brown*, 991 F.2d at 898 (internal quotation marks omitted).

14. *Cohen* v. *Brown*, 101 F.3d at 195, 193 (Torruella dissenting).

15. *Pederson* v. *Louisiana State University*, 912 F. Supp. 892, 910–14 (M.D. La. 1996).

16. See cases cited in note 2 above.

17. *Neal* v. *Board of Trustees* at note 14.

18. Quoted in Gavora, *Tilting the Playing Field*, p. 76.

19. "Brown University Files Appeal in Title IX Athletics Discrimination Case," News from Brown, Brown University News Service, April 19, 1995.

20. Quoted in Karla Haworth, "Brown U. Gets Broad Support in Appeal of Title IX Case," *Chronicle of Higher Education*, April 4, 1997. Conspicuously absent from this group of supporters were the other members of the Ivy League.

21. Quoted in ibid. See also Jim Naughton, "Foes in Title IX Lawsuit Look to Supreme Court for Resolution," *Chronicle of Higher Education*, April 25, 1997.

22. Quoted in Gavora, *Tilting the Playing Field*, p. 86.

23. Andrew Zimbalist, *Unpaid Professionals: Commercialism and Conflict in Big-Time College Sports* (Princeton University Press, 1999), p. 58.

24. Jim Naughton, "Judge Approves Settlement of Brown U.'s Title IX Case," *Chronicle of Higher Education*, July 3, 1998.

25. Suggs, *A Place on the Team*, p. 123.

26. Quoted in Lisa Guernsey, "Many Female Athletes at Brown U. Are Ambivalent about Ruling," *Chronicle of Higher Education*, December 6, 1996.

27. "Clarification of Intercollegiate Athletics Policy Guidance: The Three-Part Test," January 16, 1996, p. 1 (www2.ed.gov/about/offices/list/ocr/docs/clarific.html).

28. Ibid., pp. 10–12.

29. Dear Colleague Letter: Bowling Green State University, July 23, 1998 (www2.ed.gov/about/offices/list/ocr/docs/bowlgrn.html#bowlgrn1).

30. Quoted in Jim Naughton, "Clarification of Title IX May Leave Many Colleges in Violation over Aid to Athletes," *Chronicle of Higher Education*, July 31, 1998.

31. GAO Report 01-297, "Intercollegiate Athletics: Four-Year Colleges' Experiences Adding and Discounting Teams" (March 2001), pp. 11, 13; Suggs, *A Place on the Team*, p. 139; Gavora, *Tilting the Playing Field*, pp. 52–53.

32. These cases are examined in Brenda Ambrosius, "Title IX: Creating Unequal Equality through Application of the Proportionality Standard in Collegiate Athletics," 46 *Valparaiso University Law Review* 576 (2012).

33. Welch Suggs, "Most Americans Favor Cutting Men's Sports to Add Women's, Poll Finds," *Chronicle of Higher Education*, June 23, 2000.

34. Suggs, *A Place on the Team*, pp. 153–55.

35. Quoted in ibid., p. 155. It should be noted that this assumes both that Title IX is primarily about sports and that more college resources should be devoted to athletics.

36. Ibid.

37. Ibid., p. 158.

38. The Secretary of Education's Commission on Opportunity in Athletics, "'Open to All' Title IX at Thirty," February 28, 2003 (www2.ed.gov/about/bdscomm/list/athletics/report.html); Donna de Varona and Julie Foudy, "Minority Views on the Report of the Commission on Opportunities in Athletics," February 26, 2003 (http://scholarship.law.marquette.edu/sportslaw/vol14/iss1/32). Whether Foudy and de Varona continued to agree with the recommendations they had initially supported was unclear.

39. "Open To All," Recommendations #21, #14, and #23.

40. "Open To All," Recommendation #2.

41. Quoted in Suggs, *A Place on the Team*, p. 172.

42. Dear Colleague Letter, "Further Clarification of Intercollegiate Athletic Policy Guidance regarding Title IX Compliance," July 11, 2003 (www2.ed.gov/about/offices /list/ocr/title9guidanceFinal.html).

43. Ibid., p. 2.

44. The 2005 DCL has been removed from OCR's website. The letter and the department's technical document are available at www.feminist.org/education/pdfs/Addn ClarificationInterCollegiateAthleticsPolicy.pdf.

45. The agency also clarified the burden of proof in athletics cases. If a school claims it has "fully and effectively accommodated the interests and abilities" of the "underrepresented sex," the burden of proof rests on OCR or the complaining student "to show by a preponderance of the evidence that the institution is not in compliance with part three." To do so, OCR or the complainant must demonstrate (1) that among current or admitted students there is enough "unmet interest" and "sufficient ability" to "sustain a varsity team" in a particular sport, and (2) a "reasonable expectation of intercollegiate competition" for that team "within the school's normal competitive region." The NWLC and others argued that this unfairly reversed the burden of proof. Arthur Coleman, who had been the number two person in OCR during the Clinton administration, disagreed, claiming that the burden of proof had always fallen on those challenging schools' practices. Welch Suggs, "New Policy Clarifies Title IX Rules for Colleges; Women's Group Objects," *Chronicle of Higher Education*, April 1, 2005.

46. NCAA Executive Committee Resolution, April 28, 2005, reprinted in U.S. Commission on Civil Rights, *Title IX Athletics: Accommodating Interests and Abilities*, Briefing before the United States Commission on Civil Rights (2010), pp. 65–66.

47. Dear Colleague Letter, "Intercollegiate Athletics Policy Clarification: The Three-Part Test—Part Three," April 20, 2010 (www2.ed.gov/about/offices/list/ocr /letters/colleague-20100420.pdf).

48. Jamie Schuman, "House Democrats Urge the Bush Administration to Rescind New Guideline on Title IX Compliance," *Chronicle of Higher Education*, June 23, 2005.

49. de Varona and Foudy, "Minority Views on the Report of the Commission," p. 16. Additional references to court decisions appear on pp. 3, 6, and 17.

50. Statement to Commission on Civil Rights, *Title IX Athletics: Accommodating Interests and Abilities*, pp. 51–53.

51. Dear Colleague Letter, "Guidance on Accommodating Students' Athletic Interests and Abilities: Standard for Part Three of the 'Three-Part Test,'" April 20, 2010 (www2.ed.gov/about/offices/list/ocr/letters/colleague-201010.pdf). The letter refers to its guidance as "Intercollegiate Athletics Policy Clarification: The Three-Part Test— Part Three." That is how this DCL will be referred to in the text.

52. Quoted in Katie Thomas, "Rule Change Takes Aim at Loophole in Title IX," *New York Times*, April 20, 2010. These developments are described in Libby Sander, "Joe Biden, No. 1 Fan of Women's Sports," *Chronicle of Higher Education*, April 20,

2010; Sander, "Education Department Nixes Bush-Era Policy on Title IX Compliance," *Chronicle of Higher Education*, April 20, 2010; Libby Sander and Peter Schmidt, "Stepping Up the Pace at the Office for Civil Rights," *Chronicle of Higher Education*, April 15, 2010.

53. "Intercollegiate Athletics Policy Clarification," pp. 5–8.

54. Ibid., p. 11, n25.

55. Rutgers Resolution Letter (www2.ed.gov/about/offices/list/ocr/docs/investigations /02086001.html).

56. Ibid., pp. 41–44.

57. Merrimack College Resolution Letter (www2.ed.gov/about/offices/list/ocr /docs/investigations/01106001.html).

58. Suggs, *A Place on the Team*, ch. 9.

59. Alia Wong, "Where Girls Are Missing Out in High School Sports," *The Atlantic*, June 26, 2015.

60. National Women's Law Center, "Center Files Title IX Complaints Against 12 School Districts," November 10, 2010 (https://nwlc.org/press-releases/center-files-title -ix-complaints-against-12-school-districts/).

61. Portland Resolution Letter (www2.ed.gov/about/offices/list/ocr/docs/investigations /01115001.html).

62. Hingham Resolution Letter (www2.ed.gov/about/offices/list/ocr/docs/investi gations/01105003.html).

63. Indianapolis Resolution Letter (www2.ed.gov/about/offices/list/ocr/docs /investigations/05105002.html); see also, for example, the Resolution Letters for Idaho Falls, Idaho (www2.ed.gov/about/offices/list/ocr/docs/investigations/10095002.html) and Evansville Vanderburgh School Corp., Indiana (www2.ed.gov/about/offices/list /ocr/docs/investigations/05115002.html).

64. *Cmtys. for Equity* v. *Michigan High School Athletic Association*, 178 F. Supp. 2d 805 (W.D. Mich. 2001), upheld, 377 F.3d 504 (6th Cir. 2004). Similarly, a federal district judge in New York (upheld by the Second Circuit) required two school districts to move girls' soccer to the fall so that the schools could participate in state championships— even though it was highly unlikely that either school would do well enough to qualify. *McCormick* v. *School District of Mamaroneck*, 370 F.3d 275 (2d Cir. 2004).

65. *Parker* v. *Franklin County Community School Corp.*, 667 F.3d 910, 913, 923 (7th Cir. 2012).

66. Ibid. at 923–24. See also Joshua Dunn and Martha Derthick, "Title IX at Trial: If You Schedule It, Will They Come?" *Education Next* 12 (Fall 2012) (http:// educationnext.org/title-ix-at-trial/).

Chapter Eight

1. These themes are examined in Daniel Carpenter and David Moss, eds., *Preventing Regulatory Capture: Special Interest Influence and How to Limit It* (Cambridge University Press, 2013), esp. chs. 13–15.

2. William G. Bowen and Sarah A. Levin, *Reclaiming the Game: College Sports and Educational Values* (Princeton University Press, 2003); James L. Shulman and William G. Bowen, *The Game of Life: College Sports and Educational Values* (Princeton University Press, 2001).

3. Welch Suggs, *A Place on the Team: The Triumph and Tragedy of Title IX* (Princeton University Press, 2005), p. 175.

4. Susan Ware, *Title IX: A Brief History with Documents* (Long Grove, Ill.: Waveland Press, 2007), pp. vi, 23.

5. Gerald Gurney, Donna A. Lopiano, and Andrew Zimbalist, *Unwinding Madness: What Went Wrong with College Sports and How to Fix It* (Brookings, 2017), pp. 156–61.

6. Katie Thomas, "College Teams, Relying on Deception, Undermine Gender Equity," *New York Times*, April 25, 2011. Thomas faults schools for "padding women's teams rosters" with "underqualified athletes." The underlying assumption is that the only females who should "count" are those who are highly competitive.

7. Quoted in Linda Flanagan and Susan H. Greenberg, "How Title IX Hurt Female Athletes: The Groundbreaking Legislation, Which Was Supposed to Help Women Thrive in Sports, Has Had Several Unintended, Negative Consequences," *The Atlantic*, February 27, 2012, p. 4.

8. R. Vivian Acosta and Linda Jean Carpenter, "Women in International Sport: A Longitudinal, National Study Thirty-Seven Year Update, 1977–2014," p. E (http://acostacarpenter.org/AcostaCarpenter2012.pdf).

9. Flanagan and Greenberg, "How Title IX Hurts Female Athletes," p. 5.

10. Christine Hauser, "Report on Sexual Abuse in USA Gymnastics Urges 'Culture Change,'" *New York Times*, June 27, 2017.

11. Bowen and Levin, *Reclaiming the Game*, p. 105.

12. Debra Blum, "The Battle for Gender Equality," *Chronicle of Higher Education*, May 26, 1995.

13. Statement of Vice Chair Abigail Thernstrom, in *Title IX Athletics: Accommodating Interests and Abilities*, Briefing before the United States Commission on Civil Rights (2010), p. 85; Jim Naughton, "Title IX Poses a Particular Challenge at Predominantly Black Institutions," *Chronicle of Higher Education*, February 20, 1998.

14. Katie Thomas, "At Two-Year Colleges, Less Scrutiny Equals Less Athletic Equality," *New York Times*, July 16, 2011.

15. Quoted in Welch Suggs, "Education Dept. Offers U. of New Mexico Another Way to Comply with Title IX," *Chronicle of Higher Education*, May 5, 2000. Senator Paul Wellstone once proposed legislation to prohibit colleges from cutting funds for athletics without public justification. Shulman and Bowen, *The Game of Life*, p. 14.

16. Resolution Agreement, Chicago Public School District #299, OCR Case Nos. 05-11-1034 and 05-89-1020, p. 9 (www2.ed.gov/documents/press-releases/chicago-public-schools-agreement.pdf).

17. Gurney, Lopiano, and Zimbalist, *Unwinding Madness*, p. 204.

18. Ibid., pp. 21–24.

19. Knight Commission on Intercollegiate Athletics, *Restoring the Balance: Dollars, Values, and the Future of College Sports*, 2010, p. 7 (http://knightcommission.org /images/restoringbalance/KCIA_Report_F.pdf).

20. Ibid., pp. 4–5.

21. Brad Wolverton, Ben Hallman, Shane Shifflett, and Sandhya Kambhampati, "How Students Are Funding Athletics Arms Race," *Chronicle of Higher Education*, November 15, 2015.

22. Knight Commission, *Restoring the Balance*, p. 6.

23. Gurney, Lopiano, and Zimbalist, *Unwinding Madness*, p. 202.

24. Ibid., p. 146.

25. Ibid., p. 162.

26. Ibid., p. 157.

27. "The 25 Schools Stocked with Jocks," *Newsweek*, September 12, 2010.

28. Shulman and Bowen, *The Game of Life*, p. 146.

29. Ibid., pp. 160–61.

30. Bowen and Levin, *Reclaiming the Game*, p. 77.

31. Ibid., pp. 92–93.

32. Shulman and Bowen, *The Game of Life*, p. 131.

33. Ibid., p. 148.

34. Bowen and Levin, *Reclaiming the Game*, ch. 6.

35. Ibid., p. 150.

36. Ibid., pp. 161–67.

37. Ibid., p. 250.

38. Quoted in ibid., p. 114.

39. National Women's Law Center, "The Next Generation of Title IX: Athletics," June 2012, p. 3 (nwlc.org/wp-content/uploads/2015/08/nwlcathletics_titleixfactsheet.pdf).

40. See Suggs, *A Place on the Team*, ch. 11.

41. Flanagan and Greenberg, "How Title IX Hurt Female Athletes."

42. Diane Auer Jones, "More on Athletics and Title IX," *Chronicle of Higher Education*, April 26, 2010.

43. Ware, *Title IX*, p. 24.

44. Suggs, *A Place on the Team*, p. 186; Flanagan and Greenberg, "How Title IX Hurts Female Athletes."

45. Jane Eisner, "Female Athletes Gain Equality—But Also Help Erode Standards," January 25, 2001 (http://articles.philly.com/2001-01-25/news/25308916_1_college -sports-athletes-liberal-arts).

46. *Reclaiming the Game*, p. 214.

47. Mary Jo Festle, *Playing Nice: Politics and Apologies in Women's Sports* (Columbia University Press, 1996), p. 225.

48. Quoted in ibid., p. 137. See also Ying Wushanley, *Playing Nice and Losing: The Struggle for Control of Women's Intercollegiate Athletics, 1960–2000* (Syracuse University

Press, 2004); Shulman and Bowen, *The Game of Life*, pp. 119–25; and Suggs, *A Place on the Team*, pp. 45–65.

49. Festle, *Playing Nice*, p. 171.

50. Suggs, *A Place on the Team*, p. 61.

51. Quoted in Patricia Ann Rosenbrock, "Persistence and Accommodation in a Decade of Struggle and Change," Ph.D. dissertation (University of Iowa, 1987), p. 53; and Suggs, *A Place on the Team*, pp. 61–62.

52. Festle, *Playing Nice*, chs. 7–8; Wushanley, *Playing Nice and Losing*, chs. 9–11; Shulman and Bowen, *The Game of Life*, pp. 15–18.

53. Jeffrey Orleans, "An End to the Odyssey: Equal Athletic Opportunities for Women," 3 *Duke Journal of Gender Law and Policy* 139 (1996).

54. Suggs, *A Place on the Team*, pp. 95–96; Gurney, Lopiano, and Zimbalist, *Unwinding Madness*, pp. 31–33.

55. Quoted in Katie Thomas, "No Tackling, but a Girl's Sport Takes Some Hits," *New York Times*, May 15, 2010.

56. Bowen and Levin, *Reclaiming the Game*, pp. 184–91.

Chapter Nine

1. U.S. Department of Justice (DOJ), "Not Alone: The First Report of the White House Task Force to Protect Students from Sexual Assault," April 2014, p. ii (www .justice.gov/ovw/page/file/905942/).

2. According to commonly repeated statistics cited in the report, 20 percent of women and 6 percent of men are the victims of sexual assault while in college. About 10 million women and 8 million men have been attending college in recent years. Taking the conservative assumption that all these students spend four years in college, this would mean that from 1998 to 2014, 8 million female college students and nearly 2 million male college students have been the victims of sexual assault, with an annual rate over 600,000. The Bureau of Justice Statistics has estimated that the *total* number of rapes, attempted rapes, and sexual assaults (not the reported number, which is much smaller) in the United States (population approximately 300 million) is 200,000. This means that the number of assaults on college campuses alone is three times the Justice Department's estimate for the entire United States. Either the statistics used in the White House report or the estimates offered by the Bureau of Justice Statistics are deeply flawed.

3. *TIME* magazine cover, May 26, 2014. The *Huffington Post* series is called "Breaking the Silence" (www.huffingtonpost.com/topic/breakingthesilence). On Columbia student Emma Sulkowicz, see Roberta Smith, "In a Mattress, a Lever for Art and Political Protest," *New York Times*, September 21, 2014. In July 2017, Columbia University settled a case with the student accused by the "mattress woman," Emma Sulkowicz. Paul Nungesser had previously been acquitted of sexual assault charges by the university's grievance panel. After the school gave Sulkowicz course credit for her mattress-carrying "performance art project" (which included carrying the mattress

onstage at graduation), he accused the school of supporting what he called an "outrageous display of harassment and defamation." The terms of the settlement were not made public. See Kate Taylor, "Columbia Settles with Student Cast as a Rapist in Mattress Art Project," *New York Times*, July 14, 2017.

4. Max Kutner, "The Other Side of the College Sexual Assault Crisis," *Newsweek*, December 10, 2015; K. C. Johnson and Stuart Taylor Jr., *The Campus Rape Frenzy: The Attack on Due Process at America's Universities* (New York: Encounter Books, 2017); Laura Kipnis, *Unwanted Advances: Sexual Paranoia Comes to Campus* (New York: Harper-Collins, 2017); Emily Yoffe, "The College Rape Overcorrection," *Slate* (www.slate.com/articles/double_x/doublex/2014/12/college_rape_campus_sexual_assault_is_a_serious_problem_but_the_efforts.html); Yoffe, "The Uncomfortable Truth About Campus Rape Policy, *The Atlantic*, September 6, 2017; Yoffe, "The Bad Science Behind Campus Response to Sexual Assault," *The Atlantic*, September 8, 2017; and Yoffe, "The Question of Race in Campus Sexual-Assault Cases," *The Atlantic*, September 11, 2017.

5. Los Angeles Times Editorial Board, "Sex and College Students: Should the Legislature Be in the Mix, Too?" *Los Angeles Times*, May 28, 2014; New York Times Editorial Board, "When Yes Means Yes," September 8, 2014.

6. Ezra Klein, "'Yes means Yes' Is a Terrible Law, and I Completely Support It," *Vox*, October 13, 2014 (www.vox.com/2014/10/13/6966847/yes-means-yes-is-a-terrible-bill-and-i-completely-support-it).

7. Johnson and Taylor, *The Campus Rape Frenzy*, p. 221.

8. The most important guidelines issued by the Office for Civil Rights are, in chronological order, the following: "Revised Sexual Harassment Guidance: Harassment of Students by School Employees, Other Students, or Third Parties," January 19, 2001 (www2.ed.gov/about/offices/list/ocr/docs/shguide.html); Dear Colleague Letter on Bullying and Harassment, October 26, 2010 (www2.ed.gov/about/offices/list/ocr/letters/colleague-201010.html); Dear Colleague Letter on Sexual Violence, April 4, 2011 (www2.ed.gov/about/offices/list/ocr/letters/colleague-201104.html); and "Questions and Answers on Title IX and Sexual Violence," April 29, 2014 (www2.ed.gov/about/offices/list/ocr/docs/qa-201404-title-ix.pdf).

9. Quoted in Tyler Kingkade, "Colleges Warned They Will Lose Federal Funding for Botching Campus Rape Cases," *Huffington Post*, July 14, 2014 (https://www.huffingtonpost.com/2014/07/14/funding-campus-rape-dartmouth-summit_n_5585654.html).

10. *Chronicle of Higher Education* keeps a running total of the number of investigations, the number resolved, and the length of each. It is commonly referred to as the "Title IX Tracker" (https://projects.chronicle.com/titleix/).

11. Press release, "U.S. Department of Education Releases List of Higher Education Institutions with Open Title IX Sexual Violence Investigations," May 1, 2014 (www.ed.gov/news/press-releases/us-department-education-releases-list-higher-education-institutions-open-title-ix).

12. Resolution Agreement, Tufts University, Complaint No. 01-10-2089 (www2.ed.gov/documents/press-releases/tufts-university-agreement.pdf).

13. Ariel Kaminer, "Princeton Mishandled Sexual Misconduct and Discrimination Cases, U.S. Inquiry Finds," *New York Times*, November 5, 2014.

14. University of Pennsylvania, Student Disciplinary Charter Amendment, January 27, 2015 (http://online.wsj.com/public/resources/documents/2015_0218_upenn _policy.pdf).

15. Quoted in Susan Kruth, "It Doesn't Matter What Your Reason Is for Not Having Sex—Unless You're at Michigan," *Huffington Post*, October 1, 2014 (www .huffingtonpost.com/susan-kruth/university-of-michigan-sexual-violence_b_5910788 .html).

16. For a summary of the litigation, see SAVE (Stop Abusive and Violent Environments), "Special Report: Six-Year Experiment in Campus Jurisprudence Fails to Make the Grade," 2017, pp. 5–6. (www.saveservices.org/wp-content/uploads/Six-Year -Experiment-Fails-to-Make-the-Grade.pdf). Many of these cases are described in Johnson and Taylor, *The Campus Rape Frenzy*.

17. "The NCHERM Group Whitepaper: Due Process and the Sex Police" (www .ncherm.org/wordpress/wp-content/uploads/2017/04/TNG-Whitepaper-Final -Electronic-Version.pdf).

18. Quoted in Johnson and Taylor, *The Campus Rape Frenzy*, p. 12.

19. Quoted in SAVE, "Six-Year Experiment," p. 6.

20. Senator Patty Murray and others, letter to Secretary DeVos, June 27, 2017 (https://assets.documentcloud.org/documents/3878460/Betsy-DeVos-ED-Office-of -Civil-Rights-OCR.pdf).

21. Dear Colleague Letter on Sexual Violence, p. 1, n1.

22. 61 *Federal Register* 52172 (October 4, 1996); 62 *Federal Register* 12034 (March 13, 1997); 65 *Federal Register* 66092 (November 2, 2000); 66 *Federal Register* 5512 (January 19, 2001).

23. Reva B. Siegel, "Introduction: A Short History of Sexual Harassment," in Catharine A. MacKinnon and Reva B. Siegel, eds., *Directions in Sexual Harassment Law* (Yale University Press, 2004), p. 18.

24. Ibid., p. 26.

25. Catharine MacKinnon, *Sexual Harassment of Working Women* (Yale University Press, 1979), p. 174.

26. Elizabeth Bartholet and others, "Rethink Harvard's Sexual Harassment Policy," *Boston Globe*, October 15, 2014; see also "Open Letter from Members of the Penn Law School Faculty" (http://media.philly.com/documents/OpenLetter .pdf).

27. American College of Trial Lawyers, "White Paper on Campus Sexual Assault Investigations" (http://www.nacua.org/docs/default-source/new-cases-and-developments /New-Cases-April-2017/white-paper-re-sexual-assault-investigations.pdf).

28. ABA Criminal Justice Section Task Force on College Due Process Rights and Victim Protections, "Recommendations for Colleges and Universities in Resolving Allegations of Campus Sexual Misconduct," June 2017, p. 2 (www.americanbar.org

/content/dam/aba/publications/criminaljustice/2017/ABA-Due-Process-Task-Force
-Recommendations-and-Report.authcheckdam.pdf).

29. Elizabeth Bartholet, Nancy Gertner, Janet Halley, and Jeannie Suk, "Fairness
for All Students under Title IX," September 21, 2017, pp. 2, 4–5 (https://dash.harvard
.edu/handle/1/33789434).

30. Kipnis, *Unwanted Advances*; Johnson and Taylor, *The Campus Rape Frenzy*.

31. Samantha Harris provides a description of many of these cases in two articles
on the website of the Foundation for Individual Rights in Education (FIRE): "Due
Process Legal Update: Students' Title IX and Due Process Claims Move Forward, but
Challenges Remain," March 1, 2016 (www.thefire.org/due-process-legal-update-students
-title-ix-and-due-process-claims-move-forward-but-challenges-remain); and "Due
Process Legal Update: Settlements, Trials, and More," July 27, 2016 (www.thefire.org
/due-process-legal-update-settlements-trials-and-more). Several of these cases are also
described in Johnson and Taylor, *The Campus Rape Frenzy*, ch. 4.

32. "Not Alone," p. 14.

33. Quoted in Johnson and Taylor, *The Campus Rape Frenzy*, p. 163.

34. Bartholet and others, "Fairness for All Students," p. 3.

35. Dear Colleague Letter on Sexual Violence, p. 6.

36. Ibid., p. 10.

37. Sexual and Gender-Based Harassment Policy and Procedures for the Faculty of
Arts and Science, Harvard University, pp. 4–5 (http://www.fas.harvard.edu/files/fas
/files/fas_sexual_and_gender-based_harassment_policy_and_procedures-1-13-16
.pdf).

38. The Marshall quotation is taken from FIRE letter to Assistant Secretary for Civil
Rights Russlynn Ali, January 6, 2012 (www.thefire.org/fire-coalition-open-letter-to
-office-for-civil-rights-assistant-secretary-russlynn-ali-january-6-2012/); the Colorado
State University–Pueblo definition appears in *Code of Student Conduct & Adjudication*
(www.csupueblo.edu/StudentLife/StudentJudicialAffairs/Documents/Codeof
StudentConduct2011.pdf).

39. For example, in 2015 an undergraduate at Colorado College was suspended for
two years for posting an offensive six-word joke on social media (http://gazette.com
/student-suspended-from-colorado-college-for-social-media-posts-speaks-out/article
/1564644).

40. Dear Colleague Letter, First Amendment, July 28, 2003 (www2.ed.gov/about
/offices/list/ocr/firstamend.html).

41. Andrew Kloster, "DOJ and Department of Education Mandate Orwellian
Speech Restrictions on College Campuses," May 16, 2013 (www.thefire.org/doj-and
-department-of-education-mandate-orwellian-speech-restrictions-on-college
-campuses/).

42. Nadine Strossen, *Eighth Annual Richard S. Salant Lecture on Freedom of the
Press* (Cambridge, Mass.: Shorenstein Center on Media, Politics and Public Policy,
Harvard Kennedy School, 2015).

43. Bartholet and others, "Fairness for All Students," p. 2.

44. American Association of University Professors, "The History, Uses, and Abuses of Title IX," March 24, 2016, p. 33 (www.aaup.org/report/history-uses-and-abuses -title-ix).

45. "Not Alone," p. 2. This claim is repeated in White House Council on Women and Girls, "Rape and Sexual Assault: A Renewed Call to Action," January 2014, p. 1 (www .knowyourix.org/wp-content/uploads/2017/01/sexual_assault_report_1-21-14.pdf).

46. See, for example, the website of the advocacy group One in Four (www .oneinfourusa.org/).

47. The following quotation is included in a statement explaining the Campus Accountability and Safety Act: " 'We should never accept the fact that women are at a greater risk of sexual assault as soon as they step onto a college campus. But today they are. And it has to end,' said Senator Gillibrand" (www.mccaskill.senate.gov/media -center/news-releases/campus-accountability-and-safety-act). Facing criticism of her claim that one in four college women is the victim of sexual assault, Senator Gillibrand removed that claim from her official website. *Politico, Morning Education,* December 19, 2014.

48. Quoted in Yoffe, "The College Rape Overcorrection."

49. James Alan Fox and Richard Moran, "Sex Assault Surveys Not the Answer: Column," *USA Today,* August 10, 2014. Similar problems beset a widely reported 2014 MIT survey finding that 17 percent of female students and 5 percent of males have been sexually assaulted. Richard Pérez-Peña, "Rare Survey Examines Sexual Assault at M.I.T.," *New York Times,* October 27, 2014; and Batya Ungar-Sargon, "Why Doesn't MIT Trust Its Own Students to Recognize Sexual Assault? The Problems with the University's New Survey," *New Republic,* October 28, 2014.

50. Callie Marie Rennison and Lynn Addington, "Violence against College Women: A Review to Identify Limitations in Defining the Problem and Inform Future Research," *Trauma, Violence, and Abuse* 15, no. 3 (2014), pp. 159–69.

51. Bureau of Justice Statistics, "Rape and Sexual Assault: Victimization among College-Age Females, 1995–2013" (www.bjs.gov/content/pub/pdf/rsavcaf9513.pdf). Although this report explored an issue at the heart of the sexual assault controversy, it received little media attention. I first heard about it on National Public Radio (NPR), *All Things Considered,* which to its credit devoted a lengthy segment to the DOJ findings. NPR's online story, though, gave it this misleading spin: "Study: Just 20 Percent of Female Campus Sexual Assault Victims Go to Police" (www.npr.org/sections/thetwo -way/2014/12/11/370093706/study-just-20-percent-of-female-campus-sexual-assault -victims-go-to-police). The *New York Times,* which runs many stories on sexual assault, to its discredit completely ignored it. The *Huffington Post* did cover the report. After featuring the 20 percent statistic in many of its stories, it gave this one an unexpected title: "Sexual Assault Statistics Can Be Confusing, but They're Not the Point" (www .huffingtonpost.com/2014/12/15/sexualassaultstatistics_n_6316802.html?utm_hp _ref=breakingthesilence). They have their story, and they are sticking to it.

52. Callie Marie Rennison, "Privilege among Rape Victims: Who Suffers Most from Rape and Sexual Assault in America?" *New York Times*, December 21, 2014.

53. David Cantor and others, "Report on the AAU Climate Survey on Sexual Assault and Sexual Misconduct, Prepared for the Association of American Universities by Westat," September 21, 2015, pp. viii–ix (www.aau.edu/sites/default/files/%40 Files/ClimateSurveyAAU_Campus_Climate_Survey_12_14_15.pdf).

54. Ibid., p. 36

55. Ibid., pp. vi–vii, v.

56. Emily Yoffe, "The Problem with Campus Sexual Assault Survey," *Slate*, September 24, 2015 (www.slate.com/articles/double_x/doublex/2015/09/aau_campus_sexual _assault_survey_why_such_surveys_don_t_paint_an_accurate.html); Stuart Taylor Jr., "The Latest Big Sexual Assault Survey Is (Like Others) More Hype Than Science," *Washington Post*, September 23, 2015.

57. Matt Rocheleau, "Campus Sex Assault Reports Climbing," *Boston Globe*, October 6, 2014. This assumes, of course, that all the reports were well-founded.

58. Quoted in Carrie N. Baker, *The Women's Movement against Sexual Harassment* (Cambridge University Press, 2008), pp. 20–21. Other early opinions dismissing sexual harassment complaints are reviewed in MacKinnon, *Sexual Harassment of Working Women*, ch. 4.

59. The column is discussed in Baker, *The Women's Movement*, p. 22.

60. *Vinson* v. *Taylor*, dissent from denial of rehearing en banc, 760 F.2d 1330 (D.C. Cir. 1985).

61. Ibid. at 1332, n7.

62. 523 U.S. 75 (1998).

63. *Oncale* v. *Sundowner Offshore Services*, 523 U.S. 75, 81 (1998) (emphasis added).

64. Katherine Franke, "What's Wrong with Sexual Harassment," in MacKinnon and Siegel, *Directions in Sexual Harassment Law*, p. 172.

65. Margaret A. Crouch, *Thinking about Sexual Harassment: A Guide for the Perplexed* (Oxford University Press, 2001), p. 9. William Eskridge presents a similar view of the "liberal" approach in "Theories of Harassment 'Because of Sex,'" in MacKinnon and Siegel, *Directions in Sexual Harassment Law*, p. 161.

66. Judith Resnik, "The Rights of Remedies: Collective Accounting for and Insuring against the Harm of Sexual Harassment," in MacKinnon and Siegel, *Directions in Sexual Harassment Law*, pp. 250–51.

67. MacKinnon, *Sexual Harassment of Working Women*, p. 172.

68. Ibid., pp. 174–75.

69. Ibid., p. 88.

70. Ibid., p. 172 (emphasis added).

71. Ibid., p. 5.

72. Siegel, "Introduction," p. 18.

73. Franke, "What's Wrong with Sexual Harassment," p. 173.

74. White House Council on Women and Girls, "Rape and Sexual Assault: A Renewed Call to Action," p. 6 (www.knowyourix.org/wp-content/uploads/2017/01 /sexual_assault_report_1-21-14.pdf).

75. See Emily Yoffe, "*The Hunting Ground*: The Failures of a New Documentary about Rape on College Campuses," *Slate*, February 27, 2015 (www.slate.com/articles /double_x/doublex/2015/02/the_hunting_ground_a_campus_rape_documentary _that_fails_to_provide_a_full.html).

76. Sara Agnew, "Sally Mason Apologizes for Sexual Assault Remark," *Des Moines Register,* February 26, 2014; and Vanessa Miller, "Regents Scold University of Iowa President Mason for Poor Communication," February 28, 2014 (http://thegazette .com/2014/02/28/regents-express-concern-about-iowa-president-masons-sexual -assault-comments).

77. Quoted in Bazelon, "The Return of the Sex Wars," *New York Times Magazine*, September 10, 2015.

78. Know Your IX, "Our Values" (www.knowyourix.org/our-values/).

79. MacKinnon, "Afterword," in MacKinnon and Siegel, *Directions in Sexual Harassment Law*, p. 673.

80. Joanna Grossman, "The Culture of Compliance: The Final Triumph of Form over Substance in Sexual Harassment Law," 26 *Harvard Women's Law Journal* 1 (2001).

81. Joseph Biden, "A Call to Action for College and University Presidents, Chancellors, and Senior Administrators: Step Up on Sexual Assault," April 23, 2015 (medium.com/@VPOTUS44/a-call-to-action-for-college-and-university-presidents -chancellors-and-senior-administrators-52865585c76d#.bqz9pvciz/).

82. Baker, *The Women's Movement*, p. 191.

Chapter Ten

1. *Davis* v. *Monroe County Board of Education*, 526 U.S. 629, 675 (1999) (Kennedy dissenting).

2. Sean Farhang, *The Litigation State: Public Regulation and Private Lawsuits in the U.S.* (Princeton University Press, 2010), p. 3.

3. *Gebser* v. *Lago Vista Independent School District*, 524 U.S. 274 (1998) and *Davis* v. *Monroe County School Board*, 526 U.S. 629 (1999).

4. Carrie N. Baker, *The Women's Movement against Sexual Harassment* (Cambridge University Press, 2008), p. 1.

5. Ibid., ch. 5; and Charles R. Epp, *Making Rights Real: Activists, Bureaucrats, and the Creation of the Legalistic State* (University of Chicago Press, 2009), ch. 8.

6. Anne Simon, "*Alexander* v. *Yale University*: An Informal History," in Catharine MacKinnon and Reva Siegel, eds., *Directions in Sexual Harassment Law* (Yale University Press, 2004); Catharine MacKinnon, *Sexual Harassment of Working Women* (Yale University Press, 1979).

7. Baker, *The Women's Movement*, chs. 1 and 2. Today, the Legal Defense and Education Fund is called Legal Momentum.

8. *Williams* v. *Saxbe*, 413 F. Supp. 654, 657 (D. D.C. 1976).

9. *Barnes* v. *Costle*, 561 F.2d 983, 989–90 (D.C. Cir. 1977). A copy of Catharine MacKinnon's as yet unpublished manuscript was covertly slipped to law clerks in the case.

10. Ibid. at 992.

11. Ibid. at 995 and 1001 (MacKinnon dissenting).

12. *Bundy* v. *Jackson*, 641 F.2d 934, 944 (D.C. Cir. 1981).

13. Ibid. at 945–46.

14. Catharine MacKinnon, "The Logic of Experience: Reflections on the Development of Sexual Harassment Law," 90 *Georgetown Law Journal* 813, 816 (2001).

15. See Richard Stewart, "Reformation of American Administrative Law," 88 *Harvard Law Review* 1667 (1976).

16. *Hobson* v. *Hansen*, 269 F. Supp. 401 (D.D.C. 1967).

17. See, for example, *Vermont Yankee* v. *NRDC*, 435 U.S. 519 (1978).

18. *Bundy* at 945, n10, 947.

19. Baker, *The Women's Movement*, p. 19.

20. Quoted in ibid., p. 58.

21. 45 *Federal Register* 74676 (November 10, 1980). The proposal was published in 45 *Federal Register* 25024 (April 11, 1980).

22. Although this distinction between "quid pro quo" and "hostile environment" harassment was for many years a staple of sexual harassment law, it eventually became unmanageable and was replaced by the distinction between harassment that culminates in a "tangible employment action" and harassment that does not.

23. Epp, *Making Rights Real*, pp. 174–75, and Baker, *The Women's Movement*, pp. 139–40.

24. Baker, *The Women's Movement*, pp. 120–22.

25. *Henson* v. *City of Dundee*, 682 F.2d 897 (11th Cir. 1982).

26. *Meritor Savings Bank* v. *Vinson*, 477 U.S. 57 (1986).

27. Ibid. at 72.

28. Ibid. at 73.

29. David Oppenheimer, "Employer Liability for Sexual Harassment by Supervisors," in MacKinnon and Siegel, *Directions in Sexual Harassment Law*, p. 287.

30. *Harris* v. *Forklift Systems*, 510 U.S. 17 (1993).

31. Ibid. at 19, 21 (1993) (internal punctuation and citations omitted).

32. Ibid. at 22.

33. Ibid. at 22–23.

34. Ibid. at 24–25 (Scalia concurring).

35. Charles Clark, "Sexual Harassment," *CQ Researcher*, August 9, 1991, p. 61; Sarah Glazer, "Crackdown on Sexual Harassment," *CQ Researcher*, July 19, 1996, p. 642.

36. For the effect of this change on Title VII litigation, see Farhang, *The Litigation State*, ch. 6.

37. For a good example, see Martha Derthick, *Agency under Stress: The Social Security Administration in American Government* (Brookings, 1990) (both the Social Security Administration and the Internal Revenue Service).

38. "Policy Guidance on Current Issues of Sexual Harassment," March 19, 1990 (www.eeoc.gov/policy/docs/currentissues.html); "Enforcement Guidance on Harris v. Forklift Sys., Inc.," March 8, 1994 (www.eeoc.gov/policy/docs/harris.html); "Enforcement Guidance: Vicarious Employer Liability for Unlawful Harassment by Supervisors," June 18, 1999 (www.eeoc.gov/policy/docs/harassment.html).

39. *Faragher* v. *City of Boca Raton*, 524 U.S. 775, 785 (1998).

40. *Burlington Industries* v. *Ellerth*, 524 U.S. 742 (1998).

41. 524 U.S. 775 (1998).

42. *Burlington Industries* at 771–73 (Thomas dissenting).

43. Ibid. at 751.

44. *Jansen* v. *Packing Corporation of America*, 123 F.3d 490, 512 (7th Cir. en banc 1997).

45. *Jansen* at 509.

46. *Jansen* at 511, 513.

47. Epp, *Making Rights Real*, p. 227.

48. Oppenheimer, "Employer Liability," p. 287.

49. Michael Harper and Joan Flynn, "*Burlington v. Ellerth* and *Faragher v. Boca Raton*: Federal Common Lawmaking for the Modern Age," in Joel Friedman, ed., *Employment Discrimination Stories* (New York: Foundation Press, 2006), pp. 226–27.

50. Linda Greenhouse, "Supreme Court Weaves Legal Principles from a Tangle of Litigation," *New York Times*, June 30, 1998.

51. Barbara Mantel, "Sexual Harassment," *CQ Researcher*, April 27, 2012, pp. 380, 384, 389; Glazer, "Crackdown on Sexual Harassment," p. 630.

52. MacKinnon, "Afterword," in MacKinnon and Siegel, *Directions in Sexual Harassment Law*, p. 673.

53. Joanne Grossman, "The Culture of Compliance: The Final Triumph of Form over Substance in Sexual Harassment Law," 26 *Harvard Women's Law Journal* 1, 4 (2003). Grossman also presented her pessimistic assessment in an interview with Barbara Mantel, "Sexual Harassment," p. 382.

54. Stephen Henrick, "A Hostile Environment for Student Defendants: Title IX and Sexual Assault on College Campuses," 40 *Northern Kentucky Law Review* 49, 56–57 (2013).

55. *Alexander* v. *Yale*, 631 F.2d 178 (2nd Cir. 1980).

56. Jodi Short, "Creating Peer Sexual Harassment: Mobilizing Schools to Throw the Book at Themselves," 28 *Law and Policy* 31, 40 (2006).

57. I describe these cases in R. Shep Melnick, "Deregulating the States: The Political Jurisprudence of the Rehnquist Court," in Thomas Ginsburg and Robert Kagan, eds., *Institutions and Public Law* (New York: Peter Lang, 2005).

58. *Cannon* v. *University of Chicago*, 441 U.S. 677 (1979).

59. *Franklin* v. *Gwinnett*, 503 U.S. 60, 78 (1992) (Scalia dissenting).

60. For the backstory, see Stephen Wermiel's informative essay, "A Claim of Sexual Harassment," in Rodney Smolla, ed., *A Year in the Life of the Supreme Court* (Duke

University Press, 1995). The teacher continued to proclaim his innocence, and the case was finally settled with a nondisclosure provision.

61. *Franklin* v. *Gwinnett* at 75.

62. Wermiel, "A Claim of Sexual Harassment," p. 249.

63. *Doe* v. *Petaluma City School District*, 830 F. Supp. 1560 (N.D. Cal. 1993).

64. Short, "Creating Peer Sexual Harassment," p. 40. Many of the decisions are listed by Judge DiClerico in *Doe* v. *Londonderry School District*, 970 F. Supp. 64, 71 (D. N.H. 1997).

65. *Rowinsky* v. *Bryan Independent School District*, 80 F.3d 1006, 1016 (1996).

66. *Doe* v. *Londonderry School District* at 71–72. The court took note of OCR's 1997 guidelines, but declined to follow them in full, adopting a standard closer to that eventually announced by the Supreme Court.

67. Short, "Creating Peer Sexual Harassment," p. 44.

68. OCR first announced that it was about to propose guidelines in 61 *Federal Register* 42728 (August 16, 1996). It published its proposal in 61 *Federal Register* 52172 (October 4, 1996). Final guidelines were announced in 62 *Federal Register* 12034 (March 13, 1997). The quotation in the text comes from 61 *Federal Register* 42728 (emphasis added).

69. 61 *Federal Register* 42728, 52172.

70. By contrast, in 2004 the Bush administration used notice-and-comment rule-making to make a relatively small change in the Title IX rules first promulgated in 1975. This was the only use of notice-and-comment rulemaking under Title IX since 1975. OCR received 5,860 public comments—73 times as many as it received on its ambitious 1997 sexual harassment rules. Completing the process took the Bush administration two years. 71 *Federal Register* 62530 (October 25, 2006).

71. 62 *Federal Register* 12036 (March 13, 1997).

72. One way that Title IX guidelines diverged from those developed under Title VII was by recognizing that school policies must take into account the ages of their students. OCR "will never view sexual conduct between an adult school employee and an elementary school student as consensual." But for postsecondary students many more factors would need to be considered.

73. OCR, "Sexual Harassment Guidance 1997," p. 4 (www2.ed.gov/about/offices /list/ocr/docs/sexhar01.html1997 guidelines). The availability of this document was announced in the March 13, 1997, *Federal Register* notice, but not included in it.

74. 61 *Federal Register* 52174 (October 4, 1996).

75. OCR, "Sexual Harassment Guidance 1997," p. 10.

76. *Gebser* v. *Lago Vista Independent School District*, 524 U.S. 274, 277 (1998) (emphasis added).

77. Ibid. at 289.

78. Ibid. at 289, 287.

79. Ibid. at 304–06 (Stevens dissenting).

80. *Davis* v. *Monroe County School Board*, 526 U.S. 629, 651 (1999).

81. Ibid. at 644.

82. Ibid. at 648–49.

83. Ibid. at 651–52.

84. Ibid. at 649.

85. Ibid. at 652–53.

86. Ibid. at 653.

87. Ibid. at 657.

88. Ibid. at 684.

89. Justin Paget, "Did *Gebser* Cause the Metastasization of the Sexual Harassment Epidemic in Educational Institutions? A Critical Review of Sexual Harassment under Title IX Ten Years Later," 42 *University of Richmond Law Review* 1257 (2008).

90. Anne D. Byrne, "School District Liability under Title IX for Sexual Abuse by a Teacher: Why Has the Supreme Court Allowed Schools to Put Their Heads in the Sand?" 22 *Hamline Law Review* 587 (1998–99).

91. Meghan Cherner-Ranft, "The Empty Promise of Title IX: Why Girls Need Courts to Reconsider Liability Standards and Preemption in School Sexual Harassment Cases," 97 *Northwestern University Law Review* 1891, 1910 (2003).

92. *United States* v. *Morrison*, 529 U.S. 598 (2000).

93. The proposal appeared in 65 *Federal Register* 66092 (November 2, 2000). On January 19, 2001, OCR published a half-page "Notice of availability," explaining that "revised guidance" was available from the Department of Education. 66 *Federal Register* 5512. That document is now available at www2.ed.gov/about/offices/list/ocr/docs /shguide.pdf.

94. 65 *Federal Register* 66093.

95. Ibid.

96. Kristin Jones, "Lax Enforcement of Title IX in Campus Assault Cases," Center for Public Integrity, February 25, 2010 (www.publicintegrity.org/2010/02/25/4374 /lax-enforcement-title-ix-campus-sexual-assault-cases-0); and e-mail correspondence with Todd Jones, August 8, 2017.

97. Dear Colleague Letter on First Amendment, July 28, 2003 (www2.ed.gov /about/offices/list/ocr/firstamend. html).

98. Dear Colleague Letter from Assistant Secretary Stephanie Monroe, January 25, 2006 (www2.ed.gov/about/offices/list/ocr/letters/sexhar-2006.pdf).

99. *Annual Report to Congress, FY 2001–2002*, p. 15 (www2.ed.gov/print/about /offices/list/ocr/AnnRpt2002/index.html).

100. *Annual Report to Congress of the Office for Civil Rights, Fiscal Years 2008–09* (www2.ed.gov/about/reports/annual/ocr/annrpt2007-08/annrpt2007-08.pdf), pp. 12, 13, 28.

101. Fatima Goss Graves, "Restoring Effective Protections against Sexual Harassment in Schools: Moving Beyond the *Gebser* and *Davis* Standards," 2 *Advance: The Journal of the ACS Issue Groups* 135, 136, 143 (2008).

102. Ibid., at 136 (emphasis added).

103. Quoted in Grayson Sang Walker, "The Evolution and Limits of Title IX Doctrine on Peer Sexual Assault," 45 *Harvard Civil Rights–Civil Liberties Law Review* 94, 132 (2010).

Chapter Eleven

1. "Crossing the Next Bridge: Secretary Arne Duncan's Remarks on the 45th Anniversary of 'Bloody Sunday' at the Edmund Pettus Bridge, Selma, Alabama," March 8, 2010 (www.ed.gov/news/speeches/crossing-next-bridge-secretary-arne-duncan's-remarks -45th-anniversary-bloody-sunday-edmund-pettus-bridge-selma-alabama).

2. Dear Colleague Letter on Sexual Violence, April 4, 2011 (www2.ed.gov/about /offices/list/ocr/letters/colleague-201104.pdf).

3. Montana Letter of Finding, p. 1 (www2.ed.gov/documents/press-releases /montana-missoula-letter.pdf). The Resolution Agreement can be found at www .justice.gov/iso/opa/resources/52820135914432954596.pdf. OCR later backed away from this "blueprint" claim, writing that the agreement "represents the resolution of that particular case and not OCR or DOJ policy" (www.thefire.org/letter-from-department -of-education-office-for-civil-rights-assistant-secretary-catherine-e-lhamon-to-fire/).

4. "Questions and Answers on Title IX and Sexual Violence," April 29, 2014 (www2.ed.gov/about/offices/list/ocr/docs/qa-201404-title-ix.pdf).

5. Both the initial 2010 report and subsequent reports by the Center for Public Integrity can be found at www.publicintegrity.org/accountability/education/sexual -assault-campus. A transcript of NPR's first story can be found at www.npr.org/templates /story/story.php?storyId=124001493.

6. Kristen Lombardi, "Education Department Touts Settlement as 'Model' for Campus Sex Assault Policies," Center for Public Integrity, December 8, 2010 (www .publicintegrity.org/2010/12/08/2266/education-department-touts-settlement-model -campus-sex-assault-policies). For a discussion of the evidence on the extent of sexual assault on campus, see chapter 9.

7. Dear Colleague Letter on Sexual Violence, pp. 3–4; and Dear Colleague Letter on Bullying and Harassment, October 26, 2010, pp. 2, 6–8 (www2.ed.gov/about /offices/list/ocr/letters/colleague-201010.html).

8. Dear Colleague Letter on Bullying and Harassment, pp. 7–8; Dear Colleague Letter on Sexual Violence, p. 3, n9.

9. Dear Colleague Letter on Bullying and Harassment, p. 8.

10. Montana Resolution Agreement, pp. 8–9.

11. Ibid., p. 9.

12. The narrow meaning of "environment" is evident in the following example from an OCR pamphlet: "Throughout the school year, Student A repeatedly passed sexually explicit photographs to Student B during class. The photographs are offensive to Student B, and, consequently, Student B is unable to concentrate during class or focus on the subject. Student A has created a hostile environment that limits Student B's ability

to participate in the class." OCR, "Sexual Harassment, It's Not Academic," September 2008, p. 12 (www2.ed.gov/about/offices/list/ocr/docs/ocrshpam.html).

13. Dear Colleague Letter on Sexual Violence, p. 4.

14. OCR, "Questions and Answers on Title IX and Sexual Violence," p. 9.

15. Dear Colleague Letter on Sexual Violence, p. 1.

16. The most thorough comparison of OCR's definition of sexual assault with state criminal law is provided by Jacob Gersen and Jeannie Suk, "The Sex Bureaucracy," 104 *California Law Review* 881 (2016), especially pp. 892–97, 905–08, 919–23.

17. Ibid., p. 896.

18. Quoted in ibid., p. 930.

19. Quoted in ibid., pp. 925–26. See also the definitions of consent adopted by the University of Michigan quoted in chapter 9.

20. Quoted in Emily Yoffe, "The Uncomfortable Truth about Campus Rape Policy," *The Atlantic*, September 6, 2017.

21. Gersen and Suk, "The Sex Bureaucracy," pp. 930–31.

22. In 1996, shortly after OCR issued its initial guidance on sexual harassment, a North Carolina school disciplined a six-year-old for kissing another student on the cheek. Shortly thereafter, OCR stated that "a kiss on the cheek by a first grader does not constitute sexual harassment," but did little to explain where schools should draw the line. 62 *Federal Register* 12034 (March 13, 1997).

23. *Davis* v. *Monroe County Board of Education*, 526 U.S. 629, 648–49 (1999).

24. See, for example, the University of New Mexico Letter of Finding, April 22, 2016, pp. 23–25 (www.justice.gov/crt/file/843926/download).

25. Robin Wilson, "Colleges Call in Legal Pros to Handle Sexual-Assault Cases," *Chronicle of Higher Education*, February 16, 2015.

26. "Not Alone: The First Report of the White House Task Force to Protect Students from Sexual Assault," April 2014, p. 14 (www.justice.gov/ovw/page/file/905942).

27. Brett Sokolow, president of National Center for Higher Education Risk Management, quoted in Wilson, "Colleges Call in Legal Pros."

28. "Sexual and Gender-Based Harassment Policy and Procedures for the Faculty of Arts and Sciences, Harvard University," pp. 18–19 (www.fas.harvard.edu/files/fas/files /sexual_and_genderbased_harassment_policy_and_procedures_for_the_fas_.pdf).

29. Janet Halley, "A Call to Reform the New Harvard University Sexual Harassment Policy and Procedures," p. 25 (http://orgs.law.harvard.edu/acs/files/2014/10 /ACSPost.o14.pdf).

30. ABA Criminal Justice Section Task Force on College Due Process Rights and Victim Protections, "Recommendations for Colleges and Universities in Resolving Allegations of Campus Sexual Misconduct," June 2017, p. 3 (www.americanbar.org /content/dam/aba/publications/criminaljustice/2017/ABA-Due-Process-Task-Force -Recommendations-and-Report.authcheckdam.pdf).

31. "Questions and Answers," p. 31; Tufts University Resolution Letter, Complaint No. 01-10-2089, p. 9 (www2.ed.gov/documents/press-releases/tufts-university -agreement.pdf).

32. Tufts University Resolution Letter, pp. 10–11.

33. White House Task Force, "Not Alone," p. 9.

34. Resolution Agreement with Ohio State University, part IV (http://titleix.osu.edu/PDFs/OCRResolutionAgreement).

35. Resolution Agreement with Ohio State, sections IV D, E, F, and G. Similar provisions appear in the 2014 agreement with Harvard Law School, pp. 6–7 (www2.ed.gov/documents/press-releases/harvard-law-agreement.pdf).

36. Quoted in K. C. Johnson and Stuart Taylor, *The Campus Rape Frenzy: The Attack on Due Process in America's Universities* (New York: Encounger Books, 2017), p. 150.

37. Emily Yoffe, "The Bad Science Behind Campus Response to Sexual Assault," *The Atlantic*, September 8, 2017.

38. Johnson and Taylor, *The Campus Rape Frenzy*, p. 150.

39. Violence Against Women Act regulation, 34 *C.F.R.* section 668.46(j)(2)(iv), quoted in Gerson and Suk, "The Sex Bureaucracy," p. 912.

40. Ibid., section 668.46(a), quoted in Gersen and Suk, "The Sex Bureaucracy," p. 913, n.149.

41. Centers for Disease Control and Prevention, "Sexual Violence: Risk and Protective Factors" (www.cdc.gov/violenceprevention/sexualviolence/riskprotectivefactors.html).

42. These are all reported and cited in Gersen and Suk, "The Sex Bureaucracy," pp. 925–28.

43. Ibid., pp. 924–25.

44. White House Task Force, "Not Alone," pp. 7–8.

45. Tufts University Resolution Agreement, section VIII (F) (www2.ed.gov/documents/press-releases/tufts-university-agreement.pdf).

46. "U.S. Department of Education Releases List of Higher Education Institutions with Open Title IX Sexual Violence Investigations," OCR Press Release, May 1, 2014.

47. Quoted in Juliet Linderman, "Broader Problems of Campus Sex Assaults Leave Victims Hanging," *Washington Times*, June 8, 2015.

48. Quoted in Robin Wilson, "Colleges under Investigation for Sexual Assault Wonder What Getting It Right Looks Like," *Chronicle of Higher Education*, August 11, 2015.

49. Robin Wilson, "As Federal Investigations of Sex Assault Get Tougher, Some Ask if That's Progress," *Chronicle of Higher Education*, October 8, 2015.

50. Sara Lipka, "An Arc of Outrage: Despite the Clamor, the Real Conversation about Campus Assault Has Hardly Begun," *Chronicle of Higher Education*, April 13, 2015.

51. Quoted in Wilson, "As Federal Investigations of Sex Assault Get Tougher."

52. Yoffe, "The Uncomfortable Truth about Campus Rape Policy."

53. Wilson, "Colleges under Investigation."

54. Anonymous, "Essay: OCR Guidelines on Sexual Assault Hurt Colleges and Students," *Inside Higher Ed*, October 28, 2011.

55. Doug Lederman, "'A New Day at OCR,'" *Inside Higher Ed*, June 28, 2017.

56. Colby Bruno, attorney for the Victim Rights Law Center, quoted in Linderman, "Broader Problems of Campus Sex Assaults Leave Victims Hanging."

57. Alyssa Peterson and Olivia Ortiz, "A Better Balance: Providing Survivors of Sexual Violence with 'Effective Protection' against Sex Discrimination Through Title IX Complaints," 125 *Yale Law Journal* 2121, 2134 (2016).

58. Letter from Candice Jackson to Regional Directors, June 8, 2017, OCR Instructions to the Field re Scope of Complaints (www.propublica.org/documents/item /3863019-doc00742420170609111824).

59. New York Times Editorial Board, "Another Sign of Retreat on Civil Rights," *New York Times*, June 27, 2017.

60. Letter to Secretary DeVos from Senator Patty Murray and others, June 27, 2017 (https://assets.documentcloud.org/documents/3878460/Betsy-DeVos-ED-Office-of -Civil-Rights-OCR.pdf).

61. "74 Interview: Catherine Lhamon Takes On Trump With Probe Into Cutbacks on Student Civil Rights," June 27, 2017 (www.the74million.org/article/74-interview -catherine-lhamon-takes-on-trump-with-probe-into-cutbacks-on-student-civil-rights).

62. Gersen and Suk, "The Sex Bureaucracy," pp. 883–84.

63. Frank Dobbin, *Inventing Equal Opportunity* (Princeton University Press, 2009); Charles Epp, *Making Rights Real: Activists, Bureaucrats, and the Creation of the Legalistic State* (University of Chicago Press, 2009).

64. Dobbin, *Inventing Equal Opportunity*, p. 193.

65. Epp, *Making Rights Real*, pp. 177–78.

66. Dear Colleague Letter on Sexual Violence, April 4, 2011, p. 7

67. Dear Colleague Letter on Title IX Coordinators, April 24, 2015, pp. 1–3 (www2 .ed.gov/about/offices/list/ocr/letters/colleague-201504-title-ix-coordinators.pdf).

68. Dear Colleague Letter on Title IX Coordinators, p. 4.

69. James Q. Wilson, *Bureaucracy: What Government Agencies Do and Why They Do It* (New York: Basic Books, 1989), p. 60.

70. Tufts University Resolution Agreement, p. 12.

71. Audrey Williams June, "Overseeing Sex-Assault Cases Is Now a Full-Time Job," *Chronicle of Higher Education*, October 31, 2014.

72. Quoted in Robin Wilson, "Culture of Consent: Colleges Focus on Preventing Sex Assault before They Happen," *Chronicle of Higher Education*, February 29, 2016, and Lipka, "An Arc of Outrage."

73. Quoted in June, "Overseeing Sex-Assault Cases."

74. Swarthmore Sexual Harassment/Assault Resources & Education, "History (College Action Steps)" (www.swarthmore.edu/share/history-college-action-steps).

75. Anemona Hartocollis, "Colleges Spending Millions to Deal with Sexual Misconduct Complaints," *New York Times*, March 29, 2016.

76. Johnson and Taylor, *The Campus Rape Frenzy*, pp. 154–55.

77. Voluntary Resolution Agreement, The George Washington University, August 31, 2011, OCR Complaint #11-11-2079, p. 6 (www2.ed.gov/about/offices/list/ocr /docs/investigations/11112079-b.pdf). A similar provision can be found in the Resolution Agreement with Ohio State University, part V(D) (http://titleix.osu.edu/PDFs /OCRResolutionAgreement).

78. University of Mississippi Resolution Agreement, OCR Ref. 06102069, December 19, 2011, p. 5.

79. University of New Mexico Resolution letter, April 22, 2016, pp. 31–32 (www .justice.gov/crt/file/843926/download).

80. Quoted in Allie Grasgreen, "Disagreement on Campus Judicial Systems," *Inside Higher Ed*, February 12, 2014.

81. Laura Bennett, "Sexual Assault on Campus: 9 Views of What Will Signal Progress, When the Student Culture Changes," 2015 (http://chronicle.com/interactives /assault_views).

82. These quotations come from the OSAPR website, http://osapr.harvard.edu/.

83. The job description was posted on LinkedIn (www.linkedin.com/jobs/view /398908055).

84. Kimberly Hefling, "Congress Faces Deadline to Save Education Programs," *Politico*, September 27, 2017 (www.politico.com/tipsheets/morning-education/2017 /09/27/congress-faces-deadline-to-save-education-programs-222505).

Chapter Twelve

1. Catherine Lhamon (OCR) and Vanita Gupta (DOJ), Dear Colleague Letter on Transgender Students, May 13, 2016 (www2.ed.gov/about/offices/list/ocr/letters /colleague-201605-title-ix-transgender.pdf).

2. Ibid., p. 2.

3. Republican Platform, 2016, p. 35 (www.gop.com/the-2016-repubican-party -platform/).

4. DCL on Transgender Students, May 13, 2016, p. 1.

5. For many years *Ulane* v. *Eastern Airlines, Inc.*, 742 F.2d 1081 (7th Cir. 1984) was considered the leading case.

6. In 2016 the Equal Employment Opportunity Commission (EEOC) provided a useful list of federal court decisions in "Examples of Court Decisions Supporting Coverage of LGBT-Related Discrimination under Title VII." Of the twenty-nine district and circuit court opinions, only one predated 2000 (www.eeoc.gov/eeoc/newsroom /wysk/lgbt_examples_decisions.cfm).

7. *Price Waterhouse* v. *Hopkins*, 490 U.S. 228, 235–36 (1989).

8. Ibid. at 251 (internal quotation marks and citations omitted).

9. See the cases cited in EEOC, "Examples of Court Decisions."

10. Executive Order #13672, 79 *Federal Register* 42971 (July 23, 2014).

11. Memorandum from the attorney general to U.S. attorneys, "Treatment of Transgender Employment Discrimination Claims under Title VII of the Civil Rights Act of 1964," December 15, 2014 (www.justice.gov/file/188671/download).

12. Jaime Fuller, "Holder Calls LGBT Rights One of the 'Civil Rights Challenges of Our Time,'" *Washington Post*, February 4, 2014.

13. Department of Labor, Employment and Training Administration, Guidance Letter 37-14 (May 29, 2015), p. 1; OFCCP, Directive 2014-02, August 19, 2014.

14. Jackie Calmes, "Obama Won't Order Ban on Gay Bias by Employers," *New York Times*, April 11, 2012.

15. See Timothy Phelps, "Gay Rights Groups Press Obama for Anti-Discrimination Order," *Los Angeles Times*, March 14, 2014; and "Exec. Order No. 13672," 128 *Harvard Law Review* 1304 (2015).

16. Dear Colleague Letter on Bullying and Harassment, October 26, 2010, pp. 8–9 (www2.ed.gov/about/offices/list/ocr/letters/colleague-201010.html).

17. These agreements are cited in DCL on Transgender Students, n19.

18. 40 *Federal Register* 24141 (June 4, 1975), section 86.33.

19. The first quotation comes from "Questions and Answers on Title IX and Sexual Violence," April 29, 2014, p. 5 (www2.ed.gov/about/offices/list/ocr/docs/qa-201404-title-ix.pdf); the second from "Questions and Answers on Title IX and Single-Sex Elementary and Secondary Schools and Extracurricular Activities," December 1, 2014, question 31, p. 25 (www2.ed.gov/about/offices/list/ocr/docs/faqs-title-ix-single-sex-201412.pdf).

20. Letter from James A. Ferg-Cadima to Emily T. Prince, Esq., January 7, 2015. Unlike most OCR policy statements, the letter is not available through the OCR website. It can be found on the website of a law firm that specializes in education law (www.bricker.com/documents/misc/transgender_student_restroom_access_1-2015.pdf). On her personal Twitter account Prince describes herself as "Beltway lawyer; Sworn Knight of the Transsexual Empire; one of the worst girls since Eve."

21. *G. G.* v. *Gloucester County School Board*, 822 F.3d 709, 715 (4th Cir. 2016). Since Emily Prince's e-mail to OCR focused on the controversy in Gloucester County, it is likely that everyone knew that OCR's response would be used in that litigation.

22. Ibid. at 731.

23. Dear Colleague Letter on Transgender Students, nn5–11.

24. 136 S.Ct. 2442 (Mem., August 3, 2016). Four of the eight justices on the Court voted to grant certiorari. Justice Stephen Breyer, who did not vote for certiorari, agreed to "preserve the status quo" pending the Court's consideration. Justices Ginsburg, Sotomayor, and Kagan objected to the stay.

25. *Texas* v. *United S*tates, 201 F. Supp. 3d 810 (N.D. Tex. 2016).

26. Dear Colleague Letter from Sandra Battle (OCR) and T. E. Wheeler II (DOJ), February 22, 2017 (www2.ed.gov/about/offices/list/ocr/letters/colleague-201702-title-ix.pdf).

27. Jeremy W. Peters, Jo Becker, and Julie Hirschfeld Davis, "Trump Rescinds Rules on Bathrooms for Transgender Students," *New York Times*, February 22, 2017.

28. OCR Instructions to the Field re Complaints Involving Transgender Students, June 6, 2017 (www.documentcloud.org/documents/3866816-OCR-Instructions-to-the-Field-Re-Transgender.html).

29. "Amici Curiae Brief for Secretary of Education Arne Duncan, Secretary of Education John B. King Jr. and Other Former Officials" in *G. G.* v. *Gloucester* (http://www.scotusblog.com/wp-content/uploads/2017/03/16-273_bsac_secretaries.pdf), p. 5.

30. Ibid., pp. 7–8.

31. *Texas* v. *United States* at 832–33.

32. Brief for National Education Association and others, p. 26 (www.aclu.org /legal-document/gg-v-gloucester-county-school-board-national-education-association -et-al). All the briefs are available at www.aclu.org/cases/gg-v-gloucester-county-school -board.

33. Supplemental Brief of Plaintiff-Appellant, filed May 8, 2017, p. 34 (www.aclu .org/legal-document/gg-v-gloucester-county-school-board-supplemental-brief -plaintiff-appellant).

34. Supplemental Brief of Gloucester County School Board, filed May 8, 2017, p. 27 (www.aclu.org/legal-document/gg-v-gloucester-county-school-board-supplemental -brief-defendant-appellee).

35. *Hively* v. *Ivy Technical College of Indiana*, 853 F.3d 339 (7th Cir. 2017).

36. *Whitaker by Whitaker* v. *Kenosha Unified School District Board of Education*, 858 F.3d 1034 (7th Cir. 2017).

37. *Whitaker* at 1047 (quoting *Price Waterhouse* v. *Hopkins*, 490 U.S. 228, 251 [1989]).

38. Ibid. at 1048.

39. Ibid. at 1049.

40. Ibid. at 1050, 1052.

41. *Congressional Record*, February 28, 1972, p. 5804 (daily edition) (statement of Senator Bayh).

42. Andrew Fishel and Janice Pottker, *National Politics and Sex Discrimination in Education* (Lexington, Mass.: Lexington Books, 1977), pp. 111–12.

43. 40 *Federal Register* 24135 (June 4, 1975).

44. *Cohen* v. *Brown*, 101 F.3d 155, 179 (1st Cir. 1996).

45. Ibid. at 180–81.

46. *Neal* v. *Board of Trustees of California State Universities*, 198 F.3d 763, 769, n4 (9th Cir. 1999).

47. *Parker* v. *Franklin County Community School Corp.*, 667 F.3d 910, 923–24 (2012).

48. See Joshua Dunn and Martha Derthick, "Title IX at Trial: If You Schedule It, Will They Come?" *Education Next* 12, no. 4 (Fall 2012).

49. Erin Buzuvis, a law professor who writes frequently on Title IX issues and runs the "Title IX Blog," reviews the debate among Title IX activists on the cheerleading issue in "The Feminist Case for the NCAA's Recognition of Competitive Cheer As an Emerging Sport for Women," 52 *Boston College Law Review* 439 (2011). On the one hand, for many years, "Cultural pressure to polarize femininity and masculinity constructed cheerleading as the primary location for hegemonic feminization. But to pre serve the gender hierarchy, this hegemonic femininity was trivialized (through the deployment of the ditzy cheerleader stereotype, for example) as well as sexualized. It also presented obstacles to girls who did desire to compete in traditional sports, because the contrast called the athletes' femininity into question." Thus the feminist hostility to considering cheerleading a "sport." On the other hand, Buzuvis argues, "There is symbolic power in the transformation of cheerleading from an activity that 'ghettoized' women into non-sport activities, to one that displays women's competitive athletic ability. By promoting and supporting the growth of competitive cheer, the

NCAA could contribute to the destabilization of many negative stereotypes" (at 463, 441). In other words, the key question is not what students want, but what is most effective in changing public attitudes about femininity.

50. The phrase comes from Justice Scalia's opinion in *Oncale* v. *Sundowner Offshore Services, Inc.*, 523 U.S. 75, 80–81 (1998).

51. Quoted in Kristen Lombardi, "Education Department Touts Settlement As 'Model' for Campus Sex Assault Policies," Center for Public Integrity, December 8, 2010 (www.publicintegrity.org/2010/12/08/2266/education-department-touts-settlement -model-campus-sex-assault-policies/).

52. Jacob Gersen and Jeannie Suk, "The Sex Bureaucracy," 104 *California Law Review* 881, 924–31 (2016).

53. White House Council on Women and Girls, "Rape and Sexual Assault: A Renewed Call to Action," January 21, 2014, p. 6 (www.knowyourix.org/wpcontent /uploads/2017/01/sexual_assault_report_1-21-14.pdf).

54. 2014 Department of Education Rules Issued under Violence Against Women Act, section 668.46(j)(2)(iv), quoted in Gersen and Suk, "The Sex Bureaucracy," p. 912.

55. "74 Interview: Catherine Lhamon Takes On Trump with Probe into Cutbacks on Student Civil Rights," June 27, 2017 (www.the74million.org/article/74-interview -catherine-lhamon-takes-on-trump-with-probe-into-cutbacks-on-student-civil-rights).

56. Dear Colleague Letter on Bullying and Harassment, October 26, 2010, p. 8.

57. Richard Stewart, "The Reformation of American Administrative Law," 88 *Harvard Law Review* 1669, 1712 (1975).

58. William N. Eskridge Jr., *Dynamic Statutory Interpretation* (Harvard University Press, 1994), p. 49.

59. *United Steelworkers of America* v. *Weber*, 443 U.S. 193, 226 (1979) (Rehnquist dissenting).

60. Ibid. at 201, quoting *Church of the Holy Trinity* v. *United States*, 143 U.S. 457 (1892).

61. Paul Frymer, *Black and Blue: African Americans, the Labor Movement, and the Decline of the Democratic Party* (Princeton University Press, 2008), p. 87.

62. *Alexander* v. *Sandoval*, 532 U.S. 275, 306–07 (2001) (Stevens dissenting).

63. Alexander Bickel, *The Supreme Court and the Idea of Progress* (New York: Harper and Row, 1970), pp. 13, 19.

64. Order in *G.G.* v. *Gloucester County School Board*, #16-733, April 7, 2017, amended April 18, 2017 (www.ca4.uscourts.gov/Opinions/Published/161733R1.P.pdf).

Chapter Thirteen

1. *Motor Vehicle Manufacturers Ass'n* v. *State Farm Mutual Automobile Insurance Co.*, 463 U.S. 29 (1983).

2. Letter from Candice Jackson to Regional Directors, June 8, 2017, OCR Instructions to the Field re Scope of Complaints (www.propublica.org/documents/item /3863019-doc00742420170609111824).

3. "Secretary DeVos Prepared Remarks on Title IX Enforcement," September 7, 2017 (www.ed.gov/news/speeches/secretary-devos-prepared-remarks-title-ix-enforcement).

4. Robin Wilson, "Trump Administration May Back Away from Title IX, but Campuses Won't," *Chronicle of Higher Education*, November 11, 2016.

5. Benjamin Wermund, "New Marching Orders for Civil Rights Probes," *Politico Morning Education*, June 16, 2017 (www.politico.com/tipsheets/morning-education /2017/06/16/new-marching-orders-for-civil-rights-probes-220882).

6. Paul Pierson, *Dismantling the Welfare State? Reagan, Thatcher, and the Politics of Retrenchment* (Cambridge University Press, 1994); Eric Patashnik, *Reforms at Risk: What Happens after Major Policy Changes Are Enacted* (Princeton University Press, 2008); R. Kent Weaver, "The Politics of Blame Avoidance," *Journal of Public Policy* 6 (1986), p. 371.

7. Stephen B. Burbank and Sean Farhang, *Rights and Retrenchment: The Counter-revolution against Federal Litigation* (Cambridge University Press, 2017); Sarah Staszak, *No Day in Court: Access to Justice and the Politics of Judicial Retrenchment* (Oxford University Press, 2015).

8. Ross Sandler and David Schoenbrod, *Democracy by Decree: What Happens When Courts Run Government* (Yale University Press, 2003).

9. Daniel Kahneman, *Thinking, Fast and Slow* (New York: Farrar, Straus and Giroux, 2011), p. 305.

10. Pierson, *Dismantling the Welfare State?*, p. 18.

11. Michael Lipsky, *Street-Level Bureaucracy* (New York: Russell Sage Foundation, 1980); James Q. Wilson, *Bureaucracy: What Government Agencies Do and Why They Do It* (New York: Basic Books, 1989), chs. 3–6.

12. I address this argument in R. Shep Melnick, "Gridlock and the Madisonian Constitution," in Benjamin Wittes and Pietro Nivola, eds., *What Would Madison Do? The Father of the Constitution Meets Modern American Politics* (Brookings, 2015).

13. William Safire, *Safire's Political Dictionary* (Oxford, 2008), p. 423.

14. Charles Lindblom, "The Science of 'Muddling Through,'" *Public Administration Review* 19 (1959), pp. 79–88; Aaron Wildavsky, *The Politics of the Budgetary Process* (Boston: Little, Brown, 1964).

15. *United States* v. *Virginia*, 518 U.S. 515 (1996); *Sessions* v. *Morales-Santana*, 137 S. Ct. 1678 (June 12, 2017).

16. *Romers* v. *Evans*, 517 U.S. 620 (1996); *Lawrence* v. *Texas*, 539 U.S. 558 (2003); *United States* v. *Windsor*, 133 S. Ct. 2675 (2013); and *Obergefell* v. *Hodges*, 135 S.Ct. 2584 (2015).

17. Burbank and Farhang, *Rights and Retrenchment*, p. 3.

18. Jeffrey Berry, *The New Liberalism: The Rising Power of Citizen Groups* (Brookings, 1999), p. 2.

19. Bernice Resnick Sandler, "Title IX: How We Got It and What a Difference It Made," 55 *Cleveland State Law Review* 473, 477 (2007).

20. Quoted in Emily Wilkins, "GOP Looks to Curb Education's Civil Rights Office," *CQ Roll Call*, November 17, 2016.

21. Wilson, "Trump Administration May Back Away from Title IX."

22. R. Douglas Arnold, *The Logic of Congressional Action* (Yale University Press, 1990), pp. 68–71.

23. Lloyd A. Free and Hadley Cantril, *The Political Beliefs of Americans: A Study of Public Opinion* (Rutgers University Press, 1967).

24. James Q. Wilson, "American Politics, Then and Now," *Commentary*, February 1979.

25. Pew Research Center, "Beyond Distrust: How Americans View Their Government," November 23, 2015 (www.people-press.org/2015/11/23/beyond-distrust-how-americans-view-their-government/).

26. Frank Newport, "Half in U.S. Continue to Say Government Is an Immediate Threat," Gallup, September 21, 2015 (www.gallup.com/poll/185720/half-continue-say-gov-immediate-threat.aspx).

27. Nick Anderson, Emma Brown, and Moriah Balingit, "Trump Could Reverse Obama's Actions on College Sexual Assault, Transgender Rights," *Washington Post*, November 23, 2016.

Index